SSC

Staff Selection Commission

Junior Engineer

Recruitment Examination

Electrical Engineering

Paper II

Conventional Solved Papers 2007-2017

Includes
2 Practice Papers with Solutions

G K Publications (P) Ltd

CL MEDIA (P) LTD.

First Edition : 2019

ISBN : **978-93-89310-95-5**

Typeset by : *CL Media DTP Unit*

Administrative and Production Offices

Published by : **CL Media (P) Ltd.**
A-45, Mohan Cooperative Industrial Area,
Near Mohan Estate Metro Station,
New Delhi - 110044

Marketed by : **G.K. Publications (P) Ltd.**
A-45, Mohan Cooperative Industrial Area,
Near Mohan Estate Metro Station,
New Delhi - 110044

For product information :
Visit ***www.gkpublications.com*** or email to ***gkp@gkpublications.com***

Preface

GK Publications has been the "publisher of choice" to aspirants preparing for Staff Selection Commissions' coveted Junior Engineer recruitment examination. Our SSC JE series for this exam has been segmented into study guides and practice papers in Hindi and English modes for Civil, Electrical and Mechanical streams. With last year's exam going online, we put in effort to help students prepare better with our online test series. Our web portal gave access to full length mock tests which imitated the actual exam and helped students get familiar with online exam environment & improved analytics.

Our electrical stream study guide is vastly popular among candidates taking up Paper II - Conventional of SSC JE. The study guide comprises of numerous practice questions, adhering to the exam pattern, as laid out by SSC. Complete solutions to these questions have been given towards end to help students assess the actual level of their preparation.

This book has solved papers of last 11 years, from 2007 to 2017 with exhaustive explanatory solutions to all questions. This valuable practice material help students become acquainted with exam pattern and have better understanding, study and self-practice to face Paper - II with confidence. Timing while practicing with this textbook will also escalate their speed and always accuracy.

We hope that the book meets expectations of future Junior Electrical Engineers. Due care has been taken to keep the book error free. However, any and all erroneous statements and feedback to improve the book are always welcome.

Wishing a prestigious career to all students,

All the Best!

Team GKP

Contents

Exam Pattern

Papers	Subject	Maximum Marks	Duration
Paper – I **Objective Type** (Computer Based Test)	(*i*) General Intelligence & Reasoning (*ii*) General Awareness (*iii*) General Engineering	50 50 100	**2 Hours**
Paper – II **Conventional Type** (Paper Based Test)	General Engineering	300	**2 Hours**

Cut-offs Marks

Paper I Electrical

Category	2017		2016		2015		2014	
	Cut-off Marks	Candidates Available	Cut-off Marks	Candidates Available	Cut-off Marks	Candidates Available	Cut-off Marks	Candidates Available
SC	120.00	235	99.00	369	114.75	261	102.50	243
ST	114.50	139	94.50	176	105.50	191	93.75	123
OBC	133.25	413	109.50	1094	125.25	888	109.50	1068
OH	113.00	18	87.00	40	100.00	39	93.00	27
HH	83.50	18	54.00	36	80.50	15	69.00	25
UR	136.25	599	115.00	725	131.00	407	117.50	649
Total		**1422**		**2440**		**1801**		**2135**

Paper II Electrical

Category	2017		2016		2015	2014	
	Cut-off Marks	Candidates Available	Cut-off Marks	Candidates Available	Cut-off Marks	Cut-off Marks	Candidates Available
SC	268.50	44	210.50	169	50	149	108
ST	265.50	21	206.50	81	50	126	55
OBC	299.00	110	245.75	285	62	180	471
OH	303.50	132	205.25	15	40	124	16
HH	247.50	3	126.00	16	40	64	10
UR	164.75	9	285.75	610	107	215	190*
Total		**319**		**1176**			**850**

Syllabus

Basic Concepts

Concepts of resistance, inductance, capacitance, and various factors affecting them. Concepts of current, voltage, power, energy and their units.

Circuit Law

Kirchhoff's law, Simple Circuit solution using network theorems.

Magnetic Circuit

Concepts of flux, mmf, reluctance, Different kinds of magnetic materials, Magnetic calculations for conductors of different configuration e.g. straight, circular, solenoidal, etc. Electromagnetic induction, self and mutual induction.

AC Fundamentals

Instantaneous, peak, R.M.S. and average values of alternating waves, Representation of sinusoidal wave form, simple series and parallel AC Circuits consisting of R.L. and C, Resonance, Tank Circuit. Poly Phase system – star and delta connection, 3 phase power, DC and sinusoidal response of R-L and R-C circuit.

Measurement and Measuring Instruments

Measurement of power (1 phase and 3 phase, both active and re-active) and energy, 2 wattmeter method of 3 phase power measurement. Measurement of frequency and phase angle. Ammeter and voltmeter (both moving oil and moving iron type), extension of range wattmeter, Multimeters, Megger, Energy meter AC Bridges. Use of CRO, Signal Generator, CT, PT and their uses. Earth Fault detection.

Electrical Machines

(a) **D.C. Machine** – Construction, Basic Principles of D.C. motors and generators, their characteristics, speed control and starting of D.C. Motors. Method of braking motor, Losses and efficiency of D.C. Machines.

(b) **1 phase and 3 phase transformers** – Construction, Principles of operation, equivalent circuit, voltage regulation, O.C. and S.C. Tests, Losses and efficiency. Effect of voltage, frequency and wave form on losses. Parallel operation of 1 phase /3 phase transformers. Auto transformers.

(c) 3 phase induction motors, rotating magnetic field, principle of operation, equivalent circuit, torque-speed characteristics, starting and speed control of 3 phase induction motors. Methods of braking, effect of voltage and frequency variation on torque speed characteristics.

Fractional Kilowatt Motors and Single Phase Induction Motors: Characteristics and applications.

Synchronous Machines

Generation of 3-phase e.m.f. armature reaction, voltage regulation, parallel operation of two alternators, synchronizing, control of active and reactive power. Starting and applications of synchronous motors.

Generation, Transmission and Distribution

Different types of power stations, Load factor, diversity factor, demand factor, cost of generation, inter-connection of power stations. Power factor improvement, various types of tariffs, types of faults, short circuit current for symmetrical faults. Switchgears – rating of circuit breakers, Principles of arc extinction by oil and air, H.R.C. Fuses, Protection against earth leakage / over current, etc. Buchholtz relay, Merz-Price system of protection of generators & transformers, protection of feeders and bus bars. Lightning arresters, various transmission and distribution system, comparison of conductor materials, efficiency of different system. Cable – Different type of cables, cable rating and derating factor.

Estimation and Costing

Estimation of lighting scheme, electric installation of machines and relevant IE rules. Earthing practices and IE Rules.

Utilization of Electrical Energy

Illumination, Electric heating, Electric welding, Electroplating, Electric drives and motors.

Basic Electronics

Working of various electronic devices e.g. P N Junction diodes, Transistors (NPN and PNP type), BJT and JFET. Simple circuits using these devices.

Solved Paper 2017

Electrical Engineering

(Paper II)

1. (a) The resistance of copper winding of a motor at room temperature of 25°C is 3.0Ω. After an extended operation of the motor at full load, the winding resistance increases to 4.0 Ω. Find the temperature rise. Give that the temperature coefficient of copper at 0°C is 0.00426 Ω/°C/Ω. (15)

   (b) A toaster rotted at 2000 W, 240 V is connected to a 230 V supply. Will the toaster be damaged? Will its rating be affected? (15)

   (c) Define the following terms: (20)

   (i) Drift velocity

   (ii) Current density

   (iii) Power

   (iv) Electromotive force

   (d) The domestic power load in a house comprises the following:

   (i) 10 lamps of 100 W each

   (ii) 5 fans of 80 W each

   (iii) 1 refrigerator of 0.5 hp

   (iv) 1 heater of 1 kW

   Calculate the total current taken from the supply of 230 V. (10)

2. (a) Using Kirchhoff's law, determine the current I_A and I_B in the network shown in Figure 1. (15)

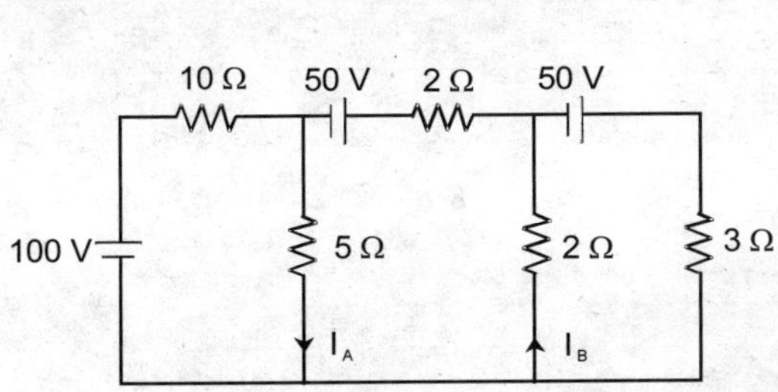

Figure 1

   (b) For the circuit shown in Figure 2, find I such that current in the 100 Ω resistor is zero. (10)

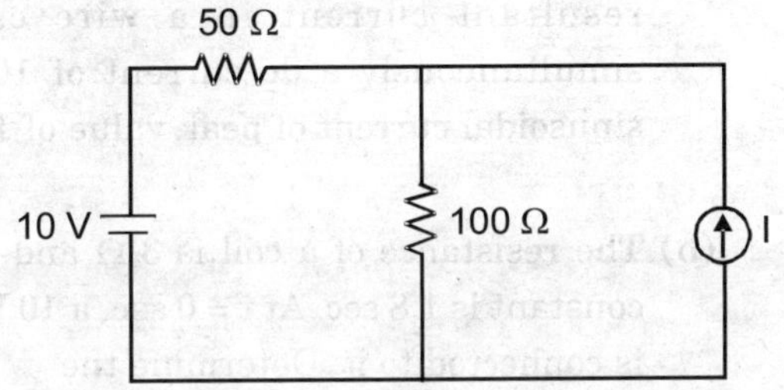

Figure 2

   (c) A series combination of two capacitances $C_1 = 5$ F and $C_2 = 10$ F is connected across a dc supply of 300 V. Determine the

   (i) charge

   (ii) voltage

   (iii) energy stored in each capacitor (15)

   (d) Define the following terms: (15)

   (i) Self-inductance

   (ii) Flux

   (iii) RMS value of alternating waves

3. (a) A circular coil of area 300 cm² and 25 turns rotates about its vertical diameter with an angular speed of 40 rad/sec in a uniform horizontal magnetic field of magnitude 0.05 T. Find the maximum voltage induced in the coil.

   (b) Define the following terms:

   (i) Reluctance

   (ii) Permeance

   (iii) Magnetic Field Strength

   (c) A coil has 1000 turns enclosing a magnetic circuit of 20 cm² in cross-section with 4A current in the coil, the flux density is 1.5 Wb/m², and with 8A current, it is 1.9 Wb/m². Find the mean value of inductance between these current limits and the induced emf if the current decreases from 8 A to 4 A in 0.06 sec. (15)

(d) A coil A of 1200 turns and another coil B of 800 turns lie near each other so that 60 percent of the flux produced in one links with the other. It is found that a current of 5 A in coil A produces a flux of 0.25 mWb, while the same current in coil B produces a flux of 0.15 mWb. Determine the mutual inductance and coefficient of coupling between the coils. **(20)**

4. (a) Determine the average and rms value of the resultant current in a wire carrying simultaneously a dc current of 10 A and sinusoidal current of peak value of 1.414A. **(10)**

(b) The resistance of a coil is 3 Ω and its time constant is 1.8 sec. At t = 0 sec, a 10 V source is connected to it. Determine the **(15)**

(i) current at t = 1 sec

(ii) time at which the current attains half of its final value

(iii) initial rate of growth of current

(c) Explain in brief the following: **(20)**

(i) Energy meter

(ii) CRO

(iii) 2 wattmeter method

(iv) Multi-meter

(d) In a moving coil instrument, the coil has a length of 5 cm, a width of 4 cm and 100 turns. The magnetic flux density in the air gap is 0.2 Wb/m^2. The hair spring provides a controlling torque of 0.5×10^{-7} Nm/degree deflection of the coil. What current will be required to give a deflection of 60°? **(15)**

5. (a) A shunt generator gives full load output of 30 kW at a terminal voltage of 200 V. The armature and shunt field resistances are 0.01 Ω and 100Ω respectively. The iron and friction losses are 1000 W. Calculate the

(i) emf generated

(ii) copper losses

(iii) efficiency

(b) Explain dynamic braking of 3-phase induction motor. **(15)**

(c) Explain in brief the following:

(i) Fractional kilowatt motors

(ii) Auto transformers

(iii) S. C. test of 3-phase transformer

(d) Explain parallel operation of two alternators. **(15)**

6. (a) Explain in brief of the following: **(30)**

(i) Merz-price system of protection

(ii) Short-circuit current for symmetrical faults

(iii) Electric welding

(b) How is the rating of a cable determined? **(10)**

(c) What are the different configurations of BJT? Explain each with suitable circuit diagram. **(10)**

(d) Explain electric installation of machines and relevant IE rules in brief. **(10)**

EXPLANATIONS

1. (a) $R_{25°c} = 3\Omega, R_T = 4\Omega$

Resistance at Temperature 'T'

$R_T = R_0 (1 + \alpha_0 (T_2 - T_1)$

α_o = Temperature coefficient of copper at 0°C

$R_{25°} = R_{0°} (1 + \alpha_0 (25 - 0))$

$3 = R_0 (1 + 00426 \times 25)$

$$R_0 = \frac{3}{1.1065} = 2.711\ \Omega$$

$R_T = R_0 (1 + \alpha_0 (T - 0))$

$4 = 2.71 (1 + 00426\ T)$

$1.47533 = 1 + 00426\ T$

$00426\ T = 47533$

$T = 111.57981°C$

Temperature Rise = T – 25°

= 111.58° – 25° = 86.58°C

(b) Given, Rating of toaster = 2000W, 240V

So, Resistance of toaster

$$(R) = \frac{V^2}{p} = \frac{(240)^2}{2000}$$

R = 28.8Ω

Maximum allowed current through toaster (I_{max})

$$I_{max} = \frac{P_{(rating)}}{V_{(rating)}} = \frac{2000}{240} = 8.33 \text{ Amp}$$

So, if current through toaster is $I > I_{max}$ then toaster will get damage otherwise will work.

$$I = \frac{\text{Supply voltage}(V)}{\text{Resistance of Toaster}(R)}$$

$$= \frac{230}{28.8} = 7.98$$

i.e. $I < I_{max}$

Therefore, toaster will not get damage.

(c) (i) Drift velocity- The Drift velocity is the average velocity that a particle, such as an electron, attains in a material due to an electrical field. It can also be referred to as axil drift velocity. In general, an electron will propagate randomly in a conductor at the fermi velocity. An applied electric field will give this Random motion a small net flow velocity in one direction.

Because current is proportional to drift velocity, which is a resistive material is in turn proportional to the magnitude of an external electric field, Ohm's law can be explain in term of drift velocity.

$u = \ E$

where u is the drift velocity, is the electron mobility (m²/v.s) of the material and E is the electric field (v/m).

(ii) Current density is the electrical current per unit area of cross section.

Current density is the ratio of electrical current flowing in a particular point in a conductor to the cross sectional area of the current taken perpendicular to the current flow at that point. It is measured in amperes per square meter.

$$J = \frac{I}{A} \text{ 'J' current density } \left(\frac{\text{Ampere}}{m^2}\right)$$

(iii) Electrical power, like mechanical power, is the rate of doing work, measured in watt and represented by latter 'P'. The electrical power in watt produce by an electric current 'I' consisting of a charge Q coulombs every 't' seconds passing through an electric potential difference of 'V'.

$$P = \text{work done per unit time} = \frac{vQ}{t}$$

Q = is electric charge in coulombs

t = is time in seconds

I = is electric current in ampere

v = is electric potential or voltage in volts.

(iv) Electric force is not a force (measured in Newtons) but a potential, or energy per unit of charge, measured in volts. EMF is the external work expended per unit of charge to produce an electric potential difference across two open-circuited terminal.

(d) (i) Domestic load (L_1)= 10 × 100 W = 1000 W

(ii) Domestic load (L_2) = 105 × 80 = 400 W

(iii) Domestic load (L_2)= 0.5 HP × 1 = 0.5 HP

1 HP = 746 W

746 × 0.5 = 373 W

(iv) Demotions Load (L_4) = 1 × 1 kW
= 1000 W

Total load (L) = $L_1 + L_2 + L_3 + L_4$
= 100 + 400 + 373 + 100
= 2773 W

$$\text{Current (I)} = \frac{\text{Power}}{\text{voltage}}$$

$$= \frac{2773}{230} = 12.05652\,A$$

$$\text{efficiency} = \frac{\text{Power out put}}{\text{Power out put + Copper Loss + iran+friction}}$$

$$= \frac{30000}{30000 + 1000 + 631.4}$$

$$= \frac{30,000}{31631.4} = 94.8455\%$$

2. (a)

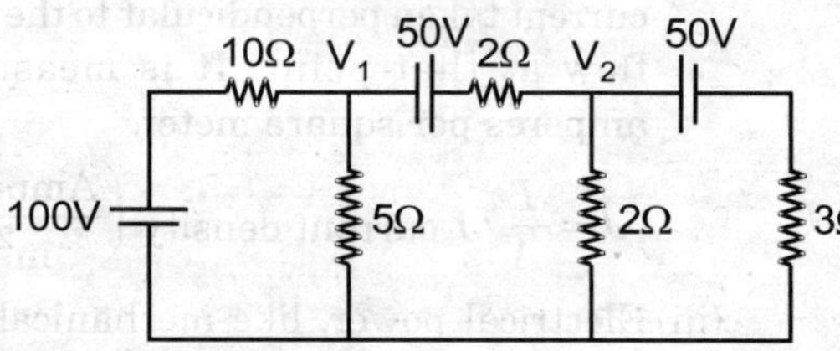

Applying kirchhoff's current law.

$$\frac{V_1 - 100}{10} + \frac{V_1}{5} + \frac{V_1 + 50 - V_2}{2} = 0$$

$V_1 - 100 + 2V_1 + 5V_1 - 5V_2 + 250 = 0$

$8V_1 - 5V_2 + 150 = 0$ ....(1)

$$\frac{V_2 - 50 - V_1}{2} + \frac{V_2}{2} + \frac{V_2 + 50}{3} = 0$$

$3V_2 - 150 - 3V_1 + 3V_2 + 2V_2 + 100 = 0$

$8V_2 - 3V_1 - 50 = 0$ ....(2)

After solving (1) & (2)

$V_1 = -19.38$ (V)

$V_2 = -1.02$ (V)

$$I_A = \frac{V_1}{5} = \frac{-19.38}{5} = -3.8775$$

$$I_B = \frac{-V_2}{2} = \frac{1.02}{2} = 51 \text{ Amp}$$

(b)

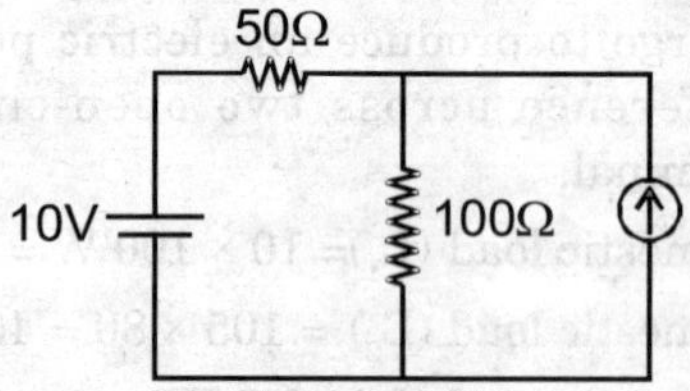

Applying super position theorem let current source open circuit.

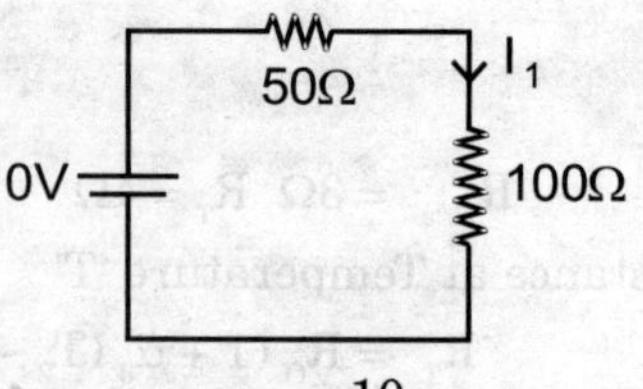

$$I_1 = \frac{10}{150}\,A$$

Let voltage source short circuit after applying superposition theorem.

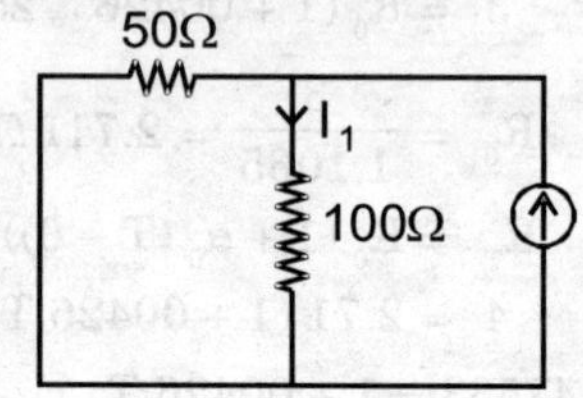

$$I_1 = \frac{50}{(50+100)}\,I$$

$$I_1 = \frac{1}{3}\,I$$

for current a in 100 Ω resistance is zero.

$I_1 + I_2 = 0$

$$\frac{10}{150} + \frac{1}{3}I = 0$$

$$\frac{1}{15} = \frac{1}{3}I$$

$$\boxed{I = -\frac{1}{5}\,A}$$

(c)

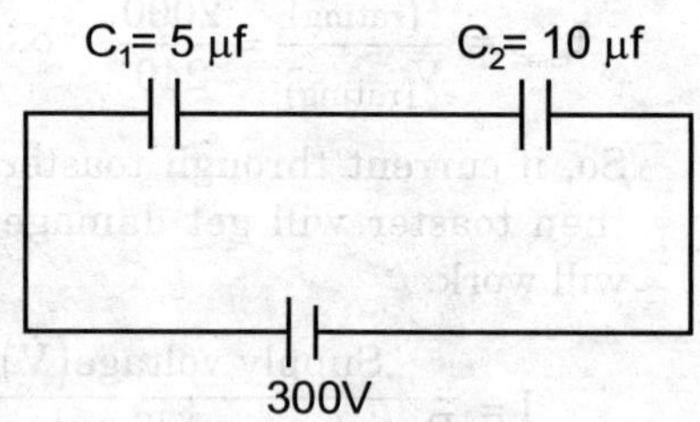

$$C_{eq} = \frac{C_1 \times C_2}{C_1 + C_2}$$

$$= \frac{5 \times 10}{5 + 10} = \frac{10}{3}\,f$$

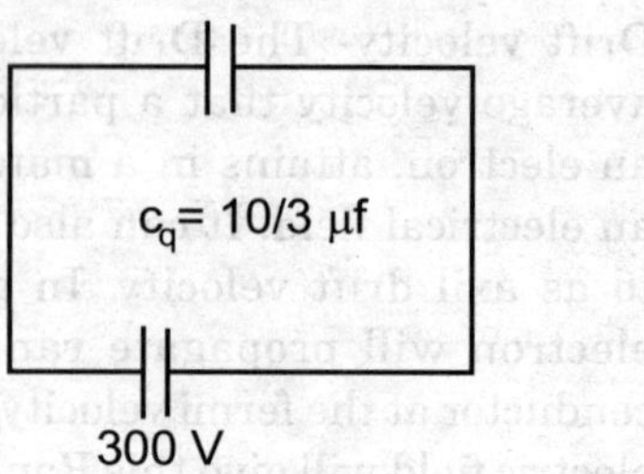

(i) $q = cv$

$$\text{charge} = \frac{10}{3} \times 300 = 100 \quad c \quad ....(1)$$

charge flow in C_1 & C_2 is 1 mc

(ii) voltage across

$$\text{'C'} = \frac{C_2}{(C_1 + C_2)} \times v$$

$$V_1' = \frac{10}{10+5} \times 300 = 200 \text{ V}$$

$$\text{voltage across } (C_2) = \frac{C_1}{(C_1 + C_2)} V$$

$$V_2' = \frac{5}{10+5} \times 300 = 100 \text{ V.}$$

(iii) energy store in 'C_1' $= \frac{1}{2} C_1 V_1^2$

$$= \frac{1}{2} \times 5 \quad F \times (200)^2 = 100 mJ$$

energy store in 'C_2' $= \frac{1}{2} C_2 V_2^2$

$$= \frac{1}{2} \times 10 \quad F \times (100)^2 = 50 \text{ mJ}$$

(d) (i) Self inductance of a coil is defined as the property of the coil due to which it opposes the change of current flowing through it. Inductance is attained by a coil due to the self-inductance emf produced in the coil itself by changing the current flowing through it.

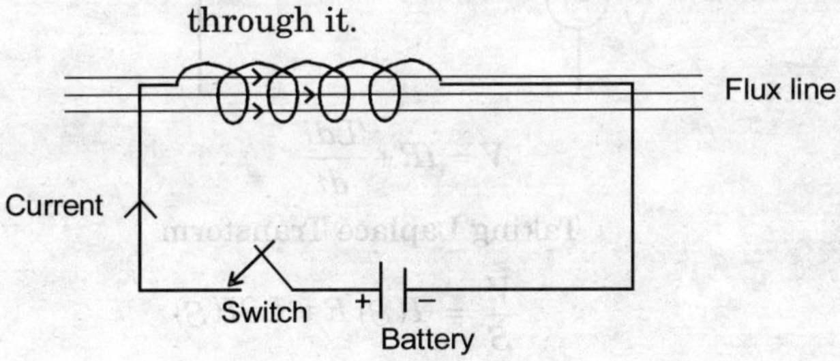

If the current in the coil in increasing, the self induced emf produced in the coil will oppose the Rise of current, that means the direction of the induced emf is opposite to the applied voltage. If the current in the coil is decreasing, the emf induce in the coil is such as direction of to opposes the fall of current this means the direction of self induce voltage is in same direction of applied voltage.

Self inductance does not affect the steady current.

$$E = L\frac{dI}{dt}$$

E = magnetic of self inductance (v/m)

$\frac{dI}{dt}$ = Rate of change of current $\left(\frac{A}{\text{sec}}\right)$

L = Self inductance (Henry 'H').

(ii) Flux is the presence of a force filed in a specified physical medium. or the flow of energy through a surface. In electronics, the term applies to any electrostatic field and any magnetic field. flux is depicted as 'lines' in a plane that contains or intersects electric charged poles or magnetic poles.

(iii) RMS value is based on the heating effect of the wave (current or voltage). It is defined as the amount of heat produced across a resistor. When an A.C. is applied produced heat is equal to the heat produced by DC across the same value of resistor and operated for the same time

$$\boxed{H_{ac} = D_{DC}}$$

3. (a) Given, flux density (B) = $0.05\,T$.

Area (A) = 300 cm² = $300 \times 10^{-4}\,\text{m}^2$

Number of turns = 25

Angular velocity (w) = 40 rad/sec

Maximum induced EMf (E_m) = NwAB.

$$= 25 \times 40 \times 300 \times 10^{-4} 0.05 = 1.5 \text{ volt}$$

(b) (i) The obstruction offered by a magnetic circuit to the magnetic flux is known as Reluctance. As in electric circuit, these is Resistance similarly in the Magnetic circuit, there is a Reluctance, but resistance in an electric circuit dissipates the electric energy and the reluctance in magnetic circuit store the magnetic energy.

$$\text{Reluctance } (S) = \frac{\text{MMF}}{\text{flux}}$$

SI unit of magnetic reluctance is

$$\left(\frac{\text{AT}}{\text{Webere}}\right)$$

(ii) The Permeance of the magnetic circuit is the reciprocal of the reluctance. It is defined as the property of the magnetic circuit due to which it allows flow of the magnetic flux through it.

$$\text{Permeance} = \frac{1}{\text{Reluctance}}\left(\frac{\text{Weber}}{\text{AT}}\right)$$

(iii) Magnetic field strength = It is defined as the magnetic flux density per unit permeability of material used.

$$H = \frac{B}{\mu} = \frac{NI}{l}$$

(c) Given, Number of turn (N) = 1000

Area (A) = 20 cm² = 20 × 10^{-4} m².

Magnetic flux (ϕ) = Flux density × Area = B. A

B_1 = 1.5 Wb/m².

B_2 = 1.9 Wb/m².

$$\phi_1 = 1.5 \times 20 \times 10^{-4}$$
$$= 30 \times 10^{-4} \text{ Wb}$$
$$\phi_2 = 1.9 \times 20 \times 10^{-4}$$
$$= 38 \times 10^{-4} \text{ Wb}$$
$$I_1 = 4A$$
$$I_2 = 8A$$

So inductance

$$(L_1) = \frac{N\phi_1}{I_1} = \frac{1000 \times 30 \times 10^{-4}}{4} = 0.75\ H$$

$$L_2 = \frac{N\phi_2}{I_2} = \frac{1000 \times 38 \times 10^{-4}}{8} = 0.475\ H$$

$$L_{eq} = \sqrt{L_1\ L_2} = 0.597 \text{ Henery}$$

and induced emf

$$= L_{eq}\frac{di}{dt} = \frac{0.597(4.8)}{0.06} = 39.72 \text{ volt}$$

(d) Given, flux ϕ_1 = 0.25 × 10^{-3} Wb

flux ϕ_2 = 0.15 × 10^{-3} Wb

Number of turn 'N_1' = 1200

N_2 = 800

Current in coils = 5A.

$$L_1 = \frac{NI_1}{I_1} = \frac{1200 \times 0.25 \times 10^{-3}}{5}$$
$$= 0.6 \text{ Henry}$$

$$L_2 = \frac{800 \times 0.15 \times 10^{-3}}{5}$$
$$= 0.24 \text{ Henry}$$

Therefore $M = K\sqrt{L_1\ L_2}$

$$= 0.6\sqrt{0.06 \times 0.24}$$
$$= 0.228 \text{ Henry}$$

4. (a) As given DC current and sinusoidal AC current carrying simultaneously

$$I_{\text{resultant}} = I_{DC} + I_{AC}$$
$$I_{AC} = I_m \sin \omega t$$
$$I_m = 1.414\ A.$$
$$Iav = I_{DC} + I_{AC}$$
$$= 10 + 1.414 \sin \omega t$$

Average value of sinusoidal signal is zero

$$I_{av} = 10$$

$$I_{rms} = \sqrt{(I_{DC})^2 + (I_{AC})^2}$$

$$I_{rms} = \frac{I_{\max}}{\sqrt{2}} = \frac{1.414}{\sqrt{2}} = 1$$

$$I_{AC(rms)} = 1$$

$$I_{rms} = \sqrt{(10)^2 + 1} = 10.049\ A$$

(b) Resistance (R) = 3Ω.

Time constant = 1.8 sec

$$\text{Time constant} = \frac{L}{R}$$

$$L = 1.8 \times 3 - 5.4$$

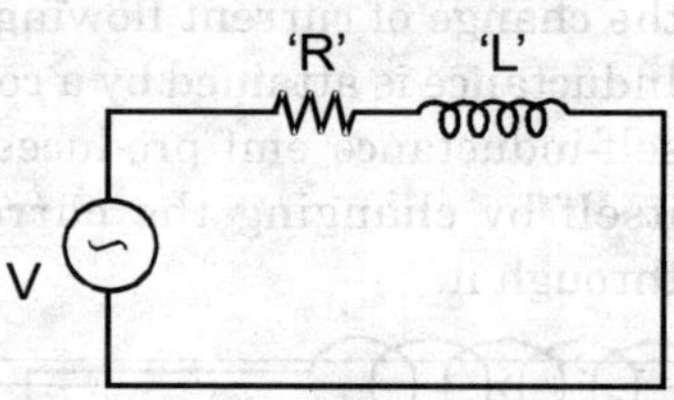

$$V = IR + \frac{Ldi}{dt}$$

Taking Laplace Transform

$$\frac{V}{S} = I(S)\,R + LSI(S)$$

$$= I(S) = \frac{V}{S(R + LS)}$$

$$= \frac{V}{LS\left(\frac{R}{L} + S\right)}$$

$$= \frac{V}{R}\left[\frac{1}{S} - \frac{1}{\left(S + \frac{R}{L}\right)}\right]$$

$$I(t) = \frac{V}{R}\left(1 - e^{\frac{Rt}{L}}\right) \quad \text{....(1)}$$

(i) Current at t = 1 sec

$$\frac{10}{3}\left(1-e^{-\frac{1}{1.8}}\right) = 3.33\,(1-.57) = 1.43\,A.$$

(ii) Final value is at infinite

$$I(\infty)=\frac{V}{R}\left(1-e^{-\frac{\infty R}{L}}\right)$$

$$I(\infty)=\frac{V}{R}$$

time at which current attains half of its final value

$$\frac{1}{2}\frac{V}{R}=\frac{V}{R}\left(1-e^{-\frac{t}{2}}\right)$$

$$e^{-\frac{t}{2}}=\frac{1}{2}$$

$$t = 2\ln 2 = 1.248 \text{ sec}$$

(iii) Initial rate of growth of current

$$\frac{dI(t)}{dt}=\frac{V}{R}e^{-\frac{tR}{L}}\times\frac{R}{L}=\frac{V}{L}e^{-\frac{tR}{L}}$$

$$\frac{dI(t)}{dt}-\frac{V}{L}e^{-.56t}=\frac{10}{5.4}e^{-.56t}\,\frac{A}{S}$$

$$=1.867e^{-.56t}\left(\frac{A}{S}\right)$$

(c) (i) Energy meter-

- Energy

$$\text{Power}\times\text{time}=\int_0^1 p\,dt$$

$$=\int_0^1 v(t).\,i(t)\,dt = VIt$$

If v is expressed in volt (v) current (I) in A and time in second (s) than, unit of energy = Joule or watt second. If V is expressed in volt (v), current (i) in A and time in hour then.

unit of energy = watt hours

- For a.c. circuits, energy is measured in items of KWh (kilowatt hour)
- For DC circuits energy is measured in terms of AH (Ampere hour)
- Energy meter is used to measure energy in a.c. circuit which is an integrating instrument and works on the principal of induction motor.

$$Td_1 \propto \phi_C J_P \cos\angle\phi_C - J_P$$

$$Td_2 \propto \phi_P I_c \cos\angle\phi_p - J_C$$

$$\boxed{Td \propto Td_1 - Td_2}$$

Requirement

1. Driving Mechanism - A shunt magnet *M1* is wound with a coil called P.C which measures the voltage of load. The series magnet M_2 carries the load current to the current coil. This current I_1 lags the voltage by an angle ϕ.

$$Td \propto VL_1 - \cos\phi$$

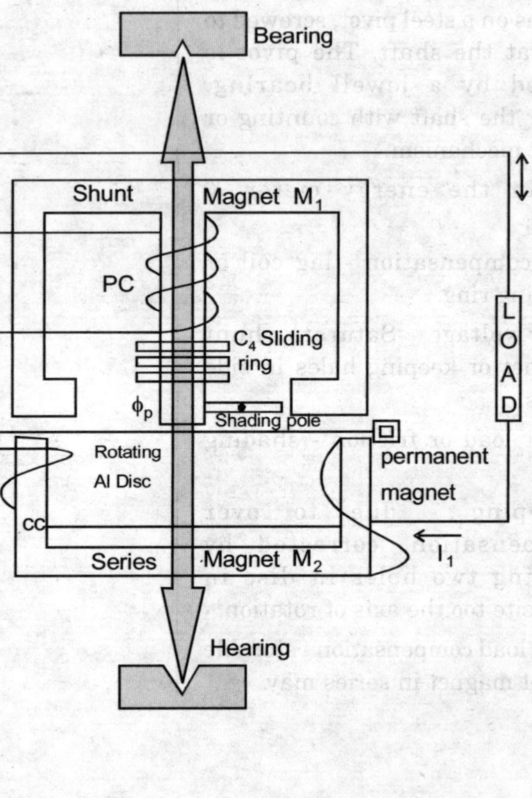

2. Breaking Mechanism - A percent magnet is used which producing a constant term in the rotating disc and this flux is induced an eddy voltage which is directly proportional to the speed of disc and this eddy voltage produce a current and interaction of this current with the flow produce a breaking torque which is directly proportional to the speed of the disc. This braking torque in opposition to the driving torque which keeps the rotation to the driving torque which keeps the rotation of disc constant

   N. dt = P.dt = Energy

3. Recording Mechanism - Reduced gears mechanism are used to record the number of revolution made by the disc. The painters in the great wheel changes the numbers in deals.

   Note - Shading rings made of copper is kept in the P.C to adjust the ϕ angle between I_2 & V so that the energy meter record correctly.

   $$t = \frac{t}{3600}\text{hr.}$$

4. Moving Mechanism - This consists at an Al disc unwanted an a light alloy shaft. The disc is positioned in air gap between series & shunt magnets. The rotor turns on a steel pivot, screwed to the foot at the shaft. The pivot is supported by a jewell bearing. A pioneer the shaft with counting or recording mechanism.

   Errors in the energy meter & correction-

   1. Lag compensation - lag coil or shading ring.
   2. Over voltage - Saturate shunt magnet or keeping hales in side limbs.
   3. Light load or friction - shading loop.
   4. Creeping - due to over compensation, corrected by making two holes in disc in opposite too the axis of rotation.
   5. Over load compensation - storable shunt magnet in series may.
   6. Speed adjustment-

      By adjusting P. magnet position near to shaft - speed high

      By adjusting P.P. away from shaft speed slow
   7. Temperature compensation - Mu-metal material used.

   Note. It the C.C. or P.C coil terminal are reversed the disc will rotate in opposite direction.

(ii) CRO

Basis of CRO (Cathode Ray Oscilloscope)

- It is a very useful and versatile laboratory instrument used for display measurement and analysis of waveforms.
- Normal from of a CRO uses a horizontal input voltage, which is an internally generated ramp voltage, called time base. This move the luminous spot periodically in a horizontal direction from left to right over screen.
- Vertical input to the CRO is the voltage under investigation. This moves luminous spot up and down with current value of the voltage.
- CRO operates on voltage. But is possible to convert current, strain acceleration, and pressure into voltage with the help of transducers.
- Used to investigation waveforms transient phenomenal, for very low frequency range to the radio frequencies.
- CRO mainly consist of CRT (Cathode Ray Tube) which is heart of CRO.

(i) Frequency and time period can be measured.

(ii) It has X-Y scale waveforms pattern.

(iii) H can display two or more input waveforms simultaneously.

(iv) It can measure the voltage like V_m. V_{pp}, V_{rms} and V_{avg}.

(v) Phase angle can be measured with the help of CRO

(vi) Sensitivity is high.

(vii) It can study the quantities from a low frequencies (20 Hz) to a very high frequency (Up to GHz)

(viii) H can be used for high applications (i.e. sampling oscilloscope)

(ix) It has high precision.

(iii) 2 wattmeter method-

For measurement of power in n^th wire system the minimum no. of wattmeter required is (n – 1).

For 3 – ϕ, 3 – wire system the minimum wattmeter required is 3 – 1 = 2

Measurement of power by two wattmeter method is given below.

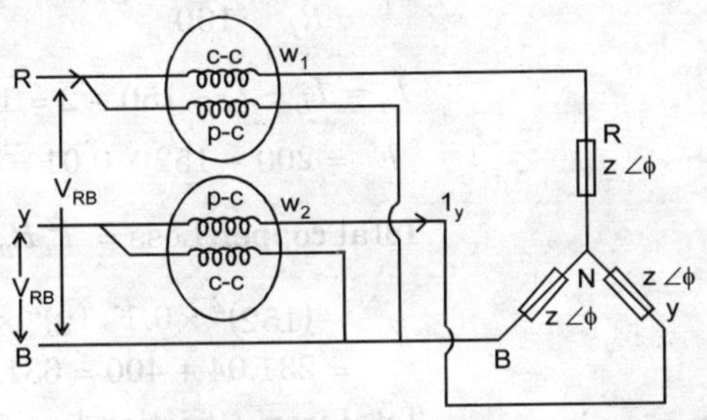

Fig. Phasor for a star load

Reading of wattmeter 1

$$W_1 = V_{RB} I_R \cos\angle(V_{RB} - I_g)$$

$$W_1 = V_L I_L \cos(30 - \phi) \qquad \text{......(1)}$$

Reading to wattmer 2

$$W_2 = V_{YB} I_Y \cos\angle(V_{YB} - I_Y)$$

$$W_2 = V_L I_L \cos(30 - \phi) \qquad \text{......(2)}$$

Now an adding equations (1) & (2), we get

$$W = W_1 + W_2.$$

$$= V_L I_L \cos(30 - \phi) + V_L I_L \cos(30 - \phi)$$

$$= V_L I_L \left[\cos(30 - \phi) + \cos(30 - \phi)\right]$$

$$\boxed{w = \sqrt{3} V_L I_L \cos\phi} \qquad \text{.....(3)}$$

This result shows that it is the power for 3 – ϕ system.

Now on subtracting equations (1) & (2), we get

$$W_1 - W_2 = V_L I_2 \cos(30 - \phi) - V_1 I_2 \cos(30 + \phi)$$

$$= V_L I_L . 2 \sin 30. \sin \phi.$$

$$\boxed{W_1 - W_2 = V_L I_L \sin\theta}$$

On dividing equation (4) by equation (3), we get

$$\frac{W_1 - W_2}{W_1 + W_2} = \frac{V_L I_L \sin\theta}{\sqrt{3} V_L I_L \cos\theta}$$

$$\tan\phi = \sqrt{3}\frac{(W_1 - W_2)}{(W_1 + W_2)}$$

Power factor angle

$$\boxed{\phi = \tan^{-1}\left\{\sqrt{3}\frac{W_1 + W_2}{W_1 + W_2}\right\}}$$

Power factor,

$$\boxed{\cos\phi = \cos\left\{\tan^{-1}\left(\sqrt{3}\frac{W_1 - W_2}{(W_1 + W2_2)}\right)\right\}}$$

Variation in Wattmeter reading

pf angle (ϕ)	*P.F* (cos ϕ)	W_1 $[V_L I_2 \cos(30 + \phi)]$	W_2 $[V_L I_2 \cos(30 - \phi)]$	$W = W_1 + W_2$ $[W = \sqrt{3} V_L \cos\phi]$	Observation
0°	1	$\frac{\sqrt{3}}{2} V_L I_L$	$\frac{\sqrt{3}}{2} V_L I_L$	$\sqrt{3} V_L I_L$	$W_1 = W_2$
30°	0.866	$\frac{V_L I_L}{2}$	$V_L I_L$	$1.5 V_L I_L$	$W_2 = 2W_1$
60°	0.5	0	$\frac{\sqrt{3}}{2} V_L I_L$	$\frac{\sqrt{3}}{2} V_L I_L$	$W_1 = 0$
90°	0	$\frac{-V_L I_L}{2}$	$\frac{V_L I_L}{2}$	0	$W_1 = W_2$

(iv) Multi-meter - The ammeter, the voltage and the ohmmeter all use a basic D's Arsonval movement the deference between these instruments is the circuit in which the basic movement is used. It is therefore obvious that an instrument can be designed to perform these measurement function. This instrument which contains a function switch to connect the appropriate circuits to the d's Arsonval movement is called a "multi-meter" or volt-ohm-milli-ammeter" (V.O.M)

A representative example of a commercial multi-meter is the simpson model 260 whose complete combination of a d.c milliammeter, a d.c voltmeter an a.c voltmeter a multi-range chapter and an output meter.

This multi-meter uses a D's Arsonval movement that has a resistance of 200 Ω and a full scale current of 500

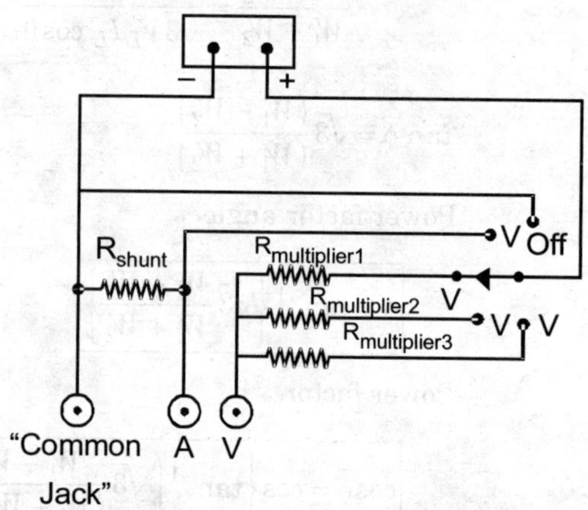

This instrument is provided with selector switch which can be set for different modes of operation like measurement of voltage, current resistance etc. and also for various ranges of these quantities.

(d) Given that,

length of coil, $l = 5$ cm $= 5 \times 10^{-2}$ cm

Number of turn $(N) = 100$

Width of the coil $(\alpha) = 4 \times 10^{-2}$ m

Magnetic flux density in air gap, $B = 2$ Wb/m^2.

Spring constant $(K) = 5 \times 10^{-7}$ Nm/degree

deflection of the coil, $\theta = 60°$

At equilibrium $T_c = T_\alpha$

$$K\theta = BINA = BIN\,(l \times d)$$

$$\boxed{A = l \times d}$$

then, $$I = \frac{K\theta}{BINld}$$

$$= \frac{5 \times 10^{-7} \times 60}{2 \times 100 \times 5 \times 10^{-2} \times 4 \times 10^{-2}}$$

$$= 7.5 \times 10^{-5} A = 75 \times 10^{-6} A = 75\ \mu A.$$

5. (a)

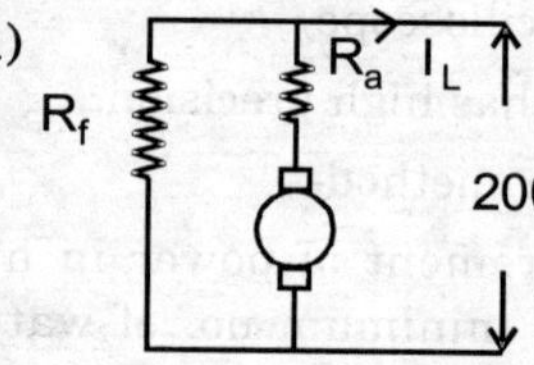

$$R_f = 100\Omega,\ R_a = 0.01\Omega$$

$$30 \text{ kW} = 200\, I_L.$$

$$I_L = 150A.$$

$$\text{EMF } 'E_b' = V + I_a R_a.$$

$$I_f = \frac{V}{R_f} = \frac{200}{100} = 2A$$

$$I_a = I_L + I_f = 150 + 2 = 152$$

$$E_b = 200 + 152 \times 0.01 = 201.52 \text{ volt}$$

$$\text{Total copper Loss} = I_a^2 R_a + I_f^2 R_f$$

$$= (152)^2 \times 0.1 + (2)^2 \times 100$$

$$= 231.04 + 400 = 631.04 \text{ w}$$

Total iron + friction loss = 1000 w

5. (b) Dynamic breaking of induction motor.

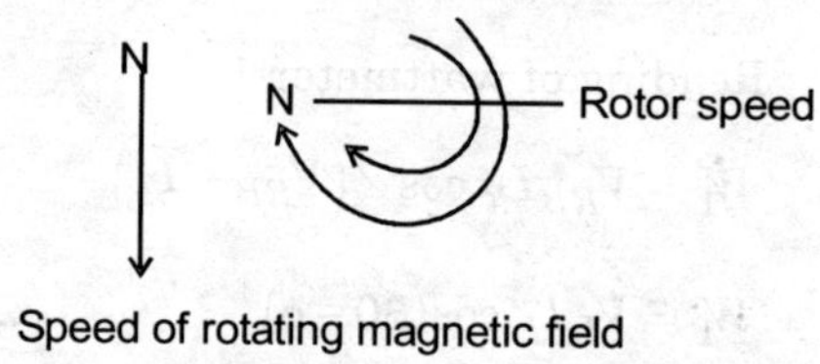

In case of dynamic breaking three phase supply is cut so rotating field is getting vanished now we apply the d.c. supply.

- This d.c. supply will produce constant magnetic field and this will be cut by the rotating magnetic field.
- According to Faraday's law an emf will be induced and it will oppose the motion by Len'z law.
- Due to opposite force machine will stop.

(c) (i) **Fractional kilowatt motors-**

- Small motors which has power rating less than 1 kW is fractional kilowatt.
- This type of motors are normally used for domestic application.

- Type of fractional kilowatt motors

(A) 1 ϕ induction motors

(1) Split phase induction motor

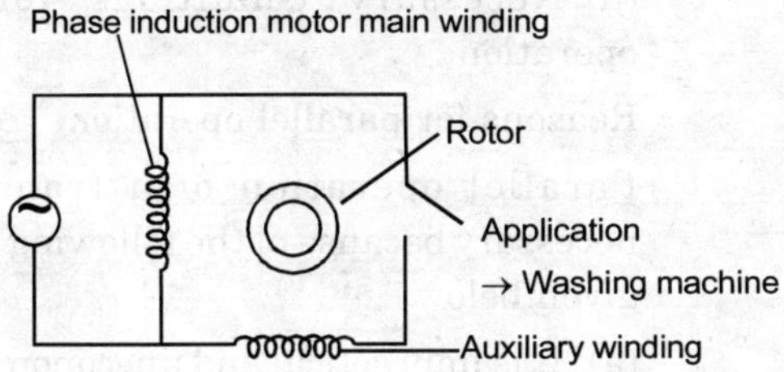

Capacitor Type

(a) Capacitor start induction motor

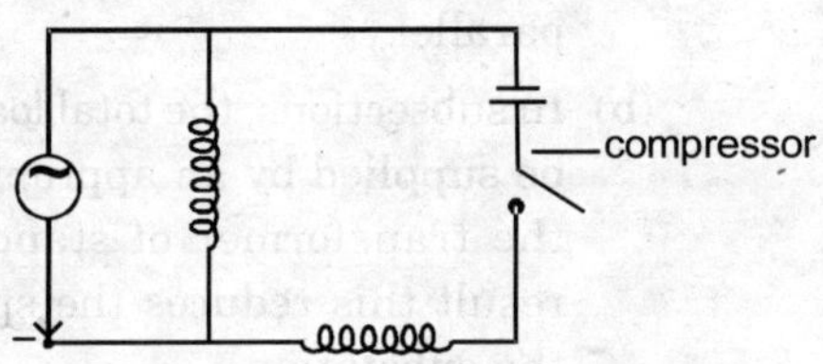

(b) Capacitor run induction motor

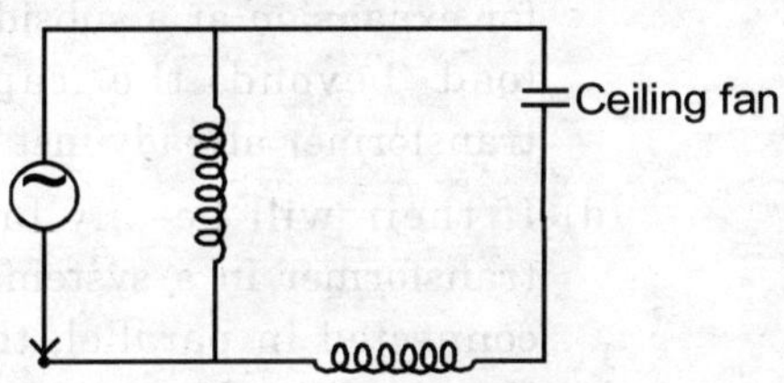

(c) Capacitor start capacitor run

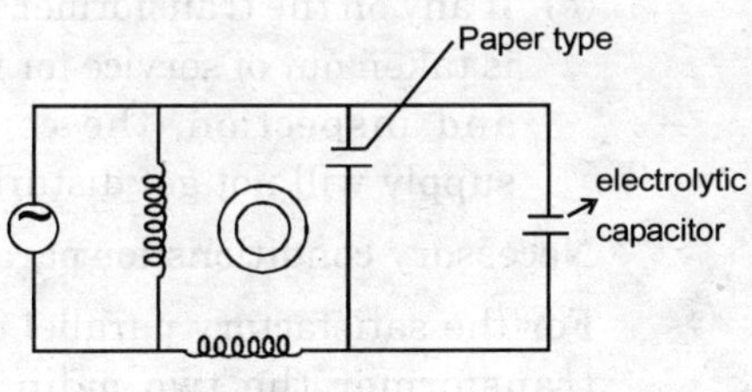

Example → refrigerator

Shaded pale indication motor

Example → toys

(2) 1-Q synchronous motor

(a) Reluctance motor

Example timing and signal line

(b) **hysteresis motor**

Example → Sound - Tap recorder.

(3) Universal motor → This is a series type of motor which can work with both A.C as well as d.c

- It can run upto a speed of 20000 rpm.
- It has high starting torque and high speed/
- Smaller in size.

Application →

(i) Vaccum cleaner

(ii) mixer

(iii) saving machine

4. Repulsion motor-

- This type of motor is operated by brush shifting
- This direction of rotation is along the shifting of brush.

Types-

(i) Repulsion motor.

(ii) compensated type repulsion motor

(iii) Repulsion start induction run

(iv) Repulsion - Induction motor.

(ii) An Auto-transformer (some times called auto-step down transformer) is an electrical transformer with only one winding. The "auto" (Greek for "self") prefix refers to the signal coil acting alone and not to any kind of automatic mechanism. In an autotransformer, portions of the some winding act as both the primary and secondary sides of the transformer. In contract, an ordinary transformer has separate primary and secondary winding which are not electrically connected.

The winding has at lest three taps where electrical connections are made. Since part of the winding does "double duty".

Autotransformers have the advantages of often being smaller. lighter and cheaper than typical dual winding transformers but the disadvantage of not providing electrical isolation between primary and secondary circuits. Other advantages of autotransformers include lower leakage reactance, lower losses, lower excitation current, and increased VA rating for a given size and mass.

(iii) **Short circuit test of 3-ϕ transformers-**

These test is conducted to find

(i) Copper loss

(ii) Series parameter like winding resistant leakage reactance.

(iii) Voltage regulation

Conditions-

(i) It is operated at rated current and from high voltage side.

(ii) Low voltage is short circuited in order to ensure that the power consumed is only due to copper loss.

- During this test the current blowing through shunt parameter is even lower so the core loss can be neglected.

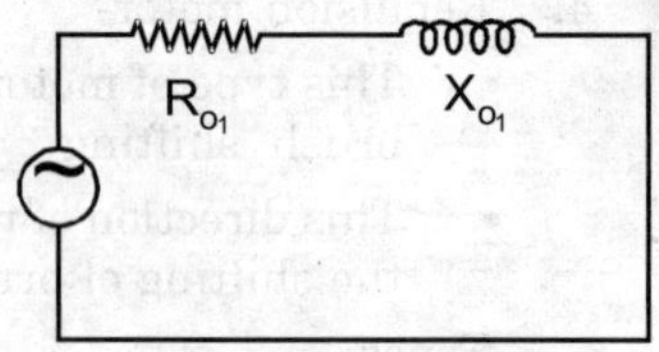

Equivalent circuit

Testing arrangement

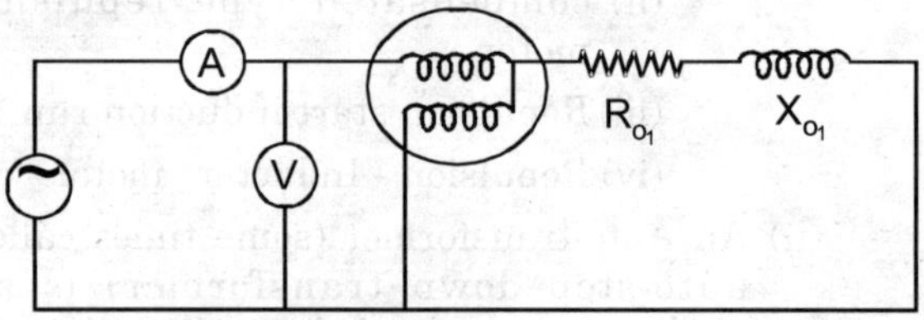

Result of testing

reading (w) → copper loss

$$\text{Impudence} = \frac{\text{Voltmeter reading}}{\text{ammeter reading}}$$

$$\text{Wattmeter reading} = (\text{ammeter reading})^2 \times R.$$

$$X = \sqrt{Z^2 - R^2}$$

(d) Parallel operation of a transformer-

The transformer is said to be in parallel operation when their primary windings are connected to a common voltage supply, and the secondary windings are connected to a common load. The connection diagram of the parallel operation of a transformer is shown in the figure below.

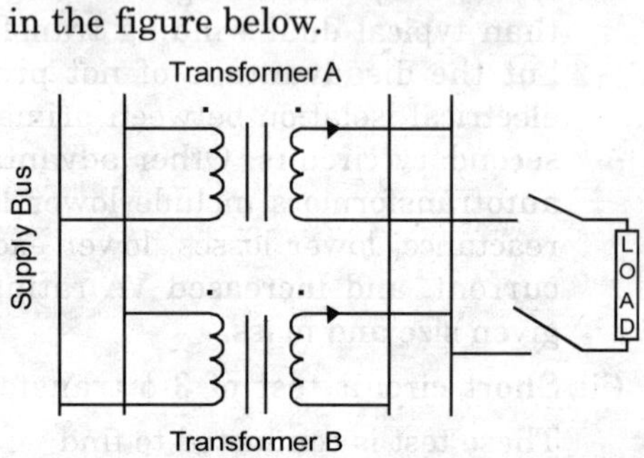

The parallel operation of a transformer has some advantages likes it increases the efficiency of the system makes the system more flexible and reliable but increases the short - circuit current of the transformers.

Contents-

(i) Reasons for parallel operation

(ii) Necessary conditions for parallel operation

Reasons for parallel operation-

Parallel operation of a transformer is necessary because of the following reasons are given below

(a) It is impractical and uneconomical to have a single large transformer for heavy and large loads. Hence it will be a wise decision to connect a number of transformers in parallel.

(b) In subsections, the total load required may be supplied by an appropriate number of the transformer of standard size. As a result this reduces the spare capacity of the substation.

(c) It is transformers are connected in parallel, so their will be scope in future, for expansion at a subsiding to supply a load beyond the capacity of the transformer already installed.

(d) If their will be any breakdown of a transformer in a system of transformer connected in parallel, there will be no interruption of power supply, for essential services.

(e) If any on the transformer from the system is taken out of service for its maintenance and inspection, the continuity of the supply will not get disturbed.

Necessary conditions for parallel operation-

For the satisfactory parallel operation of the transformer the two main conditions are necessary one is that the politics of the transformers must be same. Another condition is that the turn rate current to flow through CT_1 than CT_2 consequently, there secondary voltage becomes unequal and air circulating current flows through the pilot wires and relays. The circuit breakers at both ends of the line will trip out and the faulty line will be isolated.

Figure shows the connections of Mertz-Price voltage balance for all the three phase of the line.

Advantages-

(i) This system can used for ring mains as will as parallel feeders.

(ii) This system provides instantaneous protection of ground faults. This decreases the possibility of these faults involving other phases.

(iii) This system provides instantaneous relaying which reduces the amount of damage to overhead conductors resulting from arcing faults.

Disadvantages-

(i) Accurate matching of current transformers is very essential.

(ii) If there is a break in the pilot wire circuit, the system will not operate.

(iii) This system is very expensive owing to the greater length of pilot wires required.

(iv) In case of long line charging current due to pilot-wire capacitance "effects may sufficient of the transformer should be equal.

The other two desirable conditions are as follows-

(i) The voltage at full load across the transformer internal impedance should be equal

(ii) The ratio of their winding resistances to reactance should be equal for both the transformers. This condition ensures that both transformers operate at the same power factor thus sharing their active power and reactive volt-amperes according to their ratings.

6. (a) (i) **Merz- price of protection** - Figure shows the single line diagram of mercerize voltage balance system for the protection of a 3 phase line. Identical current transformer are placed in each phase at both ends of the line. The pair of CTs in each line is connected in series with a relay in such a way that under normal condition their secondary voltages are equal and in opposition i.e. they balance each other.

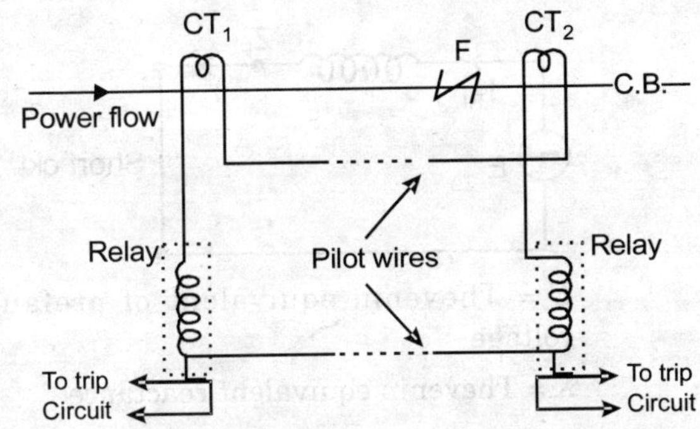

Under healthy conditions current entering the line at one-end is equal to the leading it at the other end. Therefore, equal and opposite voltages are induced in the secondary of the CTs at the two ends at the line. The result is that no current flows through the relays. Suppose a fault occurs at point F on the line as shown in Figure This will cause a greater to cause relay operation relay operation even under normal conditions.

This system can not be used for line voltages beyond 33KV because of constructional difficulties in matching the current transformers.

(ii) **Short circuit current for symmetrical faults-**

A fault in which all the three phases in involving known as symmetrical fault.

(i) All the three phase to earth (L.L.L.G.)

(ii) All the three short circuited (L.L.L)

3% chances of occurrence

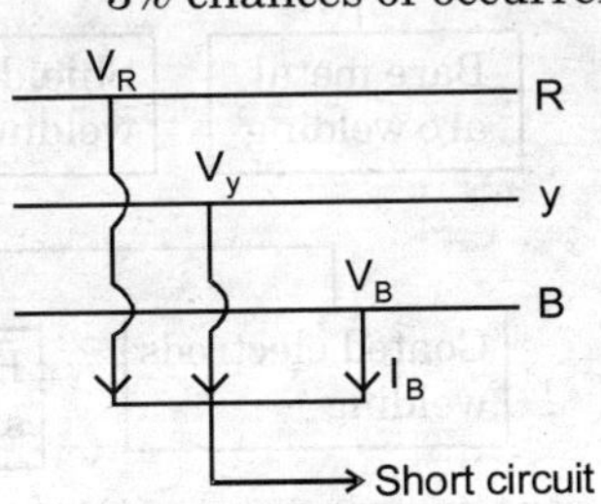

(L.L.L fault)

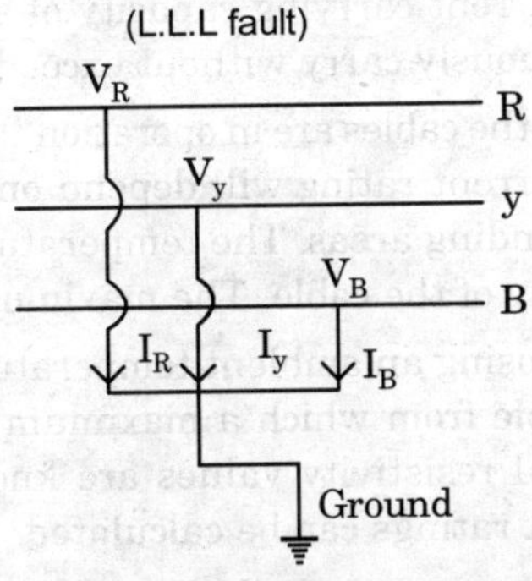

(L.L.I.G fault)

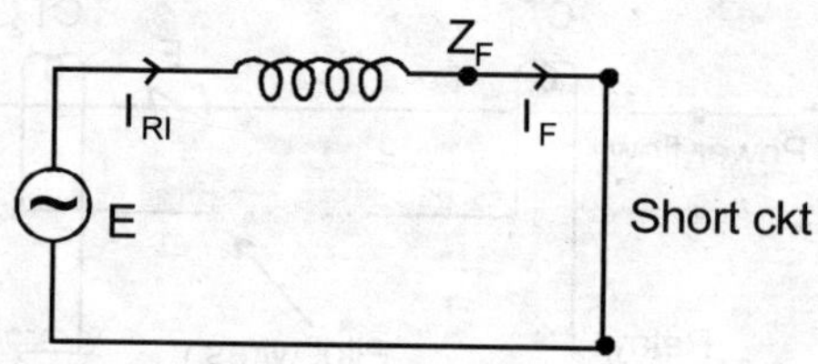

E = Thevenin equivalent of prefault voltage

X = Thevenin equivalent reactance

$$I_F(3\phi) = \frac{E}{X}$$

Let E = IPU

then $\Rightarrow I_F(3\phi) = I_{SC} = \frac{1}{X}$

(iii) **Electric Welding–**

It is metallurgical union of metals brought about by the application of heat and pressure so that welded joint should have, as for as possible, same properties as the parent metal in adjacent parts of weld. Depending upon how the heat applied is created. We get different types of welding such as thermal welding, gas welding and electric welding. Electric welding will be gone through in details with some introduction to other modern welding techniques.

Classification of electrical welding-

Electric welding is classified as electric area welding and electric resistance welding electron beam welding. There are further sub-classified as:

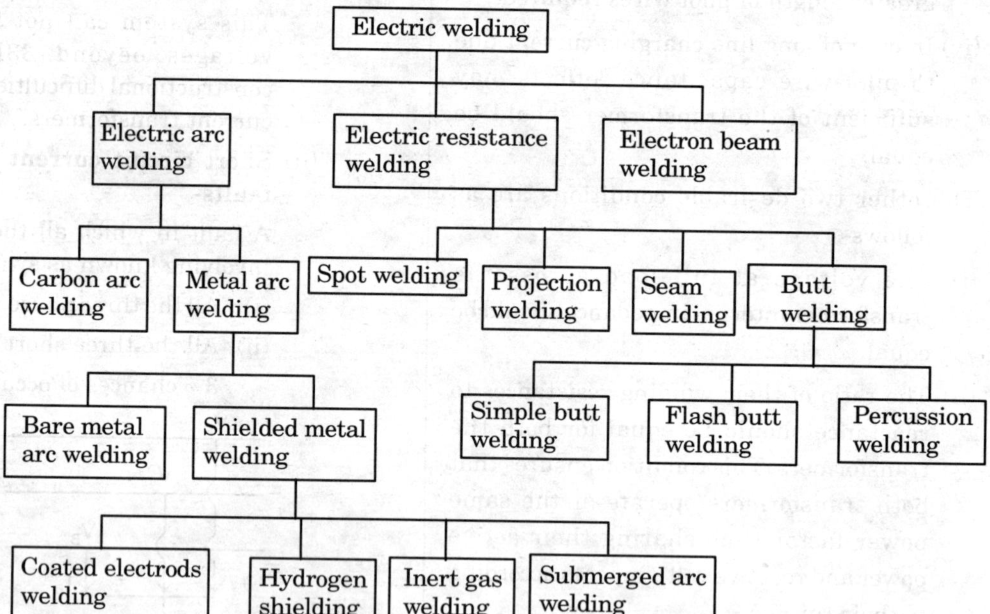

(b) The current carrying capacity of an insulated conductor or cable is the maximum current that it can continuously carry without exceeding its temperature rating. It is also known as ampacity.

Whilst the cables are in operation they suffer electrical losses. Which manifest as heat in the construction. The current rating will depend on how this heat is dissipated through the cable surface and into the surrounding areas. The temperature rating of the cable is a determining factor in the current carrying capacity of the cable. The maximum temperature as a base for the insulation material.

By choosing an ambient temperature as a base for the surroundings, a permissible temperature rise is available from which a maximum cable rating can be calculated for a particular environment. If the thermal resistivity values are known for the layers of materials in the cable construction then the current ratings can be calculated.

The formula for calculating current carrying capacity is

$$1 = \left\{ \frac{\Delta\theta - W_d\left[\frac{1}{2}T_1 + n(T_2 + T_3 + T_4)\right]}{RT1 + N_R(1+\lambda_1)T_2 + nR(1+\lambda_1+\lambda_2)(T_3+T_4)} \right\}^{\frac{1}{2}}$$

1 = permissible current rating

$\Delta\phi$ = conductor temperature rise in (K)

R = Alternating current resistance per unit length of the conductor at maximum per unit length of the conductor at maximum operating temperature (Ω/m)

W_d = dielectric loss per unit length for the insulating surrounding the conductor (W/m)

T_1 = Thermal resistance per unit length between one conductor and the sheath (Kw/w)

T_2 = Thermal resistance per unit length of the bedding between sheath and the amount (Km/w)

T_3 = Thermal resistance per unit length of the external sheath of the cable (Km/w)

T_4 = Thermal resistance per unit length between the cable surface and the surrounding medium (Km/.w)

n = number of load carrying conductors in the cable (conductors of equal size and carrying the same load.

λ_1 = Ratio of losses in the metal sheath to total losses in all conductors in that cable.

λ_2 = ratio of losses in the armouring to total losses in all conductors in that cable.

(c) The terminology used for denoting the three basic transistor configurations indicates the transistor terminal that is common to both input and output circuits. The gives rise to the three terms common base, common collector and common emitter.

The term grounded, i.e. grounded base, grounded collector and grounded emitted may also be used on occasions because the common element signal is normally grounded.

The three different transistor configurations are....

Common base- This transistor configuration provides a low input impedance while offering a high output impedance. Although the voltage is high, the current gain is also low when compared to the other transistor configurations available. The other salient feature of this configuration is that the input and output are in phase.

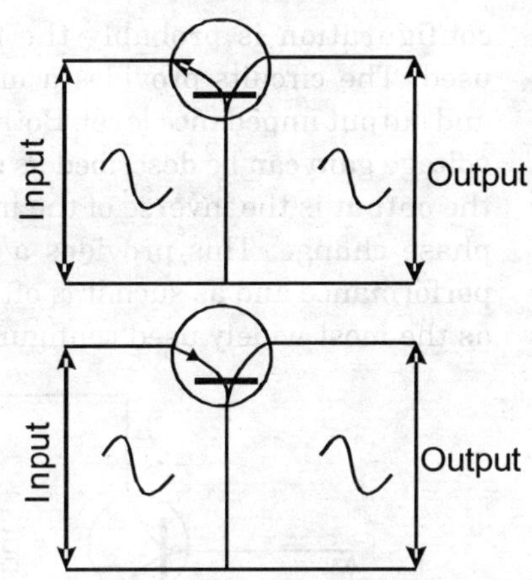

PNP

As can be seen from the diagram, in this transistor configuration, the base electrode is common to both input and output circuits. Read more about the common base amplifier.

Common Collectors - This transistor configuration is also known as the emitter follower because the emitter voltage follows that of the base. Offering a high input impedance and a low output impedance it is widely used a buffer. The voltage gas in is unity. Although current gain is high. The input and output signals are in phase.

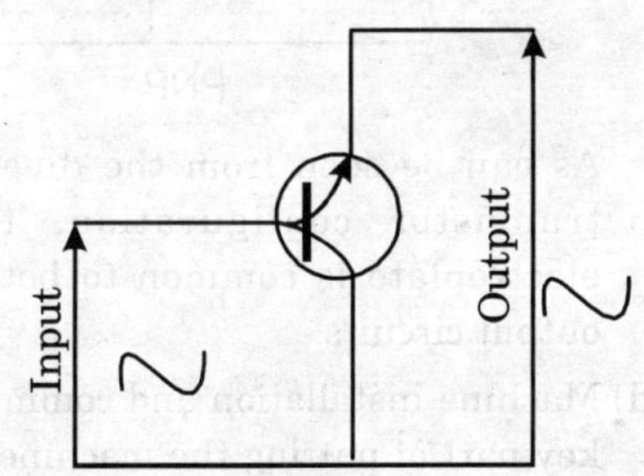

NNP

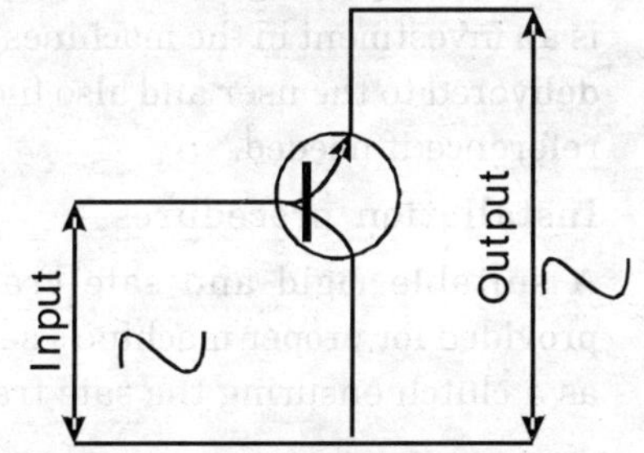

PNP

As can be seen from the diagram, in this transistor configuration the collector electrode is common to both input and output circuits.

Common emitter - The transistor

configuration is probably the most widely used. The circuits provides a medium input and output impedance level. Both current and voltage gain can be described as medium. But the output is the inverse of the input i.e. 180° phase change. This provides a good overall performance and as such it is often though at as the most widely used configuration.

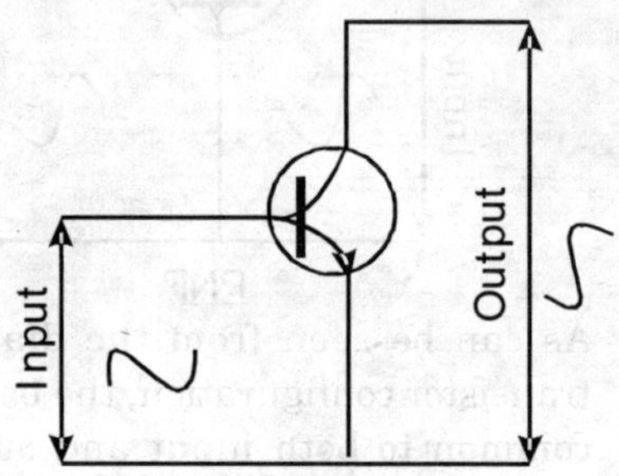

NNP

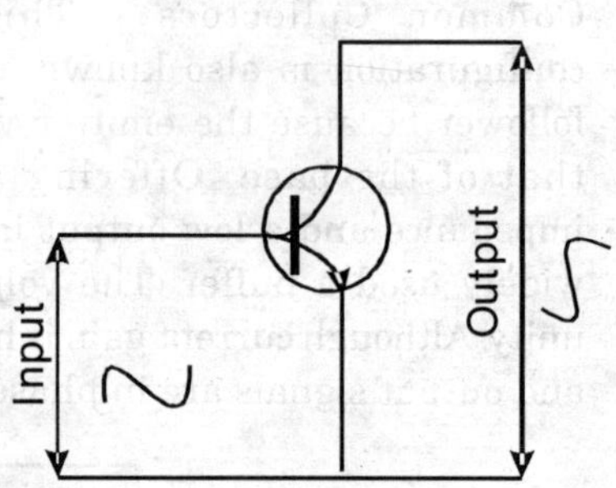

PNP

As can be seen from the diagram, in this transistor configuration, the emitter electroplate is common to both input and output circuits.

(d) Machine installation and commissioning is a key part of putting the machine into service. If installation and commissioning is carrying out carefully using the correct procedures, it is an investment in the machines are recorded, delivered to the user and also filed for further reference if needed.

Installation procedures -

A suitable rigid and safe cradle must be provided for proper machine's seating, as well as a clutch ensuring the safe transmission of torque from the driving to the driven equipment, our engineering check whether the clutch allows the required axial and radial clearances to compensate for the thermal dilation of the machine's and the bearing lift in sliding bearings.

Main tasks carried out-

Visual inspection of the cradle

Inspection of the clutch

Proper machine axial alignment checking and correction checking the main and auxiliary electric circuit connection

Checking the cooling circuit connection

Checking the lubricating circuit connection commissioning

Mechanism and electrical installations are inspected first to check parameters are kept.

Subsequently, all auxiliary and supervisory circuits required for machine starting and operation are checked.

Main tasks carried out-

Visual inspection of the main cooling and lubricating systems

Check out of the cooling main cable terminals electrical measurement and check of all the machine's wiring

Testing and calibrating setup parameters protection testing

Excitation system and Automatic voltage regulation (AVR) setting.

Checking the idle running load running and connecting the generator phases to the grid checking the operating parterres - load sharing checking operation temperatures and vibration

As soon as the prearranges set and the current operation tested and confirmed the commissioning work is completed and the equipment is handed over to the customer with a record (description of the work, set values, summary recommendation for the further use of the machines.)

Solved Paper 2016

Electrical Engineering

(Paper II)

1. (*a*) A conducting wire has a resistance of 5Ω. What is the resistance of another wire of the same material but having half the diameter and four times the length? (15)

(*b*) Two coils connected in parallel across a 100 V dc supply, take 10 A current from the supply. Power dissipated in one coil is 600W. What is the resistance of each coil? (15)

(*c*) Determine the current through the 5Ω resistor in the circuit of Figure 1. (15)

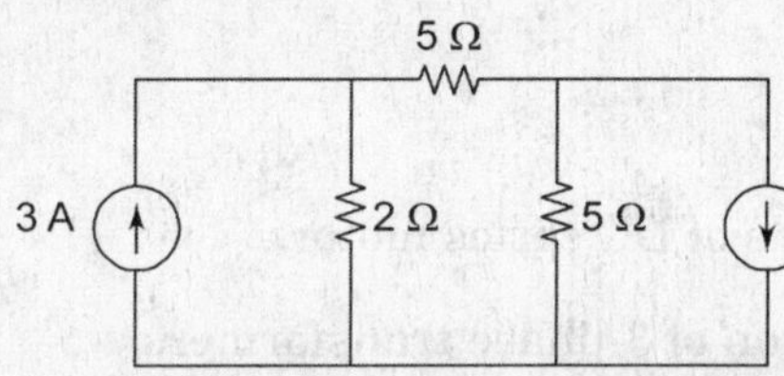

(*d*) Find the voltage across the 5Ω resistance in the network shown in Figure 2 using Thevenin's theorem. (15)

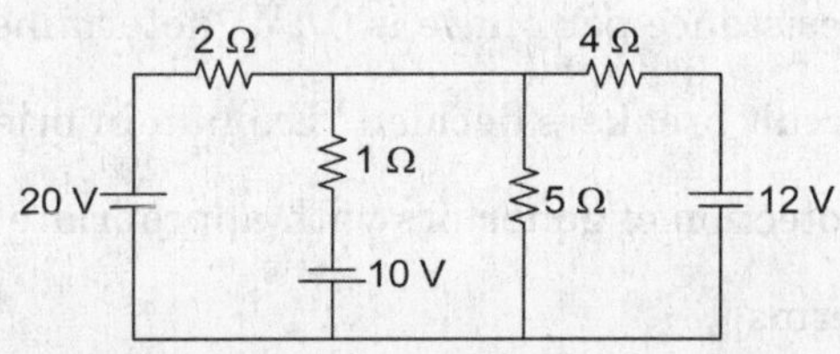

2. (*a*) An aeroplane with a wing span of 52 metres is flying horizontally at 1100 km/h. If the vertical component of the earth's magnetic field is 38×10^{-6} T. Find the emf generated between the wing-tips. (10)

(*b*) A coil of 200 turns is wound uniformly over a wooden ring having a mean circumference of 60 cm and a uniform cross-sectional area of 500 mm^2. If the current through the coil is 4 A, calculate the (i) magnetic field strength, (ii) flux density, and (iii) total flux. (10)

(*c*) An iron choke takes 4 A current when connected to a 20 V dc supply. When connected to a 65V, 50Hz as supply, it takes 5A current. Determine the power drawn by the coil (15)

(*d*) Define the following terms

(*i*) Mutual inductance

(*ii*) Resonance

(*iii*) MMF

(*iv*) Q-factor

3. (*a*) Prove that the reactive power in ac circuit is equal to VI sin ϕ.

(*b*) A 50 μA meter movement with an internal resistance of 1 kΩ is to be used as a dc voltmeter of range 50V. Calculate the

(i) multiplier resistance required and

(ii) voltage multiplying factor. (10)

(*c*) In a gravity controlled instrument the controlling weight is 0.005 kg and acts at a distance of 2.4 cm from the axis of the moving system. Determine the deflection in degrees corresponding to deflecting torque of 1.05×10^{-5} kgm.

(*b*) Explain in brief (30)

(*i*) Megger

(*ii*) Two-wattmeter method

(*iii*) Signal generator

(*iv*) Earth fault detection

(*v*) AC bridge

4. (*a*) Explain the braking methods of DC series motors. (20)

(*b*) Explain the parallel operation of 3-phase transformers. (10)

(*c*) Draw and explain equivalent circuit of a 1-phase transformer. Draw its phasor diagram for leading power factor load. (20)

(*d*) A 3-phase 400V, 50 Hz 6-pole star connected induction motor develops maximum torque at a speed of 940 rpm. If the rotor resistance per phase is 0.1W, determine the standstill rotor reactance. (10)

5. (*a*) How is the rating of circuit breakers decided? Explain in brief. (10)

(*b*) Explain Merz-Price protection of genertors with appropriate circuit diagram. (10)

(*c*) Define the following terms (30)

(*i*) Demand factor

(*ii*) Tariff

(*iii*) HRC fuses

(*iv*) Diversity factor

(*v*) Derating factor of a cable

(*d*) What are the different methods of power factor improvement? (10)

6. (*a*) Explain earthing practices in brief. (15)

(*b*) With the help of neat and labelled circuit diagram. explain the process of electroplating. (15)

(*c*) How is the synchronous motor started? Explain the various methods of starting of a synchronous motor in brief. (15)

(*d*) What are the different configurations of an NPN transistor? Explain each in brief with neat and labelled circuit diagram. (15)

EXPLANATIONS

1. (*a*) **The ratio of resistance of second wire to that of first wire is**

$$\frac{R_2}{R_1} = \frac{e(L_2/A_2)}{e(L_1/A_1)} = \frac{L_2}{L_1} \times \frac{A_1}{A_2}$$

$$\therefore \quad \frac{L_2}{L_1} = \frac{\pi d_1^2/4}{\pi d_2^2/4} = \left(\frac{d_1}{d_2}\right)^2$$

According to above relationship

$$\frac{L_2}{L_1} = \left(\frac{d_1}{d_2}\right)^2 = \frac{4}{1} = \left(\frac{1}{2}\right)^2 = 16$$

$$\frac{L_2}{L_1} = 16$$

And we already know that

$$\frac{R_2}{R_1} = \frac{L_2}{L_1} \Rightarrow \frac{R_2}{R_1} = 16$$

$$R_2 = 16\,R_1$$

$$\Rightarrow \quad \boxed{R_2 = 16 \times 5 = 80}$$

(*b*) **According to question we can make circuit diagram as follows**

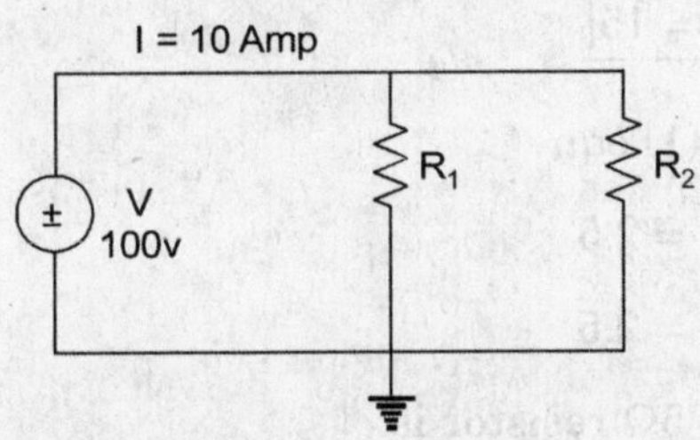

Voltage across both resistance is 100V since they are parallel, and power through one of them say R_1 is 600w

$$P_1 = V^2/R_1$$

$$R_1 = \frac{100 \times 100}{600} = 16.667W$$

Net power form source is $P = V.I = 100 \times 10 = 1000$

Power dissipated in R_1 is $P_1 = 600$ **W**

So power dissipated in R_2 is $P_2 = 1000 - 600$

Again $P_2 = V^2/R_2$

$$R_2 = V^2/P_2 = 100 \times 100/400$$

$$\boxed{R_2 = 25\Omega}$$

$$\boxed{R_1 = 16.667\Omega}$$

(*c*) Given circuit,

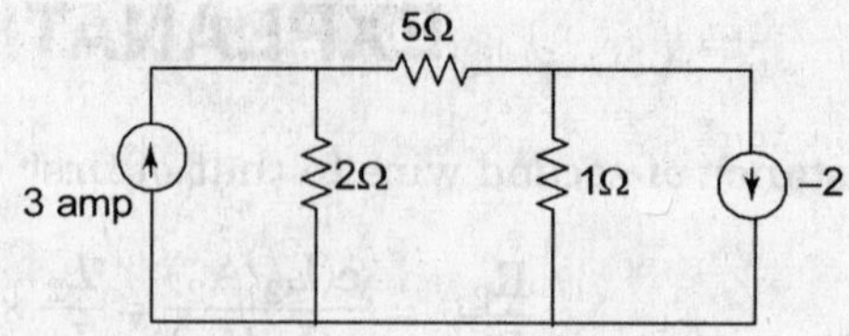

We want to know the value of current in 5Ω resistor

Now we can easily do the current distribution in given circuit diagram

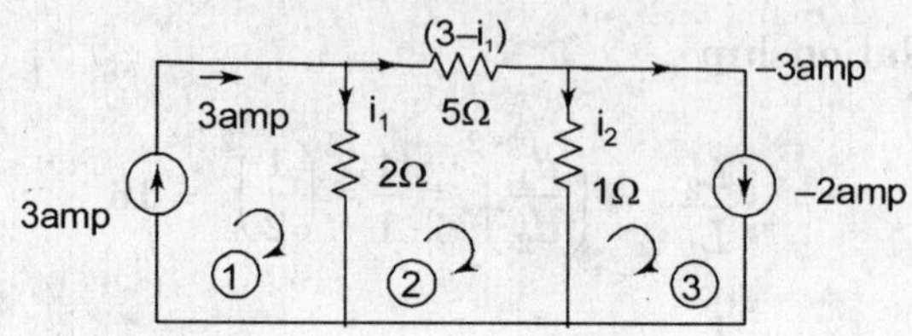

Now according to the circuit diagram

We want to find out the value of $3 - i_1$

$\Rightarrow \quad 3 - i_1 - i_2 = -2\text{amp}$

$\Rightarrow \quad \boxed{i_1 + i_2 = 5}$ ...(1)

Now apply KVL in loop 2

$$2i_1 - i_2 - 5(3 - i_1) = 0$$

$$\boxed{7i_1 - i_2 = 15} \quad ...(2)$$

After solving there (2) and (1) eqn

we get $i_1 = 2.5$

$i_2 = 2.5$

And the value of current in 5Ω resistor is

$$\boxed{3 - i_1 = 3 - 2.5 = 0.5\text{amp}}$$

(*d*) Given circuit,

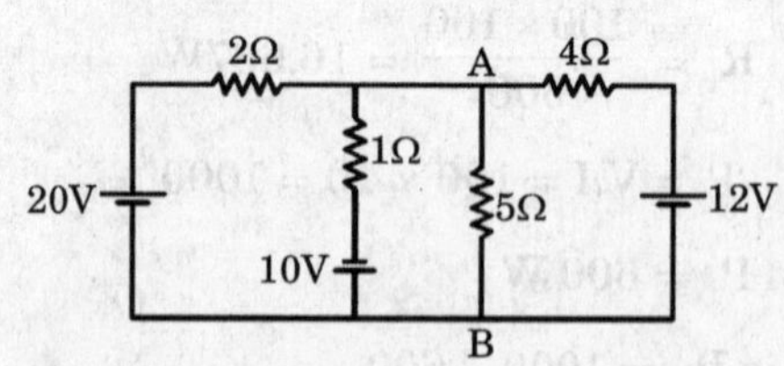

Find V_{TH} across 5W register voltage across V_{AB} = ?

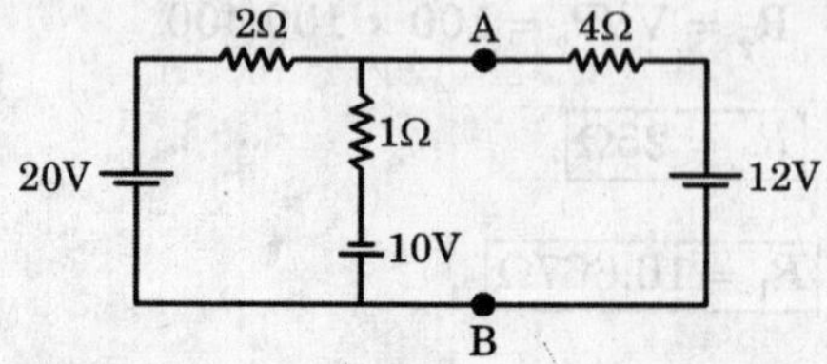

$$\frac{V_{AB}-20}{2}+\frac{V_{AB}+10}{1}+\frac{V_{AB}-12}{4} = 0$$

$$2V_{AB}-40+4V_{AB}+40+V_{AB}-12 = 0$$

$$V_{AB} = 12\text{ V}$$

2. (*a*) **Here we have to find out the generated emf between the wing tips**

Given $B = 38 \times 10^{-6}$

$l = 52$ **meter**

$\theta = 1100$**km/h (have to convert in m/s)**

We know that $\boxed{e = Blv}$

$$e = 38\times10^{-6}\times52\times\frac{1100\times100}{3600}$$

$$\boxed{e = 0.060377\text{V}}$$

(*b*) **Here Given data is**

$$N = 200$$

$$S = 60\text{cm} = 0.6\text{m}$$

$$A = 500\text{mm}^2$$

$$i = 4\text{ amp}$$

For magnetic field strength we know that

$$B = \frac{\mu_0 NI}{2\pi r} \quad \mu_0 = 4\pi\times10^{-7}$$

Now we have to find out r

$$r = s/2\pi$$

$$r = 0.6/2\times3.19 = 6.095 = 0.1\text{m}$$

$$B = \frac{4\pi\times10^{-7}\times200\times4}{2\pi(0.1)}$$

$$\boxed{B = 1.6\times10^{-3}\,w.b/m^2}$$

So we get magnetic field

For finding the magnetic flux density

$$\boxed{\text{magnetic flux} = \text{magnetic field}\times\text{area}}$$

$$\text{magnetic flux} = 1.6\times10^{-3}\times0.5\times10^{-3}$$
$$= 0.8\times10^{-6}\text{weber}$$

Now flux density = magnetic flux/area

$$\boxed{\text{flux density} = 1.6\times10^{-3}\text{web/m}^2}$$

(*c*) Given condition, I = 4 A, V = 20 V R = ?

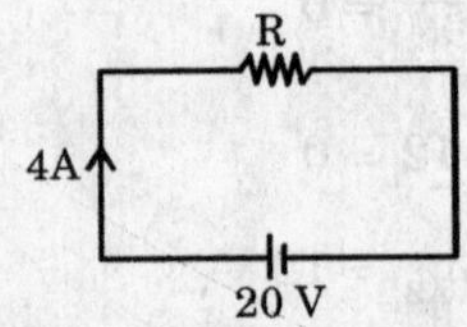

$$R = \frac{20}{4} = 5A$$

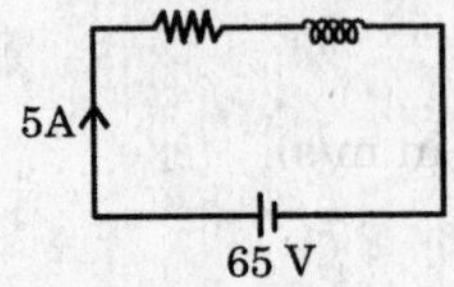

$$Z = \frac{65}{5} = 13\ \Omega$$

$$X_L = \sqrt{Z^2 - R^2}$$

$$X_L = \sqrt{(13)^2 - 5^2}$$

$$X_L = 12$$

$$P_C = VF \cos\phi = 65 \times 5 \times \frac{5}{13}$$

$$P_C = 125$$

(*d*) (*i*) **Mutual inductance:** Mutual inductance between the two coils is defined as the property of coil due to which it opposes the change of current in the other coil or you can say in the neighbouring coil. When the current in the neighbouring coil changes, the flux set up in coil and because of this changing flux emf is induced in the coil called mutually induced emf and the phenomenon is known as mutual inductance.

(*ii*) **Resonance:** Resonance occurs in an electric circuit at a particular resonant frequency when impedance of circuit is at a minimum in a series circuit or maximum in a parallel circuit or when the transfer function is maximum.

(*iii*) **MMF:** The current flowing in an electric circuit due to existance of electromotive force similarly magnetomotive force (MMF) is required to drive the magnetic flux in a magnetic circuit is called MMF. The SI unit of MMF is Ampere-turn (AT)

(*iv*) **θ - factor:** θ factor is a parameter that discribes the resonance behaviour of an undamped harmonic oscillator. The θ factor of oscillator varies substantially form system to system depending on their construction.

$$\boxed{\theta_{factor} = \frac{fr}{\Delta f}}$$

3. (*b*) $I_m = 50\ \mu A$, $R_i = 1\ k\Omega$, V = 50 V

From given condition,

Now, multiplier resistance, is

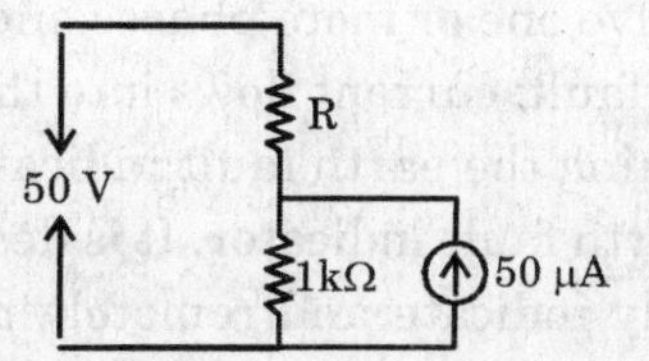

From circuit, $50 \times 10^{-3} = \left(\frac{1K}{1K + R}\right)50$

$$R = 10^6 - 10^3 = 999 \text{ K}$$

(*d*) **Megger :** Megger or ohmeter megger is a protable instrument which is used to measure insulation resistance of cable or electric machinery or system. It can be battery oprated or mechanically oprated and gives direct reading in ohms.

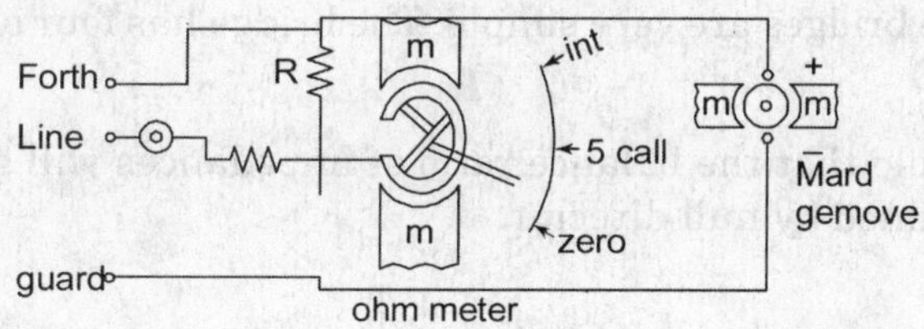

Consurction :

1. **Control** and diflecting coil
2. Permanent magnet
3. Pointer or scale
4. D.O generator or battery connection
5. Pressure coil and current cail.

Working principle : A test voltage of 500 *V* d.c is suitable testing strips equipment operating at 440 V.

The current carrying coil is connected in series and carries the current taken by the circuit under test. The pressure end is connected across the circuit the current limiting resistor are connected in series with pressure coil and current coil to prevent the damage. In hand generator, the armature is moving in the field of permanent magnet or vice-versa to gnerate a test voltage by electromagnetic induction with an increase of potential difference across the external circuit, the diflection of pointer decreases and with an increase of current. The diflection of pointer decreases so the resultant torque on the movement is directly proportional to potential differnce and inversely proportional to the rasistance. When the external circuit is open torque due to voltage cail will be maximum and the pointer will read infinity when there in short circuit pointer will read zero.

Signal generator : A signal generator is an electronic device that generates repeating or non repeating electronic signals in either the along or the digital domain. It is generally used in designing testing trouble shorting and reparing electronic or electrostatic device.

There are many different types of signal generator with different purpose and applications and at varying level of expense. These types includes function generator RF and microwave signal generator, pitch generators, arbitrary waveform generator and frequency generator in general no device is suitable for all purposes.

Traditionally, signal generator have been simulated hardware units, but since the age of multimedia and PC's flexible, programmable software tone generator have also been avaible.

Earth fault direction : An open circuit fault occurs if a circuit is intrrupted by same failure. In three phase system, a faul may involve one or more phases and ground, or earth fault, current flows into the earth. For detecting the earth fault, current flows into the earth. For detecting the earth fault, current flows into the earth. For detching the earth fault indicator there is an device called "The EARTH 4.0" Which is behave likes as an earth fault indicator. It is designed to detect, locally indicate and indicator. It is designed to detect, locally indicate and remotely report earth fault current in medium voltage remotely report earth fault current in medium voltage distribution network. For finding out the earth fault.

First isolate the complete group start panel for a lightning division one by one. Check the earth fault indicator for status (still faulty or normal). If faulty, then put on the breaker which is putt off earlier and isolate the other group start parel for lightning circuit.

A-C bridge : The bridges used measuring the value of unknown resistance, inductance and capacitance is known as A.C bridge. The AC bridge are very convinient and give accurate result of the measurement. The construction of the bridges are very simple. The bridge has four arms one AC supply source and the balance detector.

It works on the principle that the balance ratio of impedances will give the balanced condition to the circuit which is ditermined by null director.

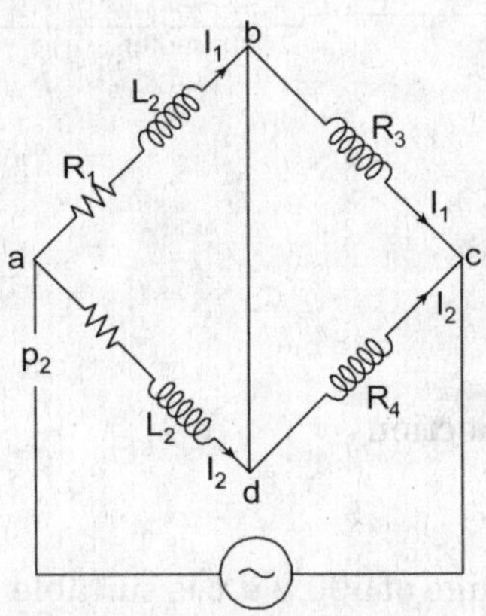

General equation for AC bridges : The bridge have four arms, too have non inductive resistance and other two have inductances with negligible resistance when the bridge is in balance condition

$$Z_1 Z_4 = Z_2 Z_3$$

$$(R_1 + jw L_1) R_4 = (R_2 + jw L_2) R_3$$

$$\boxed{R_1 = \frac{R_3}{R_4} R_2} \quad ...(i)$$

$$jwL_1 R_4 = jw L_2 R_3$$

$$\boxed{L_1 = \frac{R_3}{R_4} L_2}$$

4. (*a*) Basically, there are three types of electrical breaking done in a D.C. motor.

1. Regenerative breaking
2. Dynamic breaking
3. Plugging

Regenerative breaking : It is a form of breaking in which kinetic energy of the motor is returned to the power supply system. This type of breaking is possible when the driven load forces to the motor to run at a speed higher then its no load speed with a constant exitation. The motor back emf EB is grater than supply voltage V which reveres back emf Eb is greater than supply voltage. V which reveres the direction of motor armerture current. The motor begins to operate or an electric generator. Actually reginarative breaking can not be used to stop a motor but to control its speed above no load speed of motor.

Dynamic breaking : It is also known as rhostatic breaking in this type of breaking the D.C. motor is disconnected from the supply and the breaking resistor RL is immedisly connected across the armature. The kinetic energy stored in rotating part of the motor and a connected load is converted into electrical energy. It is dissipated as heat in the breaking resistance R_b and armature circuit resistance R_q.

Plugging : It is also known as reverse current breaking the armature terminal or supply polarity of a seperately excited d.c. motor or shunt d.c. motor when running or revers.

Therefore the supply voltage V and included voltage Eb i.e. back emf will act is the same direction. The effective veltage across the armature will the V + E_b which is almost twice is supply voltage. Thus armature current is replaced and high breaking larger is produced. Pluging is highly in insufficient method of bracking because in addition to the power supplied by the load power supplied by the source is wested in resistances.

(*b*) Parallel operation of 3 phase tranformer

It is economical to install number of small rotied transformer in parallel then installing a bigger rated transformer.

Conditions for parallel operation of transformers :

When two or more transfomer run in parallel they must satisfy the following condition for satisfactory performance.

These conditions are

1. Same voltage ratio of transformer
2. Same percentage impedance
3. Same polarity
4. Same phase

Same Voltage ratio : It two transformer of different valtage ratio are connected in parallel with same primary voltage there will be a difference of these tranformer are connected to same bus. There will be an circulating current between secondries and therefore between primary also as the internal impedance of transformer is small. A small voltage cause syfficiently sign circulatihng corrent causing unnecessary extra $I^2 R$ losses.

Same percentage impendance : The current shared by two transformer running in parallel should be proportional to their MVA ratings. Again current carried by these transformers are inversely proportional to their internal impendance. From these two statement it can be said that impendance of transformers running in parallel are inversely proportional to their MVA ratings.

Same Polarity : Polarity of all transformer that run in parallel should or same otherwise huge circulating current that flows in the transformer but no load will be fed from these transformer.

Same Phase Sequence : The phase sequence or the order in which the phases reach their maximum positive voltage must be indentical for two parallel transformers otherwise during the cycle, each pair of phase will be short circuited.

The above said conditions must be strictly followed for parallel operation of transformer but totally identical percentage impedance of two different transformer is diffcult to achieve practically that is why the transformer run in parallel may not have exactly same percentage impedance but the values will be as possible.

Advantages :

(*i*) To maximize electrical power system efficiency.

(*ii*) To maximize electrical power system ability

(*iii*) To maximize electrical power system reliability.

(*iv*) To maximize electrical power system flexibility.

(*c*) Equivalent circuit diagram of a 1 – ϕ transformer:

Equivalent circuit diagram of a transformer is basically a (diagram) a transfomer (diagram) which can be resolved into an equilvalent circuit in which resistance and leakage reactance of the transformer are imagined to be external to the winding.

The equivalent circuit diagram of transformer is given below:

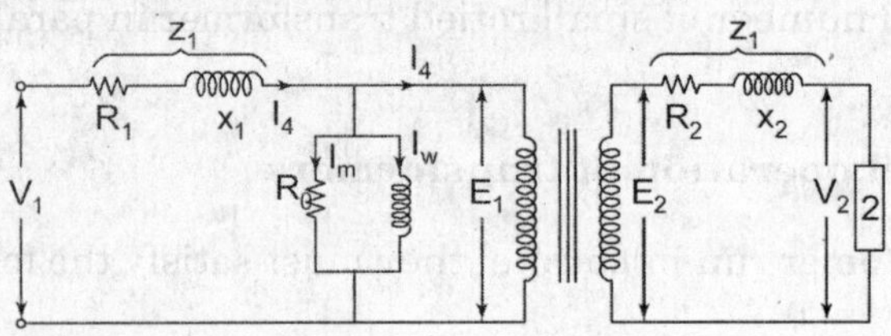

Where R_1 = Primary winding resistance

R_2 = Secondary winding resistance

I_o = load current

I_μ = Magnetizing component

I_w = Working component

This I_m and I_w are conneced in parallel across the primary circuit. The value of E_1 is obtained by subtracting viscosity I_1z_1 from v_1. The value of $X_o = E_1/I_o$ and $R_o = E_1/Iw$ we known that the relation of E_1 and E_2 *i.e.*, $E_1/E_2 = N_1/N_2 = K$ (transformation ratio).

From the equivalent circuit we can easily calculate the total impedance, transfer voltage, current, either to the primary or secondry.

Equivalent circuit referred to primary side

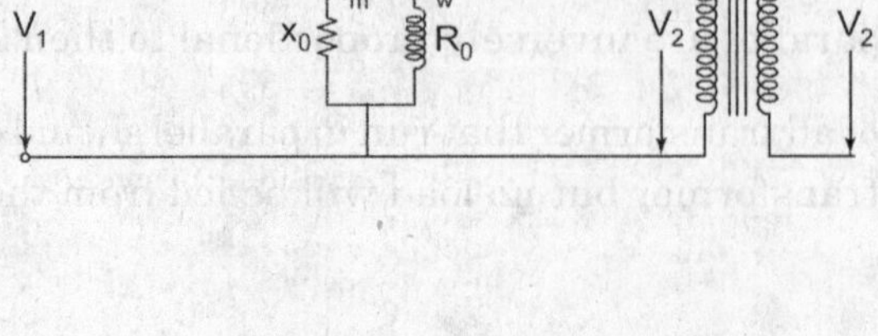

Phasor diagram of transforms on leading load:

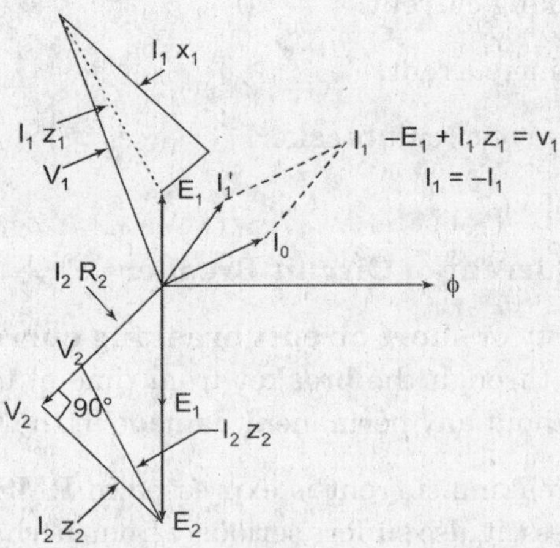

(*d*) Given condition, 3ϕ, 400 V, 50 Hz, I_M,

$$N_S = \frac{120 \times f}{P}$$

$$N_S = \frac{120 \times 50}{6}$$

$$= 1000 \text{ rpm}$$

$$S = \frac{N_S - N_r}{N_S}$$

$$= \frac{1000 - 940}{1000} = \frac{60}{1000}$$

$$S_M = \frac{R}{x}$$

$$\frac{60}{1000} = \frac{R}{x}$$

$$x = \frac{100}{6} R$$

At standstill, $S = 1$

$$S = \frac{R + 0.1}{x} = 1$$

$$R + 0.1 = x$$

$$\frac{6\,\alpha}{100} + 0.1 = x$$

$$1 = x\left(1 - \frac{6}{100}\right)$$

$$1 = x\frac{94}{100}$$

$$x = \frac{10}{94}$$

5. (*a*) The ***rating of a circuit breaker*** includes,

1. Rated short circuit breaking current.
2. Rated short circuit making current.
3. Rated operating sequence of circuit breaker.
4. Rated short time current.

Short Circuit Breaking Current of Circuit Breaker

Short circuit breaking capacity or **short circuit breaking current of circuit breaker** is defined as maximum current can flow through the breaker from time of occurring short circuit to the time of clearing the short circuit without any permanent damage in the CB.

The value of short circuit breaking current is expressed in **RMS**. During short circuit, the CB is not only subjected to thermal stress, it also suffers seriously from mechanical stresses. So during determining short circuit capacity, the mechanical strength of the CB is also considered. So for choosing suitable circuit breaker it is obvious to determine the fault level at that point of the system where CB to be installed.

Once the fault level of any part of electrical transmission is determined it is easy to choose the correct rated circuit breaker for this part of network.

Rated Short Circuit Making Capacity

The short circuit making capacity of circuit breaker is expressed in peak value not in **rms value** like breaking capacity.

Theoretically at the instant of fault occurrence in a system, the fault current can rise to twice of its symmetrical fault level. At the instant of switching on a circuit breaker in faulty condition, of system, the short circuit portion of the system connected to the source. The first cycle of the current during a circuit is closed by circuit breaker, has maximum amplitude. This is about twice of the amplitude of symmetrical fault current waveform.

The breaker's contacts have to withstand this highest value of current during the first cycle of waveform when breaker is closed under fault.

On the basis of this above mentioned phenomenon, a selected breaker should be rated with short circuit making capacity.

As the rated **short circuit making current of circuit breaker** is expressed in maximum peak value, it is always more than rated short circuit breaking current of circuit breaker. Normally value of short circuit making current is 2.5 times more than short circuit breaking current.

Rated Operating Sequence or Duty Cycle of Circuit Breaker

This is mechanical duty requirement of circuit breaker operating mechanism. The sequence of rated operating duty of a circuit breaker has been specified as O – t – CO – t′ – CO Where, O indicates opening operation of CB.CO represents closing operation time which is immediately followed by an opening operation without any intentional time delay.t' is time between two operations which is necessary to restore the initial conditions and / or to prevent undue heating of conducting parts of circuit breaker. t = 0.3 sec for circuit breaker intended for first auto re closing duty, if not otherwise specified.

Rated Short Time Current

This is the current limit which a circuit breaker can carry safely for certain specific time without any damage in it. The circuit breakers do not clear the short circuit current as soon as any fault occurs in the system. There always some intentional and an intentional time delays present between the instant of occurrence of fault and instant of clearing the fault by CB. This delay is because of time of operation of **protection relays**, time of operation of circuit breaker and also there may be some intentional time delay imposed in relay for proper coordination of **power system protection**. Even a circuit breaker fails to trip, the fault will be cleared by next higher positioned circuit breaker. In this case the fault clearing time is longer. Hence, after fault, a circuit breaker has to carry the short circuit for certain time. The summation of all time delays should not be more than 3 seconds; hence a circuit breaker should be capable of carrying a maximum faulty current for at least this short period of time.

Rated Voltage of Circuit Breaker

Rated **voltage** of circuit breaker depends upon its insulation system. For below 400 KV systems, the circuit breaker is designed to withstand 10% above the normal system voltage. For above or equal 400 KV system the insulation of circuit breaker should be capable of withstanding 5% above the normal system voltage. That means, rated voltage of circuit breaker corresponds to the highest system voltage. This is because during no load or small load condition the voltage level of power system is allowed rise up to highest voltage rating of the system.

(*b*) **Merz-Prize protection scheme**

In this scheme of protection, currents at the ends of the protected sections compare. When the system is in normal operating condition, the magnitude of currents is equal on the secondary windings of the current transformers. On the occurrence of the faults, the short-circuit current flows through the system and the magnitude of current become differ. This difference of current under fault conditions is made to flow through the relay operating coil.

The relay then closes its contacts and makes the circuit breaker to trip and thus isolated the protection from the system. Such a system is called a Merz-Prize circulating current system. It is very effective for earth faults and faults between phases.

Connection for Merz price protection scheme

The protection system requires two identical transformers which are mounted on both sides of the protection zone. The secondary terminals of the current transformers are connected in stars, and their end terminals are connected through the pilot wire. The relay coils are connected in delta. The neutral of the current transformer and the relay are connected to the common terminal.

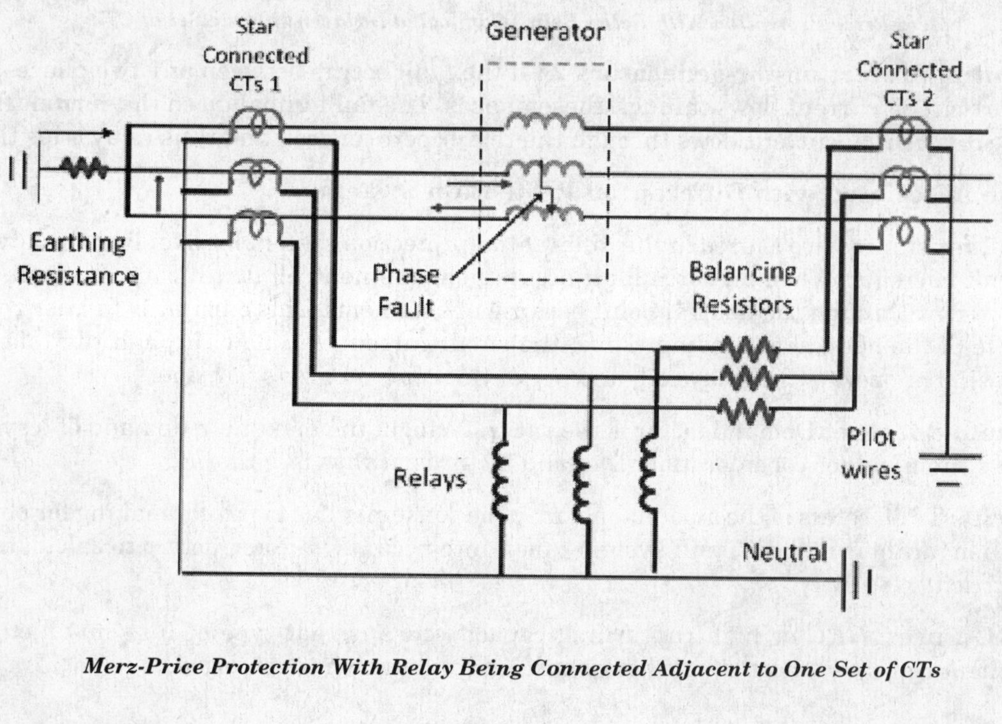

Merz-Price Protection With Relay Being Connected Adjacent to One Set of CTs

Generator-protection : The relay is connected across equipotential points of the three pilot wires so that the burden on each current transformer is same. The equipotential point of the pilot wire is its centre, so the relay is located at the midpoint of pilot wires.

For proper working of the differential protection system, it is essential to locate the relay coils adjacent to the current transformer near the main circuit. This can be done by inserting the balancing resistance series with the pilot wires to make equipotential points located near the main circuit breaker.

Working on Differential Protection System

Consider the fault occurs on the R phase of the network because of the insulation breakdown. Because of the fault, the current in the secondary of the transformer becomes unequal. The differential currents flow through the relay coil. Thus, the relay becomes operative and gives the command to the circuit breaker for operation.

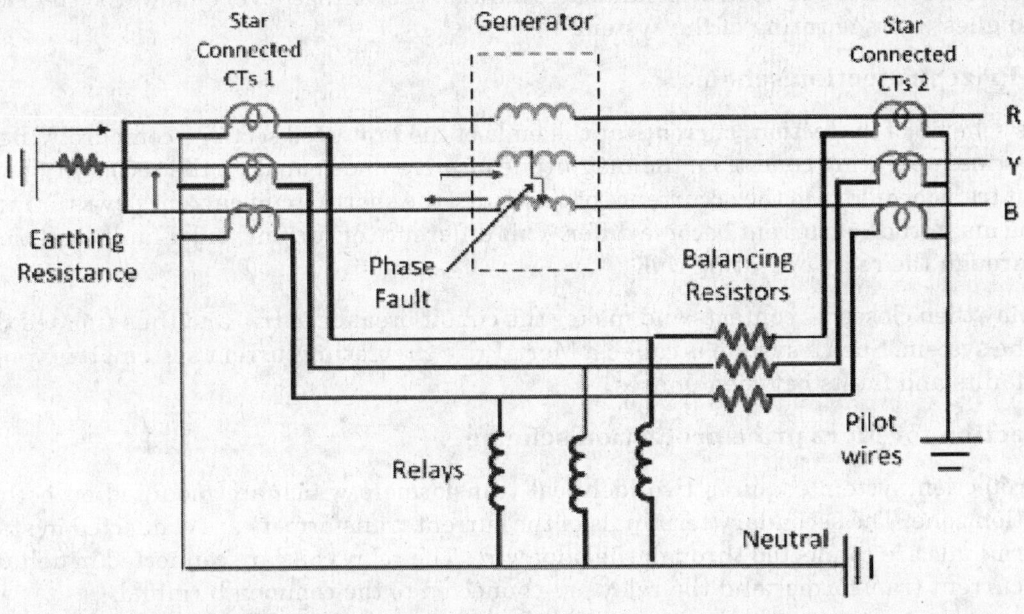

Merz-Price Protection With Relay Being Connected Adjacent to One Set of CTs

Differential-protection-for-generators-2 : If the fault occurs between any two phases, say Y and B then short-circuit current flows through these phases. The fault unbalanced the current flows through CTs. The differential current flows through the relay operating coil and thus relay trips their contacts.

Problem Associated with Differential Protection System

A neutral resistance wire is used in the differential protection system for avoiding the adverse effect of earth fault currents. When an earth fault occurs near the neutral, it will cause a small, short circuit current to flow through the neutral point because of small emf. This current is further reduced by the resistance of the neutral grounding. Thus, the small current will flow through the relay. This small current will not operate the relay coil, and hence the generator gets damage.

(*c*) (*i*) **Demand factor :** Demand factor is the ratio of sum of the maximum demand of a system (as part of a system) under consideration. Demand factor is always less than 1.

(*ii*) **Tariff :** Traiff refers to the amount of money the consumer has to pay for making for power available to them at their homes. Traiff system taken into accunts various factors to calculate total cost of electricity.

(*iii*) **HRC Fuse :** *HRC* or high rupturing capacity fuse is that type of fuse in which fuse wire or element can carry short circuit heavy current for a known time period.

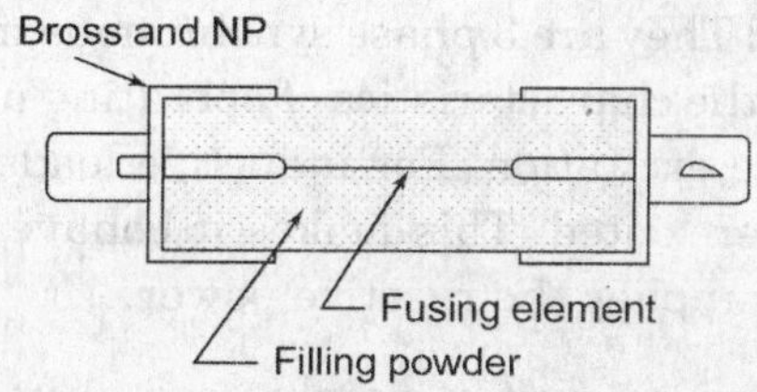

(*iv*) **Diversity factor :** It is ratio of the sum of the individual maximum demands of varrious subdivision of system (or part of system) under consideration. It is usually more than one.

(*v*) **De-rating Factor :** A power cable designed with standard operating conditions may not operate so in practical. Therefore, the current carrying capacity may get impacted due to this. Some examples of this: Cables installed deep under the ground will have reduced current carrying capacity than cables installed in air. This is impacted due to multiple factors like soil temperature, soil thermal resistivity etc.

In order to deal with this, a DE rating Factor is associated with cables to arrive at actual value of current carrying capacity.

Actual Current Carrying Capacity = DE rating Factor x Cable current carrying capacity under std. conditions.

(*d*) **Power Factor Improvement**

The term power factor comes into picture in AC circuits only. Mathematically it is cosine of the phase difference between source voltage and current. It refers to the fraction of total power (apparent power) which is utilized to do the useful work called active power.

$$\cos\phi = \frac{\text{Active power}}{\text{Apparent power}}$$

Need for Power Factor Improvement

- **Real power** is given by P = VI cos φ. To transfer a given amount of power at certain voltage, the electrical current is inversely proportional to cos φ. Hence higher the pf lower will be the current flowing. A small current flow requires less cross sectional area of conductor and thus it saves conductor and money.

- From above relation we saw having poor power factor increases the current flowing in conductor and thus copper loss increases. Further large voltage drop occurs in **alternator**, **electrical transformer** and transmission and distribution lines which gives very poor voltage regulation.

- Further the KVA rating of machines is also reduced by having higher power factor as,

$$\text{KVA} = \frac{\text{KW}}{\cos\phi}$$

Hence, the size and cost of machine also reduced. So, electrical power factor should be maintained close to unity.

Methods of Power Factor Improvement

- **Capacitors :** Improving power factor means reducing the phase difference between voltage and current. Since majority of loads are of inductive nature, they require some amount of reactive power for them to function. This reactive power is provided by the capacitor or bank of capacitors installed parallel to the load. They act as a source of local reactive power and thus less reactive power flows through the line. Basically they reduces the phase difference between the voltage and current.

- **Synchronous Condenser :** They are 3 phase synchronous motor with no load attached to its shaft. The synchronous motor has the characteristics of operating under any power factor leading, lagging or unity depending upon the excitation. For inductive loads, synchronous condenser is connected towards load side and is overexcited. This makes it behave like a capacitor. It draws the lagging current from the supply or supplies the reactive power.
- **Phase Advancer :** This is an ac exciter mainly used to improve pf of induction motor. They are mounted on shaft of the motor and is connected in the rotor circuit of the motor. It improves the power factor by providing the exciting ampere turns to produce required flux at slip frequency. Further if ampere turns are increased, it can be made to operate at leading power factor.

6. (*b*) **Electroplating** is a process that uses electric current to reduce dissolved metal cations so that they form a thin coherent metal coating on an electrode. The term is also used for electrical oxidation of anions on to a solid substrate, as in the formation of silver chloride on silver wire to make silver/silver-chloride electrodes. Electroplating is primarily used to change the surface properties of an object (such as abrasion and wear resistance, corrosion protection, lubricity, aesthetic qualities), but may also be used to build up thickness on undersized parts or to form objects by electroforming.

The cations associate with the anions in the solution. These cations are reduced at the cathode to deposit in the metallic, zero valence state. For example, for copper plating, in an acid solution, copper is oxidized at the anode to Cu^{2+} by losing two electrons. The Cu^{2+} associates with the anion $SO2^{-4}$ in the solution to form copper (II) sulfate. At the cathode, the Cu2+ is reduced to metallic copper by gaining two electrons. The result is the effective transfer of copper from the anode source to a plate covering the cathode.

The plating is most commonly a single metallic element, not an alloy. However, some alloys can be electrodeposited, notably brass and solder.

Many plating baths include cyanides of other metals (such as potassium cyanide) in addition to cyanides of the metal to be deposited. These free cyanides facilitate anode corrosion, help to maintain a constant metal ion level and contribute to conductivity. Additionally, non-metal chemicals such as carbonates and phosphates may be added to increase conductivity.

When plating is not desired on certain areas of the substrate, stop-offs are applied to prevent the bath from coming in contact with the substrate. Typical stop-offs include tape, foil, lacquers, and waxes.[4]

The ability of a plating to cover uniformly is called *throwing power* ; the better the throwing power the more uniform the coating.[5]

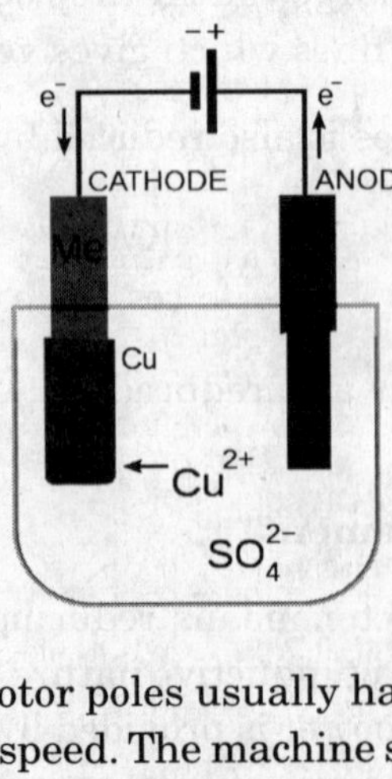

(*c*) This cannot start the motor, so the rotor poles usually have squirrel-cage windings embedded in them, to provide torque below synchronous speed. The machine starts as an induction motor until it approaches synchronous speed, when the rotor "pulls in" and locks to the rotating stator field.

As seen earlier, synchronous motor is not self starting. It is necessary to rotate the rotor at a speed very near to synchronous speed. This is possible by various method in practice. The various methods to start the synchronous motor are,

1. Using pony motors
2. Using damper winding
3. As a slip ring induction motor
4. Using small d.c. machine coupled to it.

1. **Using pony motors :** In this method, the rotor is brought to the synchronous speed with the help of some external device like small induction motor. Such an external device is called 'pony motor'.

   Once the rotor attains the synchronous speed, the d.c. excitation to the rotor is switched on. Once the synchronism is established pony motor is decoupled. The motor then continues to rotate as synchronous motor.

2. **Using Damper Winding :** In a synchronous motor, in addition to the normal field winding, the additional winding consisting of copper bars placed in the slots in the pole faces. The bars are short circuited with the help of end rings. Such an additional winding on the rotor is called damper winding. This winding as short circuited, acts as a squirrel cage rotor winding of an induction motor. The schematic representation of such damper winding is shown in the Fig.1.

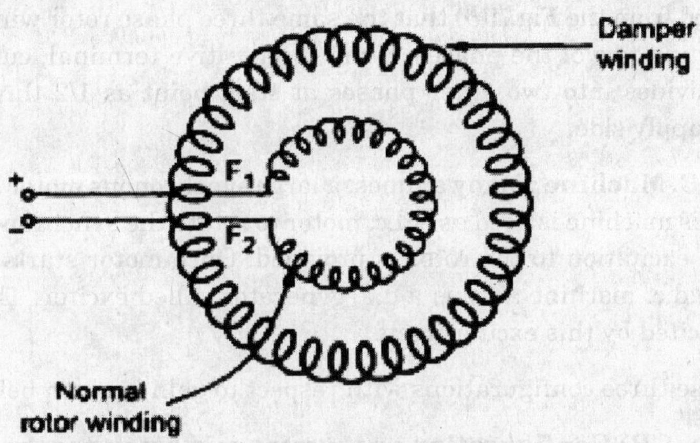

Fig. 1 Starting as a squirrel cage I.M.

   Once the rotor is excited by a three phase supply, the motors starts rotating as an induction motor at sub synchronous speed. Then d.c. supply is given to the field winding. At a particular instant motor gets pulled into synchronism and starts rotating at a synchronous speed. As rotor rotates at synchronous speed, the relative motion between damper winding and the rotating magnetic field is zero. Hence when motor is running as synchronous motor, there can not be any induced e.m.f. in the damper winding. So damper winding is active only at start, to run the motor as an induction motor at start. Afterwards it is out of the circuit. As damper winding is short circuited and motor gets started as induction motor, it draws high current at start so induction motor starters like star-delta, autotransformer etc. used to start the synchronous motor as an induction motor.

3. **As a Slip Ring Induction Motor :** The above method of starting synchronous motor as a squirrel cage induction motor does not provide high starting torque. So to achieve this, instead of shorting the damper winding, it is designed to a form a three phase star or delta connected winding. The three ends of this winding are brought out through slip rings. An external rheostat then can be introduced in series with the rotor circuit. So when stator is excited, the motor starts as a slip ring induction motor and due to resistance added in the rotor provides high starting torque. The resistance is then gradually cut off, as motor gathers speed. When motor attains speed near synchronous. d.c. excitation is provided to the rotor, then motors gets pulled into synchronism ans starts rotating at synchronous speed. The damper winding is shorted by shorting the slip rings. The initial resistance added in the rotor not only provides high starting torque but also limits high inrush of starting current. Hence it acts as a motor resistance starter.

The synchronous motor started by this method is called a slip ring induction motor is shown in the Fig.1(*b*).

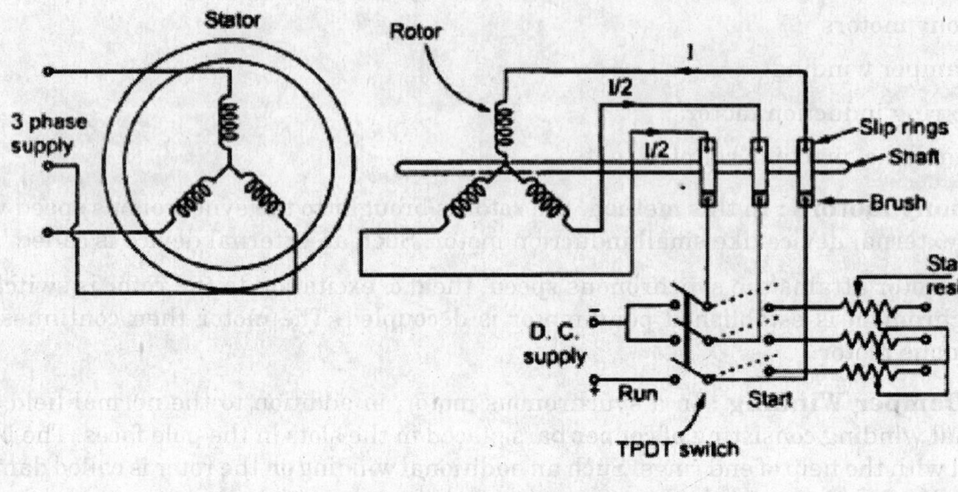

Fig. 2 Starting as a squirrel cage I.M.

It can be observed from the Fig. 1(*b*) that the same three phase rotor winding acts as a normal rotor winding by shorting two of the phases. From the positive terminal, current 'I' flows in one of the phases, which divides into two other phases at start point as 1/2 through each, when switch is thrown on d.c. supply side.

4. **Using Small D.C. Machine :** Many a times, a large synchronous motor are provided with a coupled d.c. machine. This machine is used as a d.c. motor to rotate the synchronous motor at a synchronous speed. Then the excitation to the rotor is provided. Once motor starts running as a synchronous motor, the same d.c. machine acts as a d.c. generator called exciter. The field of the synchronous motor is then excited by this exciter itself.

(*d*) The behavior of these three configurations with respect to gain is given below.

- **Common Base (CB) Configuration :** no current gain but voltage gain
- **Common Collector (CC) Configuration :** current gain but no voltage gain
- **Common Emitter (CE) Configuration :** current gain and voltage gain

Now we discuss about these three configurations with their input and output characteristics in the below.

Common Base Configuration

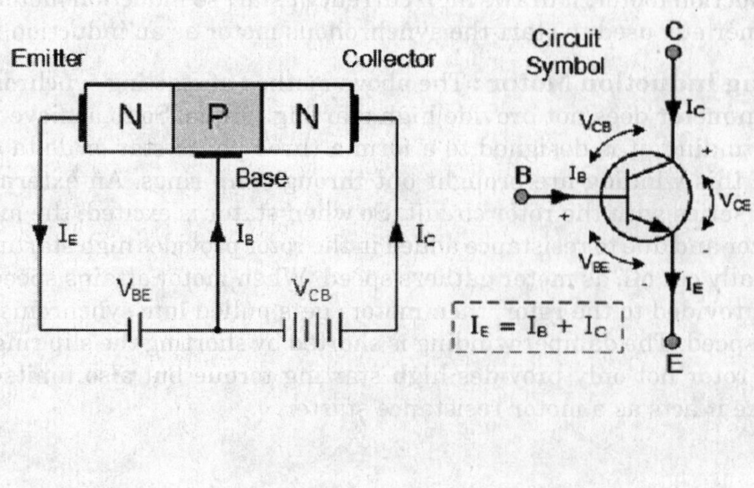

In this configuration we use base as common terminal for both input and output signals. The configuration name itself indicates the common terminal. Here the input is applied between the base and emitter terminals and the corresponding output signal is taken between the base and collector terminals with the base terminal grounded. Here the input parameters are V_{EB} and I_E and the output parameters are V_{CB} and I_C. The input current flowing into the emitter terminal must be higher than the base current and collector current to operate the transistor, therefore the output collector current is less than the input emitter current.

The current gain is generally equal or less than to unity for this type of configuration. The input and output signals are in-phase in this configuration. The amplifier circuit configuration of this type is called as non-inverting amplifier circuit. The construction of this configuration circuit is difficult because this type has high voltage gain values

The input characteristics of this configuration are looks like characteristics of illuminated photo diode while the output characteristics represents a forward biased diode. This transistor configuration has high output impedance and low input impedance. This type of configuration has high resistance gain i.e. ratio of output resistance to input resistance is high. The voltage gain for this configuration of circuit is given below.

$$AV = \frac{V_{out}}{V_{in}} = \frac{(I_C * R_L)}{(I_E * R_{in})}$$

Current gain in common base configuration is given as

$$\alpha = \text{Output current/Input current}$$

$$\alpha = \frac{I_C}{I_E}$$

Common Collector Configuration

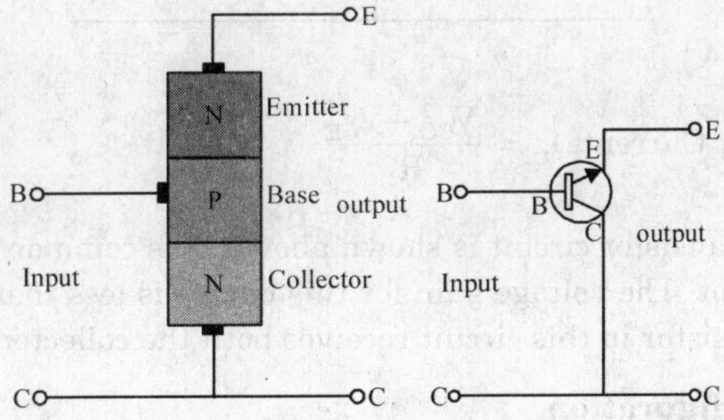

In this configuration we use collector terminal as common for both input and output signals. This configuration is also known as emitter follower configuration because the emitter voltage follows the base voltage. This configuration is mostly used as a buffer. These configurations are widely used in impedance matching applications because of their high input impedance.

In this configuration the input signal is applied between the base-collector region and the output is taken from the emitter-collector region. Here the input parameters are VBC and IB and the output parameters are VEC and IE. The common collector configuration has high input impedance and low output impedance. The input and output signals are in phase. Here also the emitter current is equal to the sum of collector current and the base current. Now let us calculate the current gain for this configuration.

Current gain, $A_i = \frac{\text{Output current}}{\text{Input current}}$

$$A_i = \frac{I_E}{I_B}$$

$$A_i = \frac{(I_C + I_B)}{I_B}$$

$$A_i = \frac{(I_C)}{(I_B)} + 1$$

$$A_i = \beta + 1$$

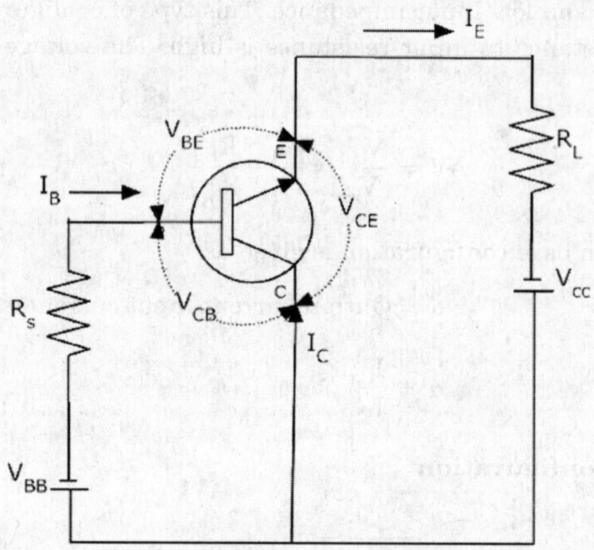

Collector Current, $I_C = \frac{V_{CC} - V_{CE}}{R_L}$

The common collector transistor circuit is shown above. This common collector configuration is a non inverting amplifier circuit. The voltage gain for this circuit is less than unity but it has large current gain because the load resistor in this circuit receives both the collector and base currents

Common Emitter Configuration

In this configuration we use emitter as common terminal for both input and output. This common emitter configuration is an inverting amplifier circuit. Here the input is applied between base-emitter region and the output is taken between collector and emitter terminals. In this configuration the input parameters are V_{BE} and I_B and the output parameters are V_{CE} and I_C.

This type of configuration is mostly used in the applications of transistor based amplifiers. In this configuration the emitter current is equal to the sum of small base current and the large collector current. i.e. $I_E = I_C + I_B$. We know that the ratio between collector current and emitter current gives current gain alpha in Common Base configuration similarly the ratio between collector current and base current gives the current gain beta in common emitter configuration.

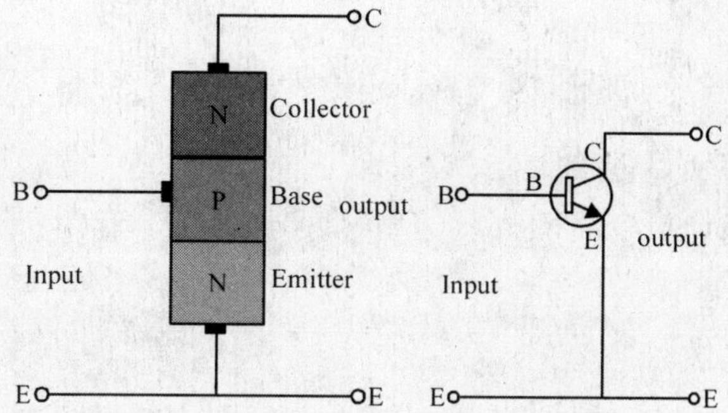

Now let us see the relationship between these two current gains.

$$\text{Current gain } (\alpha) = \frac{I_C}{I_E}$$

$$\text{Current gain } (\beta) = \frac{I_C}{I_B}$$

$$\text{Collector current } I_C = \alpha\, I_E = \beta\, I_B$$

This configuration is mostly used one among all the three configurations. It has medium input and output impedance values. It also has the medium current and voltage gains. But the output signal has a phase shift of 1800 i.e. both the input and output are inverse to each other.

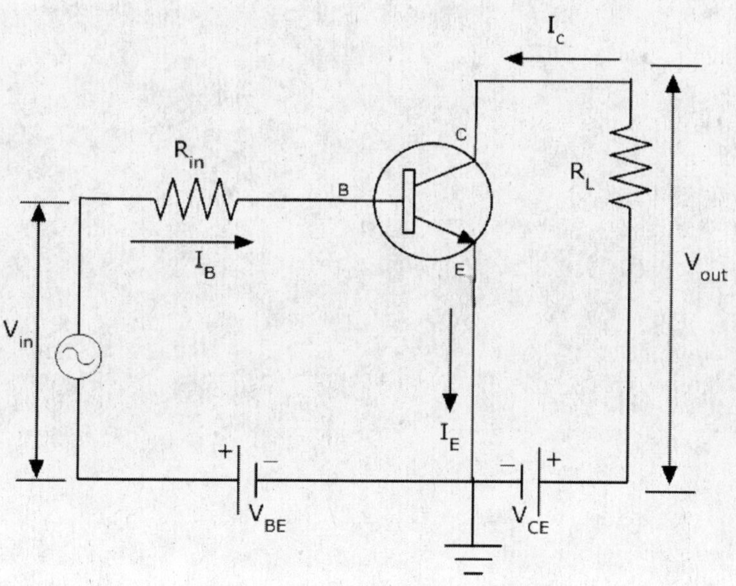

Solved Paper 2015

Electrical Engineering

(Paper II)

1. (*a*) Two conductors, one of copper and the other of iron, are connected in parallel and carry equal currents at 30°C. What proportion of current will pass through each, if the temperature is raised to 90°C? The temperature coefficients of resistance at 0°C are 0.0043/°C and 0.0063/°C for copper and iron respectively. (10)

(*b*) Determine the resistance and the power dissipation of a resistor that must be placed in series with a 50 ohm resistor across a 220 V source in order to limit the power dissipation in the 50 ohm resistor to 200 watts. (10)

(*c*) In the network shown in Figure 1, the different currents and voltages are as under:

$i_2 = 10\ e^{-4t}$; $i_4 = 6 \sin t$; $v_3 = 8e^{-4t}$

Using Kirchhoff's Current Law, find the voltage v_1. (10)

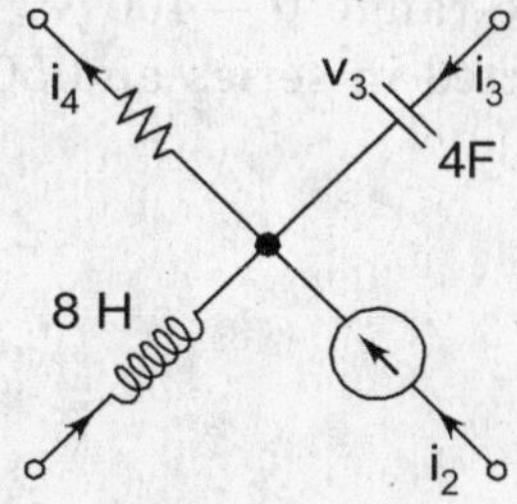

(*d*) In figure, find the current in the 10 ohm resistor using Thevenin's theorem. (20)

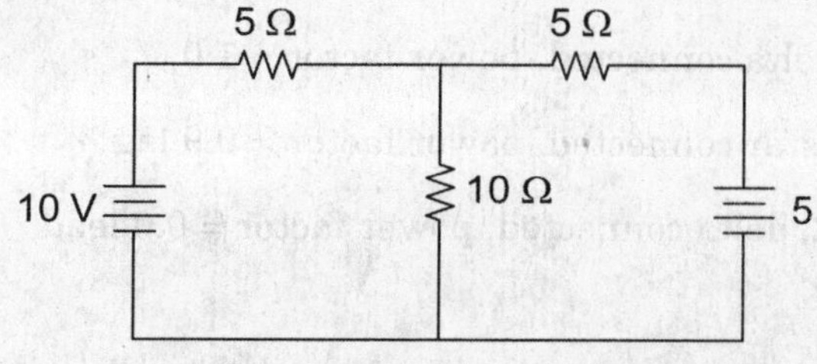

(*e*) A variable air capacitor has 10 movable plates and 11 stationary plates. The area of each plate is 0.002 m^2 and separation between opposite plates is 0.001m. Determine the maximum capacitance of this variable capacitor. (10)

2. (*a*) An iron ring has a cross-sectional area of 200 mm^2 and a mean diameter of 20 cm. It is wound with 1000 turns. If the value of relative permeability is 250. Find the total flux set up in the ring. The coil resistance is 500Ω and the supply voltage is 220 V. (10)

(*b*) Define the following terms: (5+5+5+5)

(*i*) Coefficient of magnetic coupling

(*ii*) Self-inductance

(*iii*) Electromagnetic induction

(*iv*) Time constant

(*c*) A capacitor of 10μF takes a current of 2 A when alternating voltage applied across it is 220V. Calculate:

(*i*) the frequency of the applied voltage

(*ii*) the resistance to be connected in series with the capacitor to reduce the current in the circuit to 1 A at the same frequency. (5+10)

(*d*) An RLC series circuit has R = 5Ω, C = 50 μF and a variable inductance. The applied voltage is 220 V at 100 rad/sec. The inductance is varied till the voltage across resistance is maximum. Under this condition, find the

(*i*) value of inductance

(*ii*) Q-factor

(*iii*) voltages across resistance, capacitance and inductance (5+5+5)

3. (*a*) Two voltmeters have the same range 0 – 400 V. The internal impedances are 32kΩ and 18 kΩ respectively. If they are connected in series and 500 V be applied across them, what will be their readings? (10)

(*b*) Define the following terms: (5+5+5+5)

(*i*) Deflecting torque

(*ii*) Voltmeter sensitivity

(*iii*) Shading rings

(*iv*) Power factor

(*c*) Three 3-phase balanced loads are connected in parallel across a 440 V, 3-phase 3-wire balanced supply.

Load 1 : 12,000 W, delta connected, power factor = 1.0

Load 2 : 10,000 VA, star connected, power factor = 0.9 lag

Load 3 : 10,000 VAR, delta connected, power factor = 0.0 lead

Calculate:

(*i*) the total power

(*ii*) the combined power factor

(*iii*) the current drawn from the line (10+7+8)

(*d*) What is phantom loading? With a neat diagram, explain how it is carried out. (5)

4. (*a*) A 160 Ω source is to be matched to a 40Ω, 2Ω load by means of a transformer. What is the turns ratio? Determine the primary and secondary voltages and current. (20)

(*b*) Explain the various losses in a transformer. Derive the condition for maximum efficiency of a transformer. (20)

(*c*) A direct current shunt motor develops 10 HP at 8000 rpm when drawing a line current of 40 A at 220V. Find the efficiency at this load and the useful torque. (10)

(*d*) Explain the effect of frequency variation on torque-speed characteristics of a 3-phase induction motor. (10)

5. (*a*) Explain the causes of low power factor in a power system. (10)

(*b*) Explain why a three-phase induction motor is self-starting and a single-phase induction motor is not. (15)

(*c*) Explain why a synchronous motor develops torque at synchronous speed, whereas an induction motor develops torque at all speeds except the synchronous speed. (15)

(*d*) Which fault in a power system is more severe as compared to other faults and why? (10)

(*e*) What are the necessary conditions to operate two alternators in parallel to supply a common load? (10)

6. (*a*) What are the advantages and disadvantages of BJT over JFET? (10)

(*b*) Explain clearly how a fuse rating is selected for the following: (20)

(*i*) Lighting circuit

(*ii*) Power circuit

(*c*) Name the different types of domestic wiring and compare their performance briefly. (15)

(*d*) What are the advantages and disadvantages of electric drives over conventional drives? (15)

EXPLANATIONS

1. (*a*) We have to find out the proportion of current in each conductor

Let us consider the resistance of copper and iron as r_1 and r_2 respectively at 30°C then according to question change in temp

$$\Delta t = 90° - 30° = 60°C$$

We know that

$$r_1' = r_1 (1 + \alpha_1 \Delta t)$$

$$r_1' = r_1(1 + 0.0043 \times 60)$$

$$r_1' = 1.258\, r_1 \quad ...(1)$$

$$r_1' = r_2(1 + \alpha_2 \Delta t)$$

$$= r_2 (1 + 0.0063 \times 60)$$

$$r_2' = 1.378\, r_2 \quad ...(2)$$

Currents are equal at 30°C i.e. $I_1 = I_2$

$$I \alpha \frac{1}{r} \quad \text{....(we know that)}$$

$$\frac{I_1}{I_2} = \frac{r_2}{r_1} \text{ if } I_1 = I_2$$

Hence $\boxed{r_1 = r_2}$

At 90°C

$$\frac{I_1'}{I_2'} = \frac{r_2'}{r_1'} \quad ...(3)$$

Put the value of r'_2 and r'_1 in eqn (3)

$$\frac{I_1'}{I_2'} = \frac{1.378}{1.258} = 1.175$$

(*b*) According to the question circuit diagram drawn is

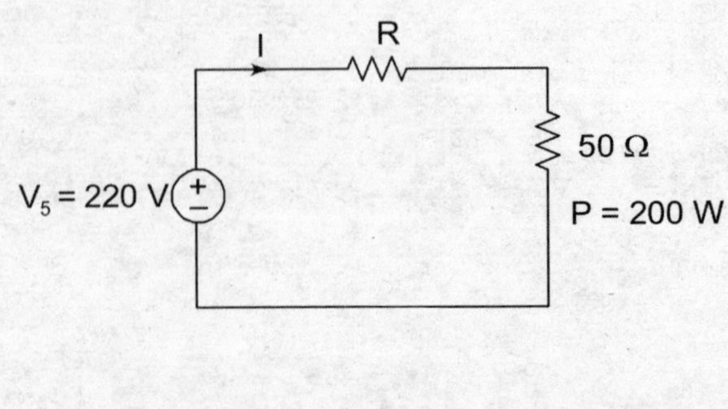

Power dissipation in 50Ω resistor is 200w

$$P = I^2R$$

$$200 = I^2 (50)$$

$$I^2 = \frac{20\not{0}}{5\not{0}} = 4 \text{ amp}$$

$$\boxed{I = 2\text{amp}}$$

We have to calculate the value of R

Now applying KVL

$$220V = (R + 50)I$$

$$220V = (R + 50)2$$

$$\boxed{R = 60\Omega}$$

Power dissipation $P = I^2R$

$$P = (2)^2 \times 60 = 240w$$

$$\boxed{P = 240w}$$

(*c*)

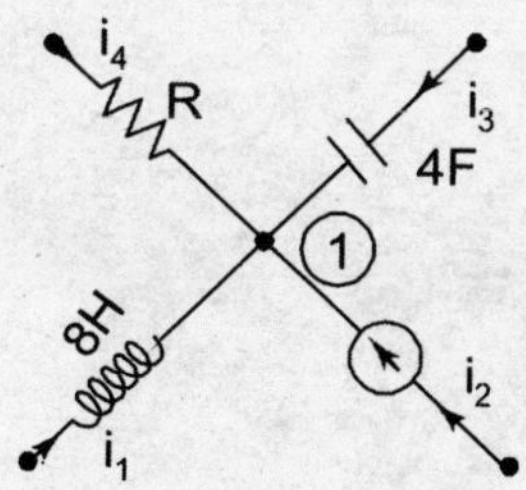

Given data:

$$i_2 = 10e^{-4t}$$

$$i_4 = 6\sin t$$

$$V_3 = 8e^{-4t}$$

Find out V_1

Apply KCL at node 1

$$i_4 = i_1 + i_1 + i_3$$

$$i_1 = i_4 - i_2 - i_3$$

$$i_3 = C\frac{dV}{dt}$$

$$= 4 \times \frac{d(8e - 4t)}{dt}$$

$$i_3 = 4.(8)(-4)e^{-4t}$$

$$= -128e^{-4t} \text{ Amp}$$

Put the value of i_3 in equation of i_1 we get

$$i_1 = 6\sin t - 10e^{-4t} + 128e^{-4t}$$

$$V_1 = L\frac{di_1}{dt}$$

$$= 8\frac{d[6\sin t - 10e^{-4t} - 128e^{-4t}]}{dt}$$

$$= 8[6\cos t - 10(-9e^{-4t}) - 128(-9e^{-4t})]$$

$$= 8[6\cos t + 40e^{-4t} + 512e^{-4t}]$$

$$\boxed{V_1 = [48\cos t + 4416e^{-4t}]\text{volts}}$$

(*d*) We have to find out current in 10Ω resistor using Thevenin theorem

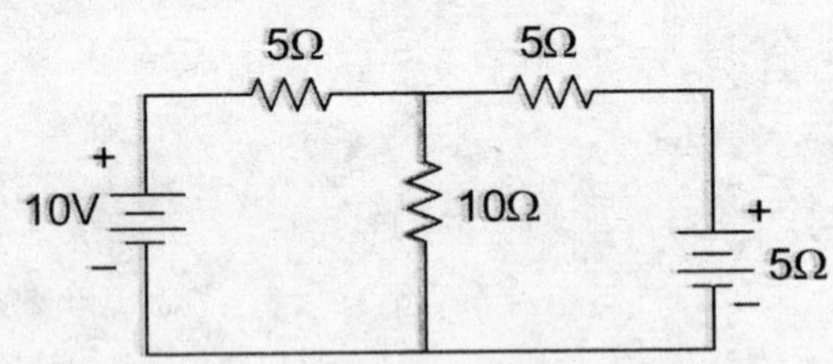

Step. 1 Remove 10Ω resistance and then find V_{TH} across it

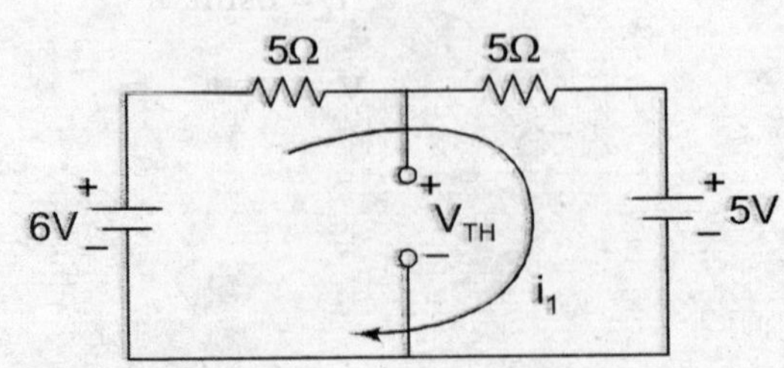

$$i_1 = \frac{10.5}{10}$$

$$= \frac{5}{10} = 0.5 \text{ amp}$$

$$V_{TH} = 10.5\,(0.5) = 7.5V$$

Step. 2 Find out R_{TH} across terminal a-b by reduce the active source ie. $V_s \rightarrow$ short circuit

C_s = open circuit

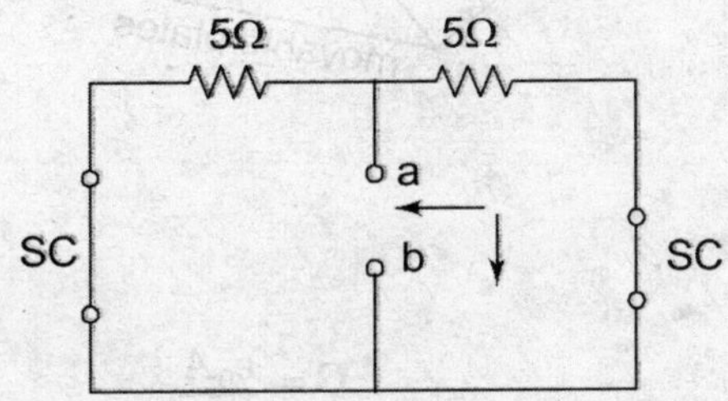

$$R_{TH} = 5/15$$

$$R_{TH} = \frac{5 \times 5}{5 + 5}$$

$$= 2.5\Omega$$

Step. 3

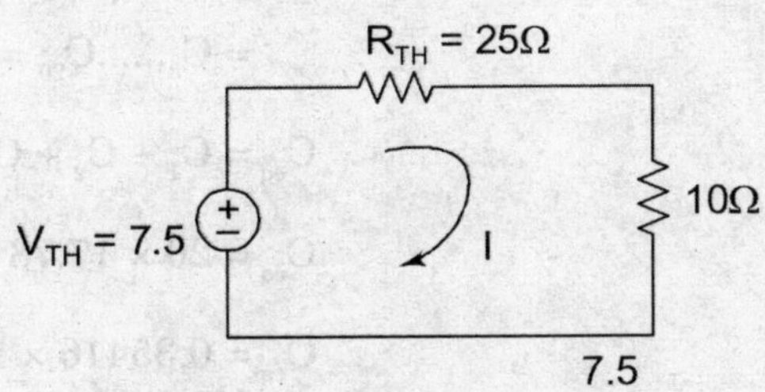

$$i = \frac{V_{TH}}{R_{TH}+10}$$

$$= \frac{7.5}{2.5 + 10} = 0.6 \text{ amp}$$

(*e*) Given data

10 movable plates

11 variable plates

$$A = 0.002 \text{ m}^2$$

$$d = 0.001 \text{ m}$$

According to the question there will be total 20 capacitor formed using 10 movable and stationary plates like this:

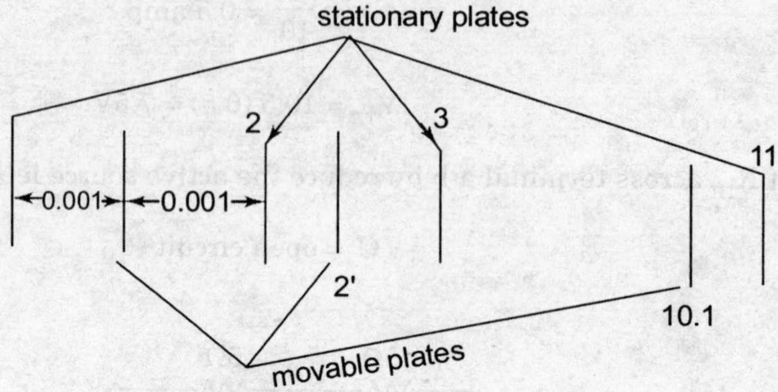

We know that

$$C = \frac{\varepsilon_0 A}{d}$$

$$= \frac{8.854 \times 10^{-12} \times 0.002}{0.001}$$

$$= 17.708 \times 10^{-12} \text{ F}$$

$$C_1 = C_2$$

$$= C_3......C_{20} = C = 17.78 \times 10^{-12}\text{F}$$

$$C_{eq} = C_1 + C_2 + C_3.....C_{20} = 20C$$

$$C_{eq} = 20 \times 17.78 \times 10^{-12}$$

$$C_{eq} = 0.35416 \times 10^{-16}$$

$$\boxed{C_{eq} = 0.359\text{nF}}$$

2. (*a*) **Given parameter:**

$$R = 500\text{W}$$

$$V_s = 220\text{V}$$

$$A = 200\text{mm}^2 = 200 \times 10^{-6}\text{m}^2$$

$$d = 20\text{cm} = 20 \times 10^{-2} \text{ m}$$

$$N = 100$$

$$\mu_r = 250$$

Total flux = ?

We know that

$$\phi = \frac{mmf}{\text{Reluctance}} = \frac{NI}{R}$$

$$R = \frac{l}{\mu_0 \mu_r A}$$

For which we have to find out l and I first

$$I = \frac{220}{500} = 0.44 \text{ amp}$$

$$\text{Mean iron length } l = \pi d = \pi \times 20 = 62.832 \text{ cm}$$

$$R = \frac{l}{\mu_0 \mu_r A}$$

$$= \frac{62.832}{4\pi \times 10^{-7} \times 250 \times 200 \times 10^{-6}}$$

$$R = 10 \times 10^6$$

$$\phi = \frac{mmf}{\text{Reluctance}}$$

$$= \frac{NI}{R} = \frac{1000 \times 0.44}{10 \times 10^6}$$

$$\boxed{\phi = 0.044 \text{wbm}}$$

2. (*b*) **Co-efficient of magnetic coupling:** The fraction of magnetic flux produced by the current in one coil that links with other coil is called coefficient of coupling between the two coils. It is denoted by k = 1 when the flux produced by one coil completely links with other coil and is called magnetically lightly coupled, and k = 0 when the flux produced by one coil does not link with the other coil and thus coil are said to be magnetically isolated as we know that

$$M = k\sqrt{L_1 L_2}$$

where k = coefficient of coupling

M = mutual inductance

L_1 = inductance of coil 1

L_2 = inductance of coil 2.

Self inductance : It is the inductance of the coil due to which it opposes the change of current flowing through it. Inductance is attained by a coil due to the self induced emf produced in the coil itself by changing the current flowing through it

$$\boxed{L = \frac{N\phi}{I}} \text{ Hencey}$$

where N = no. of turns in coil

ϕ = magnetic flux

I = current flowing through the coil

Electromagnetic induction: The induction of an electromotive force by the motion of a conductor across magnetic field or by a change in magnetic flux in a magnetic field.

$$\boxed{Emf = e = -N\frac{d\phi}{dt}}$$

where N = no. of turns

ϕ = Magnetic flux

Time constant : The time required for a changing quantity in a circuit as voltage or current to rise or fall approximately 0.632 of the difference between its new value after an impulse has been applied that induces such a change equal in seconds to the inductance of the circuit in henries divided by resistance in ohms.

It is denoted by τ

In case of inductance $\boxed{\tau = \frac{L}{R}}$

In case of capacitance $\boxed{\tau = RC}$

2. (*c*) (*i*) $V_s = 220V$

$C = 10\mu F$

$I = 2$ amp

$$|Z| = |X_c|$$

$$= \frac{V_s}{I}$$

$$= \frac{200}{2} = 110\Omega$$

$$X_c = \frac{1}{w_c} = 110\Omega$$

$$\omega = \frac{1}{110 \times 10^{-6} \times 10}$$

$$= 909.09 \text{ rad/sec}$$

$$w = 2\pi f$$

$$\Rightarrow \quad f = \frac{w}{2\pi} = \frac{909.09}{2\pi}$$

$$\boxed{f = 144.686\text{Hz}}$$

(*ii*) **Now we have to calculate the value of resistance to be connected in series with the capacitor**

$$R = ?$$

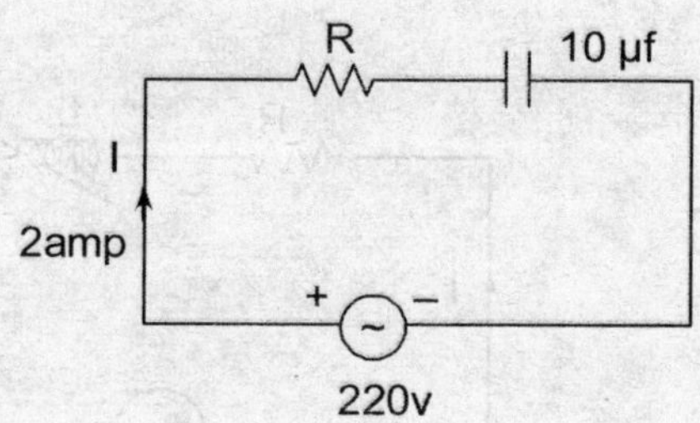

$$\omega = 909.09 \text{ rad/sec}$$

And current reduced to 1Amp

$$Z = |R - jX_c|$$

$$= \frac{V_s}{I}$$

$$= \frac{220}{1} = 220\Omega$$

$$Z^2 = R^2 + Xc^2 = (220)^2$$

$$R^2 = (220)^2 - (110)^2 = 36300$$

$$R^2 = 36300$$

$$\boxed{R = 190.525\Omega}$$

2. (*d*) Given data

$$R = 5\Omega$$

$$C = 50\mu F$$

$$\omega = 100 \text{ rad/sec}$$

$$Vs = 200V$$

Find out

(*i*) value of inductance

(*ii*) Q - factor

(*iii*) Voltage across resistance, C and L

$$Z = R + j(X_L - X_C)$$

$$Z = R + j\left(wL - \frac{1}{w_c}\right)$$

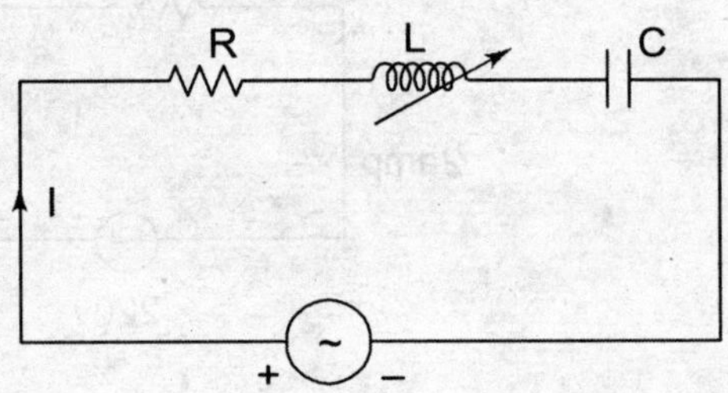

The inductance is varied till the 100 rad/sec voltage across the resistance is maximum i.e. at resonance condition

$$X_L - X_C = 0$$

$$Z = R$$

$$I = \frac{220}{R}$$

$$= \frac{220}{5} = 44\text{Amp}$$

Now $\quad X_L - X_C = 0$

$$\omega_L - \frac{1}{\omega_c} = 0$$

$$L = \frac{1}{w^2 C}$$

(*i*)

$$L = \frac{1}{(100)^2 \times 50 \times 10^{-6}}$$

$$\boxed{L = 2H}$$

(*ii*)

$$\theta = \frac{w_L}{R}$$

$$= \frac{100 \times 2}{5} = 40$$

$$\boxed{\theta = 40}$$

Voltage across capacitance

$$= I\,X_C$$

$$= 44 \times \left(\frac{1}{w_c}\right)$$

$$= 44 \times \left(\frac{1}{100 \times 50 \times 10^{-6}}\right)$$

$$= 8800V$$

$$\boxed{Vc = 8800V}$$

Voltage across inductance $= IX_L$

$$= 44 \times (\omega_L)$$

$$= 44 \times 100 \times 2$$

$$\boxed{V_L = 8800V}$$

3. (*a*) **Given that**

Internal impedance of voltmeter Vi is

$$Z_1 = 32kW$$

Internal impedance of voltmeter V_2 is

$$Z_2 = 18kW$$

Total impedance of circuit

$$\boxed{Z_T = Z_1 + Z_2}$$

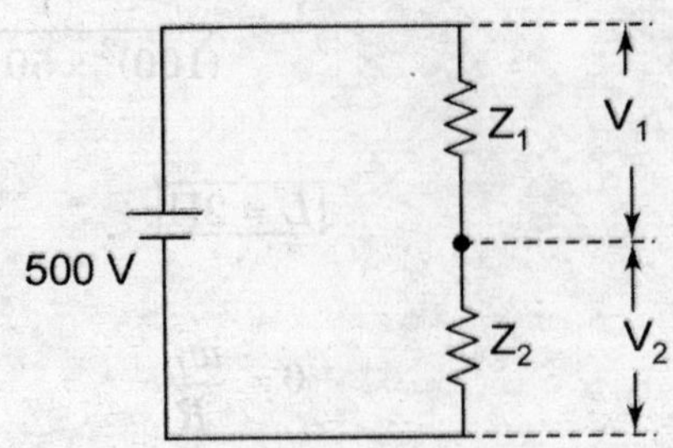

$$ZT = 32 + 18$$

$$\boxed{Z_T = 50\text{k}\Omega}$$

$$\text{Current Is} = \frac{V_s}{Z_T}$$

$$= \frac{500}{50 \times 10^3} = 10\text{mA}$$

$$\boxed{I_s = 10\text{mA}}$$

Reading of voltmeter $V_1 = I \cdot Z_1$

$$V_1 = 10 \times 10^{-3} \times (32 \times 10^{-3})$$

$$\boxed{V_1 = 320 \text{ Volts}}$$

Reading of voltmeter $V_2 = I \cdot Z_2$

$$= (10 \times 10^{-3}) \times 18 \times 10^3$$

$$\boxed{V_2 = 180V}$$

3. (*b*) (*i*) Deflecting torque: The deflecting torque is produced by making use of one of the magnetic heating, chemical electromagnetic induction effects of current and voltage and causes the moving system of instrument to move from its zero position when the instrument is connected in an electrical circuit to measure the electrical quantity. The method of producing this torque depends upon the type of instrument. It is denoted by T_d

(*ii*) Voltmeter sensitivity: Voltmeter sensitivity is the ratio of the total resistance of voltmeter to its full scale reading in volts. It is denoted by s_v

$$\boxed{S_V = \frac{R_V}{V_{FSD}}}$$

where R_V = Total resistance of voltmeter

V_{FSD} = Full scale reading of voltmeter

(*iii*) Shading rings : The copper ring used in shaded pole motor to produce rotating magnetic field for starting purpose, or used around the part of core of an alternating current relay to prevent contact chatter. Also known as shading coil.

(*iv*) Power factor : It is defined as the rartio of the real power flowing to the load to the apparent power in the circuit.

– A power factor less than one means that the voltage and current waveforms are not in phase

It is denoted by cos ϕ

$$\cos\phi = \frac{P}{S}$$

$$\boxed{S = \sqrt{P^2 + Q^2}}$$

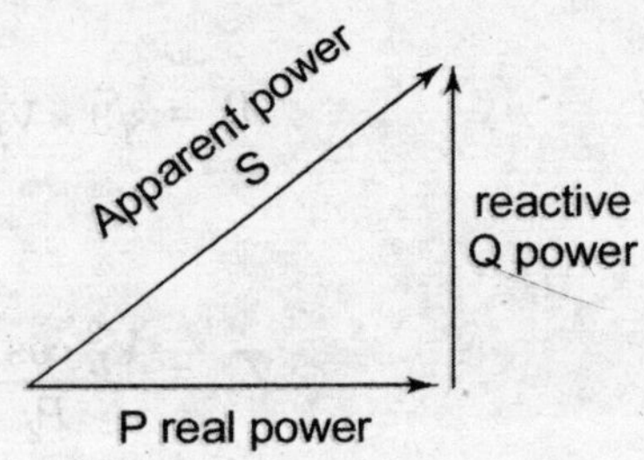

3. (*c*) Given that

Load 1 is connected as a delta connection, 12000 w

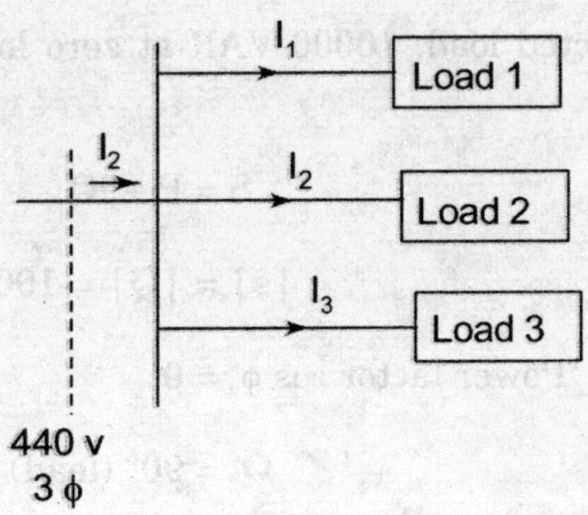

$$P_1 = \sqrt{3}\, V_L I_L \cos\phi_1$$

$$P_1 = \sqrt{3}\ V_L \left(\frac{V_{ph}}{Z\Delta_1}\right)\cos\phi_1$$

$$P_1 = \frac{\sqrt{3} \times V_L^2 \times \cos\phi_1}{Z_{\Delta 1}} \qquad \text{(In } \Delta \text{ connection } V_{ph} = V_L\text{)}$$

$$Z_{\Delta 1} = \frac{\sqrt{3} \times (440)^2 \times 1.0}{12 \times 10^3} = 2.7.977\angle 0°$$

If load Z is star connected load, 1000 VA at 0.9 lag p.f.

$$P_2 = 3 \times \cos\phi$$
$$= 1000 \times 0.9 = 900 \text{ w}$$

$$P_2 = \sqrt{3} V_L I_L \cos\phi_2 \qquad \left(\text{In } \lambda \text{ connection } V_{ph} = \frac{V_L}{\sqrt{3}}\right)$$

$$P_2 = \sqrt{3} V_L \left(\frac{V_{ph}}{Z_{Y_2}}\right) \cos\phi_2$$

$$P_2 = \sqrt{3} \times V_L \left(\frac{V_L / \sqrt{3}}{Z_{Y_2}}\right) \cos\phi_2$$

$$Z_{y2} = \frac{V_L^2 \cos\phi_2}{P_2}$$

$$= \frac{(440)^2 \times 0.9}{900}$$

$$= 19.36 \angle 25.842\ \Omega$$

And load 3 is delta connected load, 10000 VAR at zero load p.f means active power P is zero, only reactive power is present

$$S = P + jQ$$

$$\Rightarrow \quad |s| = |Q| = 10000$$

$$\text{Power factor } \cos\phi_3 = 0$$

$$\Rightarrow \quad Q_3 = 90° \text{ (lead)}$$

$$S = \sqrt{3} V_L I_3$$

$$= \sqrt{3} V_L \left(\frac{V_L}{Z_{\Delta 3}}\right) \quad \therefore (V_{ph} = V_L)$$

$$Z_{\Delta 3} = \frac{\sqrt{3}(V_L)^2}{S} = \frac{\sqrt{3}(440)^2}{10000} = 33.532 \angle -90° \Omega$$

Transforming delta load to star

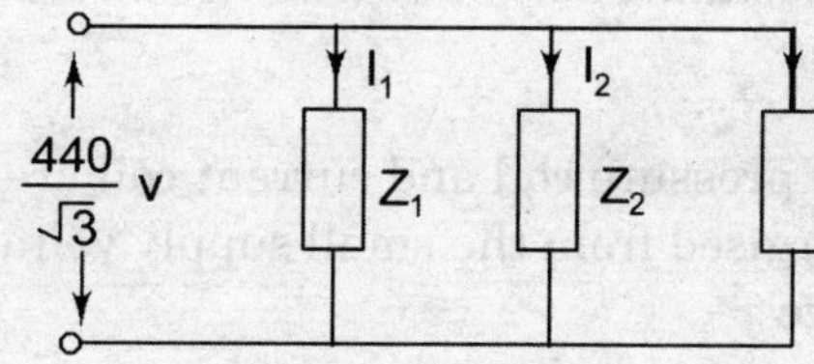

$$Z_1 = \frac{Z_{\Delta 1}}{3}$$

$$= \frac{27.944}{3}\Omega = 9.315\angle 0°\Omega$$

$$Z_2 = Z_{Y2}$$

$$= 19.36\ \angle 25.842\ \Omega$$

$$Z_3 = \frac{Z_{\Delta 3}}{3}$$

$$= \frac{33.532\angle -90°}{3} = 11.177\angle -90°\Omega$$

$$\text{Total current } I_L = I_{Ph}$$

$$= I_1 + I_2 + I_3$$

$$I_L = \frac{440/\sqrt{3}}{9.315\angle 0°} + \frac{440/\sqrt{3}}{19.36\angle 25.842} + \frac{440/\sqrt{3}}{11.177\angle 90°}$$

$$I_L = 42.62\ \angle 23.529\ A$$

$$\cos\phi_2 = 23.532 \text{ leading}$$

(i) $$\text{Total power } P_T = \sqrt{3} V_L I_L \cos\phi_2$$

$$= \sqrt{3} \times 440 \times 42.62 \times \cos(23.524°)$$

$$P_T = 2978.142\ \omega$$

$$= 29.78412\ W$$

(ii) $$\text{Power factor } \cos\phi_2 = \cos(23.529) = 0.9169 \text{ (radial)}$$

(iii) The current drawn from line

$$\boxed{I_L = 42.62 \text{ Amp}}$$

3. (*d*) Phantom loading is the phenomena in which the appliances consume electricity even when they are turn off. The disc of energy meter rotates which increases the reading of meter, but the devices do not consume power. This type of loading also known as virtual loading. The phantom loading mainly occurs in the electronic appliances.

– In phantom loading the pressure coil and current coil are seperately excited on the supply source. The pressure coil is energised from the small supply voltage and the current energises the current coil at very small voltage

Example of Phantom loading : Consider the d.c. energy meter having rating voltage 220V and current 9 amp. The resistance of presure coil and the current coil is 4400 Ω resp. The power consumption by direct and phatom loading shown below

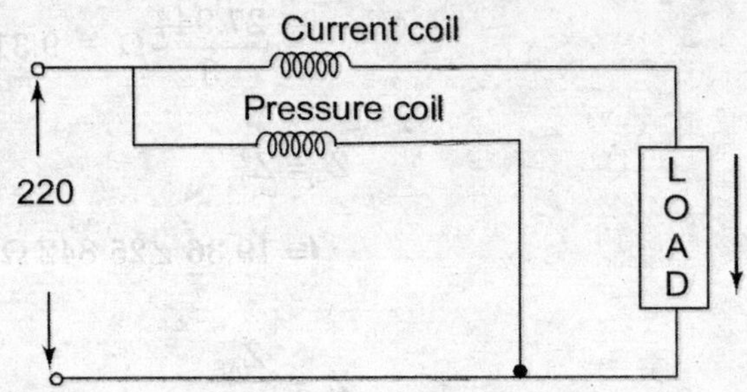

Direct loading arrangement

$$P = (220)2 /4400$$

$$= 11 \text{ watt}$$

$$\text{Power} = 220 \times 9$$

$$= 1980 \text{ watt}$$

$$\boxed{P_T = 11 + 1980 = 991 \text{ watt}}$$

Phantom loading arrangement

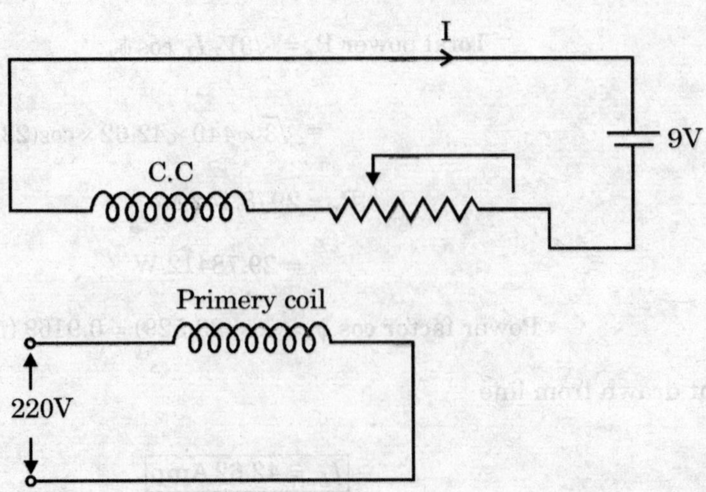

$$P = (220)2/400$$

$$= 11 \text{ watt}$$

The current coil of the phantom loading arrangement is seperately excited by the other of aV. The power of current coil is measured as

$$P = 9 \times 9 = 81 \text{ w}$$

$$\boxed{P_T = (\text{Total power}) = 11 + 81 = 91 \text{ w}}$$

The above example shows that in phantom loading the pressure and current coil is seperated excited by the meter, hence, power loss is less in phanotm loading.

4. (*a*) According to question

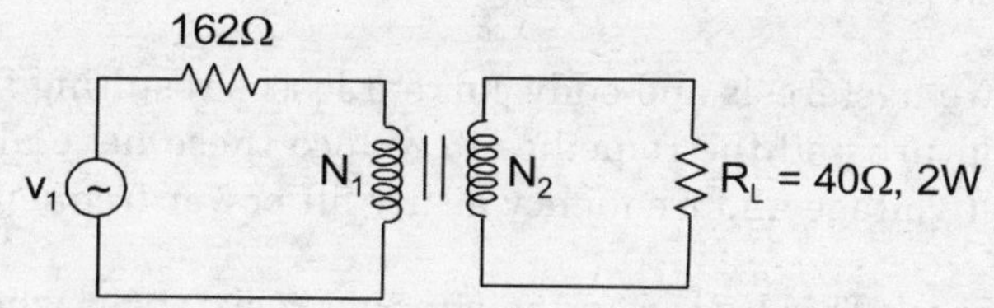

Source resistance = 160Ω is matched to a 40Ω

$$R_L' = R_L \cdot a^2$$

$$a^2 = \frac{160}{40} = 4$$

$$\boxed{a = 2}$$

$$\boxed{a = \frac{N_1}{N_2} = 2}$$

$$P_L = I_2^2 R_2$$

$$Z = (I_L)^2 \times 40$$

$$I_2^2 = \frac{2}{40}$$

$$= \frac{1}{20}$$

⇒ $$I_2 = \sqrt{\frac{1}{20}} = 0.224 \text{ Amp}$$

$$\text{Secondary voltage } V_2 = I_2R_L = 0.224 \times 40 = 8.944 \text{ volts}$$

$$\text{Primary voltage } V_1 = a.V_2 = 2\times 8.944 = 17.88 \text{ V}$$

$$\text{Primary current} = I_1 = \frac{I_2}{a} = 0.112 \text{ amp}$$

So

$$v_1 = 17.88 \text{ v}$$

$$v_2 = 8.944 \text{ v}$$

$$I_1 = 0.112 \text{ amp}$$

$$I_2 = 0.224 \text{ amp}$$

4. (*b*) **Transformer losses :** The transformor has no moving parts so that its efficiency in much higher than that of rotating machine. The various losses in transformer are enumerated below.

Core loss : These are hysteresis and eddy current losses resulting from alternations of magnetic field in the core. Their nature and the remedies to reduce these have already we know for a transformer operated at constant voltage and frequency as are all power frequency transformer.

Copper loss ($I^2{}_R$ loss) : This loss occurs in winding resistances when the tranformer carries the load current varies or a square of loading expressed as a ratio of the full load.

Load (Stray) loss : It largely results from leakage field inducing eddy currents in the tank wall and conductors.

Di-electric loss : The seat of this loss in the insulating materials, particularly in oil and solid insulation.

Note:

(*i*) The stray and dielectric losses are very small and therefore neglected.

(*ii*) $\boxed{\text{Core loss = Hysteresis loss + eddy current}}$

Hysteresis loss, $\boxed{P_h = \eta(b\max)^x.f.v}$ watts

where

f = supply frequency

v = volume of core in cubic meters

η = hysteresis cofficient

B_{max} = peak value of flux density

x = lies between 1.5 - 2.5 depending upon material

Eddy current loss]

$$\boxed{Pe = \frac{r^2}{6e} \times B^2 \max \times f^2 \times t^2 \times \text{vol.of laminations}}$$

Condition for maximum efficiency :

Transformer efficiency

$$\eta = \frac{\text{output}}{\text{Input}}$$

$$= \frac{\text{Output}}{\text{Output + losses}}$$

power output = $V_2 I_2 \cos \phi$.

losses = $P_i + P_C$ (Iron loss) + (Copper loss)

Copper loss at a load x times full load = x^2PC and hence η

$$\eta = \frac{V_2 I_2 \cos \phi}{V_1 I_2 \cos \phi + Pi + x^2 Pc}$$

$$\eta = \frac{xp}{xP + Pi + x^2 Pc} \qquad \text{...(i)}$$

where P = full load

Pi = Total iron loss

Pc = full load copper los

x = fraction of full load KVA at which η is maximum

Differentiating eqn (1)

$$\frac{d\eta}{dx} = \frac{(xp + Pi + x^2Pc).P - xP(P + 2xPc)}{(xP + Pi + x^2Pc)^2}$$

$$= \frac{P(Pi + x^2Pc)}{(xP + Pi + x^2Pc)^2}$$

η = will be maximum when $\frac{d\eta}{dx} = 0$

$$Pi - x^2 Pc = 0$$

$$\boxed{x = \sqrt{\frac{Pi}{Pc}}}$$

Hence efficiency will be maximum when variable loss is equal to constant loss (iron loss).

4. (*c*) Given that

$$\text{Developed power} = 10 \text{ HP}$$

$$P_0 = 10 \times 746$$

$$= 7460 \text{ watt}$$

$$P_{in} = V_s I_L$$

$$= 220 \times 40 = 8800 \text{ w}$$

The efficiency of shunt motor is

$$\%\eta = \frac{P_0}{P_{in}} \times 100$$

$$= \frac{7460}{8800} \times 100 = 84.77\%$$

$$\text{Torque T} = \frac{P_0}{w_m}$$

$$= \frac{7460}{\left(2\pi \times \frac{8800}{60}\right)} = 8.905 \text{ Nm}$$

4. (*d*) Effect of frequency variation on torque speed characterstic

1. Below base speed by keeping v/f constant and frequency $f \leq f_{rated}$ i.e. $\frac{v}{f}$ = constant

$\boxed{v \,\alpha\, f}$ → we know that

$$T_{max} = \frac{V_1^2}{2\omega_{sm} X_2'} \,\alpha\, \frac{1}{2} \cdot \frac{f^2}{f} = \text{constant}$$

$$S_{Tmax} = \frac{R_2'}{X_2'} \,\alpha\, \frac{1}{f}$$

$$\tan \phi_2 = \frac{SX_2'}{R_2'} \,\alpha\, Sf$$

Region 1: Normal operation region or low slip region)

i.e. $0 < S \leq S_{Tmax}$

(*i*) $$I_2' = \frac{SV_1}{RL'} \alpha\, sf$$

(*ii*) $$\frac{1}{w_{sm}} \times \frac{SV_1^2}{R_2'} \;\alpha \frac{1}{f} \times sf^2$$

Region 2: (High slip region): $S > S_{Tmax}$

(i) $$I_2' = \frac{V_1}{X_2'} \alpha \frac{f}{f} = \text{constant}$$

(ii) $$\text{Torque } T = \frac{1}{w_{sm}} \times \frac{V_1^2}{(X_1^2)^2} \times \frac{R_2'}{S}\, a \frac{1}{f} \times \frac{f_2}{f_2} \times \frac{1}{s}$$

$$T\, \alpha \frac{1}{f_s} \Rightarrow \boxed{T_{st}\ \alpha \frac{1}{f}} \text{ At starting time } \boxed{S = 1}$$

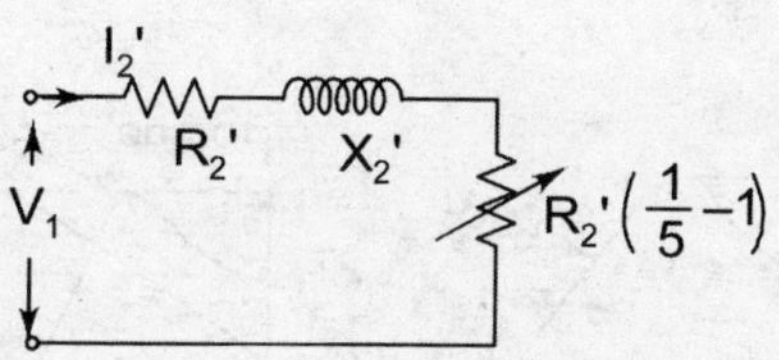

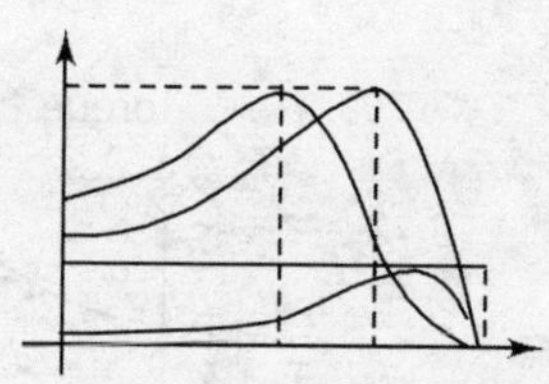

2. Above base speed by keeping supply voltage constant and supply frequency f > frated

i.e. supply voltage V1 = constant

Supply frequency $f > F_{rated}$

$$T_{max} = \frac{1}{2w_{sm}} \times \frac{V_1^2}{X_2^1} \alpha \frac{1}{f^2}$$

$$S_{Tmax} = \frac{R_2'}{X_2'} \alpha \frac{1}{f}$$

$$Ns - N = SNs\ \alpha\ sf$$

$$\tan \phi_2 = \frac{SX_2'}{R_2'} \alpha\, sf$$

Region (i)

Low slip region $0 < s \leq S_{Tmax}$

(i) $$I_2' = \frac{SV_1}{R_2^1} \alpha\, s$$

(ii) $$T = \frac{1}{w_{sm}} \times \frac{SV_1^2}{R_2^1} \times \frac{1}{f} \times s\, \alpha \frac{s}{f}$$

Region (ii) (High slip region): $s > S_{T\,max}$

(i) $$I_2' = \frac{V_1^2}{X_2^1} \alpha \frac{1}{f}$$

(ii) $$T = \frac{1}{w_{sm}} \times \frac{V_1^2}{(X_2')^2} \times \frac{R_2^1}{S} \alpha \frac{1}{f} \times \frac{1}{f^2} \times \frac{1}{s} \alpha \frac{1}{sf^3}$$

$$T_{st} = \frac{1}{f^3}$$ ....(s = 1 at starting time)

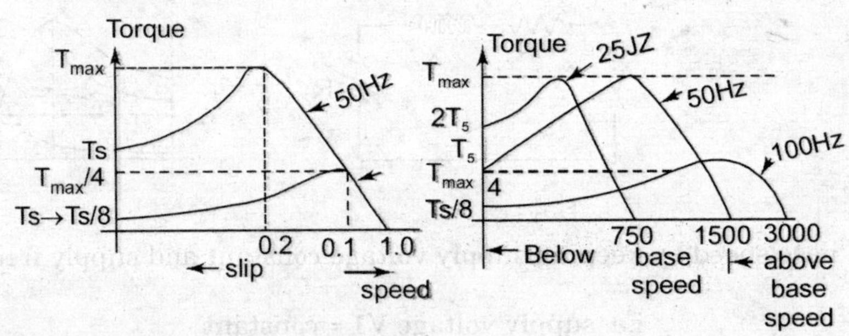

5. (*a*) Cases of low power factor in a power system:

The main cause of low power factor is inductive load As in pure inductive circuit, current lags 90° from voltage, this large difference of phase angle between current and voltage causes zero power factor. Basically all those circuit having capacitance and inductance (except resonance circuit) where $X_L = X_C$, power factor would be exist over there becouse of capacitance and inductance causes difference of phase angle θ between current and voltage.

Main causes of low power factor:

1. Single phase and three phase induction motor usually induction motor works at low p.f. i.e. at full load p.f. = 0.8 – 0.9

   Small load p.f. = 0.2 – 0.3

2. Varying load in power system: During low load period, supply voltage in increased which increased the magnetizing current which cause the decresed power factor.

3. Industrial heating furnace

4. Transformers

5. Harmonic currents.

6. Electrical discharge lamp.

5. (*b*) Let us consider a 3-ϕ induction motor first and see how it rotates. A 3-ϕ supply is given to the armature of induction motor produces a rotating megnetic speed N_S = (120 f/P). This rotating magnetic field linked to the rotor coils and induces voltage which in turn produces current in the rotor. The current carrying rotor being placed in a magetic field experiences a torque being placed in a magnetic field experiences a torque and hence begins to rotate in the direction of rotating magnetic field. Thus we can say that 3-ϕ induction motor is self starting.

Single phase induction motor has distributed stator winding and a squirrel cage rotor, when fed from a flux which is only alternating i.e. are which alternate along one space axis only. It is not synchronously revolving flux as in case of a two or a three phase stator winding fed from a 2 of 3 phase supply. Now an alternating on pulsating flux acting on a squirrel cage rotor can not produce rotation. That is why single phase induction motor is not self starting.

5. (*c*) In an electric motor torque is developed by interaction of rotor flux and the stator flux. In order to develop a continuous torque the fluxes must be fixed value relative to one another as the motor rotates. It they are not fixed then the torque fluctuates both +ve and –ve and the net torque is zero, In case of synchronous motor the position of rotor flux is fixed relative to rotor Therefore rotor speed must be same as rotational speed of stator flux and in synchronous motor rotor is magnetically locked once approches the speed of stator flux and developes the torque at synchronous speed. But in case of induction motor the rotor flux move slowly relation to rotor. Rotor flux is produced by induction which will occur only if there is some difference between the rotor speed and stator speed. it is called slip. Therefore torque developed by induction motor is proportional to slip. At synchronous speed slip is zero and hence torque developed by the induction motor is zero.

5. (*d*) In case of power syntem single line to ground fault is most severe fault at the generator terminals than three phase fault become zero sequence impedance is less at the generator and fault current in case of line to ground fault is three times of +ve sequence current

$$I_F\,(L - G) = 3I_{R1}$$

I_{R1} = +ve sequence current

And if $Zn < \frac{1}{3}\,[Z_{G1} - Z\,G_0]$ the L–G fault is more severe where Z_{G1} is +ve sequence impedance of generator.

Z_{G0} is zero sequence of generator Zn neutral grounding impedance

As the fault location moves away from generator, zero sequence impedance increases and 3–ϕ fault becomes more severe.

5. (*e*) The following conditions should be satisfied for parallel operation are as follows:

(i) The phase sequence of bus bar voltages and the incoming machine voltages must be some

(*ii*) The bus bar voltages and incoming machine terminal voltage must be in phase.

(iii) The terminal voltage of incoming machine and alternators which is to be connected in parallel or with the bus bar voltage should be equal.

(iv) The frequency of generated voltage of incoming machine and the frequency of voltage of bus bar should be equal.

6. (*a*) **Advantage of BJT over J.FET:**

(*i*) BJT having good voltage gain compared to J-FET

(*ii*) BJT having faster switching time compared to J.FET by preventing the device going into hard saturation.

(*iii*) BJT using amplifier circuit due to its high gain bandwidth product compared to J.FET

(*iv*) BJT shows good performance at high frequency compared to J.FET

Disadvantage of BJT over J-FET:

(*i*) BJT is less imune to radiation compared to J-FET

(*ii*) BJT is less stable than J-FET with respect to temperature variation

(*iii*) BJT occupies more space in integrated form compared to J-FET

(*iv*) BJT is more noisy compared to J-FET

(*v*) BJT has low input resistance compared to J-FET

6. (*b*) Fuses protect against overcurrent events by metting their elements and opening the circuit. Fuse must be applied at or below their specified voltage rating which differs between a.c and d.c currents.

Selection of fuse condition : In order to begin selecting the appropriate fuse, one needs to understand the nature of the circuit it power and protects. Basic operating factor such as maximum steady state voltage current value ambient temperature.

(*i*) **Voltage rating :** Fuses of lightning circuit are insensitive to voltage change within their ratings so selecting the proper voltage rating is necessary.

(*ii*) **Current rating :** The fuse element to be used in a fuse must be selected for a rated current large energy to ensure that the element will not fuse when the light circuit carrying its sustained maximum load current and when circuit is carrying a short time over load current

(*iii*) **Ambient temperature :** When a fuse is applied in an ambient temperature exceeding the standard 23°C. The fuse current rating should be durated

$$I_{rated} = \frac{\text{Input current (max)}}{K_{Temp}}$$

$$K_{Tempt} = \text{Temperature derating factor}$$

6. (*c*) **domestic wiring:**

1. **Lead and sheath wiring:** The wiring is similar to that of CTs but the conductors are individually insulated and convered with a common outer lead aluminium alloy sheath. The sheath protects the cable against dampness atmospheric extremities and mechanical damages. The sheath is earthed at every junction to provide a path to ground for leakage current. They are fixed by means of metal clips on wooden battens. The wiring system is very expensive It is suitable for low voltage installations.

2. **Casing and caping wiring :** As the name refered in this wiring. PVC insulated wires are placed in plastic cashing and covered with cap. The casing is of rectangular cross-section. In this wiring no risk of electric shock due to covered wires and cables in casing and caping. The cables were carried through the wooden casing enclosers.

(3) **Clear wiring :** Cleat wiring temporary electrical wiring on building and construction sites is necessary to enable lightning and power to be provided for the various points on the site

Advantages:

(i) It is simple and cheap wiring system

(ii) Inspection is simple and easy

(iii) Cables and wires of cheat wiring system is in open air

(4) **Conduit wiring :** It conduits installed on root or wall. It is known as surface conduit wiring. In this wiring method they make holes on the surface or wall on equal distances and conduit is installed then with the help of rawal plugs.

Concealed conduit wiring : If the conduit is hidden inside the wall stock with the help of plastering it is called concealed conduit wiring. In other words, the electrical wiring system inside wall, roof or floor with the help of plastic or metallic piping is called concleared conduit wiring.

Advantage:

1. It is reliable and popular wiring system
2. It is very safe wiring system
3. No risk of electric shock
4. Sustainable and long-lossing wiring system
5. Battern wiring (CTs and TRs):

Single core or double core or three core TRs cables with a circular oval shape cables are used in this kind of wiring. Mostly single core cable are prefered

Advantages

(*i*) Strong and long lasting

(*ii*) Installation of wiring is simple

(*iii*) Less chance of leakage current in batten systems

(*iv*) Repairing is easy

6. (*d*) **Advantages of Electric drive over conventional drive:**

1. Electric drive is more reliable than conventional drives
2. It is smooth and easy control
3. Facility of remote control is avilable in electric drive.
4. Having long life than conventional drives
5. Electric drive has easy starting facilities.
6. It is more compact than conventional drives
7. Having low cost than conventional drives
8. More flexible than conventional drives

Disadvantage of Electric drives over conventional drives:

1. Having noise pollution.
2. It has poor dynamic response
3. To increase torque, a larger and havier motor must be used which is costly
4. It can not be employed at distant places
5. It's non availability on failure of supply

■■

Solved Paper 2014

Electrical Engineering

(Paper II)

1. (*a*) A copper wire has a resistance of 0.85 Ω at 20°C. What will be its resistance at 40°C? Temperature coefficient of resistance of copper at 0°C is 0.004°C. (10)

(*b*) In the circuit shown in Figure, what is the value of V? (10)

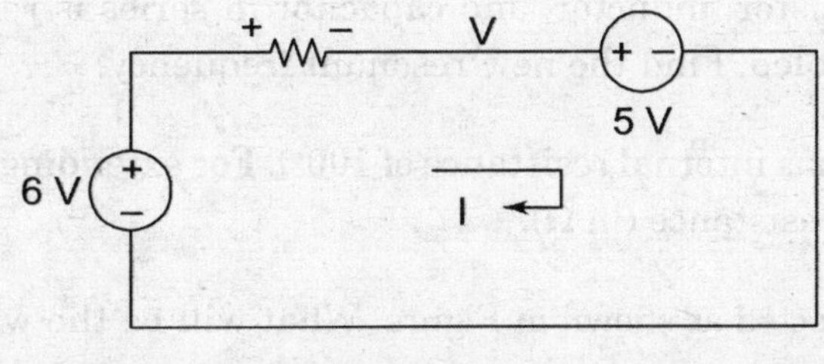

Figure 1

(*c*) What is the value of Thevenin voltage E_{Th} in the given circuit of Figure? (10)

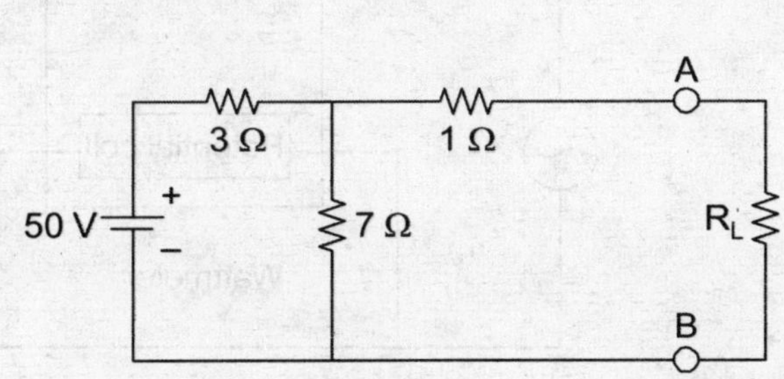

Figure 2

(*d*) In Figure, find the value of resistance R. (30)

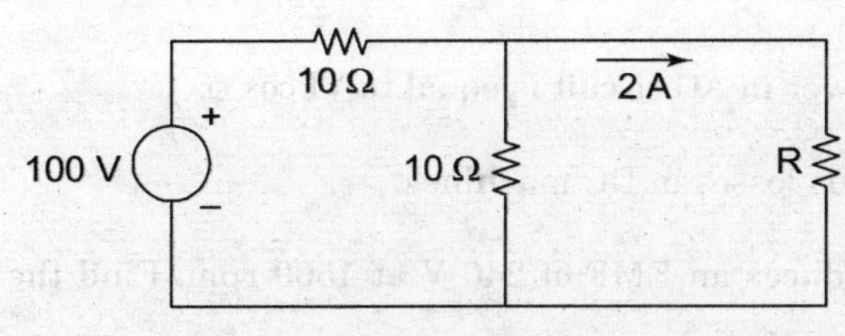

Figure 3

2. (*a*) Define the following terms: (20)

(*i*) Magnetic field intensity

(*ii*) Magnetic flux density

(*iii*) Magnetomotive force

(*iv*) Reluctance

(*b*) In a pair of coupled coils, coil 1 has a continuous current of 2A and the corresponding fluxes φ_{11} and φ_{21} are 0.3 and 0.6 mWb respectively. If the turns are N_1 = 500 and N_2 = 500, find L_1, L_2, M and K. (10)

(*c*) An AC voltage of 50 Hz has a maximum value of 50V. What will be its voltage after 1/600 second? (10)

(*d*) A circuit with a resistor, inductor, and capacitor in series is resonant of f_0 Hz. If all the component values are now doubled. Find the new resonant frequency. (20)

3. (*a*) A 100 μA ammeter has internal resistance of 100Ω. For extending its range to measure 500μA, calculate the value of shunt resistance (in Ω). (10)

(*b*) A wattmeter is connected as shown in Figure. What will be the wattmeter reading of power consumed either by Z_1 or Z_2? (10)

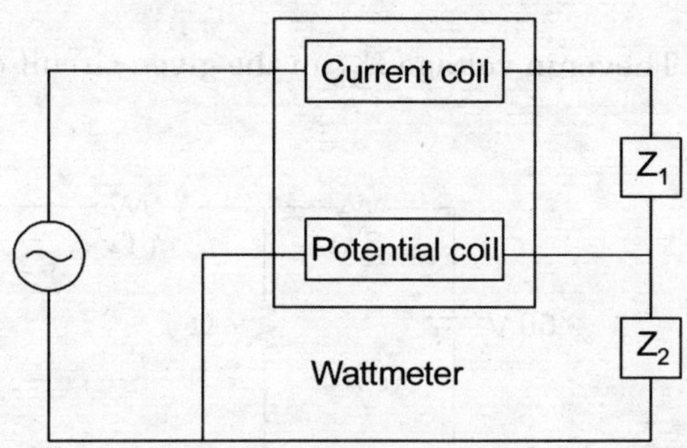

Figure 4

(*c*) A CRO screen has ten divisions on the horizontal scale. If a voltage signal 5 sin (314 t + 45°) is examined with a line base setting of 5 msec/div, find the number of cycles of signal displayed on the screen.(20)

(*d*) Prove that the power in AC circuit is equal to VI cos φ. (20)

4. (*a*) Explain the various losses in DC machines. (20)

(*b*) A DC machine induces an EMF of 240 V at 1500 rpm. Find the developed torque for an armature current of 25 A. (10)

(*c*) A 3300/300 V single phase transformer gives 0.6 A and 60 W as ammeter and wattmeter readingd when supply is given to the low voltage winding and high voltage winding is kept open. What is the power factor of no load current? (15)

(*d*) A 3 hp, 3-phase 4-pole, 400V 50Hz induction motor runs at 1440 rpm. What will be the frequency of the rotor-induced EMF? (15)

5. (*a*) Explain the need for connecting a capacitor in the auxiliary winding of a single phase induction motor. (15)

(*b*) Why are two alternators connected in parallel to supply a common load? What are the necessary conditions for parallel connection? (15)

(*c*) What are the advantages and disadvantages of AC over DC? (15)

(*d*) Overhead power transmission lines are preferred over underground power cables. Discuss. (8)

(*e*) What are the main advantages of SF6 circuit breakers? (7)

6. (*a*) A residential flat has the following average electrical consumptions per day:

(*i*) 4 tube lights of 40 watts working for 5 hours per day;

(*ii*) 2 filaments of 60 watts working for 8 hours per day;

(*iii*) 1 water heater rated 2 kW working for 1 hour per day;

(*iv*) 1 water pump of 0.5 kW rating working for 3 hours per day.

Calculate the cost of energy per month if 1 kWh of energy (i.e., 1 unit of energy) costs ` 3.50. (20)

(*b*) Cite the advantages and disadvantages of electric drives. (20)

(*c*) A silicon diode is connected across a 3V supply with a series resistance of 20Ω as shown in Figure. Neglecting diode resistance, find the diode current. (20)

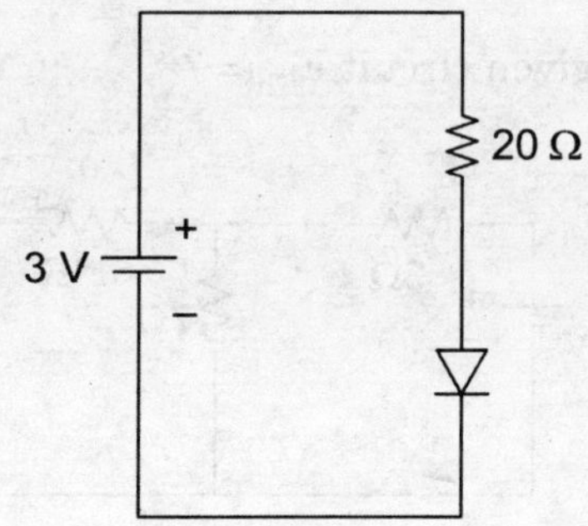

EXPLANATIONS

1. (*a*) Given:

at 20°C value of resistance is 0.85Ω

at 40°C change in temp Δt = 40–20 = 20°C

$$R_{40} = R_{20}(1 + \alpha\, \Delta t)$$

∴ $\alpha = 0.004$°C given

$$R_{40} = 0.85(1 + 0.004 \times 20)$$

$$\boxed{R_{40} = 0.91\Omega}$$

(*b*)

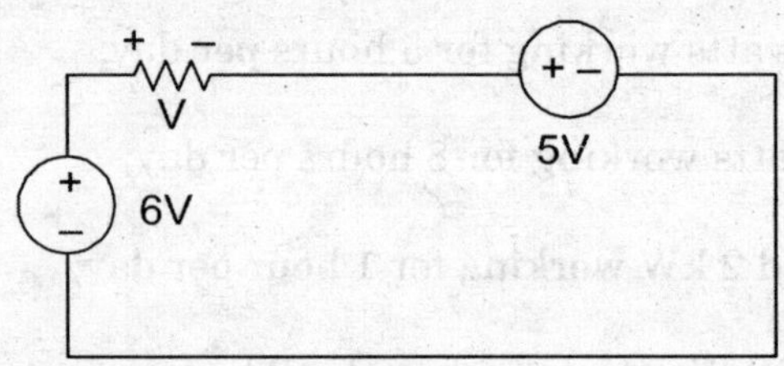

We have to find out the value of V in given circuit

On applying KVL

$$-6 + V + 5 = 0$$

$$\boxed{V = 1V}$$

(*c*) Find out the value of V_{TH} in given circuit E_{Th} = ?

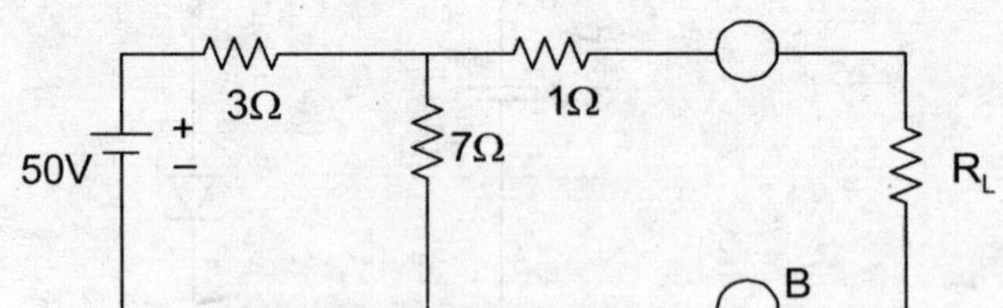

Step 1. Remove R_L

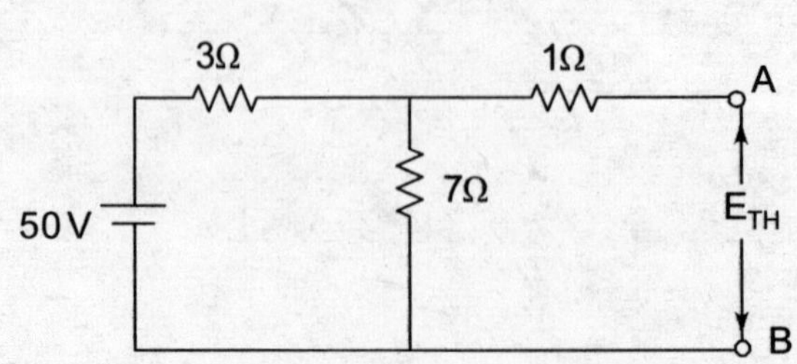

E_{TH} means voltage across 7W resistance

$$E_{TH} = \frac{7 \times 50}{7 + 3}$$

$$= 35V$$

$$\boxed{E_{TH} = 35V}$$

(*d*) We have to find out the value of R in given circuit

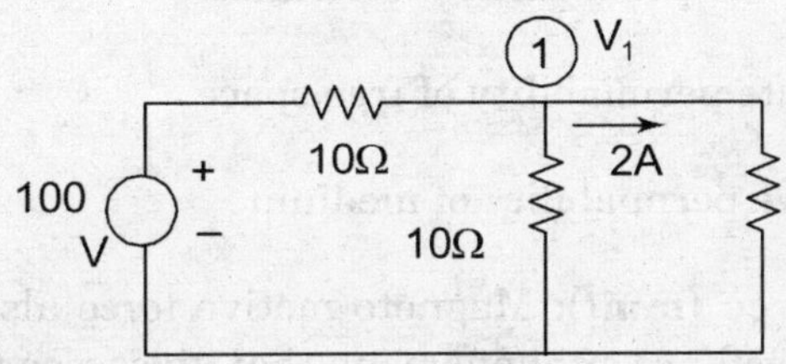

On applying KCL at node 1,

$$\frac{V_1 - 100}{10} + \frac{V_1 - 0}{10} + 2 = 0$$

$$\Rightarrow \quad 2V_1 - 100 + 20 = 0$$

$$\boxed{V_1 = 40}$$

$$\therefore \quad R = \frac{V_1}{2}$$

$$= \frac{40}{2}$$

$$= 20W$$

$$\boxed{R = 20\Omega}$$

2. (*a*) Define following turms

(*i*) **Magnetic field intensity:** Magnetic field intensity is also known as magnetizing force which is measured in A–T/m. It is denoted by H

$$\boxed{H = \frac{NI}{l}} \text{ AT/m}$$

Or we can say that the magnetic field intensity of a circuit is given by mmf per unit length (*ii*) **Magnetic flux density:** Magnetic flux density is defined as the amount of magnetic flux in an area taken perpandicular to the magnetic flux direction. Flux density B is ϕ flux per unit area. It's unit is Tesla

$$\boxed{B = \frac{\phi}{A} wb/m^2 \text{orTesla}}$$

The magnetic flux density (B) and its intensity in a medium can be related as:

$$\boxed{B = \mu H}$$

where $\mu = \mu_o \mu_r$ is the permiability of medium

μ_o = absolute permiability of free space

μ_r = relative permiability of medium

(*iii*) **Magneto motive force (mmt):** Magneto motive force also known as magnetic potential, is the property of certain substance or phenomena that gives rise to magnetic field. Magnetomotive force is anologus to electromotive force or voltage in electricity

$$\boxed{\text{MMF} = \text{NI AT}}$$

Reluctance: It is the property of the medium which opposes the passage of magnetic flux. Magnetic reductance is alnalogus to resistance in the electric circuit. It's unit is AT/wb.

$$\text{Reductance} = \frac{\text{mmf}}{\text{flux}}$$

at 40°C change in temp

(*b*) Given parameter

$$I_1 = 2 \text{ amp}$$

$$N_1 = 500$$

$$N_2 = 500$$

$$f_{12} = 0.6 \text{ mwb}$$

$$f_{11} = 0.3 \text{ mwb}$$

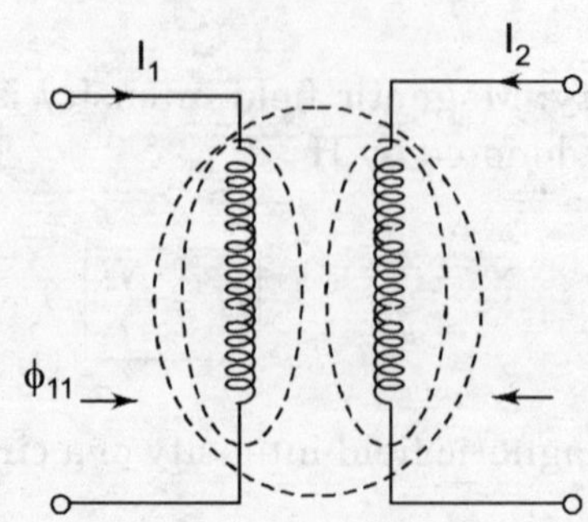

$$\phi_{12} = \phi_{21}$$

Self inductance of coil 1.

$$L_1 = \frac{N_1\phi_1}{I_1}$$

$$= \frac{500 \times 0.3 \times 10^{-3}}{2}$$

$$= 75 \times 10^{-3}$$

$$= 0.075H = 75 \text{ mH}$$

Coupling coefficient

$$k = \frac{\phi_{12}}{\phi_1}$$

$$= \frac{0.6}{0.9} = 0.607$$

Mutual inductance between two coils

$$M = \frac{N_2\phi_{12}}{I_1}$$

$$= \frac{500 \times 0.6 \times 10^{-3}}{2}$$

$$= 150 \times 10^{-3}$$

$$= 0.15H = 150 \text{ mH}$$

Self inductance of coil 2,

$$M = k\sqrt{L_1L_2}$$

$$L_2 = \frac{M^2}{K^2L_1} = \frac{(0.15)^2}{\left(\frac{2}{3}\right)^2 \times 0.225}$$

$$= 0.675H$$

$$\boxed{L_1 = 0.075H = 75mH}$$

$$\boxed{L_2 = 675mH}$$

$$\boxed{M = 150mH}$$

$$\boxed{k = 2/3 = 0.667}$$

(*c*) Given :

$$V_m = 50V \text{ at } 50Hz$$

$$V = Vm \sin\omega t$$

$$= Vm \sin(2\pi f)t$$

$$V = 50.\sin(2\pi \times 50 \times \frac{1}{600})$$

$\therefore$ $$t = 1/600$$

$$\boxed{V = 25 Volts}$$

(*d*)

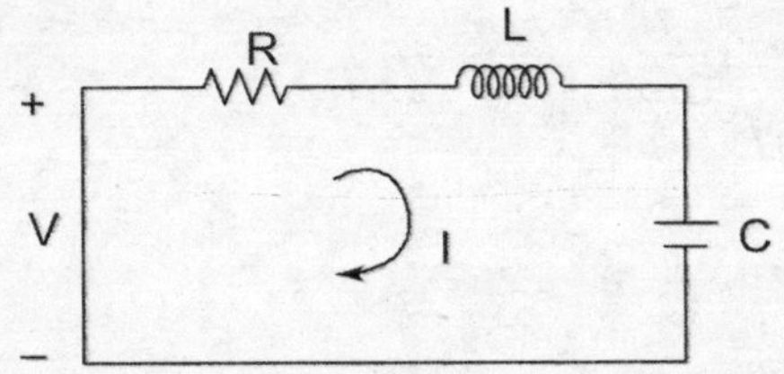

Impedance of above network is

$$Z = R + j\left(wL - \frac{1}{wc}\right)$$

$\therefore$ $$w = wr$$

At resonance condition we know that

$$w_r L - \frac{1}{w_r C} = 0$$

$$\omega_r^2 = \frac{1}{LC}$$

$$\boxed{\omega_r = \frac{1}{\sqrt{LC}}}$$

$$\text{hence } fr = \frac{1}{2\pi\sqrt{LC}}$$

If all the components values are now doubled

$$\frac{fr_{(2)}}{fr_{(1)}} = \frac{1}{2\pi\sqrt{L_2C_2}}.\left(2\pi\sqrt{L_1C_1}\right)$$

$$fr_{(2)} = fr_1\left[\frac{\sqrt{L_1C_1}}{\sqrt{2L_1, 2C_1}}\right]$$

$$= \frac{fr}{\sqrt{4}} = \frac{fr}{2}$$

And hence new resonant frequency is

$$\boxed{fr_{(2)} = \frac{fr_1}{2}}$$

3. (*a*)

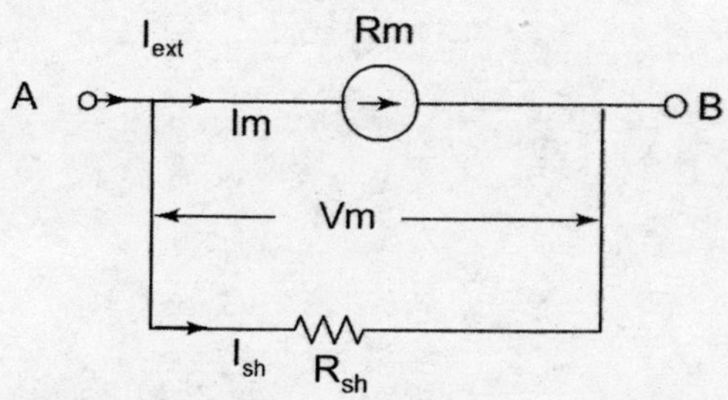

Given parameter

$$I_m = 100\mu A \rightarrow \text{ammeter current}$$

$$R_m = 100\Omega \rightarrow \text{ammeter resistance}$$

Extending range for measurement

$$I_{ext} = 500\mu A$$

From figure

$$I_{ext} = I_{sh} + I_m$$

$$I_m\left[\frac{I_{ext}}{I_m} - 1\right] = I_{sh} = \frac{V_m}{R_{sh}}$$

$\therefore$
$$m = \frac{I_{ext}}{I_m}$$

$$= \frac{500}{100} = 5$$

$\therefore$
$$R_m = \frac{V_m}{I_m}$$

$$\Rightarrow \qquad I_m(m-1) = \frac{V_m}{R_{sh}}$$

$$R_{sh} = \frac{V_m}{I_m(m-1)}$$

$$= \frac{R_m}{m-1} = \frac{100}{5-1} = \frac{100}{4}$$

$$\boxed{R_{sh} = 25\Omega}$$

(*b*)

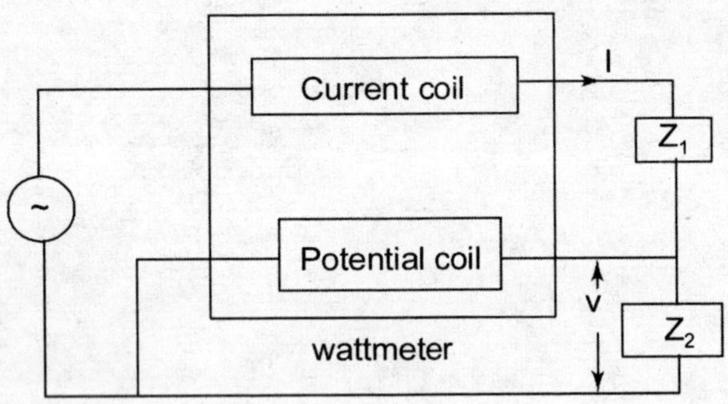

→ we have to calculate the wattmeter readings of power consumed either by Z_1 or Z_2

→ Now assume potential coil draws negligible current from the current coil C.C = I_{cc} = I

Voltage across potential coil = V_{pc} = V

i.e., voltage across Z_2 = V_{pc} = V

So wattmeter reads power consumed by Z_2 only because of potential coil connects across Z_2.

→ current through current coil (C.C) = current through Z_2 wattmeter reading of power consumed, P = V.I

(*c*) Horizontal scale division of cross screen = 10 div

Line base setting = 5msec/div

Total time period of horizontal scale = 10 × 5 = 50msec

Voltage signal V = 5sin (314π + 45°)

ω = 314rad

2πf = 314

f = 314/2π = 50Hz

Time period of signal in once cycle

$$T = 1/f = \frac{1}{50} = 20\text{msec}$$

$$\text{No. of cycles of signal displayed on the screen} = \frac{\text{Total time period of horizontal scale}}{\text{Time period of signal in one cycle}}$$

$$= \frac{50 \times 10^{-3}}{20 \times 10^{-3}}$$

$$= 2.5 \text{ cycles}$$

(*d*) **Prove:** power in AC circuit = VI cosϕ

Consider R.L circuit

$$V(t) = V\text{msin wt}$$

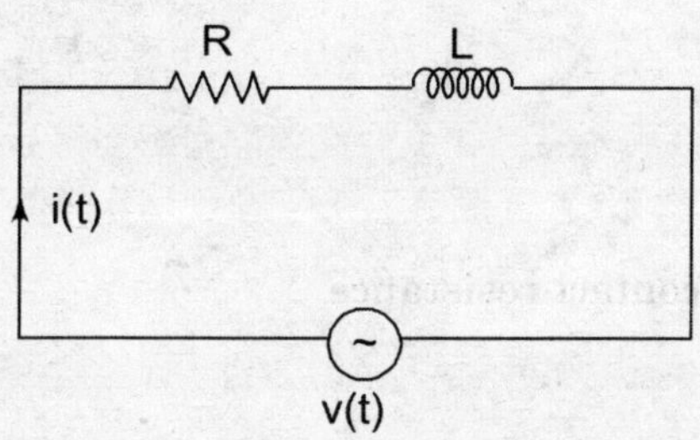

I will lag V by an angle

$$\phi = \tan^{-1}\left(\frac{wL}{R}\right)$$

$$\text{Instantaneous current i} = \text{Im sin } (\omega t - \phi)$$

$$\text{Instantaneous power P} = \text{v.i}$$

$$= [\text{Vm sin}\omega t]\ [\text{Im sin}(\omega t - \phi)]$$

$$= \text{Vm Im sin}\omega t \times \sin(\omega t - \phi)$$

$$= \frac{V_m I_m}{2}[\cos\phi - \cos(2\omega t - \phi)]$$

$$= \text{VrmsIrms } [\cos\phi - \cos(2\omega t - \phi)]$$

$$\text{Average power } P_{avg} = \frac{1}{T}\int_0^T P.d(wt)$$

$$P_{avg} = \frac{1}{2\pi}\int_0^{2\pi} VrmsIrms[\cos\phi - \cos(2wt - \phi)]d\omega t$$

$$= \frac{VrmsIrms}{2\pi}\left[\cos\phi(\omega t) - \frac{\sin(2\omega t - \phi)}{2}\right]_0^{2\pi}$$

$$= \frac{VrmsIrms}{2\pi}[\cos\phi(2\pi - \phi) - 0]$$

$$= \frac{1}{2\pi}VrmsIrms(2\pi\cos\phi)$$

$$\boxed{P = VrmsIrms\cos\phi}$$

= Active power

4. (*a*) Losses in a rotating DC machine

(*i*) Copper loss

(*a*) Armature Cu loss

(*b*) Field Cu loss

(*c*) Loss due to brush contact resistance

(*ii*) Iron losses

(*a*) Hysteresis loss

(*b*) Eddy current loss

(*iii*) Mechanical loss

(*a*) Friction loss

(*b*) Windage loss

Copper losses: These losses occur in amature and field copper windings. Copper losses consist of armature copper loss field copper loss and due to brush contach resistance

Armature copper loss: $I_a^2R_a$

∴ I_a = armature current

R_a = armature resistance

This loss contributes about 30 to 40% of full load losses. The armature copper loss is variable and depends upon the amount of loading of the machine.

Field copper loss = $I_f^2R_f$

∴ I_f = field current

R_f = field resistance

In case of shunt wounded field, field copper loss is particularly constant. It contributes about 20 to 30% to full load losses.

- Brush contact resistance also contribution to copper loss generall his loss is included armature copper loss

Iron losses (Core losses) : As the armature core is made of iron and it rotates in a magnetic field, a small current gets induced in the core itself too. Due to this current eddy current loss and hysteresis loss occur in the armature iron core. Iron losses are also called as core losses or magnetic losses.

Hysteresis loss: Hysteresis loss in due to reversal of magnetization of the armature core. When the core passes under one pair of poles it undergoes one complete cycle of magnetic reversal. The frequency of magnetic reversal is f = P.N/120. P = no. of poles. N = speed in rpm

Hysteresis coss is given by steinmetz formula

$$W_n = \eta \, B_{max}^{1.6} \, fv \text{ (watts)}$$

where η = steinmetz hysteresis constt

V = volume of core.

Eddy current loss : When armature core rotates in magnetic field, an emf is also induced in the core. according to Faraday's law of electromagnetic induction. Though this emf is smalll it causes a large current to flow in the body due to low resistance of core. This current in known as eddy current. The power loss due to this current is known as eddy current loss

$$Pe = Ke\, B^2max\, f^2t^2V \text{ watts}$$

where ke = constt

Bmax = max flux density in wf/m^2

f = frequency of magnetic reversal

t = thickness of lamination

v = volume of core

Mechanical loss: Mechanical loss consist of the losses due to friction in bearing and commutator and windie loss occurs due to air friction of rotating coil. This losses depends on the speed of machine.

(*b*) Given $E_b = 240V$

$N = 1500$ rpm

$I_a = 15$ amp

$$T = \frac{E_b I_a}{w} = \frac{E_b I_a}{2\pi N/60} = \frac{240 \times 25}{2\pi\left(\frac{1500}{60}\right)}$$

$$\boxed{T = 38.197\text{N-m}}$$

(*c*) Given $I_o = 0.6$ amp

$$P_{oc} = 60w$$

$$V_{oc} = 300V$$

$$P_{oc} = V_{oc} I_o \cos \phi_0$$

$$\cos \phi_0 = \frac{P_{oc}}{V_{oc} I_o} = \frac{60}{300 \times 0.6}$$

No load power factor $\cos\phi_0 = 0.333$

(*d*) Given

No. of poles p = 4

Supply frequency $f_s = 50Hz$

$$\text{Speed of induction motor} = \frac{120f}{P} = \frac{120 \times 50}{4}$$

$$= 1500 \text{ rpm}$$

Slip = s

$$= \frac{Ns - Nr}{Ns}$$

$$= \frac{1500 - 1440}{1500} = 0.04$$

Frequency of rotor induced emf

$$f_r = sf_s = 0.04 \times 50 = 2Hz$$

5. (*a*) **Need of capacitor in auxilcary winding of single phase induction motor:**

A single phase induction motor having a main winding and auxiliary winding feed from a 1-ϕ supply can be considered as equivalent to a two phase motor having 1 - ϕ supply.

Since the two windings are not identical the two current I_m and I_a flowing through the two windings can be made 90° and hence 1-ϕ motor

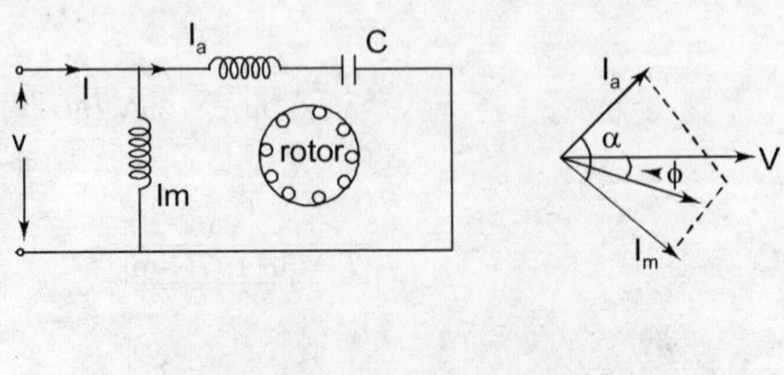

Exactly behaves like as a two phase motor the time phase displacement between the two currents I_m and I_a can be increase by using a capacitor in the auxilarly winding.

The capacitor will also improve the overall power factor of the motor. If a capacitor is using for achiving a high starting torque then the auxilary winding can be switched off when motor picks up speed.

(*b*) Reasons for parallel operation of alternators

- Several alternator can supply a bigger load than a single alternator
- One or more alternator can shunt down during the period of light loads. Thus the remaining alternator operates at near or full load with greater efficiency.
- When one machine is taken out of service for its scheduled maintenance the remaining machine maintains the continuity of supply
- If there is a breakdown of the generator, there is no intruption of power supply
- Number of machines can be added with the initial installation according to the requirement to fullfill the increasing future demand of load.
- Parallel operation of alternators reduces the operating cost and the cost of energy generation.
- It ensures the greater security of supply and enables overall economic generation.

Necessary condition for parallel operation:

- The phase sequence of the busbar voltages and the incoming machine voltage must be same
- The bus bar voltages and the incoming machine terminal voltage must be in phase
- The terminal voltage of the incoming machine and the alternator which is to be connnected in parallel or with the bus-bar voltage should be equal
- The frequency of generated voltage of the incoming machine and the frequency of busbar voltage should be equal.

(*c*) **Advantages of ac over dc**

1. We all know that we got ac supply in our homes and we got this supply by transmitting ac over long distances. Ac can be transmitted using step up transformer but dc can not be transmitted by this process.
2. The ac is easy to generate than dc
3. It is cheaper to generate ac than d.c
4. The a.c generator have higher efficiency than dc
5. The loss of energy during transmission is negligible for a.c
6. The a.c can be easily converted to d.c
7. The variation of a.c can be easily done using transformer either step up or step down.

Disadvantages of ac over dc

1. Voltage regulation is poor in a.c than d.c transmission
2. In a.c line can not rapid changes in magnitude and direction of power flow as dc line
3. Ac causes more interference with nearby communication line.
4. Peak value of a.c is high and it is dangerous to use so better insulation is required.

(*d*) The advantages of using overhead transmission line

- The main advantage is that they are easy to repair if damaged.
- They are not restricted by landscape, can easily suspended them over a motor way or river.
- The installation cost of overhead power transmission lines is less than that of underground cables
- In overhead transmission line faults can ve easily detected and repairable
- In overhead transmission line, the size of conductor for same amount of power is small but in case of underground cable size of conductor is quite large.
- Heat can be dissipated easily in overhead transmission line are open to atmosphere and in case of underground cables heat dissipated is too much difficult hence number of insulating layer is required.

(*e*) Advantage of SF_6 circuit breaker:

1. Excellent insulating are extinguishing, physical and chemical properties of SF_6 gas is greater advantage of this C.B.
2. The gas is non inflammable and chemically stable. The decomposition products are non-explosive i.e. there is no risk of fire or explosion.
3. Electrical clearance are very much reduced because of high-di-electric stregth of SF_6
4. Its performance is not affected due to variation in atmospheric condition
5. It gives noisless operations, it does not make sound like air blast circuit breaker.
6. No frequent contact replacement arcing time is small owing to outstanding arc quenching properties of SF_6 and therefore contact erosion is less. Hence contact do not suffer oxidation.
7. Therefore there is no reduction in di-electric strength of SF_6 since no carbon particle is formed during arcing.
8. Minimum maintenance the breaker may require maintenance once in four to ten years.
9. No over voltage problem. The arc is extinguished at natural current zero without current chopping and associated overvolatges originating across the circuit breaker terminal
10. The sealed construction avoids the contamination by moisture, dust, sand etc. No costly compressed air system is required as in case of air blast circuit breaker.

6. (*a*) (*i*) 4 tube light of 40w working for 5hr per day

$$\text{Power consumption} = 4 \times 40 \times 5 = 800\text{whr.}$$

(*ii*) 2 filaments of 60w working for 8 hr. per day

$$\text{Power consumption} = 2 \times 60 \times 8 = 960\text{hr.}$$

(*iii*) 1 water heater rated 2 kw working for 1hr. per day

$$\text{Power consumption} = 1 \times 2 \times 10^3 \times 1 = 2000\text{whr.}$$

(*iv*) 1 water pump of 0.58kw rating working for 3hr. per day

$$\text{Power consumption} = 1 \times 0.5 \times 10^3 \times 3$$

$$= 1500\text{whr.}$$

Total power consumption per day in (watt hr.)

$$= 800 + 960 + 2000 + 1500$$

$$= 5260 \text{ whr.}$$

$$\text{in kwhr} = \frac{52600}{1000} = 5.26 \text{ kwh}$$

$$1\text{Kwh} = 1 \text{ unit}$$

$$1 \text{ unit cost} = 3.50 \text{ rs.}$$

So the cost of energy per month (i.e. in 30 day)

$$= 3.50 \times 5.26 \times 30$$

$$= 552.30 \text{ rs.}$$

(*b*) **Advantages of electric drives:**

1. Electric drive has facility for remote control
2. Electric drive is more reliable
3. Having long life.
4. It is more flexible
5. It is more simple
6. It cost is low than conventional drives
7. Electric drive has easy starting facility
8. Electric drive is smooth and easy control
9. It is more compact.

Disadvantage of Electric drives

1. It can not be employed at distant places
2. It causes noise pollution
3. Having poor dynamic response
4. To increase torque, a larger or heavier motor must be used which is costly.
5. It's non availability on failure of supply.

(*c*)

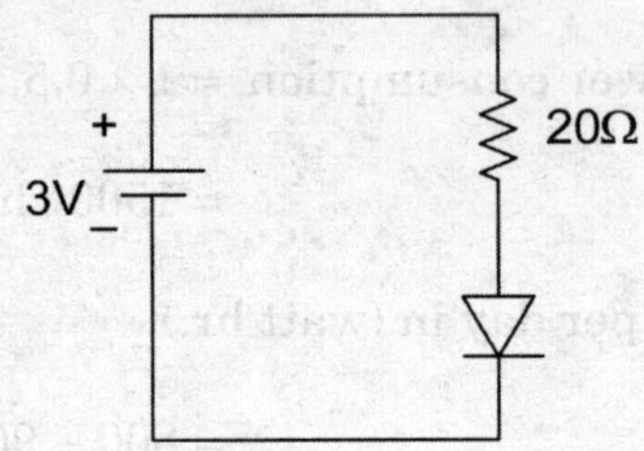

To find the diode current

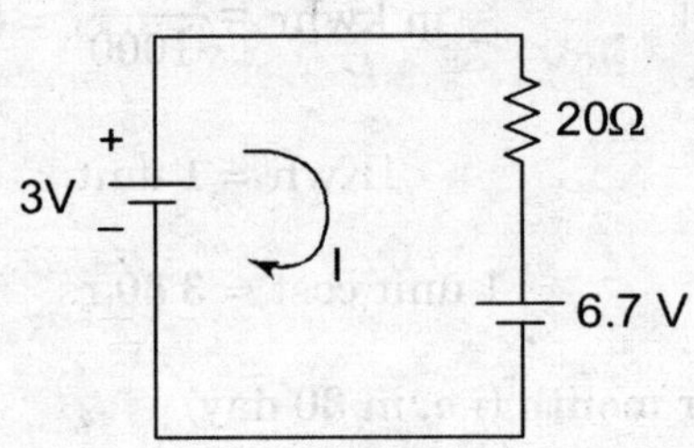

On applying KVL

$$-3 + 20I + 0.7 = 0$$

$$20I = 2.3$$

$$I_D = I$$

$$= \frac{2.3}{20} = 0.115\text{Amp}$$

$$\boxed{I_D = 115\text{mA}}$$

Solved Paper 2013

Electrical Engineering

(Paper II)

1. (*a*) (*i*) **An oven operates on a 15.0 A current from a 120 V source. How much energy will it consume in 3.0 h of operation?** **(10)**

(*ii*) **How many 100 W light bulbs connected to a 120 V supply can be turned on at the same time without blowing a 15.0 A fuse?** **(10)**

(*iii*) **3.0 A, 125 V circuit contains a 10.0 W resistor. What resistance must be added in series for the circuit to have a current of 5.0 A?** **(10)**

(*b*) **In the following circuit, find the total resistance, R_3, V_2 and I_4.** **(30)**

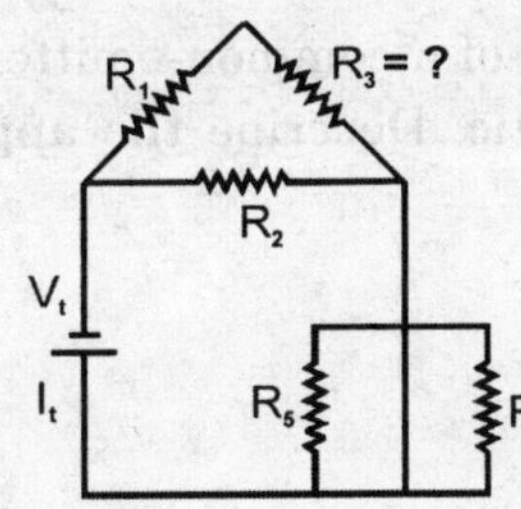

$R_1 = 9\ \Omega$

$R_2 = 4\ \Omega$

$R_4 = 12\ \Omega$

$R_5 = 36\ \Omega$

$R_t = 12\ V$

$I_t = 1.0\ A$

2. (*a*) **What do you understand by magnetic hysteresis? Differentiate between hard and soft magnetic materials.** **(30)**

(*b*) **Deduce an expression for the average power in a single phase RL circuit and hence explain the term power factor.** **(30)**

3. (*a*) **Describe the working principle and construction of an induction type wattmeter. What are the errors in induction type wattmeter, and how are they compensated?**

(30)

(*b*) The four arms of a Maxwell A.C. bridge are as follows:

AB and BC are non-inductive resistors of 100 Ω each, DA is a standard variable inductor L of resistance 32.7 Ω and CD comprises a standard variable resistor R in series with a coil of unknown impedance. Balance is obtained when L = 47.8 mH and R = 1.36 Ω. Find the resistance and inductance of the coil. (30)

4. (*a*) (*i*) What are factors that control the speed of a DC motor? (10)

(*ii*) A 500 V shunt motor runs at its normal speed of 250 rpm when the armature current is 200 A. The resistance of armature is 0.12 Ω. Calculate the speed when a resistance is inserted in the field reducing the shunt field to 80% of normal value and the armature current is 100 A. (20)

(*b*) A three phase induction motor having a 6-pole, star connected stator winding runs on 240 V, 50 Hz supply. The rotor resistance and standstill reactance are 0.12 Ω and 0.85 ohm per phase. The ratio of stator to rotor turns is 1.8. Full load slip is 4%. Calculate the developed torque at full load. (30)

5. (*a*) What is loss load factor? Explain in detail how the loss load factor can be determined. (30)

(*b*) Discuss various bus bar systems for distribution networks. (30)

6. (*a*) Discuss the laws of illumination and their limitations in actual practice. (30)

(*b*) Draw the output characteristics of a common-emitter transistor. Show various regions of operation of the BJT on this characteristic. Describe the applications of operating the BJT into different regions. (30)

EXPLANATIONS

1. (*a*) (*i*) Given data $V_s = 120V$

$$i = 15amp$$

Energy consumtion in 3hrs is

$$E = 120 \times 15 \times 3$$

$$= 5400 \text{ whr} = 5.4 \text{ k Whr.}$$

(*ii*) $V_s = 120V$

$$P_b = 100 \text{ w}$$

$$\text{Resistance of each bulb} = \frac{(120)^2}{100} = 144\Omega$$

If n no. of bulbs are connected in parallel

$$\frac{144}{n} = \frac{120}{15}$$

$$8n = 144$$

$$\boxed{n = 18}$$

and hence 18 bulbs connected to a 120V supply can be turned on at same time without blowing 15A fuse.

(*iii*)

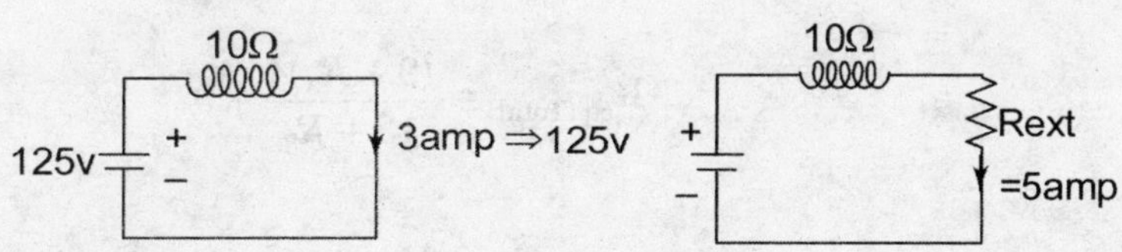

In this question given data is incorrect, because by adding a resistor in series the circuit current will decrease from 3A.

(*b*) Given

$R_1 = 9\Omega$ $R_3 = ?$

$R_2 = 4\Omega$ $V_2 = ?$

$R_4 = 12\Omega$ $I_4 = ?$

$R_5 = 36\Omega$

$V_t = 12V$

$I_t = 1.0$ Amp

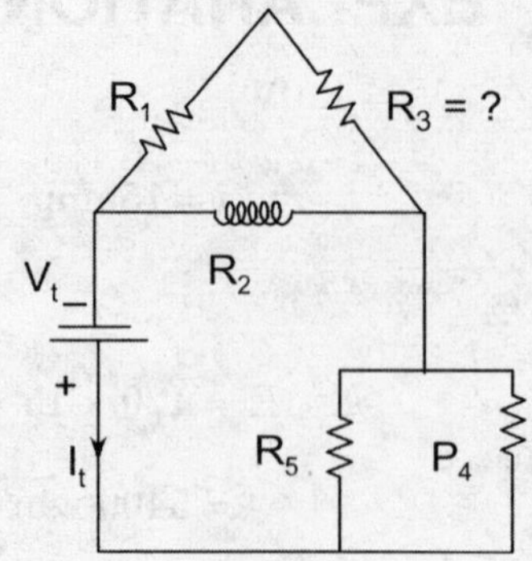

According to the diagram

R_1 and R_3 in series

$$R_{eq1} = R_1 + R_3$$

$$= (9 + R_3)\Omega$$

R_4 and R_5 in Parallel

$$R_{eq2} = \frac{R_4 \times R_5}{R_4 + R_5}$$

$$= \frac{12 \times 36}{12 + 36}$$

$$= 9\Omega$$

$$\text{Total equivalent resistance of circuit} = [(9 + R_3) \parallel 4] + R_{(eq)2}$$

$$R_{eq\ (Total)} = \frac{(9 + R_3)4}{13 + R_3} + 9$$

$$= \frac{V_t}{I_t}$$

$$= \frac{12}{1} = 12\Omega$$

$$\frac{(9 + R_3)4}{13 + R_3} + 9 = 12$$

$$\frac{9 + R_3}{13 + R_3} = 12 - 9$$

$$= \boxed{R_3 = 3\Omega}$$

Now resistance ($R_1 + R_3$) and R_2 in parallel so using current division rule

$$I_2 = I_{R2}$$

$$= \frac{1_t \times (R_1 + R_3)}{(R_1 + R_3) + R_2} = \frac{1 \times (9+3)}{(9+3)+4}$$

$$I_2 = 0.75 \text{ amp}$$

so voltage across resistance R_2

$$V_2 = I_2(R_2) = 0.75 \times 9 = 3V$$

Again applying current division rule for I_4

$$R_4 \parallel R_5$$

$$I_4 = I_{R4}$$

$$= \frac{I_t \times R_5}{R_4 + R_5}$$

$$= \frac{1 \times 36}{12 + 36} = 0.75\text{amp}$$

$$\boxed{R_3 = 3\Omega}$$

$$\boxed{V_2 = 3V}$$

$$\boxed{I_4 = 0.75\text{amp}}$$

2. (*a*) **Magnetic Hysteresis :** When a ferromagnetic material is magnetized in one direction it will not relax back to zero magnetization when the imposed magnetizing field is removed. It must be driven back to zero by a field in the opposible direction. If an alternating field is applied to the material its magnetization will trace out a loop called hysteresis loop the lack of retraceability of the magnetization curve is the property called hysteresis.

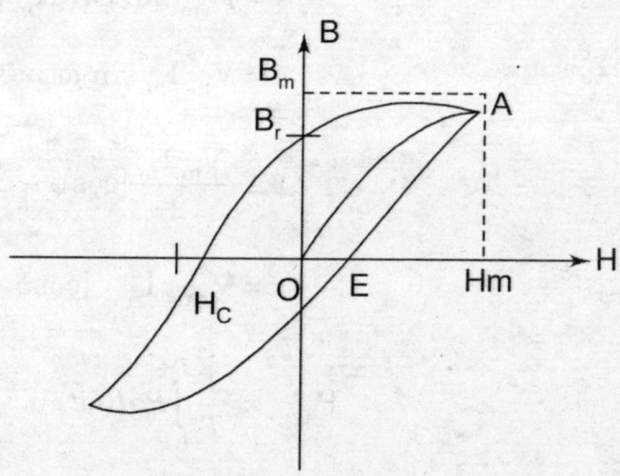

Soft magnetic material	**Hard magnetic material**
→ High permeability	→ High permeability
→ low retentivity	→ high retentivity
→ low coercivity	→ high coercivity
→ small hysteresis loop	→ large hystersis loop
→ suitable for making	→ high curve temp
→ transformer core, electromagnets (used in magnetic shielding)	→ suitable for permanent magnet Ex: Alnico

(*b*) Consider an R.L circuit shown below

V(t) = instantaneous supply voltage

V(t) = Vmsinωt

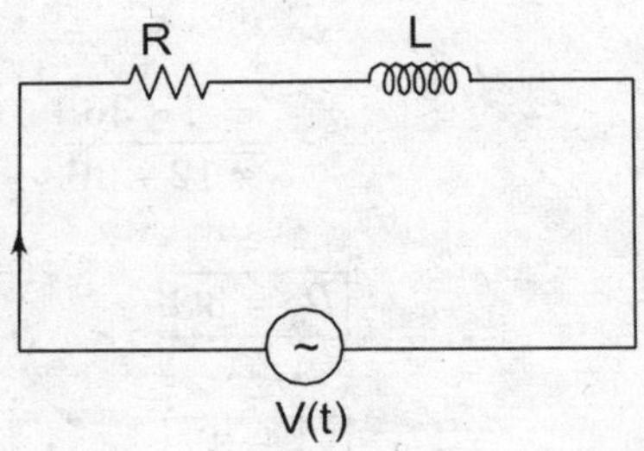

The angle between i and v which is in the Lagging nature is i.e. ϕ

$$\phi = \tan^{-1}\left(\frac{wL}{R}\right)$$

Instantaneous current i = Im sin (ωt – ϕ)

Instantaneous power p = v.i

$$= [V_m \sin \omega t]\ [I_m \sin (\omega t - \phi)]$$

$$= V_m I_m \sin \omega t \times \sin(\omega t - \phi)$$

$$= \frac{V_m I_m}{2}[\cos\phi - \cos(2\omega t - \phi)]$$

$$= V_{rms} I_{rms}\ [\cos\phi - \cos(2\omega t - \phi)]$$

Now average power $$P_{avg} = \frac{1}{T}\int_0^T P.d(\omega t)$$

$$P_{avg} = \frac{1}{2\pi}\int_0^{2\pi} V_{rms} I_{rms}[\cos\phi - \cos(2\omega t - \phi)]d(\omega t)$$

$$P_{avg} = \frac{V_{rms}I_{rms}}{2\pi}\left[\cos\phi(\omega t) - \frac{\sin(2\omega t - \phi)}{2}\right]_0^{2\pi}$$

$$= \frac{V_{rms}I_{rms}}{2\pi}\,[\cos\phi(2\pi - 0) - 0]$$

$$= \frac{1}{2\pi}V_{rms}I_{rms}(2\pi\cos\phi)$$

$$\boxed{P = V_{rms}\ I_{rms}\cos\phi}$$

Power factor: The ratio of the actual electrical power dissipated by an AC circuit to the product of the r.m.s values of current and voltage. The difference between the two is caused by reactance in the circuit and represents power that does no useful work. It is denoted by cos ϕ

$$\cos\phi = \frac{P}{S}$$

$$S = \sqrt{P^2 + Q^2}$$

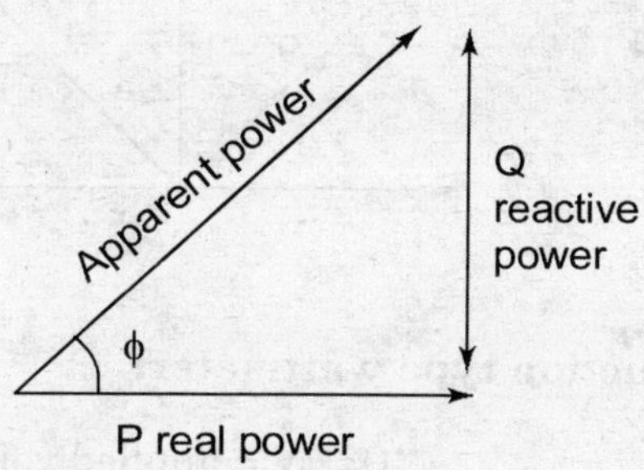

3. *(a)* **Induction type wattmeter:**

The induction type wattmeter is used to measure a.c power only

Principle of induction type wattmeters: The principle of operation of an induction type wattmeter is same as that of induction ameter and voltmeters i.e induction principle. However, it differs from induction ammeter or voltmeter in so far that separate two coils are used to produced the rotating flux in place of one coil with phase split arrangement

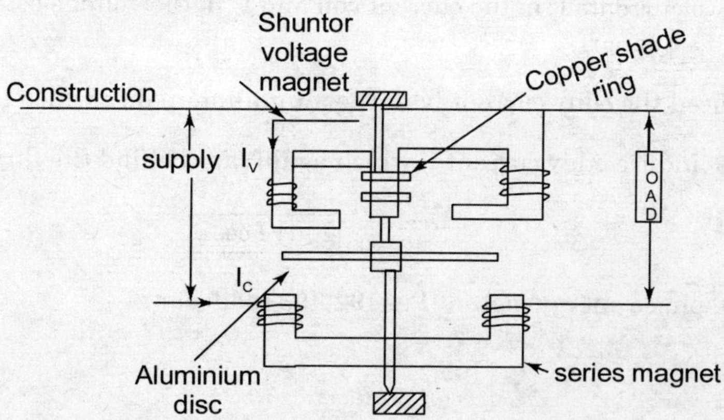

The principle parts of an induction wattmeter is shown above. It consist of two laminated electromagnets. One electromagnets called shunt magnet is connected across supply and carries current proportional to the applied voltage. The coil of this magnet is made highly inductive so that the current in it lags behind the supply and carries the load current. The coil of this magnet is made highly non inductive so that the angle of lag or lead is determined fully by load. A thin aluminium disc mounted on the spindle is placed between the twp magnets so that it cuts the fluxes of both the magnets. Thd controlling torque is provided by spiral springs. The damping is electromagnet and is usually provided by permanent magnet embracing the aluminimum disc. Two or more closed copper rings are provided on the central limb of shunt magnet. By adjunting the position of these rings, the shunt magnet flux can be made to lag behind supply voltage by 90 degree

Working of induction type wattmeter:

When the wattmeter is connected in the circuit to measure O.C power the shunt magnet carries current proportional to supply voltage and the series magnet carries the load current. The two fluxes produced by the magnet induced eddy current in aluminimum disc. The interaction between the fluxes and eddy current produce the deflecting torque system to move over the scale

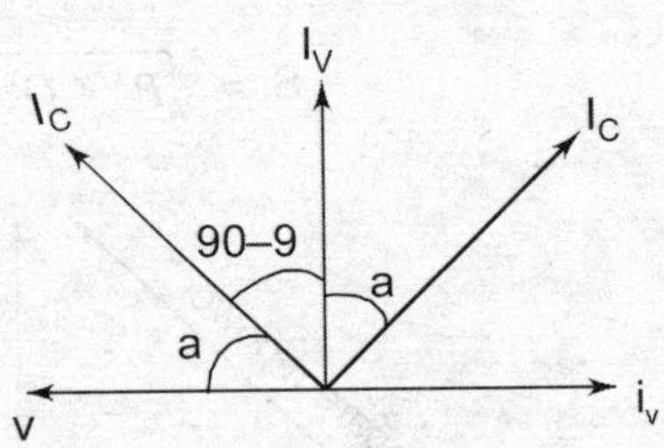

Deflecting torque of induction type wattmeter:

Let V = applied voltage

I_c = Load current carries by the series magnet

I_v = current carries by the shunt magnet

$\cos\phi$ = Lagging power factor of load.

According to the vector diagram the current I_v in the shunt magnet lags the applied voltage V by 90° degree and the flux ϕ_v produced by it. The current I_c in the series magnet is the load current and hence lags behind the applied voltage by ϕ' athe flux ϕ_c produced by this current I_c is in phase with it

Therefore the two currents I_c in the current coil and I_v in the voltage coil and also corresponding fluxes ϕ_v and ϕ_c are $(90 - \phi)$ apart.

The flux ϕ_c induced the eddy current iv in the aluminimum disc which lags behind the flux by 90°.

Similarly flux ϕ_c induce eddy current i_c which again lags behind the flux ϕ_c by 90 degrees

$$\boxed{T_d \alpha VI \cos\phi}$$

Errors in single phase energy meter. (Pg. 192-193 madeeary)

Last heading

Temp. Compensation:

(*b*)

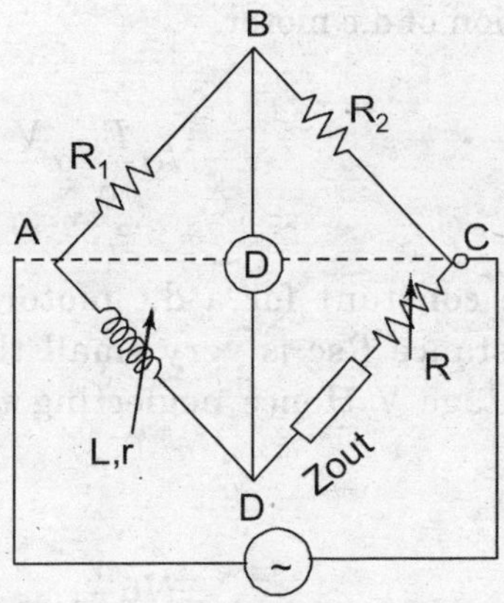

Given that

$$R_{AB} = R_{BC} = 100\Omega$$

$$r = 32.7\Omega$$

$$L = 47.8\text{mH}$$

$$R = 1.36\Omega$$

$$\text{Zcoil} = (R + jX_L)\text{coil}$$

$$\text{Assume supply frequency } f = 50\text{Hz}$$

$$X_L = 2\pi fL$$

$$= 2\pi \times 50 \times 47.8 \times 10^{-3}$$

$$= 4.78\ \pi\Omega$$

In balance condition

$$R_1[\text{Zcoil} + R] = R_2[r + jX_L]$$

$$100[\text{Zcoil} + 1.36] = 100[32.7 + j4.78\Omega]$$

$$\text{Zcoil} = 32.7 + j4.78\pi - 1.36$$

$$(R + jX_L)\text{coil} = 31.34 + j15.017$$

$$\text{Resistance of coil} = 31.34\Omega$$

$$\text{Inductance of coil} = \frac{15.017}{2\pi f}$$

$$= \frac{15.017}{2\pi \times 50}$$

$$= 47.8\text{mH}$$

4. (*a*) (*i*) **Factors affecting the speed of d.c motor:**

According to speed equation of d.c motor

$$N \alpha \frac{E_b}{\phi} \alpha \frac{V - IaRa}{\phi}$$

The factors Z, P, A are constant for a d.c motor But as the value of armature resistance Ra and series field resistance Rsc is very small the drop IaRa and (Ra + Rse) is very small compared to appiled voltage V Hence neglecting these voltage drops the speed equation can be modified as.

$$N \alpha \frac{V}{\phi} \text{ as } E_b = V$$

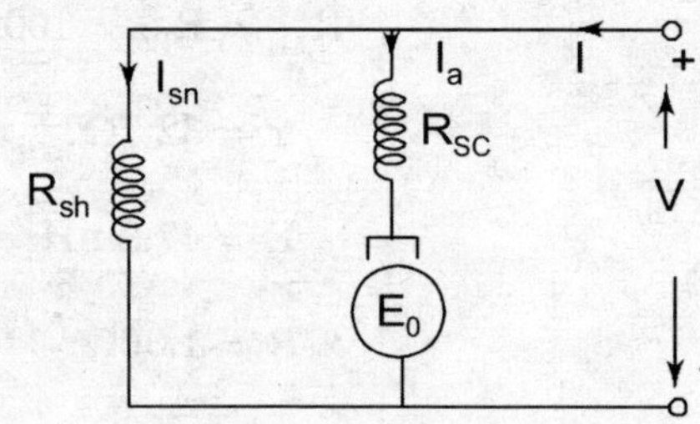

Thus the factors affecting the speed of d.c motor are

→ The flux f

→ The voltage across armature

→ The applied voltage V

Depending on these factors the various methods of speed control are:

1. Changing the flux ϕ by controlling the current through the field winding called flux control methods

2. Changing the armature path resistance which in turn changes the applied voltage across the armature called rheostatic control

3. Changing applied voltage called voltage control method.

(*ii*)

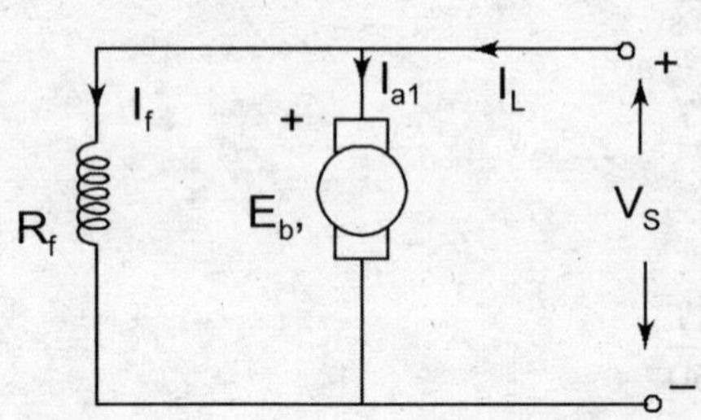

Given that

$$V_s = 500V$$

$$N_1 = 250 \text{ rpm}$$

$$Ia_1 = 200A$$

$$R_1 = 0.12\Omega$$

$$E_{b1} = V_S - Ia_1R_1$$

$$E_{b1} = 500 - 200 \times 0.12 = 478 \text{ V}$$

Now, after inserting field resistance

$$\text{Flux } \phi_2 = 0.8\phi_1$$

$$Ia_2 = 100A$$

$$E_{b2} = V_s - Ia_2 R_2$$

$$500 - 100 \times 0.12 = 488V$$

$$E \alpha N\phi$$

$$\frac{E_{b2}}{E_{b1}} = \frac{N_2}{N_1} \times \frac{\phi_2}{\phi_1}$$

$$N_2 = N_1 \times \frac{E_{b2}}{E_{b1}} \times \frac{\phi_1}{\phi_2}$$

$$= 250 \times \frac{488}{476} \times \left(\frac{\phi_1}{0.8\phi_1}\right)$$

$$\boxed{N_2 = 320.378\text{rpm}}$$

(*b*) Given parameter

$$P = 6, f = 50H$$

Hence

$$N_s = \frac{120f}{P}$$

$$= \frac{120 \times 50}{6} = 1000\text{rpm}$$

$$\text{Stator winding voltage } W_s = 2\pi \times \frac{1000}{60} = 104.72 \text{ rad/sec}$$

Standstill rotor resistance $r_2 = 0.12\Omega/\text{phase}$

Standstill rotor resistance $x_2 = 0.85\Omega/\text{phase}$

Turns ratio $a = 1.8$

Now rotor resistance refered to stator side

$$r_2' = a^2 r_2$$

$$= (1.8)^2 \times (0.12)$$

$$= 0.3888\Omega$$

Rotor reactance referred to stator side

$$r_2' = a^2 r_2$$

$$= (1.8)^2 \times (0.85)$$

$$= 2.754\ \Omega$$

Rotor reactance referred to stator side

$$x_2' = a^2 x_2$$

$$= (1.8)^2 \times (0.85)$$

$$= 2.754\Omega$$

Neglecting stator resistance and inductance

$$I_2' = \frac{V_1}{\sqrt{\left(\frac{r^1{}_2}{s}\right)^2 + (x_2^1)^2}}$$

$$= \frac{240/\sqrt{3}}{\left[\left(\frac{0.388}{0.04}\right)2 + (2.754)^2\right]^{1/2}}$$

Now full load torque

$$T_{fl} = \frac{3}{ws} \times (I_2')^2 \times \frac{r_2'}{s}$$

$$= \frac{3}{104.72} \times \frac{(240/\sqrt{3})^2}{\left(\frac{0.388}{0.09}\right)^2 + (2.754)^2} \times \left(\frac{0.388}{0.09}\right)$$

$$\boxed{T_{fl} = 52.383 N.m}$$

5. (*a*) **Loss-load factor:** It is a factor which when multiplied by energy lost at time of peak and the no. of load periods will give overall average energy lost. It is calculated as the ratio of average load loss to the peak load loss.

or

It is defined as the ratio of actual loss during a period to the loss assuming maximum current to flow over the same period. It is denoted by G

$$\text{Loss load factor} = \frac{\text{Actual loss(kwh) during a period}}{\text{loss (kwh) assuming maximum current to flow over the same period}}$$

If the load factor of the plant is 100% the copper loss will be at its full value throught the period approximately as the square of load.

The loss will occur with the same load factor it mean current flows continuosly except when a peak current I is reached movementairily and copper loss could be considered negligible under this condition

$$\text{Loss } \alpha \ I^2 F^2 = \text{where } F = \text{Load factor}$$

The greatest possible loss will occur it maximum current flow for fraction of the year and no current in the remaining part of year.

Under this condition Loss α I^2F

Now it is convieninent to neglect the effect of I^2 from both cases and express the losses as a fraction of those which would occur if the maximum current flows continuosly. This factor which is actually load factor of losses called load factor.

Loss factor formula

$$\boxed{G = 0.5F + 0.5F^2}$$

The above formula gives a relativity of high value loss.

(*b*) **Bus bar:** Bus bars are the common electrical component that connects electrically number of lines which are operating at same voltage directly.

Various bus bar distribution network are:

(*i*) single bus bar arrangement

(*ii*) single sub bar arrangement with bus sectionalized

(*iii*) Main and transfer bus arrangement

(*iv*) Double bus double breaer arrangement

(*v*) Ring main arrangement

(*vi*) Mesh arrangement

Single bus bar arrangement:

The arrangement of such type of system is very simple and easy. The system has only one bus bar along with the switch. All substation equipment like transformer, generator, the feeder is connected to this bus bar only. The advantages are

→ It has low initial cost

→ If requires less maintenance

→ It is simple in operation

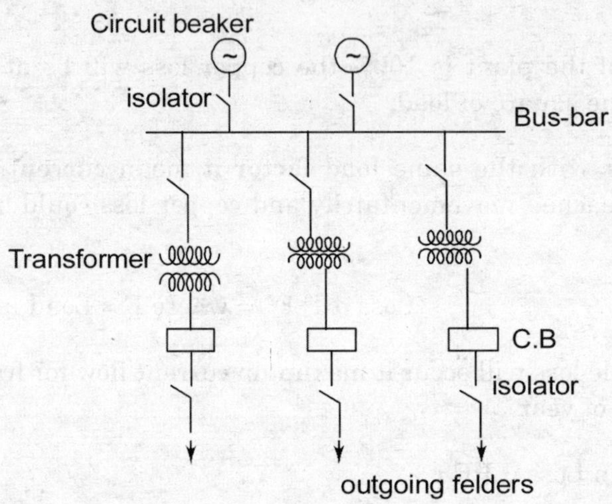

Single bus-bar arrangement with bus sectionalized:

In this type of arrangement, the C.B and isolating switches are used. The isolator disconnects the faulty section hence protect the system from complete shunt down. This type of arrangement uses one additional C.B which does not much increase the cost of system

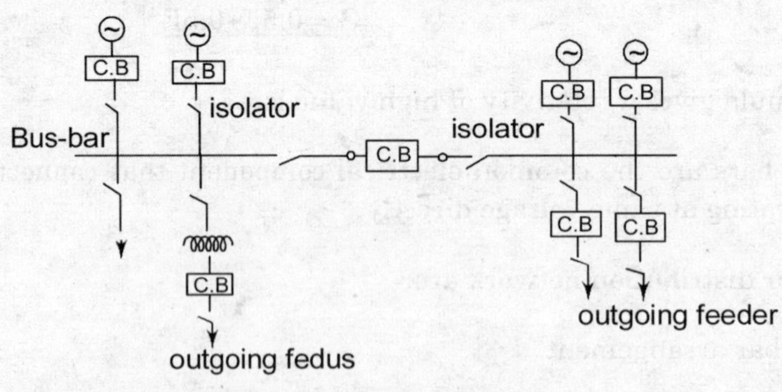

Main and transfer bus arrangement:

Such type of arrangement uses two types of bus bar mainly i.e. main bus bar and auxilary bus bar. The bus bar arrangement uses bus coupler which connects the isolating switches and circuit breaker to the bus bar. The bus coupler is also used for transfering the load from one bus to another in case of overloading. The following are the steps of transfering the load

→ The potential of both bus kept same

→ The bus bar on whcih the load is transfered kept close

→ open the main bus bar

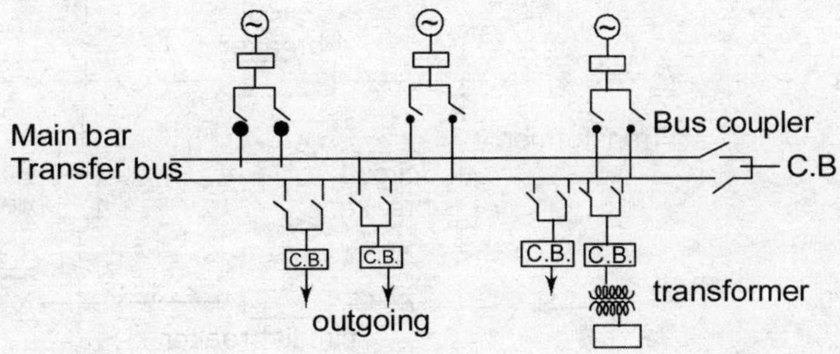

Double bus Double breaker arrangement

This type of arrangement requires two bus and two circuit breaker. It does not require any additional equiment like bus coupler and switch

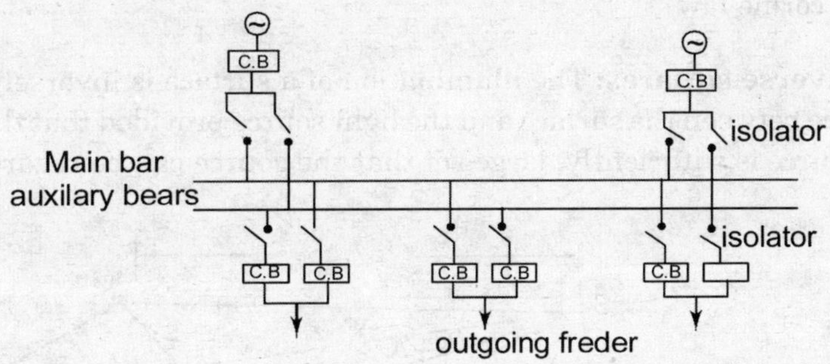

Ring main arrangement

In such type of arrangement the end of bus bar is connected back to the starting point of bus to form a ring

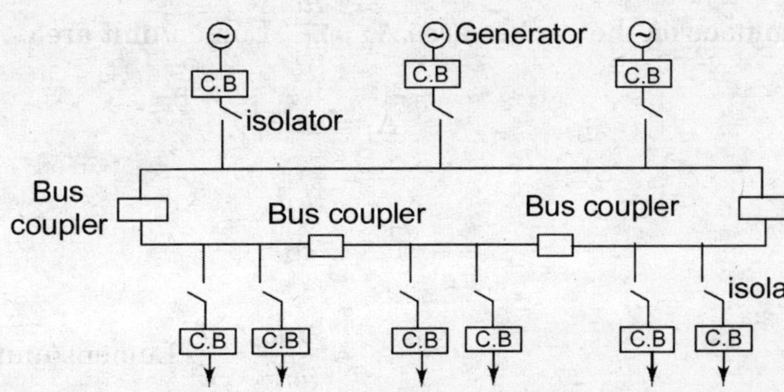

Mesh arrangement: In installed such type of arrangement the C.B are inslated in the mesh formed by the buses the circuit is tapped from the node point of mesh. such type of arrangement controlled by four C.B.

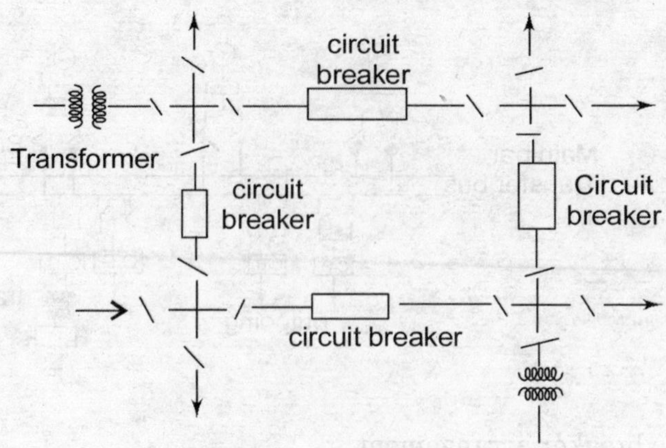

6. (*a*) Laws of illumination:

(*i*) Inverse law of square

(*ii*) Lambert's corine law

1. Law of inverse squares: The illumination of a surface is inversely proportional to the square of the distance between the surface and the light source provided that the distance between the surface and the source is sufficiently, large sot that the source can be regarded as point surface

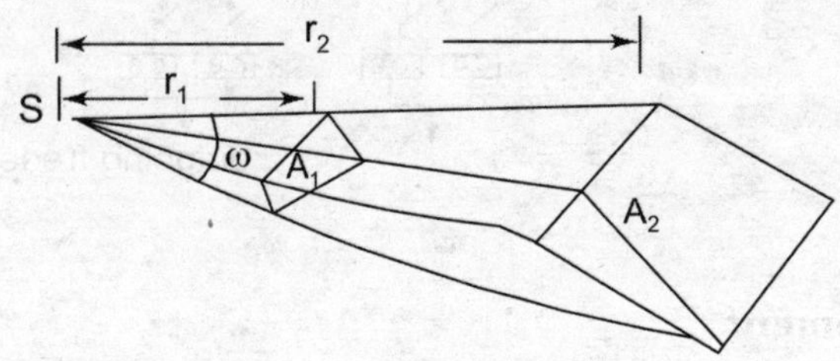

Consider surface area A_1 and the surface area A_2 at distance r_1 and r_2 respectively from the source point 's' of illumination intensity I and normal to the rays. The solid angle subtended be ω sterradian.

Iluminous on the surface area $A_1 = \dfrac{Iw}{A_1}$ Lumen/unit area

and $A_1 = \omega r_1^{\,2}$

$$E_1 = \frac{Iw}{A_1}$$

$$= \frac{Iw}{wr_1^2} = \frac{I}{r_1^2} \text{ Lumens/unit area}$$

On area A_2 $E_2 = \dfrac{Iw}{A_2}$

$$= \frac{Iw}{wr_2^2} = \frac{I}{r_2^2} \text{ Lumen/unit area}$$

2. **Lambert's cosine law:**

According to this law the illumination at any point on a surface is proportional to the cosine angle of the angle between the normal at that point and direction of luminous flux

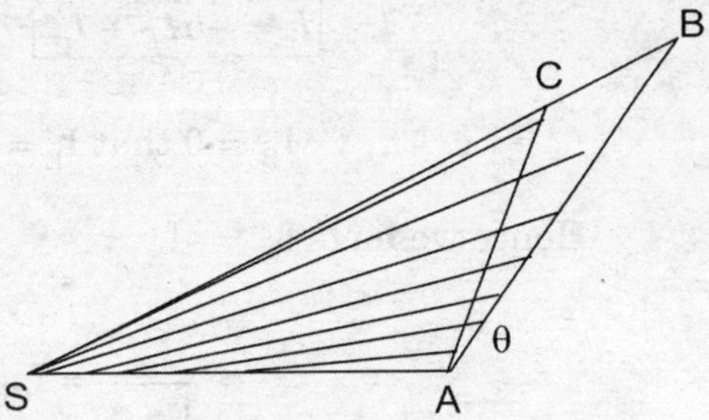

$$\frac{AB}{AC} = \frac{1}{\cos\theta} \text{ increase ratio}$$

and the illumination decreases in the ratio. Cosθ/p

$$\boxed{E = \frac{I\cos\theta}{r_2^2}}$$

(*b*) **Output characteristic of common emitter transistor**

The input is applied between base and emitter and output is taken between collector and emitter. Here emitter of the transistor is common to both input and output and hence the name common emitter contiguration.

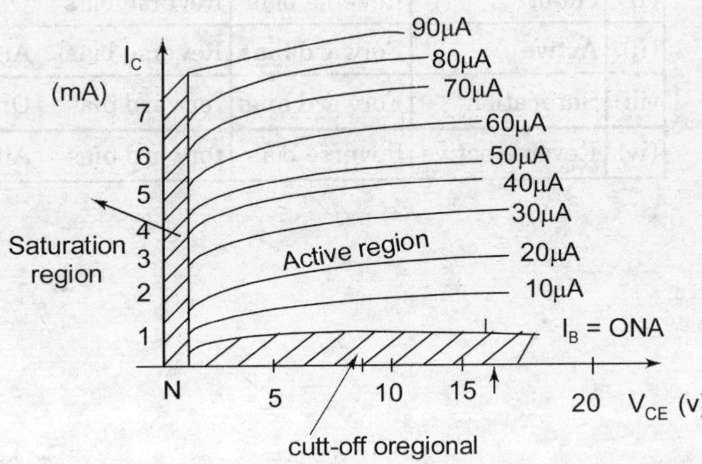

Active Region:

In this region the transistor output current respond most sensitively to an input signal. It must be operated to restric in this region if transistor is used to be an amplifying device.

According to figure, the active region is the area to the right of the ordinate V_{CE} = a few tenths of a volt and above $I_B = 0$

Cut-off region:

Cut-off region occurs at the interaction of load line with current $I_B = 0$ and hence we have to find out the collector current possible in this region

$$\boxed{I_c = -\alpha I_E + I_{co}}$$

From fig ∴ $I_B = 0$ that $I_E = -I_C$

Hence we have $I_C = -I_E$

$$= \frac{I_{co}}{1-\alpha} = I_{CEO}$$

The actual collector current with collector junction reverse biased and base open circuited is represented by symbol I_{CEO}

In order to cut-off transistor, it is not enough to reduce. I_B up to zero it is necessary to reverse bias the emitter junction slightly. Cut-off means $I_E = 0$, $I_C = I_{co}$, $I_B = -I_c = -I_{co}$ and V_{BE} is a reverse voltage whose magnitude is to the order of 0.1V for and 0 V for a silicon transistor

Saturation Region:

The saturation region may be defined as where collector junction an emitter junction is forward biased. In this region $|V_{CE}|$ drops to few tenths of a volt and collector current is approximately independent of base current

	Mode	Emitter bias	Collector base	Applications
(i)	cut-off	Reverse bias	Reverse bias	OFF switch
(ii)	Active	Forward bias	Reverse bias	Amplifier
(iii)	Saturation	Forward bias	forward bias	On switch
(iv)	Reverse active	Reverse bias	forward bias	Alternator

■■

Solved Paper 2012

Electrical Engineering

(Paper II)

1. (*a*) For the network shown in figure find the current in each resistor using super position principle. (30)

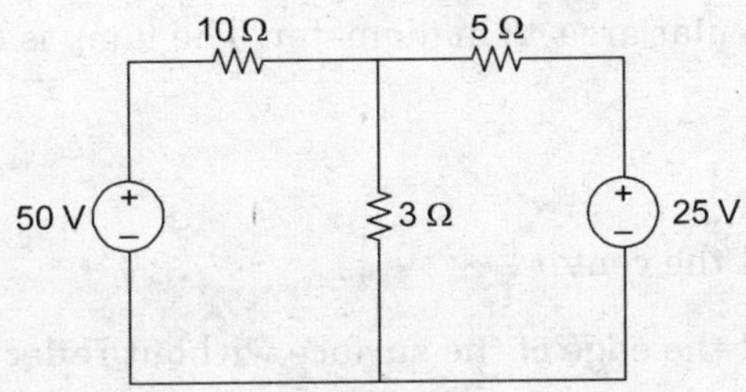

Figure

(*b*) Three impedances (6 + 15)Ω, (8 – 16)Ω and (8 + J10)Ω are connected in parallel. Calculate the current in each branch when the total current is 20 A. (30)

2. (*a*) What are the various methods for the measurement of three phase power? Explain two-wattmeter method for star-connected three phase balanced circuits. Also derive the expression for power factor. (30)

(*b*) Derive the e.m.f and torque equation of d.c. machines. Also discuss the significance of back emf in d.c. machines. (30)

3. (*a*) A 400 KV A, 5000/320 V, 1 phase transformer has a primary winding resistance of 0.5Ω and secondary winding resistance of 0.001Ω. The iron loss is 2.5 KW. Determine the efficiency of transformer at full load and half load at 0.85 p.f. lagging. (30)

(*b*) Explain the open circuit and short circuit tests on single phase transformer. (30)

4. (*a*) Explain the principle of operation of three phase synchronous motor. Discuss the various applications of three phase synchronous motor. (20)

(*b*) A 415 V, three phase, 50Hz, 4 pole star connected induction motor runs ar 24 rps on full load. The rotor resistance and reactance per phase are 0.35Ω and 3.5Ω respectively and the effective rotor - stator turns ratio is 0.85:1. Calculate

(i) synchronous speed

(ii) the slip

(iii) the full load torque

(iv) the power output if mechanical losses amount to 770 W

(v) the maximum torque. (40)

5. (*a*) Discuss the various types of transmission lines. Derive the expression for voltage regulation of single phase short transmission line. (30)

(*b*) Write short notes on any two of the following: (30)

(i) Power factor improvement

(ii) Bucholz Relay

(iii) Advantages of Inter connection of power stations

6. (*a*) Explain the various starting methods for three phase induction motors in detail. (20)

(*b*) A lamp having a Candle power of 300 in all directions is provided with a reflector that directs 70% of total light uniformly on a circular area 40 m diameter. The lamp is hung at 15 m above the area. Calculate: (40)

(*i*) The illumination

(*ii*) The illumination at the center

(*iii*) The illumination at the edge of the surface without reflector.

EXPLANATIONS

1. To find out the current in each resistor using super position principle.

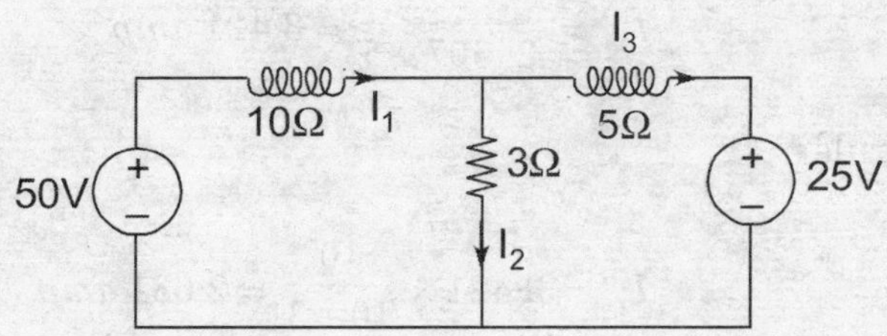

Now take 50 V source and other active sources deactivated according to this circuit

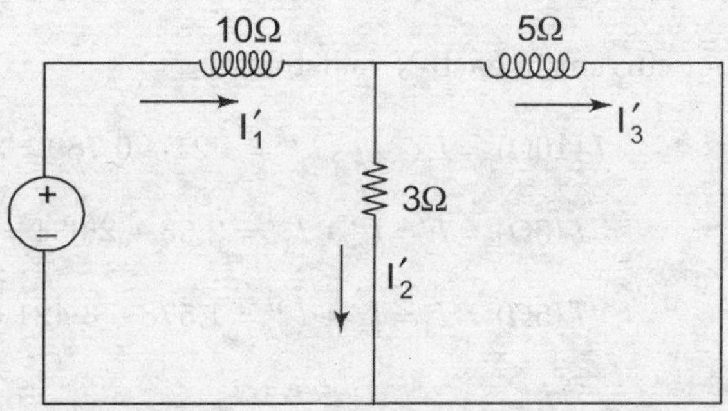

$$\text{Req} = 3 \parallel 5 = \frac{3 \times 5}{3+5} = 1{\cdot}875 \text{ W}$$

$$I_1' = \frac{50}{10 + 1{\cdot}875} = 4{\cdot}21\ Amp$$

by using corrent division rule

$$I_2' = \frac{4{\cdot}21 \times 5}{(3+5)} = 2{\cdot}63 \text{ amp}$$

$$I_3' = \frac{4{\cdot}21 \times 3}{(3+5)} = 1{\cdot}578 \text{ amp}$$

Now take 25V source and other active sources deactiveated according to this circuit.

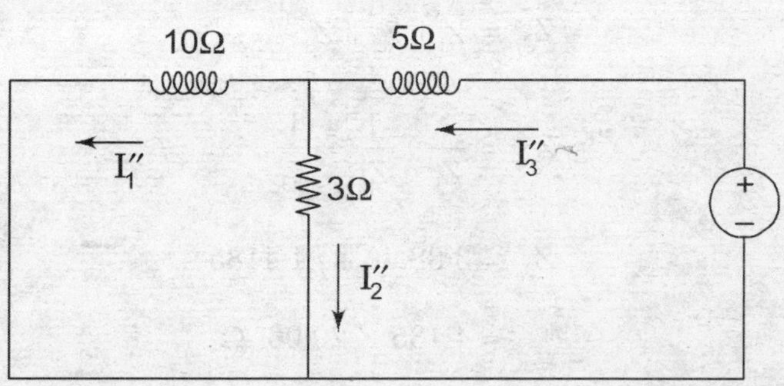

$$\text{Req} = 10 \parallel 3 = \frac{10 \times 3}{10+3} = 2{\cdot}3077\ \Omega$$

$$I_3'' = \frac{25}{2\cdot 307 + 5} = 3{\cdot}421\ amp$$

by using corrent division rule

$$I_2'' = 3{\cdot}421 \times \frac{10}{10+3} = 2{\cdot}631\ amp$$

$$I_1'' = 3{\cdot}421 \times \frac{3}{10+3} = 0{\cdot}789\ \text{amp}$$

Now we have to calculate net current in each N rasistor

$$I\,(10\Omega) = I_1 = I' - I_1'' = 4{\cdot}21 - 0{\cdot}789 = 3{\cdot}421\ amp$$

$$I\,(3\Omega) = I_2 = I_2' + I_2'' = 2{\cdot}63 + 2{\cdot}631 = 5{\cdot}261\ amp$$

$$I\,(5\Omega) = I_3 = I_3' + I_3'' = 1.578 - 3{\cdot}421 = -1{\cdot}643\ amp$$

(*b*) According to question

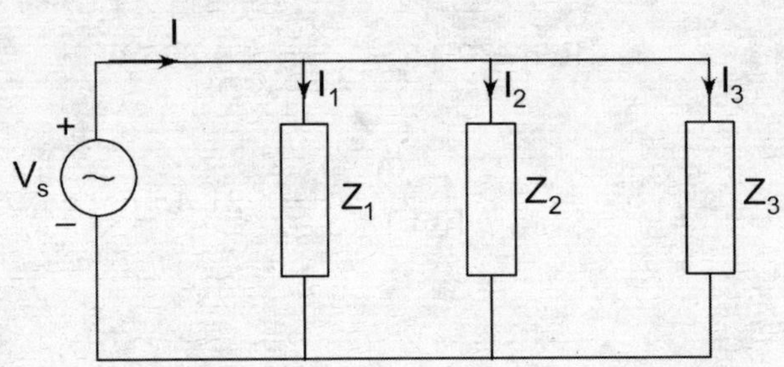

Given data:

$$Z_1 = (6 + j5)\Omega = 7{\cdot}81\ \angle 39{\cdot}8^\circ$$

$$Z_2 = (8 - j6)\Omega = 10\angle -36{\cdot}87^\circ$$

$$Z_3 = (8 + j10)\Omega = 12{\cdot}8\ \angle\ 51{\cdot}34^\circ$$

$$Z_{eq} = \overrightarrow{Z_1} \parallel \overrightarrow{Z_2} \parallel \overrightarrow{Z_3}$$

$$Z_{eq} = \frac{1}{Z_1} + \frac{1}{Z_2} + \frac{1}{Z_3}$$

$$Z_{eq} = 3{\cdot}88\,46 + j\,1{\cdot}4185$$

$$= 4{\cdot}135\ \angle\ 20{\cdot}06^\circ\ \Omega$$

assume supply voltage is taken as reference phasor current $I = \dfrac{V_S \angle 0°}{Zeq} = \dfrac{V_S \angle 0°}{4 \cdot 135 \angle 20 \cdot 06°}$

$$I = \frac{V_S \angle -20 \cdot 06°}{\angle 4 \cdot 135} = 20 \angle \phi$$

$$\frac{V_S}{4 \cdot 135} = 20 \text{ and } \phi = -20{\cdot}06$$

$$V_S = 20 \times 4{\cdot}135 = 82{\cdot}7 \text{ volts}$$

Since all the impedances are connected in parallel therefore the supply voltage $Vs = 82{\cdot}7$ volt will appear across all there,

$$I_1 = \frac{V_S}{Z_1} = \frac{82{\cdot}7 \angle 0°}{(6 + j5)} = 10{\cdot}5886 \angle -39{\cdot}8056 \; amp$$

$$I_2 = \frac{V_S}{Z_2} = \frac{82{\cdot}7 \angle 0°}{(8 - j6)} = 8{\cdot}27 \angle 36{\cdot}87° \; amp$$

$$I_3 = \frac{V_S}{Z_3} = \frac{82{\cdot}7 \angle 0°}{(8 + j10)} = 6{\cdot}458 \angle -51{\cdot}34 \; amp$$

2. (*a*) We can measure the 3-phase power by three methods generally

(*i*) One watt meter method

(*ii*) Two watt meter method

(*iii*) Three watt meter method

Now two watt meter method for star connected three phase balanced circuit

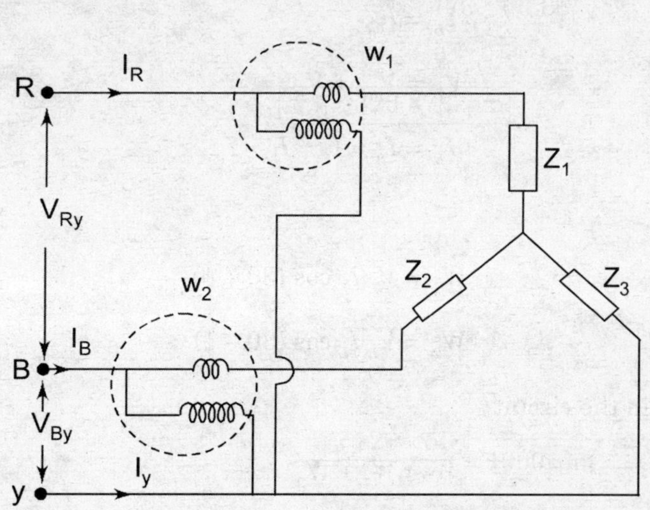

Phasor diagram for measuring 3 – phase power by two wattmeter method

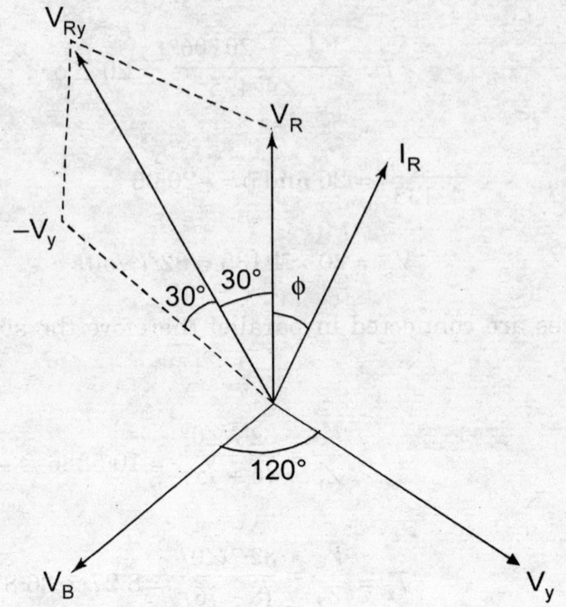

→ In this connection if load is balanced it means $Z\angle\phi$ lagging in nature

and hence watt meter reading are:

$$W_1 = V_{RY} \cdot IR \cos \text{(angle between } V_{RY} \text{ and } I_R)$$

$$W_2 = V_{BY} \cdot IB \cos \text{(angle between (} V_{BY} \text{ and } I_B).$$

For star connection we have

$$V_L = \sqrt{3}\, V_{Ph}$$

$$I_L = I_{Ph}$$

$$V_L = V_{RY} = V_{BY}$$

$$I_R = I_B = I_Y = I_L = I_{Ph}$$

Using phasor diagram

$$W_1 = V_L I_L \cos (30 + \phi)$$

$$W_2 = V_L I_L \cos (30 - \phi)$$

and hence total power in the circuit

$$W = W_1 + W_2$$

$$W = V_L I_L [\cos (30 + \phi) + \cos (30 - \phi)]$$

$$W = \sqrt{3}\, V_L I_L \cos \phi$$

$$V_L = \sqrt{3}\, V_{Ph}$$

$$\boxed{W = 3V_{Ph}\, I_{Ph} \cos\phi = \sqrt{3}V_L\, I_L \cos\phi}$$

Measurement of Power factor:

$$W_1 = V_L I_L \cos(30 + \phi)$$

$$W_2 = V_L I_L \cos(30 - \phi)$$

$$W_1 + W_2 = \sqrt{3}V_L\, I_L \cos\phi$$

$$W_2 = V_L I_L \cos(30 - \phi)$$

$$\frac{W_1 - W_2}{W_1 + W_2} = \frac{\tan\phi}{\sqrt{3}} \text{ or } \tan\phi = \sqrt{3}\left[\frac{W_1 - W_2}{W_1 + W_2}\right]$$

$$\boxed{P \cdot f = \tan^{-1}\left[\frac{\sqrt{3}\,(W_1 - W_2)}{W_1 + W_2}\right]}$$

(*b*) Emf and torque Equation of D.C motor

Assuption

No. of Poles = P

Total no. of Conductors = Z

Flux per pole = ϕ

Number of parallel path = A

and We already know that

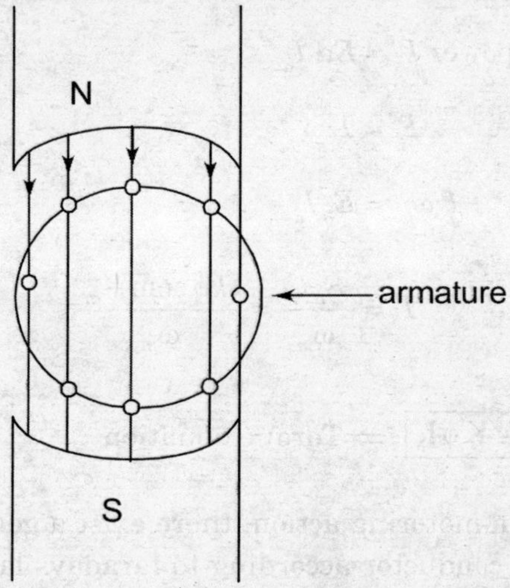

$A = 2$ for wave winding

$A = P$ for lap winding

N = Speed in *r.p.m*

Flux cut by one conductor per revolution= $P\,\phi$

Number of revolution per second = $\frac{N}{60}$

Now flux cut by one conductor in one second = $\frac{P\phi N}{60}$

Emf induced in one conductor $E_C = \frac{P\phi N}{60}$

Since no of conductors in series per parallel path = Z/A

So induced emf in the armature of *d.C* machine

$$E_a = E_C \times \frac{2}{A} = \left(\frac{P\phi N}{60}\right)\left(\frac{Z}{A}\right)$$

$$E_a = \frac{Z\,\phi\,N.P}{60 \cdot A}$$

$$N = \frac{60\omega_m}{2\pi}$$ where ω_m is angular velocity in rad/sec.

$$E_a = \left(\frac{\phi z}{60}\right)\left(\frac{60\omega_m}{2\pi}\right)\left(\frac{P}{A}\right) = \left(\frac{PZ}{2\pi A}\right) \cdot \phi.\ \omega_m$$

$\boxed{Ea = K\,\phi\,\omega_m}$ where $k = \frac{P_2}{2\pi A}$

Armature power $P = Ea\ I_a$

$$P = T \cdot \omega_m$$

$$T \cdot \omega_m = E_a I_a$$

$$T = \frac{E_a I_a}{\omega_m} = \frac{(k\phi\,\text{com})\,\text{I}_\text{m}}{\omega_m}$$

$\boxed{\text{T} = \text{K}\,\phi\,\text{I}_\text{a}}$ $\Rightarrow$ Torque equation

Back emf: In *d.C* motor after a motoring action, there exist a generating action. There is an induced emf in the rotation armature conductor according to faradays law of induction. This induced emf in armature acts in opposite direction of supply voltage. This is according to Lenz's law which states that the direction of induced emf is always so as to opposes the cause producing it. In a *d.c* motor, electrical input, *i.e.*, supply voltage is the cause and hence this induced emf oppose the supply voltage. This emf tries to set up the count in opposite direction to that, which supply voltage is forcing through the conductor. So as this emf always oppose the supply voltage, it is called back emf and denoted as E_b. actually it gets generated by generating action.

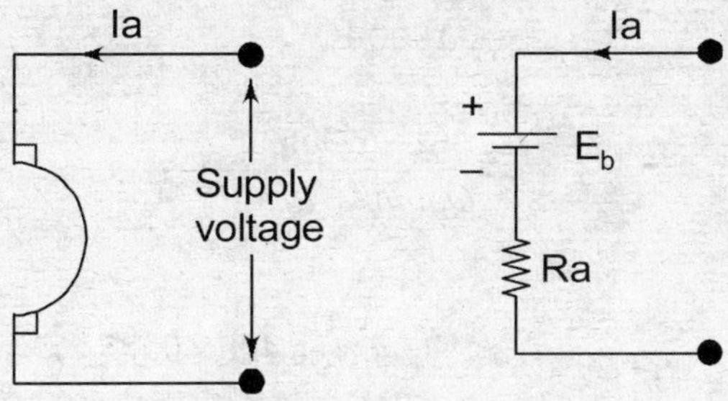

$$\boxed{E_b = \frac{\phi PNZ}{60\,A}\text{ Volts}}$$

3. (*a*) Given data

$$P_i = 2{\cdot}5 \text{ KW}$$

Primary winding resistance = 0.5 Ω

Secondry winding resistance = 0.001Ω

if $$P_i = 2.5 \text{ KW}$$

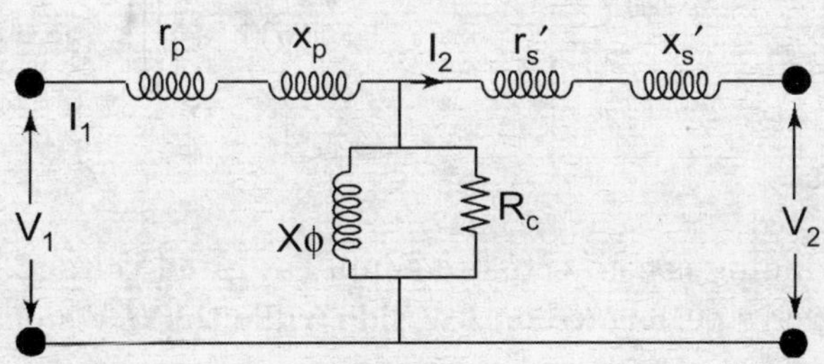

$$\text{Secondry Current } I_2 = \frac{400 \times 10^3}{320} = 1250\,A = 1{\cdot}25 \text{ KA}$$

$$\text{Primary Current } I_1 = \frac{400 \times 10^3}{5000} = 80\ amp$$

$$\text{Total copper loss at full load } = \left(I_1^2 \times r_p\right)\left(I_2^2 \times r_s\right)$$

$$= (80)^2 \times 0{\cdot}5 + (1250)^2 \times 0{\cdot}001$$

$$= 4{\cdot}7625\ kW$$

At half load

$$\text{Copper loss } (P_{cu})_{1/2} = \left(\frac{1}{2}\right)^2 P_{cu} = \frac{1}{4} \times 4{\cdot}7625$$

$$(P_{cu})_{1/2} = 1{\cdot}1906 \text{ KW}$$

$$\eta = \frac{\text{Output}}{Output + Pi + (P_{cu})_{1/2}}$$

$$\eta = \frac{\frac{1}{2} \times 400 \times 0\cdot85}{\frac{1}{2} \times 400 \times 0\cdot85 + 1\cdot1906 + 2\cdot5}$$

$$\eta = 0{\cdot}97875$$

$$\boxed{\eta = 97.8\%}$$

(*b*) Open circuit test and short circuit test of transformer:

Open circuit test: This test is also called no load test. The purpose of this test is to determine shunt branch prarameters of equivalwent circuit of tranformer.

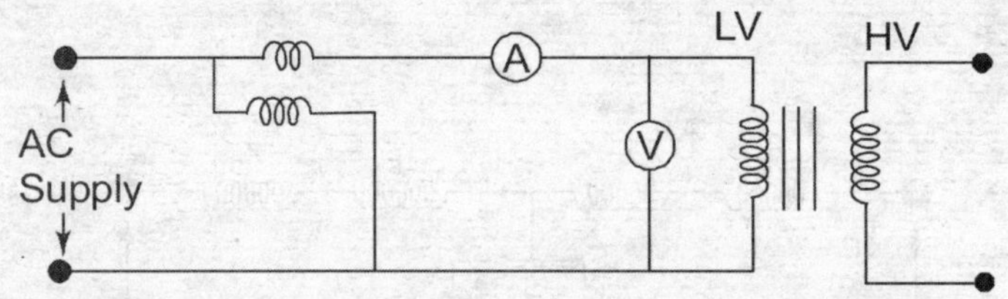

In this test one of the winding is connected to supply at rated voltage, while after winding leep open circuired. This test is always performed on *L.V* side while the *H.V* side is keep open circuited.

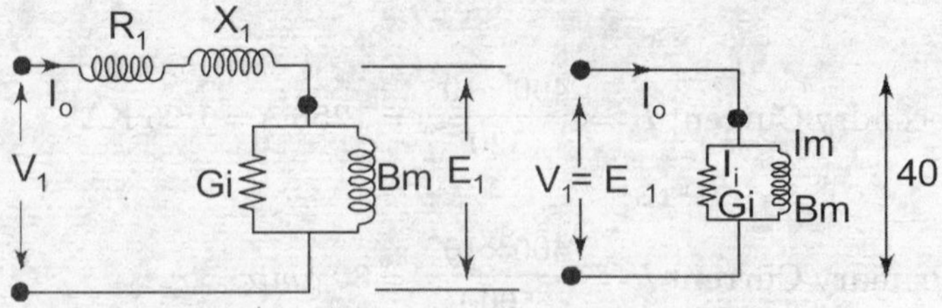

The shunt branch parameters can easily be determined from three readings.

$$Y_o = G_i - iBm$$

$$Y_o = \frac{I_O}{V_1}$$

Now $$V_1^2\ Gi = P_o\ B_m = \sqrt{Y_o^2 - G_i^2}$$

$$P_i = \frac{P_o}{V_1^2}$$

It is threfore, seen that the *OC* test yields the values of core loss parameter of shunt branch equivalent circuit.

Short Circuit Test:

This test serves the pupose of determining the series parameters of a transformer. This test usually conducted from the *HV* side of transformer while *LV* side is short cicuited. Since the transformer resistances and leakage resistances are very small. The voltage V_{sc} needed to circulate the full loasd current under short circuit as low as 5 – 8% of the rated voltage. As a result the exciting current $I_o(SC)$ Under these conditions is only about 0·1 to 0.5% of full load current.

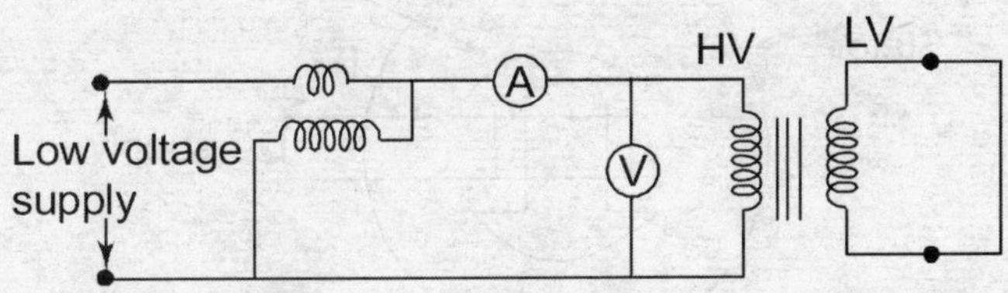

While conducting *SC* test, the supply voltage is gradually raised from zero till the transformer draw full load current.

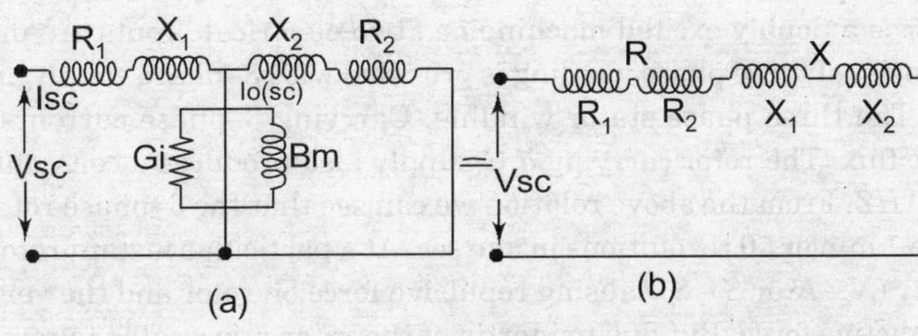

Voltage = Use Current I_{SC} power $i/p = P_{SC}$

Since the transformer is exicited at very low voltage, the iron loss is negligible, power input corresponds to copper loss.

$$P_{SC} = P_{C(\text{copper loss})}$$

$$Z = \frac{V_{SC}}{I_{SC}} = \sqrt{R^2 + X^2}$$

$$\text{equivalent resistance } R = \frac{P_{SC}}{(I_{SC})^2}$$

$$\text{Equivalent reactance } X = \sqrt{Z^2 - R^2}$$

⇒ It is to be observed that the SC test has given us the equivalent resistance and reactance of transformer.

4. (*a*) Principle of Operation of 3-phase Synchronous Motor:

First, why we called its synchronous motor because the speed of the rotor of this motor is same as the rotating magnetic field. It is basically a fixed speed rotor because it has only one speed. Basically it is in synchronism with the supply frequency. Synchrorous speed is given by

$$N_S = \frac{120f}{P}$$

where f = supply frequency

P = No. of pole.

Construction of Synchronous Motor:

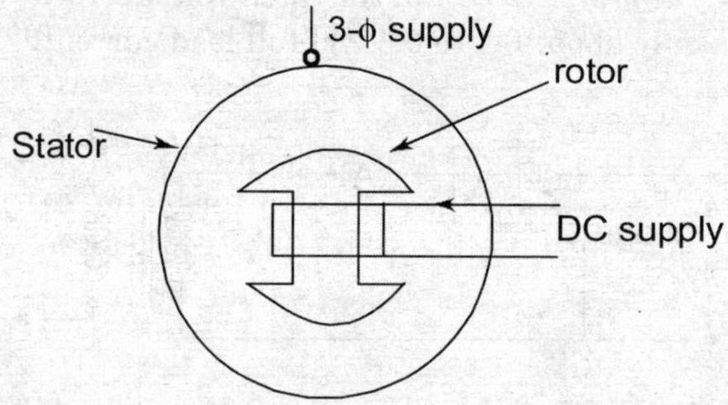

Principle of operation:

Suchronous motor is a doubly excited machine *i.e.*, two electrical inputs are provided to it. It's stator winding which consist of three phase winding is provided with 3–phase supply and the rotor is provided with *d.C* supply. The three phase stator winding. Carrying 3–phase currents produces three phase rotating magnetic flux. The rotor carrying *d.C* supply also produces a constant flux. Considering the frequency to be 50 *HZ*. From the above relation we can see that the 3–phase rotating flux rotates about 3000 revolution in 1 min or 50 revolutions in one sec. At a particular instant rotor and stator pole might be of same polarity ($N - N$ or $S - S$) causing repulsive force on rotor and the very next second it will be $N - S$ causing attractive force. But due to inertia of the rotor it is unable to rotate in any direction due to attractive or repulsive forces and remain in standstill condition. Hence it is not self starting. To overcome this inertia, rotor is initially fed some mechanical input which rotates it in same direction as magnetic field to a speed very close to synchrorous speed. After some time magnetic locking occurs and the synchronous motor rotates in synchronism with the frequency.

Application of Synchronous Motor:

1. 3-phase synchronous motor used to improve the power tacks

2. It is also used to regulate the voltage at the end of transmission line.

3. 3-phase synchronous motor used whose constant speed, constant load drives.

4. Synchronous motor having no load connected to its shaft is used for power factor improvement owing to its charactertic to behave at any electrial power factor. It is used in power systems where static capacitor are expensive.

5. Synchronous motor is used where operating speed is less and high power is required.

(*b*) Given $P = 4$

$N_r = 24\ rps$

$f_s = 50\ H$

$R_2 = 0.35\ W/\text{Phase}$

$X_2 = 3.5 W/\text{Phase}$

Effective rotor-stator ratio $(1/a) = 0{\cdot}85 : 1$

$$a = \frac{1}{0{\cdot}85} = \frac{100}{85} = \frac{20}{17}$$

Rotor resistance refered to stator side

$$R_2' = a^2 R_2' = \left(\frac{20}{17}\right)^2 \times 0{\cdot}35 = 0{\cdot}484\ \Omega$$

Rotor reactance refered to stator side

$$X_2' = a^2, X_2 = \left(\frac{20}{17}\right)^2 \times 3{\cdot}5$$

Assuming core loss, stator resistance and reactance to be negligible

(*i*) Synchronous speed $N_S = \dfrac{120 f}{P} = \dfrac{120 \times 50}{4}$

induction motor speed $N_r = 60 \times N_S = 60 \times 24 = 1440\ rpm$

(*ii*) Slip, $S = \dfrac{N_S - Nr}{Ns} = \dfrac{1500 - 1400}{15000}$

(*iii*) $I_1' = \dfrac{V_1}{\sqrt{\left(\dfrac{R_1'}{S}\right)^2 + X_2'^{\,2}}} = \dfrac{415/\sqrt{3}}{\sqrt{\left(\dfrac{0 \cdot 484}{0 \cdot 04}\right)^2 + (4 \cdot 844)^2}}$

$= 18{\cdot}383$ cm

The full load torque $T_{fl} = \dfrac{3}{W_S} \times (I_1')^2 \times R_2'\left(\dfrac{1}{S} - 1\right)$

$$= \frac{3}{\left(\dfrac{2\pi \times 1500}{60}\right)} \times (18 \cdot 383)^2 \times 0 \cdot 484\left(\frac{1}{0 \cdot 04} - 1\right)$$

$= 74{\cdot}97\ N.m$

(*iv*)

$$P_{o/p} = P_{\text{mech}} - P_{\text{friction loss}}$$

$$= 3I_1'R_2'\left(\frac{1}{S} - 1\right) - 770$$

$$= 3\times(18{\cdot}383)^2 \times 0.484\left(\frac{1}{0\cdot 04} - 1\right) - 770$$

$$= 11012{\cdot}755\text{W} = 110{\cdot}127 \text{ kW}$$

(*v*) T_{max} Occurs at S_{max}

$$S_{max} = \frac{R_2}{X_2} = \frac{0\cdot 35}{3\cdot 5} = \frac{1}{10} = 0.1$$

$$\frac{T_{fl}}{T_{max}} = \frac{2}{\dfrac{S_{max}}{S_{fl}} + \dfrac{S_{fl}}{T_{max}}} = \frac{74\cdot 97}{T_{max}}$$

$$= \frac{2}{\left(\dfrac{0\cdot 1}{0\cdot 04}\right) + \left(\dfrac{0\cdot 04}{1}\right)}$$

$$\boxed{T_{max} = 108\cdot 7065\ N-m}$$

$$\boxed{T_tl = 74\cdot 97\ N-m}$$

$$\boxed{N_S = 15000\ rpm}$$

$$\boxed{P_{O/P} = 110\cdot 127\ kW}$$

$$\boxed{S = 0\cdot 04 = 4\%}$$

5. (*a*) **Transmission line:** Depending upon the length of transmission line it can be classified into three types.

(*i*) Short transmission line

(*ii*) Medium transmission line

(*iii*) Long transmission line

Short Transmission Line: The length of this transmisson line is lesser than 80 km and operating voltage lower than 20 kV and operationg voltage lower than 20 kV and product of operating frequency and length of transmission line is less than 4000. Due to smaller distance and lower line voltage, the capacitance effects are small therefore can be neglected.

Medium Transmission Line: The length of this transmission line is in between 80 km and 200 km and line voltage between 20 kV and 100 kV, product of operating frequency and length of transmission line is between 4000 to 1000.

Long Transmission Line: The length of this transmission line is above 200 km and line voltage above 100*V*, and the product of operating frequency and length of the frequency line is above 10000.

Performance analysis of Short Transmission Line:

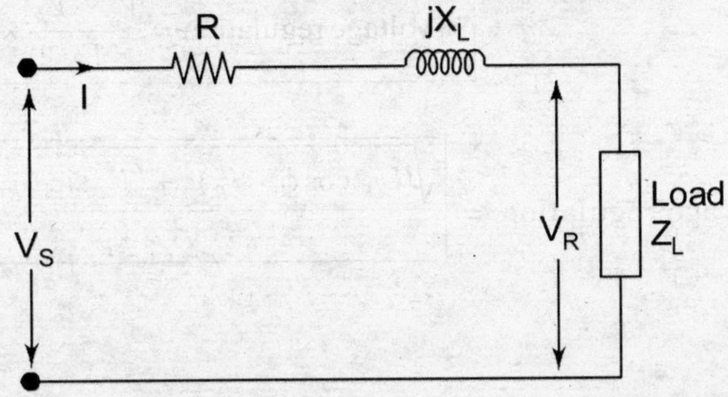

The equilent circuit for a short transmissior line is represented as shown above. In the analysis of short transmission line the capacitance effects are small and neglected. The resistance and inductance are taken into consideration.

Let I = Load current

R = Resistance of loop

X_L = Inductive loop reactance

V_R = Receving end voltage

$\cos\phi_R$ = Receivng end power factor

V_S = Sending end voltage

$\cos\phi_S$ = Sending end power factor

Z_L = Load impedance

The corresponding phasor diagram for lagging load *P.F* from the right angle triangle *OEC*

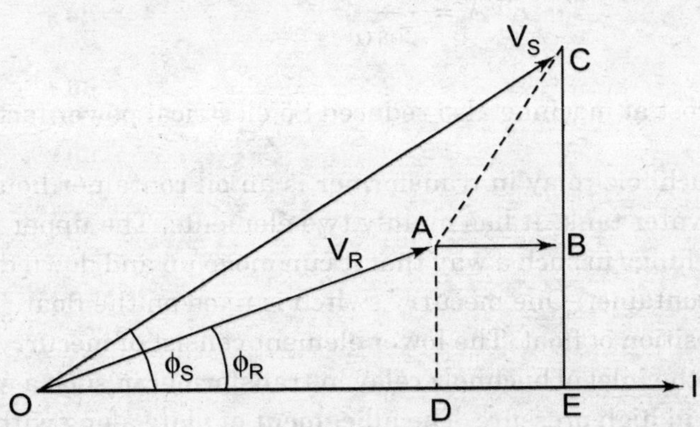

$$(OC)^2 = (OE)^2 + (EC)^2$$

$$V_S^2 = (OD + DE)^2 + (EB + BC)^2$$

$$V_S^2 = [V_R \cos\phi_R + I_R]^2 + [V_R \sin\phi_R + Ix_2]^2$$

$$V_S = \sqrt{[V_R \cos\phi_R + I_R]^2 + (V_R \sin\phi_R + Ix_2)^2}$$

$$\boxed{\% \text{ voltage regulation} = \frac{V_S - V_R}{V_R} \times 100}$$

$$\% \text{ Voltage regulation} = \boxed{\frac{\sqrt{(U_R \cos\phi + I_R)^2 + (V_R \sin\phi_R + I \times L)^2} - V_R}{V_R} \times 100}$$

(*b*) **Short Notes:**

Power factor Improvement: The terms power factor comes to the picture in *AC* circuits only. Mathematically it is cosine of the phase difference between source voltage and current. It refers to the franction of total power (apparent power) which is ulitized to do usefull work called active power.

$$\cos\phi = \frac{\text{Active power}}{\text{apparent power}}$$

Need for Power Factor Improvement:

Real Power is given by $P = VI \cos\phi$. To transfer given amount of power at certain voltage. The electrical current is inversly proportional to $\cos\phi$. Hence higher the power factor lower will be the current. A small current flow requires less cross sectional area of conductor and thus it saves conductor and money.

⇒ From the above relation we are having a poor power factor increases the current flowing in the conductor and thus copper loss increases. Further larger voltage drop occur in alternator, electrical transformer and transmission lines which gives very poor voltage regulation. Further the *KVA* rating of machine also reduced by having higher power factor

$$KVA = \frac{\text{KW}}{\cos\phi}$$

Hence the size and cost at machine also reduced So electrical power factor maintained close to unity.

Buchholoz Relay: Buchholz relay in transformer is an oil container housed the connecting pipe from main tank to conservator tank. It has mainly two elements. The upper element consists of float. The float is attached to a hinge in such a way that it cun move up and down depending upon the oil level in the Buchholz relay container. One mecurry switch is fixed on the float. The aliegnment of this switch depends upon the position of float. The lower element consist of mecurry switch. This plate fitted on a hinge just in front of the inlet of buchholz relay in transformer in such a way that when oil enters in the relay from that inlet in high pressure. The alliegment of plate along with mercurry switch attached to it will change.

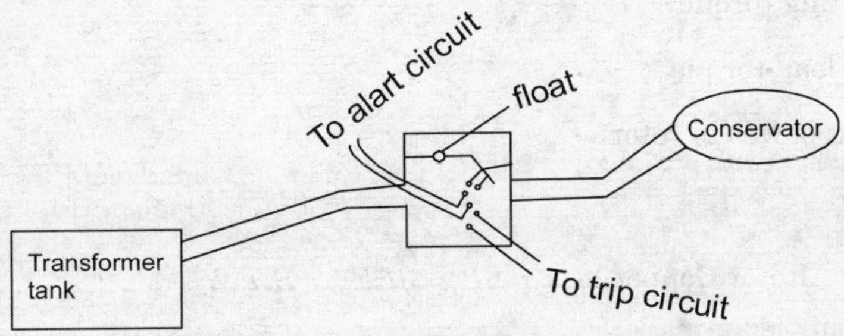

It is also called on gas actuated relay. It provides protection only against internal faults. Whenever a fault occur inside the transformer the oils of the tank get over heating and gases are generated. The generation of gases may be slow or violent depending upon the fault in minor or heavy short circuit.

(*iii*) Advantage of interconvection of Power Stations:

(*a*) The reliability and continuity of supply is improved with interconnected power stations. If faults occurs at any one station the supply can be maintained by the other station.

(*b*) Generally various interconnected power station have their different load curves due to maximum demand on the system is reduced. The effective capacity of the system increased as there is improment in diversity factor.

(*c*) If power stations are interconnected, the peak load can be exchanged between the generating stations. If there is peak load demand is more than rated capacity of plant then the excess load can be shared by other interconnected system.

(*d*) If power stations are interconnected, the economical operation of plant is possible. The total load is arranged in such a way that more efficient-plant can be used as base load stations which can work continuously throughout the year at high load factor. Also large generator unit can be employed to reduce capital cost per kW.

(*e*) In abnormal conditions every power station should have reserve stand by unit to be put in operation with interconnected system, the reserve capacity is reduced which increase efficiency of system.

6. (*a*) **Starting Methods of 3 – ϕ Induction Motor:**

Direct on line Starting Method: In this method we can directly switch the stator of the three phase squirrel cage induction motor on the supply mains. The motor at the time of starting drawn a very high value of account for the very short duration. The amount of current drawn by the motor depends upon its design and size. In this method just because of temperature rise, the mojor may get damaged it the starting period is large which may be due to excessive load, insufficient rotor resistance excussive voltage drop.

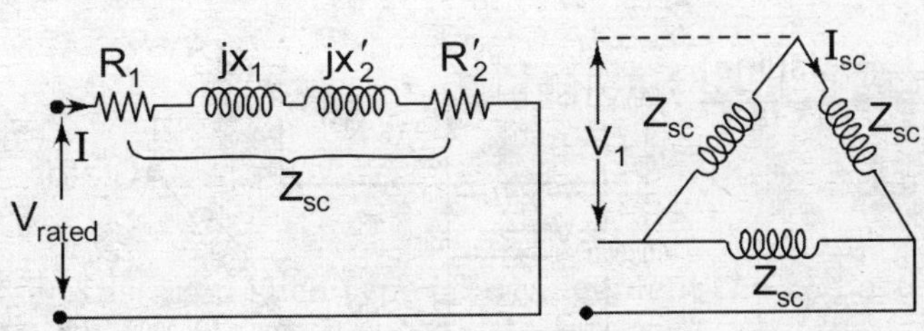

$$I_{sc} = \frac{V_{rated}}{Z_{SC}}$$

Let T_{st} = Starting torque

T_{fl} = Full load torque

P_g = input power to rotor

$P_g = TW$

$$\text{Rotor Copper loss} = SP_g = 3I^2R_2' = S.T\,W$$

$$\text{Torque developed } T = \frac{3I^2R_2'}{SW}$$

at starting slip $S = 1$

So starting torque $T_{st} = K(I_{st})^2 = K(I_{SC})^2$

Full load torque $T_{fl} = \left(\frac{KI_{fl}}{Ist}\right)^2$

So $$\frac{T_{st}}{T_{fl}} = S_{fl} \times \left(\frac{I_{SC}}{Ist}\right)^2$$

$$T_{st}\,(DOL) = \left[S_{fl} \times \left(\frac{I_{SC}}{I_{fl}}\right)^2\right] \times Tf_l$$

Auto-Transformen Starting: In this starting method reduced voltage is obtained by taking tapping at suitable point of a 3–phase auto transformer. It the voltage V.

The motor starting current.

$$I_S = xI_{SC}$$

Where, I_{SC} = starting current (line) with full load voltage.

The current drawn from the supply is

$$I_S(\text{line}) = x(xI_{SC}) = x^2\,I_{SC}$$
$$= XISC$$

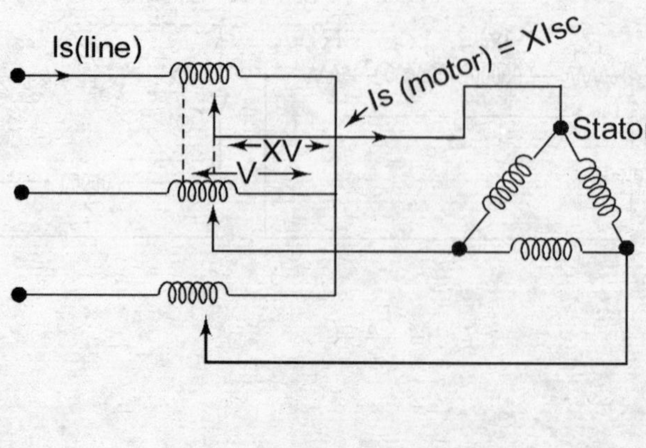

The starting 1 full load forque ratio

$$\frac{T_S}{T_{fl}} = x^2\left(\frac{I_{SC}}{I_{fl}}\right)^2 Sfl$$

Start delta Starting: The star delta starting is an inexpensive two step method of induction motor starting. The motor designed for delta running, is started across full line voltage by connecting the phases in star as shown in diagram below.

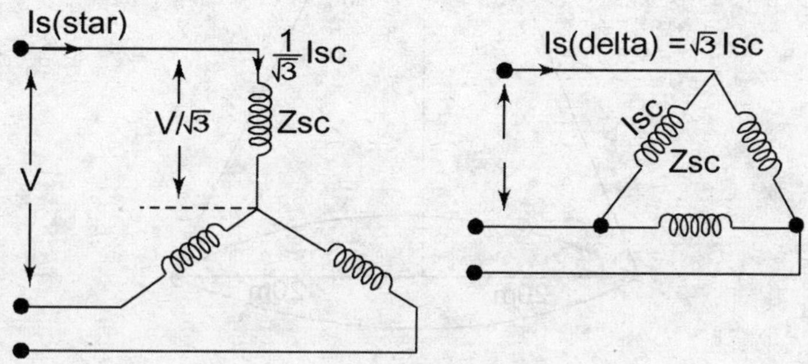

In direct delta starting

$$\text{Starting phase count } I_{SC} = V/Z_{SC}$$

∴

$$V = \text{line voltage}$$

$$\text{Starting line current } I_S \text{ (delta)} = \sqrt{3}\, I_{SC}$$

$$\text{In star starting } I_S = \frac{V/\sqrt{3}}{Z_{SC}} = \frac{1}{\sqrt{3}} I_{SC}$$

$$\frac{I_S(star)}{I_S(delta)} = \frac{1}{3}$$

$$\frac{T_S(star)}{T_{fl}} = \frac{1}{3}\left(\frac{I_{SC}}{I_{fl}}\right)^2 S_{fl}$$

It is thus seen that star delta starting reduces the starting torque to one third that obtainable by direct delter starting.

$$x = 1/\sqrt{3} = 0{\cdot}58$$

⇒ As star delta starter is much cheaper than an auto-transformer stater and is commonly employed for both small and medium size motor.

According to question

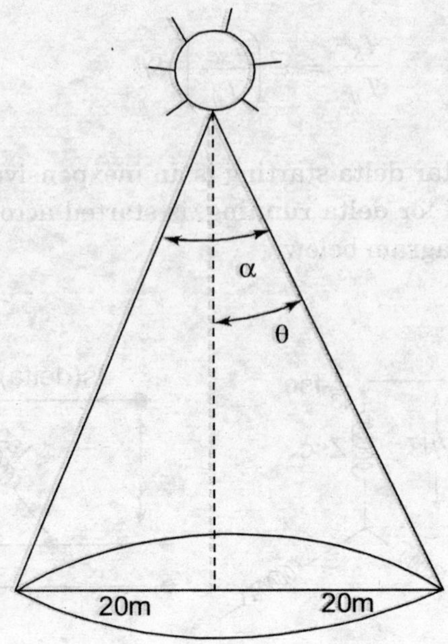

Given $d = 40$ m

$r = 20$ m

$h = 15$ m

$$\text{Candle power of the lamp} = 300$$

$$\text{Luminous output of lamp} = 4\pi \times CP = 4\pi \times 300$$

$$\text{Flux emitted by the reflector} = \text{Efficiency of reflector} \times \text{Luminous output of lamp}$$

$$= 0{\cdot}7 \times (4\pi \times 300) = 840\pi \text{ Lumens}$$

$$\text{area of circular surface} = 4\pi r^2 = \pi\,(20)^2 = 400\,\pi - m^2$$

(*i*)
$$\text{Illumination} = \frac{\text{Flux emitted by reflector}}{\text{area of circular surface}}$$

$$= \frac{840\,\pi}{400\,\pi} = 2{\cdot}1 = 2{\cdot}1 \text{ Lumens/m}^2$$

(*ii*) Since the reflector direct the light uniformly on the surface. The illumination at every point of surface including edge and centre will be same

$$\text{So illumination at centre} = 2.1 \text{ Lumen/m}^2$$

(*iii*) Illumination at edge of surface without reflector

$$= \frac{CP}{h^2} \cos^3 \theta$$

$$\cos \phi = \frac{15}{\sqrt{15^3 + 20^2}} = 0.6$$

Now we get, $\dfrac{300}{(15)^2} \times (0.6)^3 = 0{\cdot}288$ Lux.

Solved Paper 2011

Electrical Engineering

(Paper II)

1. Find I_L for the circuit shown in figure, using Superposition theorem. (30)

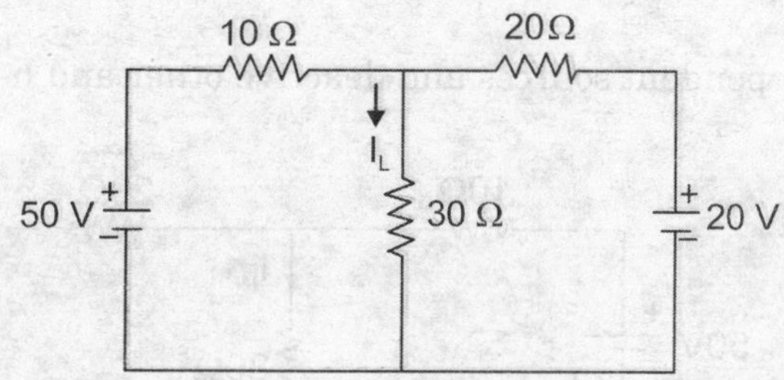

Figure

2. Two impedances $Z_1 = (8 + j6)\Omega$ and $Z_2 = (3 - j4)\Omega$ are in parallel and this combination takes 25 A. Determine the current and power taken by each branch. (30)

3. Derive and explain the two Wattmeter method of measurement of three phase power for a balanced star connected load. Discuss the variations in readings for different power factors of loads from unity to zero. (30)

4. A short shunt compound d.c. generator delivers 100 A to a load at 250 V. The generator has shunt field, series field and armature resistance, 130 Ω, 0.1 Ω and 0.1 Ω respectively. Calculate the voltage generated in armature winding. Assume 1 V drop per brush. (30)

5. Explain the working principle of three phase synchronous motor. (30)

6. Show that maximum stress in a single-core cable is $\frac{2V}{d \log_e D/d}$

Where V is the operating voltage, d and D are the conductor and sheath diameter. (30)

EXPLANATIONS

1. To find out I_L using super position theorem.

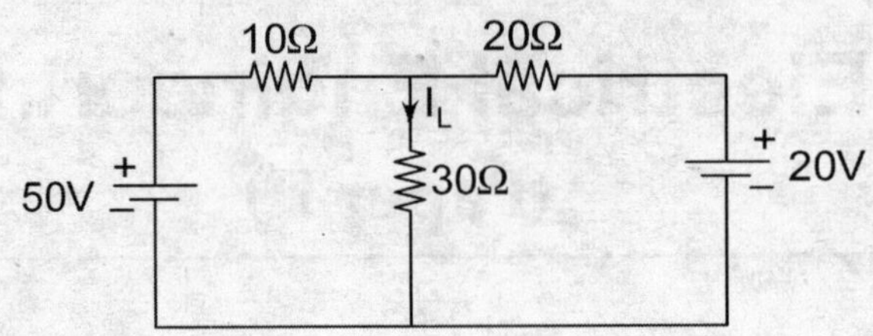

Step: 1

First we take only one independent sources and deactive other and hence first we take 50 V source.

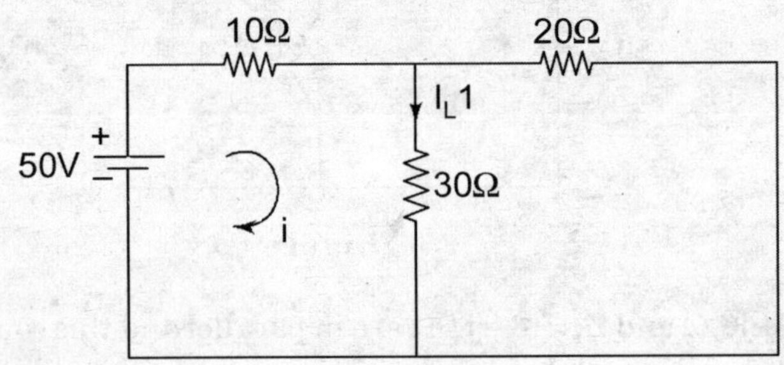

from above figure

$$R_{eq} = 20||30 = \frac{20 \times 30}{20 + 30} = 12\ \Omega$$

$$i = \frac{50}{12 + 10} = \frac{50}{22}\text{ amp}$$

Using current division rule

$$I_1' = \frac{i \times 20}{20 + 30} = \frac{\left(\frac{50}{22}\right) \times 20}{50} = \frac{20}{22}\text{ amp}$$

Step 2: Now we take 20V surce and deactivate other sources.

from this fig.

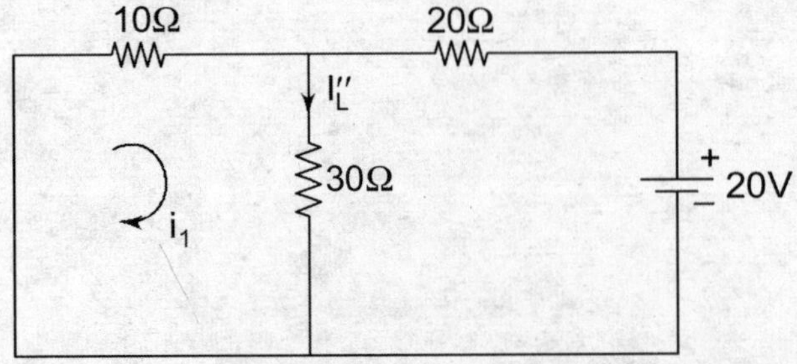

$$\text{Req} = 10 \parallel 30 = \frac{10 \times 30}{10 + 30} = 7.5\Omega$$

$$i_1 = \frac{20}{20 + 7.5} = \frac{8}{11}\text{amp}$$

Using current division rule

$$I_i'' = i_1 \times \frac{10}{10 + 30} = \frac{8}{11}\text{amp}$$

Step 3: To determine net branch current we have to add the current which we find out above.

$$I_L = I_L' + I_L''$$

$$= \frac{20}{22} + \frac{2}{11} = 1.0909 = 1.091 \text{ amp.}$$

2. Given $Z_1 = (8 + j6)\Omega = 10 \angle 36.87°\Omega$

$$Z_2 = (3 - j4)\Omega = 5 \angle -53{\cdot}13° \ \Omega$$

$$Zeq = Z_1 \,||\, Z_2$$

$$Zeq = \frac{Z_1 Z_2}{Z_1 + Z_2}$$

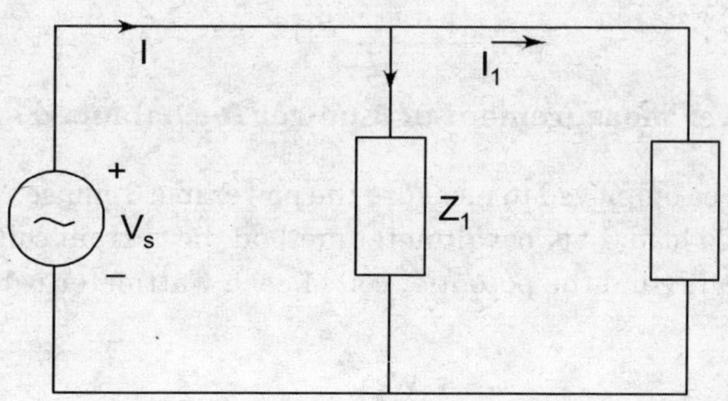

$$= \frac{(8 + i6)(3 - j4)}{(8 + i6)(3 - j4)} = (4 - j2)\Omega = 4.472 \angle -26.565°\Omega$$

If we take $V_s\angle 0°$ is a reference voltage

$$I = \frac{V_S\angle 0°}{Z_{eq}} = \frac{V_S\angle 0°}{4{\cdot}472\angle -26.5650}$$

$$25 \angle\phi = \frac{V_s \angle 26.565}{4.472}$$

$$\frac{V_S}{4\cdot 472} = 25 \text{ and } \phi = 26\cdot 565 \text{ (leading count)}$$

$$V_s = 111\cdot 8 \text{ volts}$$

Since both the impedances are connected in parallel therefore supply voltage V_s = 11·8V will appear on both

So
$$\vec{I} = \frac{\vec{V_s}}{Z_1} = \frac{111.8\angle 0°}{Z_1} = 11.18 \angle -36.87° \text{ Amp}$$

$$\vec{I_2} = \frac{\vec{V_s}}{Z_L} = \frac{111.8\angle 0°}{(3-j4)} = 22.36 \angle 53.13 \text{ Amp}$$

Now power taken by branch $\vec{Z_1}$

$$P_1 = |I_1|^2 R_1$$

$$= (11\cdot 18)^2 \times 8 = 999\cdot 932 = 1000\ W = 1\ KW$$

and power taken by oranch z_2

$$P_2 = |I_2|^2 Z_2$$

$$= (22.36)^2 \times 3 = 1499.9088 = 1500\ W$$

$$\boxed{P_2 \cong 1\cdot 5\,kW}.$$

3. Two watt method of power measurement of 3-power for balanced start connected load:-

Two wattmeter method can be employed to measure the power in a 3-phase, 3-wire star or delta, connected the balanced and unbalanced load. In two waltmeter method the current coils of watt meter are connected with any two lines say R and B and the potential coil of each wattmeter is joined on the same line.

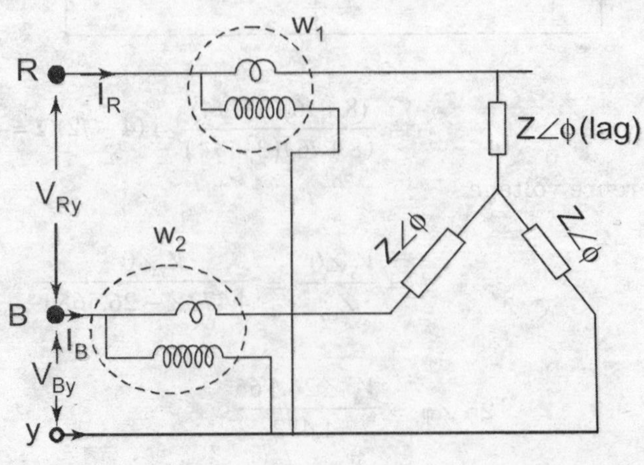

Phasor diagram

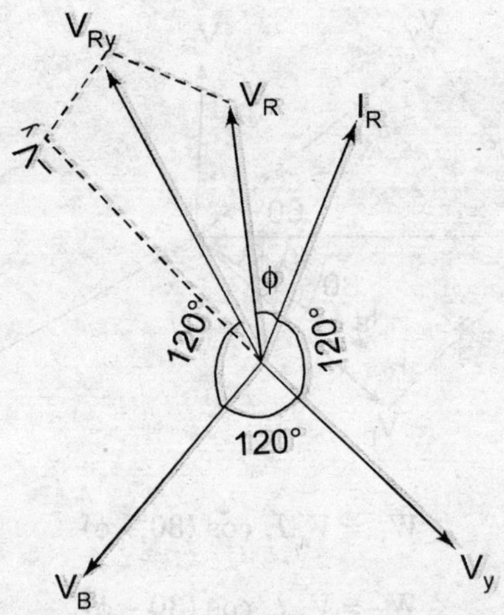

Now watt meter reading are

$$W_1 = V_{RY}\, I_R \cos(\text{angle between } V_{RY} \text{ and } I_R)$$

$$W_2 = V_{BY}\, I_B \cos(\text{angle between } V_{BY} \text{ and } I_B)$$

for star connection

$$V_L = \sqrt{3}\, V_{ph}$$

$$I_L = I_{ph}$$

$$V_L = V_{RY} = V_{BY}$$

$$I_R = I_B = I_Y = I_L = I_{Ph}$$

Now according to phasor diagram

$$W_1 = V_L\, I_L \cos(30 + \phi)$$

$$W_2 = V_L\, I_L \cos(30 - \phi)$$

Total power in the circuit

$$W = V_L\, I_L\, (\cos(30 + \phi) + \cos(30 - \phi)]$$

$$W = \sqrt{3} V_L\, I_L \cos\phi$$

$\therefore$ $V_L = \sqrt{3}\, V_{ph}$, and $I_L = I_{ph}$

$$W = 3\, V_{ph}\, I_{ph} \cos\phi = \sqrt{3}\, V_L\, I_L \cos\phi \qquad \text{...}(i)$$

Now for V_{By}

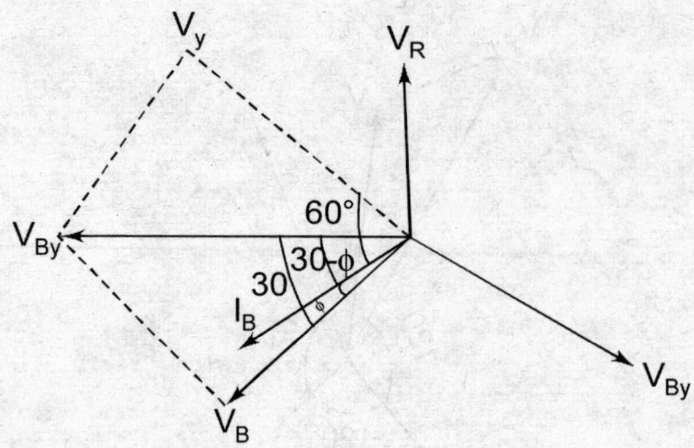

$$W_1 = V_L I_L \cos(30 + \phi)$$

$$W_2 = V_L I_L \cos(30 - \phi)$$

$$W = \sqrt{3}\ V_L I_L \cos\phi$$

$$W_1 - W_2 = V_L I_L \sin\phi \qquad ...(ii)$$

Using eqn (*i*) and (*ii*)

$$\frac{W_1 - W_2}{W_1 + W_2} = \frac{\tan\phi}{\sqrt{3}} \text{ or } \tan\phi = \sqrt{3}\left[\frac{W_1 - W_2}{W_1 + W_2}\right]$$

$$\boxed{\phi = \tan^{-1}\left[\frac{\sqrt{3}(W_1 - W_2)}{W_1 + W_2}\right]}$$

P.f of circuit = cos ϕ

Variations in wattmeter radings

P.f of angle	*P.f* cos ϕ	W_1 $I_2 \cos(30 + \phi)$	W_2 $V_L I_L \cos(30 - \phi)$	$W = W_1 + W_2$	Obseriere
0	1	$\sqrt{3}/2\ V_L I_L$	$\sqrt{3}/2\ V_L I_L$	$\sqrt{3}\ V_L I_L$	$W_1 = W_2$
30°	0.866	$V_L I_L/2$	V_{LIL}	$1.5 V_L I_L$	$W_2 = W_1$
60°	0.5	0	$\sqrt{3}/2 V_L I_L$	$\sqrt{3}/2_{V_L} I_L$	$W_1 = 0$
90°	0	$-V_L I_L/2$	$V_L I_L/2$	0	$W_1 = -ve$ $W_1 = +ve$

4. Given

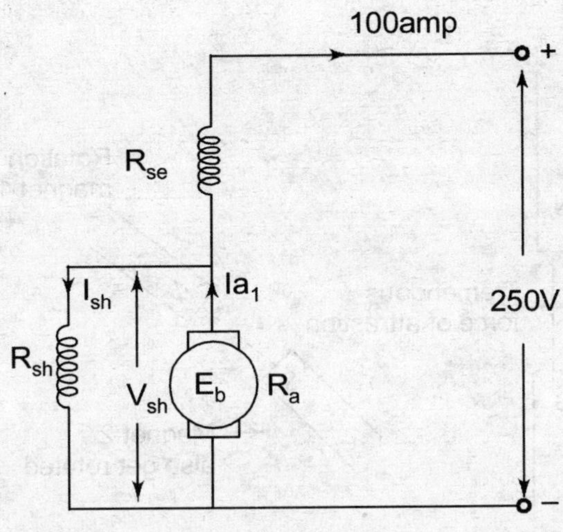

R_{se} series field resistance = 0.1 Ω

R_a carmatere resistance = 0.1 Ω

Shunt field R_{sh} = 130 Ω

Voltage drop per brush = 1V

Load current I_L = 100 A

$$I_a = I_{sh} + I_{se} \ (\therefore I_{se} = I_L)$$

$$I_{sh} = \frac{V_{sh}}{R_{sh}}$$

$$V_{sh} = 250 + I_{se} R_e = 250 + 100 \times 0.1$$

$$= 250 \text{ V}$$

$$I_{sh} = \frac{260}{130} = 2 \text{ A}$$

$$I_a = I_{sh} + I_{se} = 2 + 100 = 102 \text{ Amp}$$

$$E_a = V_{sh} + I_a R_a + 2$$

$$= 260 + 10^2 \times 0{\cdot}1 + 2 \times 1$$

$$\boxed{Ea = 272 \cdot 2\,Volts}$$

5. Principle of operation of 3-phase synchronous motor:

Sunchronous motor works on the principle of magnetic locking when two unlike poles are brought near to each other, it the magnets are strong, there exist a trumendous force of atraction between those two poles. In such condition the two magnets are soild to be magnetically localed.

It now one of two magnet is rotated, the other also rotates in the same direction, the same spend due to force of diraction. *i.e* due to magnetic locking condition. This principle show below by fig.

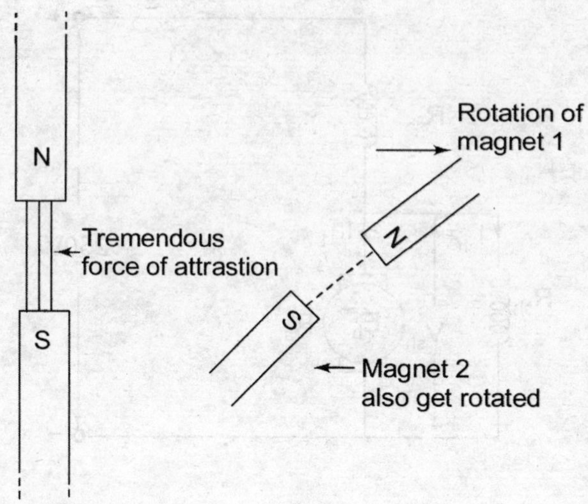

Now consider *a* 3-ϕ synchronous motor which is doubly exicited machine. Its stator winding is provided with 3 – ϕ *a.c* supply and the rotor is provided with *D.C* supply. So the poles of rotor retain the same polarity thrughout but the polarity of stator poles changes as its connected to an 3–ϕ *a.c* supply. The 3-ϕ stator winding carrying a 3-phase current produces 3-ϕ rotating flux. The rotor particular instant rotor and stator poles might be of same polarity (*N-N* or *S-S*) causing repulsive force or rotor and the very next second it will be *N-S* causing atlrative force. But due to inertia of rotor, it is unable to rotate in any direction due to attractive or repulsive force and remain in stanstill condition hence not self starting.

To overcome this inertia, rotor is intially fed with some mechanical input which rotates in same direction as magnetic field to a speed very close to synchronas speed. The main aim of doing this is reduce the speed differenic between the rotating flux and rotor poles. When the relative speed between there two reaches almost zero, the pales. When the relative speed between there two reaches almost zero, the pates of rotor gets attatched or located with rotating flux and where synchronous motor rotates in synchronism with frequency.

6. The insulation of a cable is subjected to electrostatic stress under operating conditions called the dielectric stress.

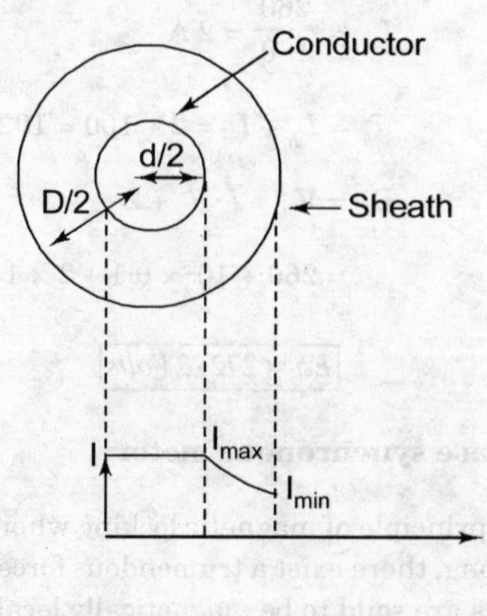

Potential gradient at any point is the same as that the di-electric stress at that point.

A cable is a form of cylindrical condenser therefore electric intensity at a distance x from the centre of cable.

$$E_x = \frac{Q}{2\pi\,\varepsilon_o\,\varepsilon_r}\cdot\frac{1}{x} U/m$$

Since potential gradient = Electric intensity

$$g = \frac{Q}{2\pi\,\varepsilon_o\,\varepsilon_r}\cdot\frac{1}{x} U/m \qquad ...(i)$$

$$v = \frac{Q}{2\pi\,\varepsilon_o\,\varepsilon_r}\cdot \ln\left(\frac{D}{d}\right)$$

$$Q = \frac{2\pi\varepsilon_o\varepsilon_r V}{\ln\left(\frac{D}{d}\right)}$$

Substituting the value of Q in eqn (i) we get

$$g = \frac{2\pi\varepsilon_o\varepsilon_r}{\ln\left(\frac{D}{d}\right)}\cdot\frac{1}{2\pi\varepsilon_o\,\varepsilon_r}\cdot\frac{1}{x} = \frac{V}{x\ln\frac{D}{d}} V/m$$

Since potential gradient 'g' is as,

$$g \propto \frac{1}{x}$$

Therefore, potential gradient will be maximum when x is minimum *i.e.*, $x = d/2$

Hence maximum value of potential gradient is

$$\boxed{g_{\max} = \frac{2V}{d\ln(D/d)} V/m}$$

Solved Paper 2010

Electrical Engineering

(Paper II)

1. (*a*) In the network shown in fig. Find resistance R_L so that maximum power is developed across R_L. (10)

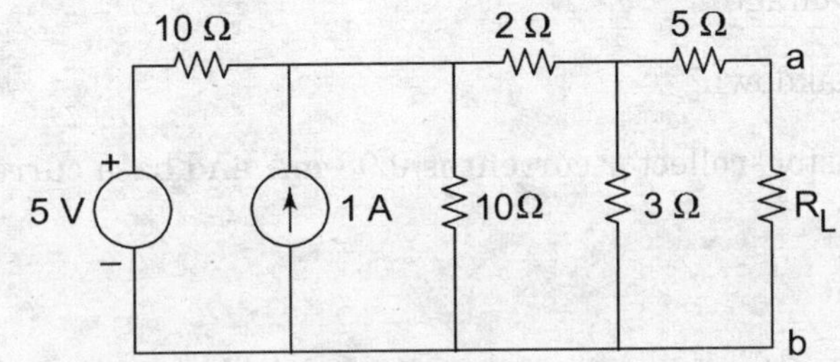

(*b*) Find current through 5Ω resistor in the circuit shown in Fig., using Thevenin's theorem. (10)

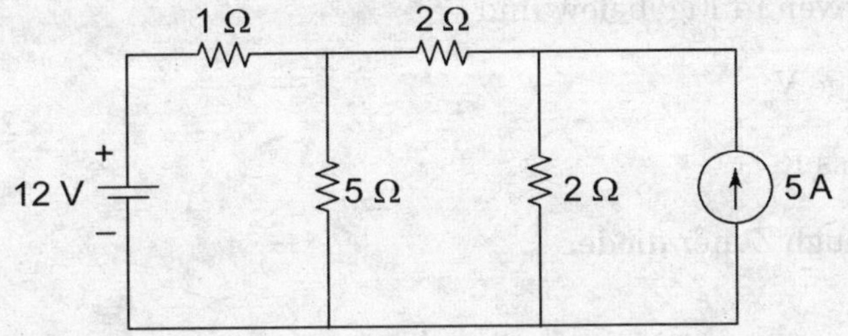

(*c*) What do you understand by statically and dynamically induced emf? Write down difference between them with example. (10)

2. (*a*) A coil of power factor 0.6 is in series with a 100 μF capacitor. When connected to a 50Hz supply the voltage across the capacitor is equal to the voltage across the coil. Find the resistance and indusctance of the coil. (15)

(*b*) Explain with neat sketch the working principle of repulsion type moving iron instrument. Prove that the deflection of the moving iron ammeter is proportional to the square of rms value of the current. (15)

3. (*a*) Describe the construction and principle of working of a capacitor-start capacitor-run single-phase induction motor. (10)

(*b*) A 11000/400 V, distribution transformer takes a no load primary current of 1 A at a power factor of 0.24 lagging. Find (10)

(*i*) core loss current and magnetising current

(ii) core loss in the transformer.

(*c*) Explain different types of distribution systems with the help of neat sketches. (10)

4. (*a*) Describe the working of vacuum tube voltmeter VTVM. State the disadvantages of VTVM. (15)

(*b*) Describe the operation of PN junction diode under forward bias condition. (5)

(*c*) What is meant by doping in a semiconductor? How does the energy band structure of a semiconductor differ from that of a conductor and an insulator? (10)

5. (*a*) What are different turn-on methods of SCR? Explain gate triggering process to turn on the SCR. Draw the gate characteristics of SCR. (15)

(*b*) Define the following terms: (6)

(*i*) Pinch-off voltage

(*ii*) Peak inverse voltage

(*iii*) Avalanche breakdown

(*c*) In a certain transistor, collector current is 0.98 mA and base current is 20 μA. Determine the values of (9)

(*i*) emitter current

(*ii*) current amplification factor

(*iii*) current gain factor.

6. (*a*) For the circuit given in Fig. below find

(*i*) output voltage V_o

(*ii*) voltage across R_S

(*iii*) current through Zener diode.

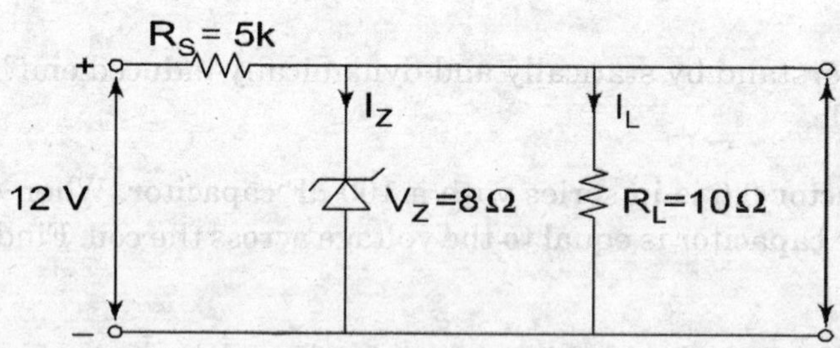

(*b*) With the help of neat diagram explain the V – I characteristics of UJT.

(*c*) Explain the following:

(*i*) Intrinsic and Extrinsic semiconductor

(*ii*) N-type and P-type semiconductor

EXPLANATIONS

1. (*a*) **Step 1.** Remove R_L and find R_{TH} of source netwrok looking through open circuit load terminals.

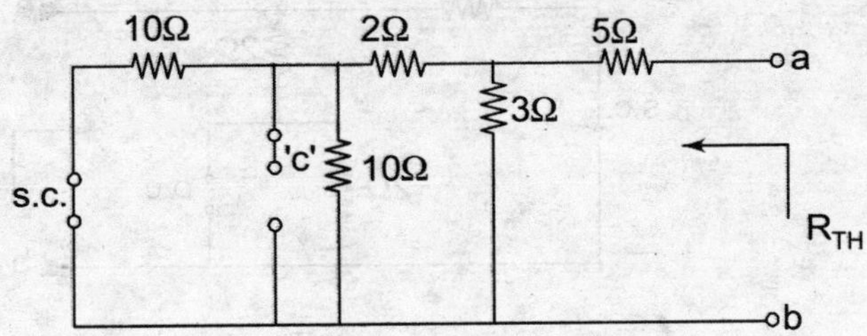

$$R_{TH} = (10 \parallel 10 + 2) \parallel 3 + 5$$
$$= (5 + 2) \parallel 3 + 5$$
$$= 7.1\Omega$$

Step 2. According to maximum power transfer theorem R_{TH} is load resistance of n/w.

$$R_{TH} = R_L = 1.7\Omega$$

(*b*) **Step 1.** Remove 5Ω and find V_{oc}

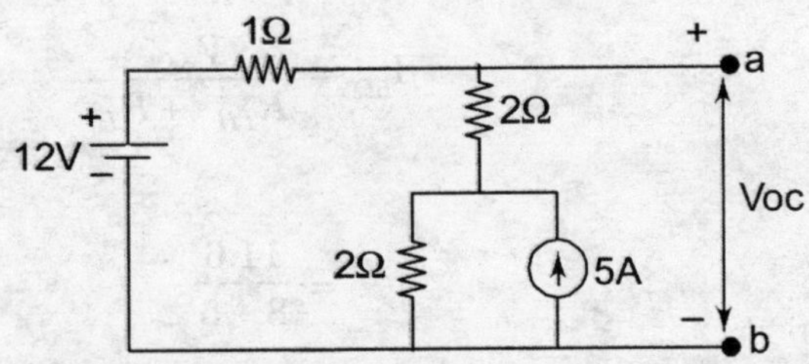

Using source transformation method,

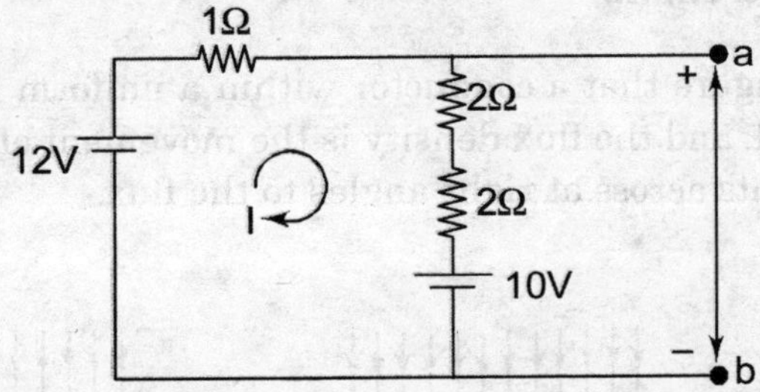

$$I = \frac{12-10}{1+2+2} = \frac{2}{5} = 0.4\text{A}$$

So, $$V_{oc} = 10 + 4 \times 0.4 = 11.6\text{V}$$

Step 2. Deactivate independent sources (voltage source) replaced by internal resistance, current source is removed & replaced by open circuit and find R_{TH}.

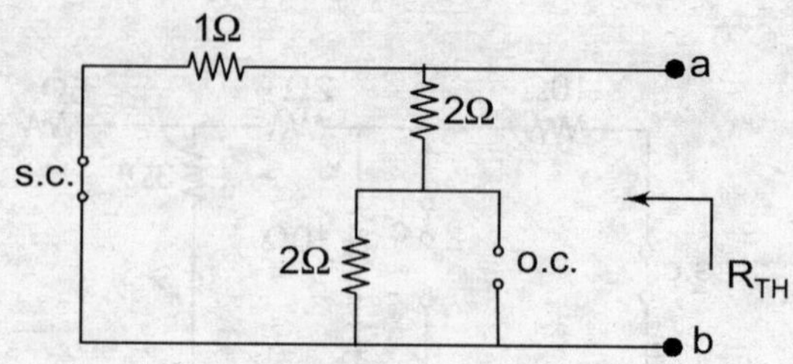

Step 3. Obtain Theveinin's equivalent circuit.

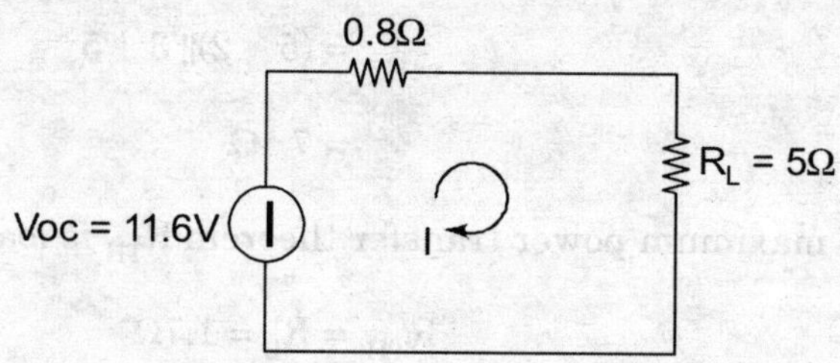

Step 4. Reconnect R_L across load terminals

$$I_{5\Omega} = \frac{V_{oc}}{R_{TH} + R_L}$$

$$= \frac{11.6}{8+5}$$

$$= 2A$$

Hence current through 5Ω is 2A.

(*c*) **Dynamically induced e.m.f.:**

We can see from the figure that a conductor within a uniform magnetic field whose flux density is a uniform magnetic field. and the flux density is the movement of the conductor is shown by arrow line. When the conductor cuts across at right angles to the flux.

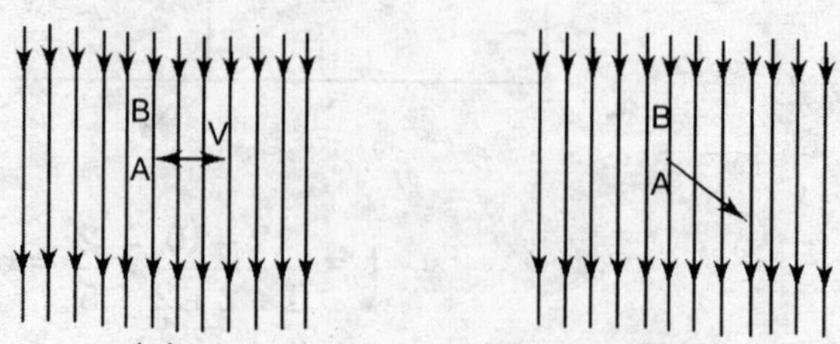

(a) (b)

Let l = Length of the conductor within the field. And it moves a distance dx in time dt, So, the area swept by the conductor is = l.dx. Hence, flux cut by the conductor = l.dxXB change in Flux = B.l.dx weber, Time = dt second

According to Faraday's laws the e.m.f. induced in the conductor. And this induced e.m.f is known as dynamically induced e.m.f.

$$\text{The rate of change of flux linkages} = \frac{Bldx}{dt}$$

$$= Bl\frac{dx}{dt} = Blv \text{ volt}$$

[where, $\frac{dx}{dt}$ is velocity]

If the conductor moves at an angle q with the direction of flux which is shown in (b).

Then the induced e.m.f. is

$$e = \text{Blvsin } \theta = \vec{l}v \times \vec{B}$$

(i.e. ds cross product vector $\vec{V}$ and $\vec{B}$)

An example, the generator works on the production of dynamically induced e.m.f. in the conductors.

Statically induced E.m.f.

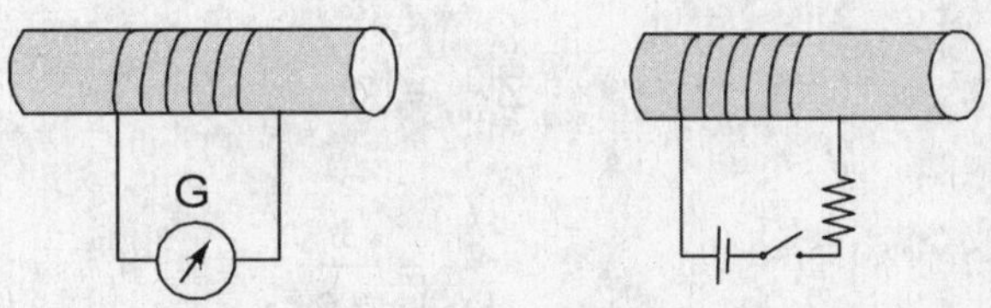

Mutually induced e.m.f: Mutually induced e.m.f. occurs in between two coils. let & are two coils which are placed close to each other. If coil is joined to a battery a switch and a variable resistance R and coil B is connected to a sensitive voltmeter G. When the switch is closed, a current will flow through the coil and produce a magnetic field in which partly links with the coil. As current through is changed, the flux linked with is also changed. According to Faraday's law, induced e.m.f is produced in the coil B and This e.m.f. know as mutually induced e.m.f.

Self-induced e.m.f:

Self-induced e.m.f is the e.m.f which is produced in the coil due to the change of its own flux linked with it. if the current of the coil is changed, then the flux linked with it own turns will also change which will produced an e.m.f. that is called self-induced e.m.f.

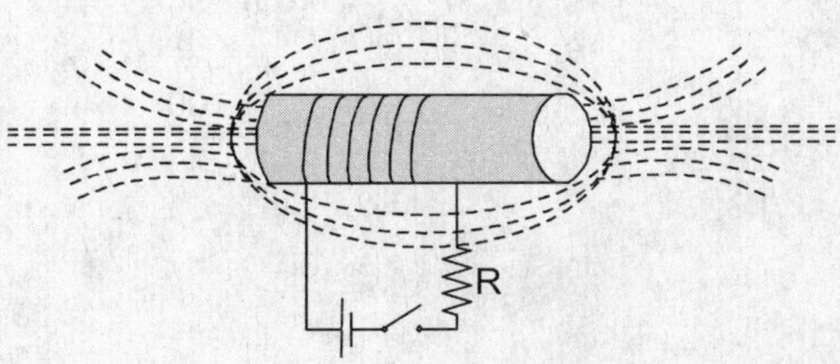

2. (*a*)

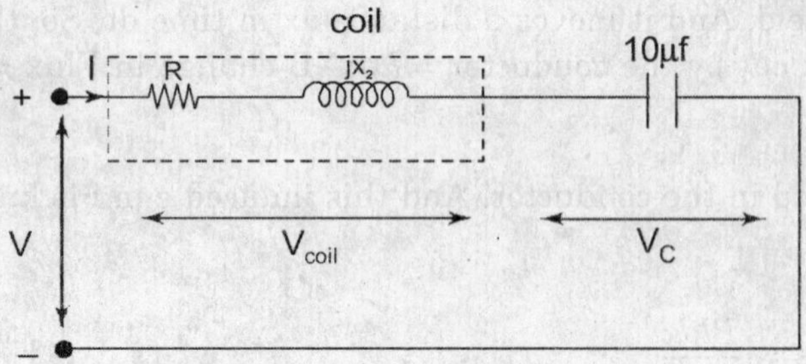

Coil of power factor

$$\cos\phi = \frac{R}{Z} = 0.6$$

$$R = 0.6\ Z$$

$$Z = \sqrt{R^2 + X_L^2}$$

$$= \sqrt{(0.6z)^2 + X_L^2}$$

or $$X_L = 0.8z$$

also, $$|V_{coil}| = |V_c|$$

$$IZ_{coil} = I|-jX_c|$$

$$Z_{coil} = X_c$$

$$= \frac{1}{wc}$$

$$= \frac{1}{2\pi fc}$$

$$= \frac{1}{2\pi \times 50 \times 100 \times 10^{-6}}$$

$$Z_{coil} = \frac{100}{\pi}$$

$$\text{Resistance of coil} = R_{coil}$$

$$= 0.6\ Z$$

$$\text{coil} = 0.6 \times \frac{100}{\pi}$$

$$= \frac{60}{\pi}$$

$$\text{Reactance of coil } X_{coil} = 0.8$$

$$Z_{coil} = 0.8 \times \frac{100}{\pi}$$

$$= \frac{80}{\pi}$$

$$X_{coil} = 2\pi f L_{coil}$$

$$= \frac{80}{\pi}$$

$$L_{coil} = \frac{80/\pi}{20\pi \times 50}$$

$$= 81\text{mH}$$

$$\text{Resistance of coil} = R_{coil}$$

$$= \frac{60}{\pi}$$

$$= 19.098\ \Omega$$

$$\text{Inductance of coil} = L_{coil} = 81\text{mH}$$

(*b*) In the repulsion type, there are two vanes inside the coil one fixed and other movable. These are similarly magnetized when the current flows through the coil and there is a force of repulsion between the two vanes resulting in the movement of the moving vane. Two different designs are in common use

(*i*) Radial Vane Type

In this type, the vanes are radial strips of iron. The strips are placed within the coil as shown in Fig. The fixed vane is attached to the coil and the movable one to the spindle of the instrument.

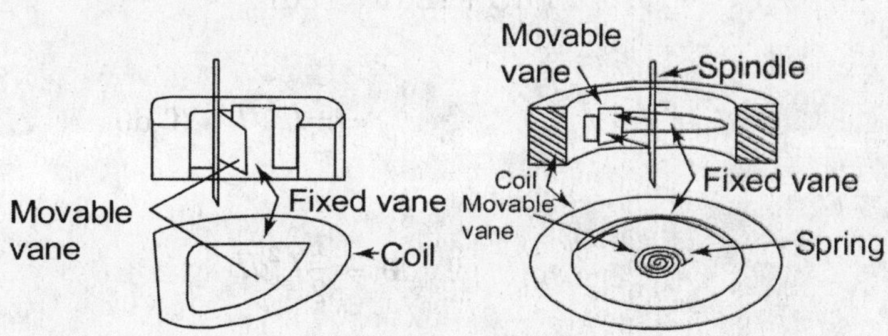

(ii) Co-axial Vane Type

In this type of instrument, the fixed and moving vanes are sections of co axial cylinders as shown in Fig.The controlling torque is provided by springs. Gravity control can also he used in vertically mounted instruments.The damping torque is produced by air friction as in attraction type instruments.

Torque Equation of Moving Iron Instrument:

An expression for the torque moving iron instrument may be derived by consid ring the energy relati ons when there is a small increment in current supplied to the instrument. When this happens there will be a small deflection ds a mechanical work will be done. Let T_d be the deflecting torque.

Mechanical work done = T_d. d_s

Alongside there will be a change in the energy stored in the magnetic field owing to change in inductance.

Suppose the initial current is I, the instrument inductance L and the deflection s. If the current is increased by di then the deflection'changes by ds and the inductance by dL. In order to affect an increment the current there must be an increase in the applied voltage given by

$$e = \frac{d}{dt}(LI)$$

$$= I\frac{dL}{dt} + L\frac{dI}{dt}$$

The electrical energy supplied eldt = I^2dl + ILdl

The stored energy changes from $= \frac{1}{2}I^2L$ to $\frac{1}{2}(I + dI)^2(L + dL)$

Hence the change in stored energy $\frac{1}{2}(I^2 + 2IdI + dI^2)(L + dL) - \frac{1}{2}I^2L$

Neglecting second and higher order terms in small quantities this becomes $ILdI + \frac{1}{2}I^2dI$

From the principle of the conservation of energy,

Electrical energy supplied = increase in stored energy + mechanical work done

$$I^2dL + ILdI = ILdI$$

$$= \frac{1}{2}I^2dL + T_d d\theta$$

Thus $$T_d\, d\theta = \frac{1}{2}I^2dL$$

or Deflecting torque $$T_d = \frac{1}{2}I^2\frac{dL}{d\theta}$$

Hence the deflection is proportional to square of the rms value of the operating cur rent. The deflecting torque is, therefore, unidirectional (acts in the same direction) whatever may be the polarity of the current.

3. (*a*) **Capacitor Start Capacitor Run Motor**

The Capacitor Start Capacitor Run Motor has a cage rotor, and its stator has two windings known as Main and Auxiliary Windings. The two windings are displaced 90 degrees in space. There are two capacitors in this method one is used at the time of the starting and is known as starting capacitor. The other one is used for continuous running of the motor and is known as RUN capacitor.

So this motor is named as Capacitor Start Capacitor Run Motor. This motor is also known as Two Value Capacitor Motor. Connection diagram of the Two valve Capacitor Motor is shown below

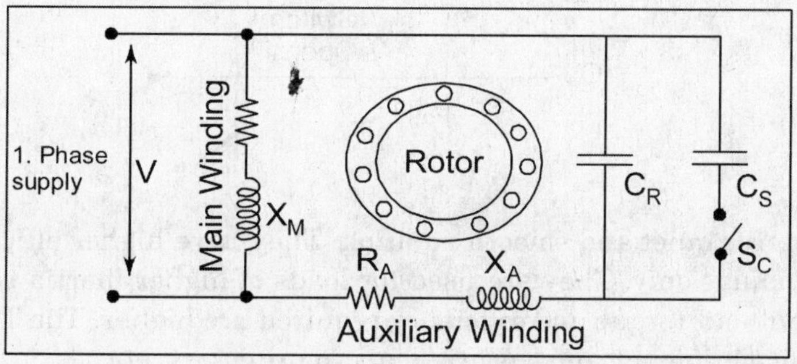

There are two capacitors in this motor represented by C_S and C_R. At the starting, the two capacitors are connected in parallel. The Capacitor Cs is the Starting capacitor is short time rated. It is almost electrolytic. A large amount of current id required to obtain the starting torque. Therefore, the value of the capacitive reactance X should be low in the starting winding. Since, $X_A = 1/2\pi fC_A$, the value of the starting capacitor should be large.

The rated line current is smaller than the starting current at the normal operating condition of the motor. Hence, the value of the capacitive reactance should be large. Since, $X_R = 1/2\pi fC_R$ the value of the run capacitor should be small.

As the motor reaches the synchronous speed, the starting capacitor Cs is disconnected from the circuit by a centrifugal switch Sc. The capacitor C_R is connected permanently in the circuit and thus it is known as RUN Capacitor. The run capacitor is long time rated and is made of oil filled paper.

The figure below shows the Phaser Diagram of the Capacitor Start Capacitor Run Motor.

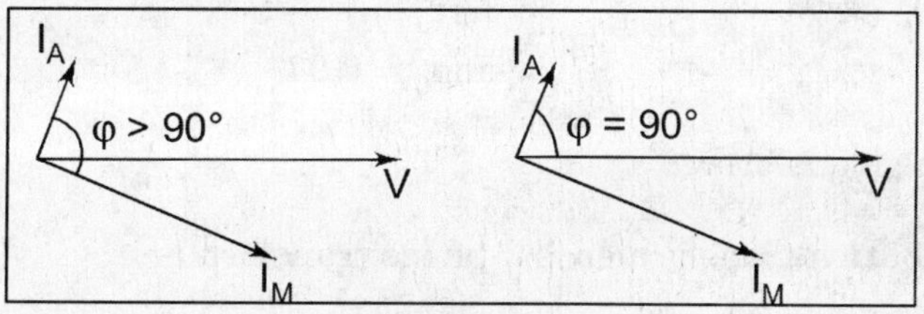

Fig. (a) shows the phasor diagram when at the starting both the capacitor are in the circuit and $\phi > 90°$. Fig

Fig. (*b*) shows the phasor when the starting capacitor is disconnected, and ϕ becomes equal to 90°.

The Torque Speed Characteristic of a Two Value Capacitor Motor is shown below.

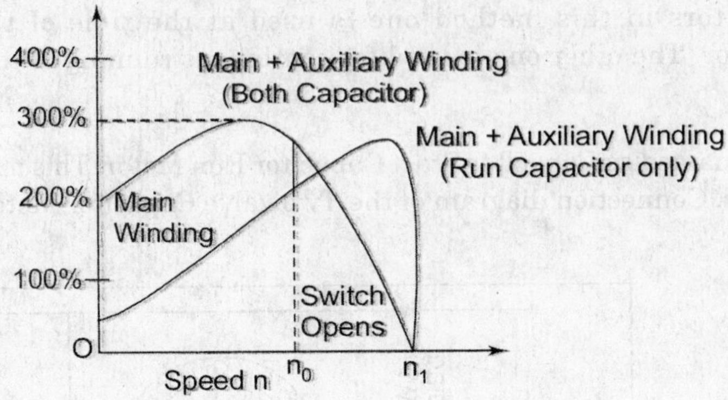

This type of motor is quiet and smooth running. They have higher efficiency than the motors that run on the main windings only. They are used for loads of higher inertia requiring frequent starts where the maximum pull-out torque and efficiency required are higher. The Two Value Capacitor Motors are used in pumping equipment, refrigeration, air compressors, etc.

(*b*) Given that :

No load curren,

$$I_0 = 1 \text{ A at power factor, } \cos\phi_0 = 0.24 \text{ (lagging)}$$

(*i*) Core loss current,

$$I_c = I_0 \cos\phi_0$$

$$= 1 \times 0.24 = 0.24\text{A}$$

Magnetising current,

$$I_\phi = I_0 \sin\phi_0$$

$$= 1 \times 0.97 = 0.97 \text{ A}$$

$$\therefore \quad \phi_0 = \cos^{-1}(0.24) = 76.113°$$

$$\sin\phi_0 = 0.97$$

(*ii*) Core loss in the transformer

Assume distribution transformer is 3-phase transformer,

$$P_0 = \sqrt{3} V_0 I_0 \cos\phi_0$$

$$= \sqrt{3} \times 11000 \times 1 \times 0.24$$

$$= 4572.614 = 4.5726 \text{ kW}$$

(*c*) Distribution systems may be classified in various ways as followed:

1. According to current, the distribution systems are two types:

(a) **dc distribution system,**

(b) **ac distribution system.**

(*a*) **dc distribution system:**

(*i*) 2-wire dc distribution system: This system of distribution consists of two wires, one is the positive and other is the negative wire.

This system is never used for transmission purpose due to low efficiency but may be employed for distribution of dc power.

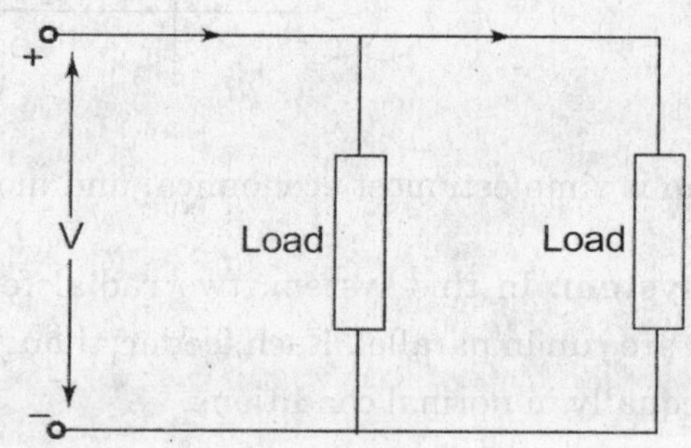

(*ii*) 3-wire dc distribution system: This system consists of two outers and a middle or neutral wire which is earthed at the substation. The voltage between the outer is twice the voltage between either outer and neutral wire.

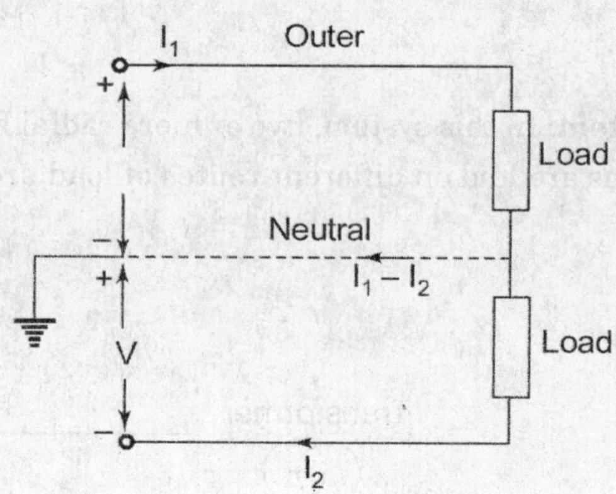

This system is used for transmission purpose.

2. According to types of construction of distribution systems:

(*a*) **Overhead**

(*b*) **Underground**

(*a*) The overhead system is generally employed for distribution as it is cheaper than underground system.

(*b*) The underground system is used at places where overhead construction is impracticable.

3. According to the scheme of connection of distribution system.

(*a*) **Radial system**

(*b*) **Parallel system**

(*c*) **Ring system**

(*d*) **Interconnected system**

(*a*) **Radial system:** In this system, separate feeder radiates from a substation and feed the distribution at one end only.

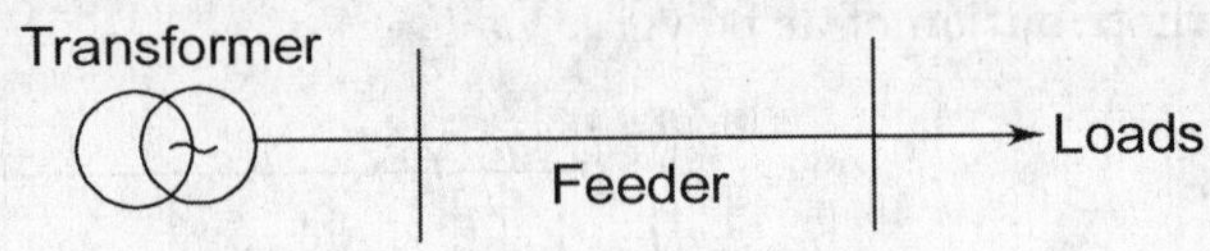

This system is simplest, most economical and most commonly used one.

(*b*) **Parallel system:** In this system, two radial feeders originated from the same or different substation are run in parallel. Each feeder, though cable of supplying the entire load, share the total and equally in normal conditions.

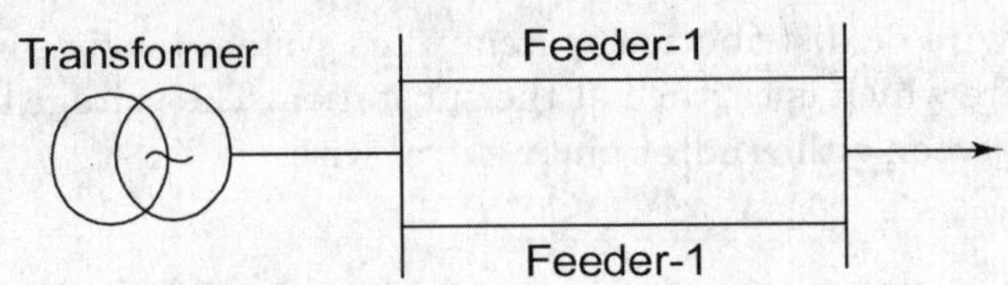

(*c*) **Ring system:** In this system, two or more radial feeders originating from the same or different substations are laid on different routes of load areas.

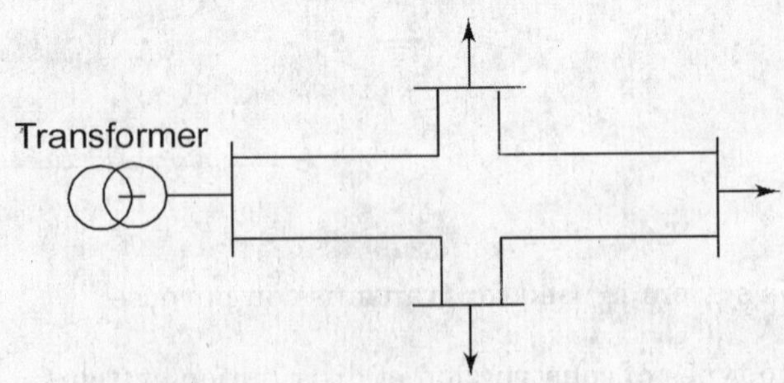

This system is most reliable for continuity of supply and gives better voltage regulation and less power losses.

(*d*) **Inter-connected system:** When the feeder of ring main is energised from two or more than two generating stations or substation it is called the interconnected system.

This system provides better reliability and flexibility and is employed is large metropolitan cities where continuity of supply is the most important.

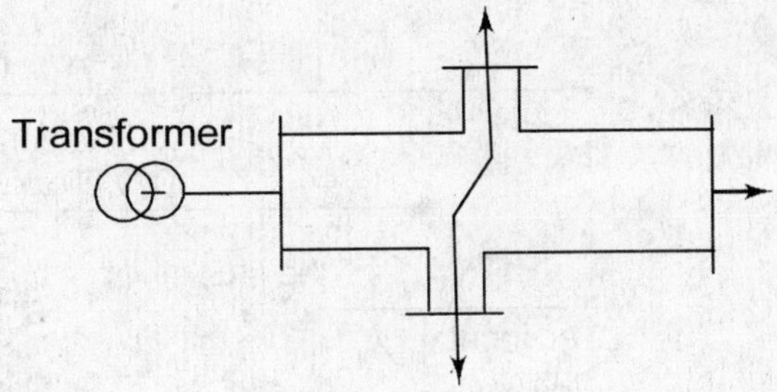

4. (*a*) **Vacuum Tube Voltmeter (VTVM)**

Definition : The voltmeter which uses the vacuum tube for amplifying the measurand AC and DC voltage is known as the vacuum tube voltmeter (VTM). The vacuum tube increases the sensitivity of the voltmeter because of which it can detect the signal of very weak strength.

The electronic voltmeter is used for measuring the voltage of direct, RMS and peak voltage of the system. The vacuum tube has many advantages like they have high input impedance, wide frequency range and high sensitivity.

The most significant advantage of the VTM is that it can draw very less current as compared to the other meter. In VTM, the measuring signal is directly supplied to the vacuum tube of the meter. The vacuum tube is amplifying the signal and pass it to the deflecting meter.

Types of Vacuum tube Voltmeter

The Vacuum Tube Voltmeter is classified into the following types.

1. Diode Type
   - Peak Reading Diode Vacuum Tube Voltmeter
2. Single Triode
3. Balanced Triode Type
4. Rectifiers Amplifier Type
5. Amplifier Rectifier Type

Simple Diode Type Voltmeter

The circuit of the diode voltmeter consists the PMMC meter, load resistor, vacuum tube diode. The vacuum tube diode connects in series with resistance raises the strength of the weak signal. Because of the vacuum tube, the system becomes more sensitive than the normal voltmeter.

For obtaining the accurate reading from the voltmeter, it is essential that their current and voltage are directly proportional to each other. This can be done by the help of the series resistor. The circuit diagram of the diode vacuum tube voltmeter is shown in the figure

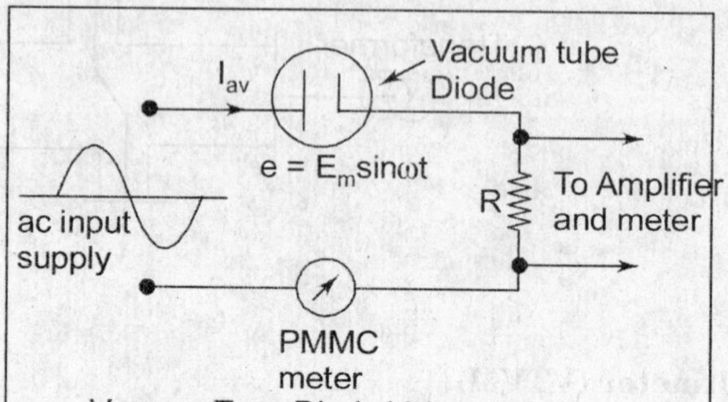

Vacuum Type Diode Voltmeter

Demerits:

* Accurate readings can be obtained only for sine waves.
* It cannot make current measurements directly. The resistance of the series resistor is very high as compared to the resistance of the vacuum tube diode. Thus the resistance of the tube is neglected. The linear relationship is obtained between the voltage and current. The input supply deflects the pointer of the PMMC meter which indicates the magnitude of the measured voltage.

In Diode vacuum voltmeter,

- The value of the input resistance of the voltmeter is equal to the series resistance because high voltage resistor decreases the sensitivity of the meter.
- The frequency range of the diode voltmeter depends on the value of the series resistance. The higher value of the series resistance decreases the frequency range of the meter.
- The vacuum tube voltmeter is used in limited applications because of the low input resistance and limited frequency range.

(*b*) **Forward Biased P-N Junction**

When we connect p-type region of a junction with the positive terminal of a voltage source and n-type region with the negative terminal of the voltage source, then the junction is said to be forward biased. At this condition, due to the attraction of positive terminal of source, electrons which participated in covalent bond creations in p-type material, will be attracted towards the terminal. As result numbers of covalent bonds are broken and, electrons are shifted towards the positive terminal. As a result, the concentration of electrons in the crystal nearer to the terminal increases and these electrons recombine with holes here. In this way, the number of holes increases in the portion of the p-type region away from the junction, and it is reduced in the portion of p-type region nearer to the terminal. As such holes are shifted from terminal to junction.

Due to the higher concentration of holes adjacent to negative impurity ions layer the electrons of negative ions come out and recombine with those holes and create new holes in the layer. Consequently, the width of this negative ions layer is reduced and finally this layer vanishes.

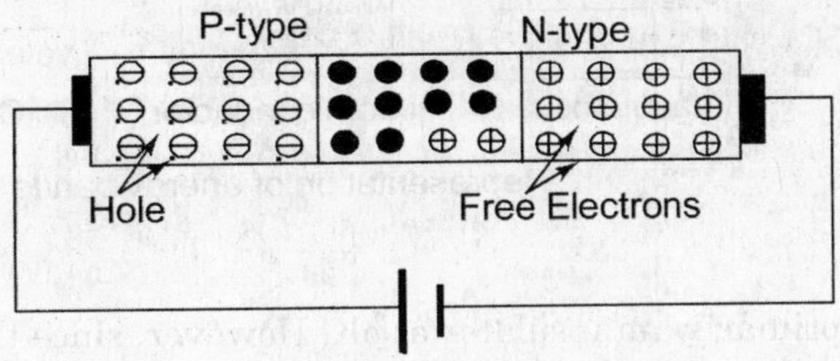

Similarly due to the negative terminal of source the free electrons in the n-type region will ripple towards junction where they will find the layer of positive impurity ions and start recombine with these ions and generate free electrons inside the layer. Consequently, the width of positive impurity ions is reduced, and finally, it vanishes.

In these ways, both layers of ions disappear, and there will be no more depletion layer. After the depletion layer disappeared, free electrons from the n-type region can easily drift to p-type region and holes from p-type region to n-type region in the crystal. Hence, ideally there will be no obstruction of flowing current and the pn junction behaves as the short circuit.

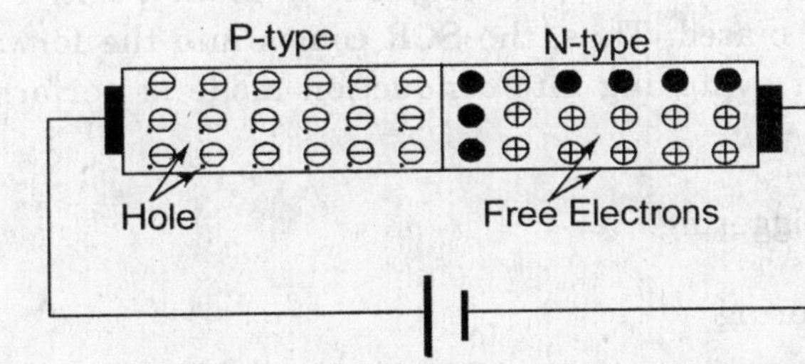

(*c*) **Doping**

In semiconductor production, doping is the intentional introduction of impurities into an intrinsic semiconductor for the purpose of modulating its electrical properties. The doped material is referred to as extrinsic semiconductors. A semiconductor doped to such high levels that it acts more like a conductor than a semiconductor is referred to as a degenerate semiconductor.

The electrical properties of a given material depend on the electronic populations of the different allowed bands. Electrical conduction is the result of electron motion within each band. When an electric field is applied to the material, electrons start to move in the direction opposed to the direction of the electric field. An empty energy band (in which there is no free electron) does not of course participate in the formation of an electric current. It is also the case for a fully occupied band. Indeed, an electron can move provided that, whenever it leaves its site, it can find some free space elsewhere (another available site within its energy band, called a "hole"), where it can go. A material with fully occupied or empty energy bands is then an insulator. This is the case when the gap energy exteeds ~9eV, because for such gaps, the thermal energy at 300K (~25 meV) is clearly insufficient to allow electrons from the valence band to be promoted to the conduction band. In this case the valence band (and all bands of lower energy) is fully occupied, and the conduction band is empty.

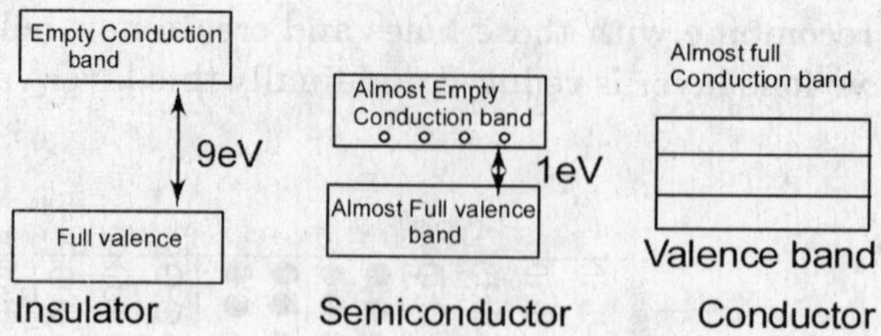

Representation of energy bands

A semiconductor is primarily an insulator at oK. However, since the energy gap is lower compared to insulators (~ leV), the valence band is slightly thermally populated at room temperature, whereas the conduction band is slightly depopulated. Since electrical conduction is directly connected to the number of electrons in the "almost empty" conduction band and to the number of holes in the "almost fully occupied" valence band, it can be expected that the electrical conductivity of such an intrinsic semiconducior will be very small.

For a conductor, conduction bands and valence bands are not separated and there is therefore no energy gap. The conduction band is then partially occupied (even at low temperatures), resulting in a "high" electrical conductivity.

5. (*a*) **SCR Triggering or Turn ON Methods**

With a voltage applied to the SCR, if the anode is made positive with respect to the cathode, the SCR becomes forward biased. Thus, the SCR comes into the forward blocking state. The SCR can be made to conduct or switching into conduction mode is performed by any one of the following methods.

1. Forward voltage triggering
2. Temperature triggering
3. Dv/dt triggering
4. Light triggering
5. Gate triggering

Gate Triggering

This is most common and efficient method to turn ON the SCR. When the SCR is forward biased, a sufficient voltage at the gate terminal injects some electrons into the junction J2. This result to increase reverse leakage current and hence the breakdown of junction J2 even at the voltage lower than the V_{BO}.

Depends on the size of the SCR the gate current varies from a few milli-amps to 200 milli amps or more. If the gate current applied is more, then more electrons are injected into the junction J2 and results to come into the conduction state at much lower applied voltage.

In gate triggering method, a positive voltage applied between the gate and the cathode terminals. We can use three types of gate signals to turn On the SCR. Those are DC signal, AC signal and pulse signal.

Dynamic Turn ON Switching Characteristics

Delay Time (t_d)

The delay time is measured from the instant at which the gate current reaches 90 percent of its final value to the instant at which anode current reaches 10 percent of its final value. It can also define as the time between which anode voltage falls from initial anode voltage value Va to 0.9 Va .

Consider the below figure and observe that, until the time td, the SCR is in forward blocking mode so the anode current is the small leakage current. When the gate signal is applied (at 90 percent of Ig) then the gate current is reached to 0.1 la and also correspondingly anode to cathode voltage falls to 0.9 VA.

With the gate signal applied, there will be non-uniform distribution of current over the cathode surface so the current density is much higher at gate terminal. And it rapidly decreases as the distance from gate increases. Hence, the delay time t_d is the time during which anode current flows in a narrow region at which current density(gate current) is highest.

Rise Time (tr)

This is the time taken by the anode current to rise from 10 percent to 90 percent of its final value. Also called as the time required for the forward blocking voltage to fall from 0.9Va to 0.1 Va. This rise time is inversely proportional to the gate current and its rate of building up.

Therefore, if high and steep current pulses are applied at the gate reduces the rise time tr. Also, if the load is inductive this rise time will be higher and for resistive and capacitive loads it is low.

During this time, turn ON losses in the SCR are high due to large anode current and high anode voltage occurs simultaneously. This can result in the formation of local hot spots and hence the SCR may be damaged.

Spread Time (ts)

This is the time taken by the anode current to rise from 0.9 Ia to Ia. Also the time required for the forward blocking voltage to fall from 0.1Va to its ON-state voltage drop which is the range of 1 to 1.5 volts. During this time anode current spread over the entire conducting region of an SCR from a narrow

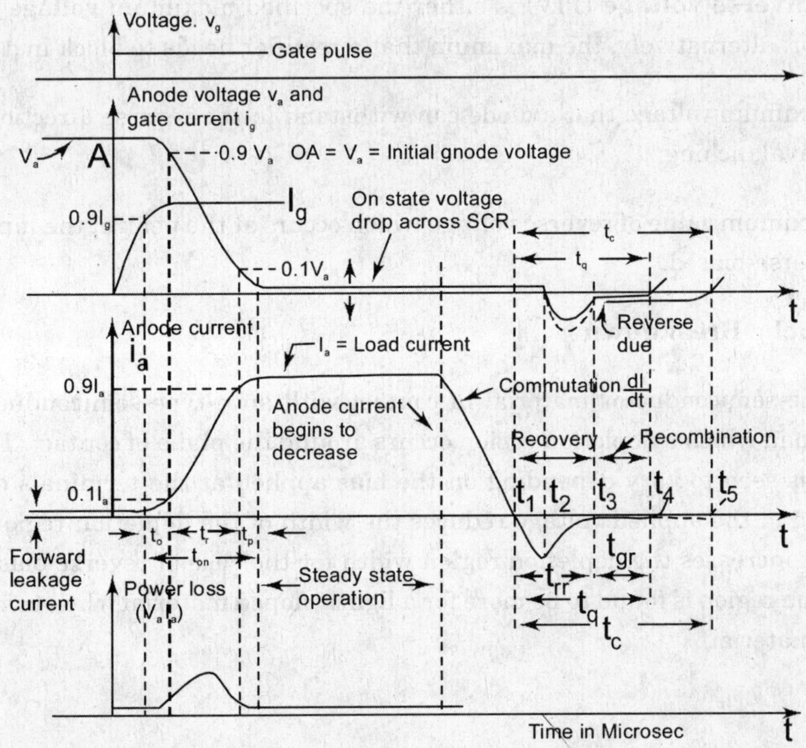

Conducting region. After spreading time, a full anode current flow through the device with small On-state voltage drop.

Therefore, the total turn ON time,

$$Ton = tr + td + ts$$

The typical value of the trun ON time is in the order of 1 to 4 micro seconds depends on the gate signal wave shapes and anode circuit parameters. To reduce the turn ON time of the SCR, the amplitude of the gate pulse should be in the order of 3 to 5 times the minimum gate current of the SCR.

(*b*) (*i*) At $V_{GS} = 0$, in response to small applied voltage V_{DS}, the n-type bar acts as a simple semiconductor resistor and the current I_D incresae linearly with V_{DS}. As V_{DS} increases, the voltage drop along the channel also increases. This increase in voltage drop increases the reverse bias on gate-source junction and causes the depletion regions to penetrate into the channel, reducing channel width. The effect of reduction in channel width provides more opposite to increase in drain current I_D. Thus, rate of increases in I_D with respect to V_{DS} in now reduced. This is shown by the curved shape in the characteristics.

At some value of V_{DS}, drain current I_D cannot be increased further, due to reduction in channel width. Any further increase in V_{DS} does not increase the drain current I_D. I_D approaches the constant saturation value. The voltage V_{DS} at which the current I_D reaches to its constant saturation level is called 'Pinch-off Voltage' V_P The pinch-off voltage V_p is given by,

$$|V_p| = qND2\varepsilon a_2$$

(*ii*) **Peak Inverse Voltage**

Peak inverse voltage (PIV) is either the specified maximum voltage that a diode rectifier can block, or, alternatively, the maximum that a rectifier needs to block in a given application.

- Maximum voltage that a diode can withstand in the reverse direction without breaking down or avalanching.
- Maximum value of reverse voltage which occurs at the peak of the input cycle when the diode is reverse-biased.

(*iii*) **Avalanche Breakdown**

A p-type semiconductor material in contact with an n-type semiconductor material forms a p-n junction in which a depletion region occurs around the plane of contact. The width of this depletion region is seen to vary depending on the bias applied at the terminals of the p-n junction i.e. an increase in the applied voltage reduces the width of the depletion region in case of forward bias, while it increases the depletion region width for the case of reverse bias. Further the span of the depletion region is found to be more for a lightly doped material when compared to that of a heavily doped material.

Figure I shows the I-V characteristics of such a p-n junction both for the case of forward- as well as reverse-bias. From the figure, it is clear that the current through the semiconductor rises with an increase in the magnitude of the applied voltage when the p-n junction is forward biased.

Further it is seen that there will be a certain amount of minimum current flowing through the p-n junction under the reverse bias condition. This current is referred to as the reverse saturation current (I_s) and is due to the minority charge carriers in the semiconductor device.

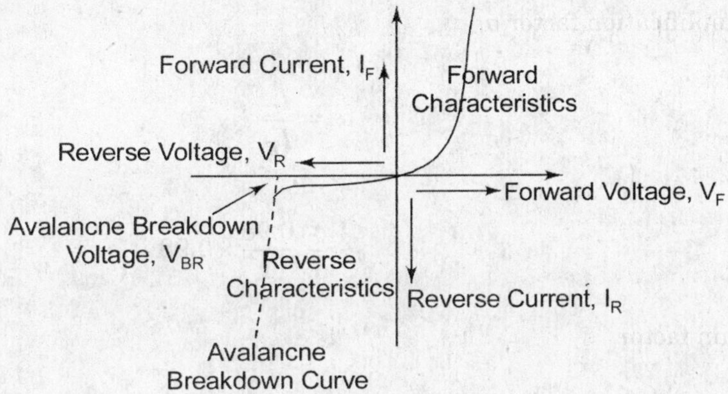

Figure 1 I-V Curve for a P-N Junction Depicting Avalanche Breakdown Phenomenon

Moreover I_s is observed to be almost independent of the applied voltage at its initial stage. However after reaching a particular point, the junction breaks-down leading to the heavy flow of reverse current through the derive. This is because, as the magnitude of the reverse voltage increases, the kinetic energy of the minority charge carries also increase. These fast moving electrons collide with the other atoms in the derive to knock-off same more electrons from them. The electrons so released further release much more eletrons from the atoms by breaking the covalent bonds. This process is termed as carrier multiplication and leads to a considerable increase in the flow of current through the p-n junction. The associated phenomenon is called Avalanche Breakdown (shown in red color in the figure) and the corresponding voltage is Avalanche Breakdown Voltage (V_{BR}).

The efficiency of Avalanche breakdown can be expressed in terms of multiplication factor, M given by

$$M = \frac{1}{1 - \left|\frac{V}{Vm}\right|^n} \quad \text{Where, } 2 < n < 6$$

Here, V and V_{BR} represent the applied voltage and the breakdown voltage, respectively.

Avalanche breakdown occurs in lightly doped p-n junctions when the reverse voltage increase beyond 5 V. Further it is difficult to control this phenomenon as the number of charge carriers generated cannot be directly controlled. Moreover the Avalanche breakdown voltage has positive temtperature coefficient meaning which the Avalanche which the Avalanche breakdown voltage increases with the increase in the junction temperature.

(*c*)

$$I_C = 0.9\text{mA}$$

$$I_B = 0.02\text{mA}$$

(*i*) Emitter current

$$I_E = I_B + I_C$$

$$= (0.98 + 0.02)\text{mA} = 1\text{mA}$$

(*ii*) Current amplification factor α

$$\alpha = \frac{I_C}{I_E}$$

$$= \frac{0.98}{1} \times 0.98$$

(*iii*) Current gain factor

$$\beta = \frac{I_C}{I_B}$$

$$= \frac{0.98}{0.02} = 49$$

6. (*a*)

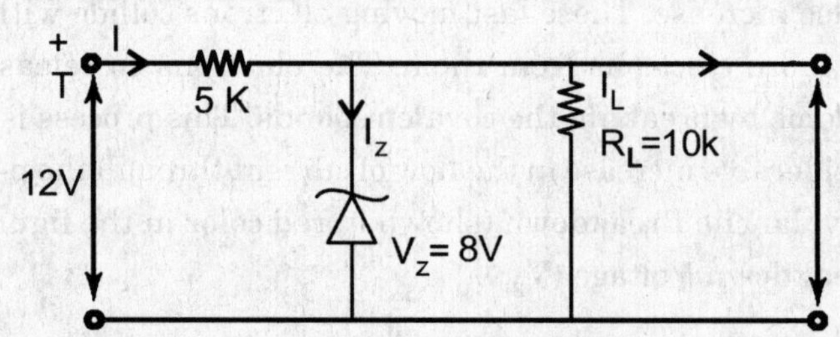

$$I = I_Z + I_L$$

$$I_L = \frac{V_L}{R_L}$$

$$I_L = \frac{8}{10} = 0.8\text{mA}$$

$$I = \frac{12 - 8}{5 \times 10^3} = 0.8\text{mA}$$

$$I_Z = I - I_L$$

$$= 0.8 - 0.8 = 0\text{mA}$$

(*i*) O/p voltage

$$V_o = 10 \times 0.8$$

$$= 8V$$

(*ii*) Voltage across

$$R_s = 5 \times 0.8$$

$$= 4V$$

(*iii*) Current through zene diode

$$I_Z = 0mA$$

(*b*) **V-I characteristic of Unijunction transistor (UJT)**

The unijunction transistor characteristic is shown in below figure,

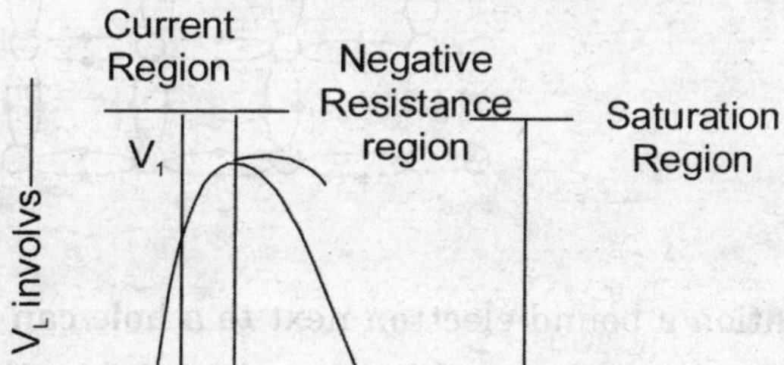

The emitter voltage V_E is applied between emitter E and base Bl. V_E is positive with respect Bl. Let increasing this voltage from zero. The P-N Junction is reverse biased and emitter current I_E is negative as long as the emitter voltage $V_E < \eta V_{BB}$ as shown by the curve PS. The current flowing are very close to the reverse leakage current of PN junction reverse biased. At point B, the emitter voltage V_E is equal to $\eta V_{BB} + V_D$ the PN junction is forward biased and UJT starts conducting. The point B is known as the peak point and the voltage and current across its known as peak point voltage (V_p) and peak point current (I_p) respectively. The emitter voltage V_E decreases with increase in emitter current I_E. Due to drop in resistance rbl with increase in the value of I_E reduction in voltage across UJT. Thus the device exhibits a negative resistance region as shown by the curve BC. The entire base region is saturated at point C and rbl does not decrease any more. As shown in curve CQ, the rise in voltage V_E so further increase in I_E. The point C is known as valley voltage and the voltage and current across is known as valley voltage (V_V) and valley current (Iv).

(c) (i) **Intrinsic or pure semiconductor:** The conduction band of silicon and germanium is empty and the valence band is fully filled up with electrons at very low temperature. Germanium and silicon have four valence electrons. Each atom of germanium silicon shares one electron with its neighboring atom. Thus covalent bond is made. So, there is no free electron in germanium and silicon. For this reason there is no conduction of electricity in them. Such pure semiconductors are known as intrinsic semiconductors. If pure semiconductors are heated at high temperature due to thermal agitation electrons of pure semiconductors becomes free by breaking the bonds. The electrons can pass forbidden gap if the energy of their electrons is very large and transferred into conduction band. When an electron goes into conduction band from valence band there a vacancy occurs. The vacancy makes a hole and this hole is equal to a positive charge.

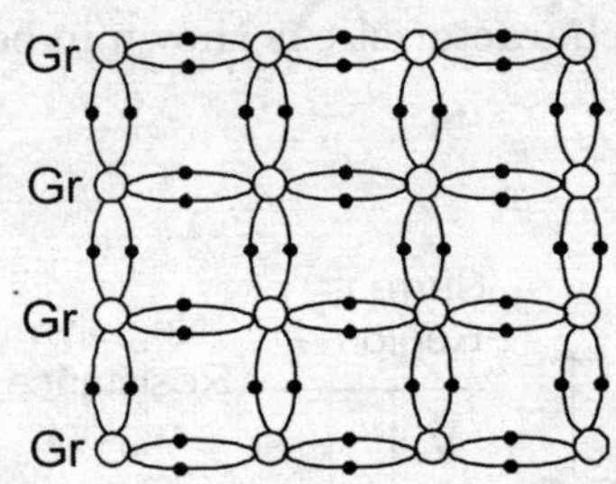

Due to thermal vibration a bound electron next to a hole can move across to fill the gap. The net motion of the negative charge from a bound position to another being in effect equivalent to the motion of a hole in the opposite direction. This means the transfer of a hole is the transfer of positive charge. A hole is positive charge so flowing of holes mean flowing of current. Holes and electrons acts as charge carriers. Transferring of a hole and electron is shown in a figure. The number of electrons and holes are equal in pure on intrinsic semiconductor. Electron-hole bond pair forms due to thermal agitation. Hence the number of holes and electrons becomes equal in pure semiconductor.

Extrinsic semiconductors or impure: We know that due to thermal agitation charger carrier are produced in pure semiconductor. At normal temperature the charge carrier in pure semiconductors is very small. So the electrical conductivity is also very low in this situation. The small current has no importance practically. It has been found that if a small amount of impurity is added with -the pure semiconductor the charge carrier increases. The mixing amount is one part in million. Hence the conductivity of the semiconductor increases. I this system of mixing suitable impurity is called doping or doping semiconductor. Semiconductor doping is the process of making impure semiconductor.

This type of mixed semiconductor is called extrinsic semiconductor or impure semiconductor. Aluminum, arsenic, antimony, gallium etc impurities are mixed in silicon or germanium.

Extrinsic or impure semiconductors are classified into two types, viz n-type and p-type semiconductors, n-type semiconductor means negative type semiconductor and p-type semiconductor means positive type semiconductor.

(*ii*) **p-type**

In a pure (intrinsic) Si or Ge semiconductor, each nucleus uses its four valence electrons to form four covalent bonds with its neighbors (see figure below). Each ionic core, consisting of the nucleus and non-valent electrons, has a net charge of +4, and is surrounded by 4 valence electrons. Since there are no excess electrons or holes In this case, the number of electrons and holes'present at any given time will always be equal.

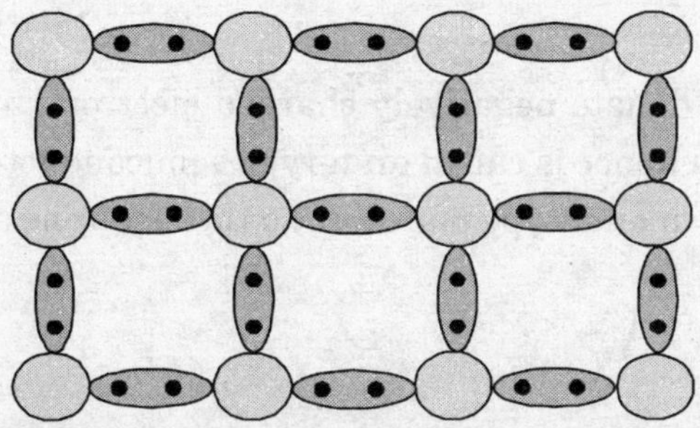

Now, if one of the atoms in the semiconductor lattice is replaced by an element with three valence electrons, such as a Group 3 element like Boron (B) or Gallium (Ga), the electron-hole balance will be changed. This impurity will only be able to contribute three valence electrons to the lattice, therefore leaving one excess hole (see figure below). Since holes will "accept" free electrons, a Group 3 impurity is also called an acceptor.

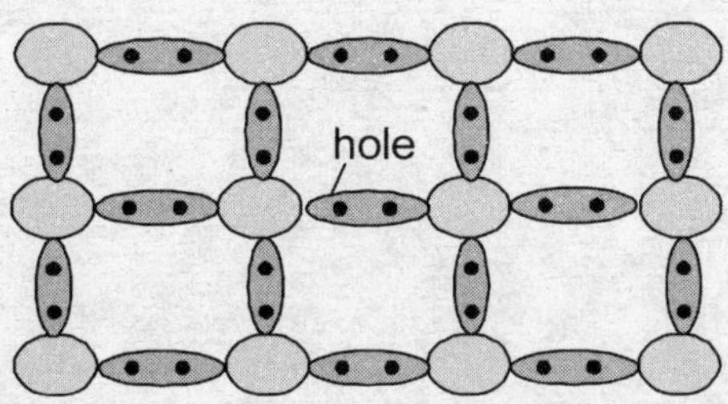

Because an acceptor donates excess holes, which are considered to be positively charged, a semiconductor that has been doped with an acceptor is called a p-type semiconductor; "p" stands for positive. Notice that the material as a hole remains electrically neutral. In a p-type semiconductor, current is largely carried by the holes, which outnumber the free electrons. In this case, the holes are the majority carriers, while the electrons are the minority carriers.

n-type

In addition to replacing one of the lattice atoms with a Group 3 atom, we can also replace it by an atom with five valence electrons, such as the Group 5 atoms arsenic (As) or phosphorus (P). In this case, the impurity adds five valence electrons to the lattice where it can only hold four. This means that there is now one excess electron in the lattice (see figure below). Because it donates an electron, a Group 5 impurity is called a donor. Note that the material remains electrically neutral.

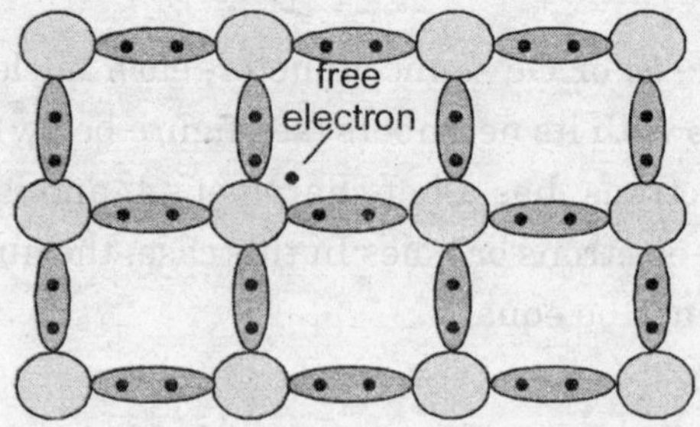

Donor impurities donate negatively charged electrons to the lattice, so a semiconductor that has been doped with a donor is called an n-type semiconductor; "n" stands for negative. Free electrons out number holes in an n-type material, so the electrons are the majority carriers and holes are the minority carriers.

■■

Solved Paper 2009

Electrical Engineering

(Paper II)

1. (*a*) State Norton's theorem. (5)

(*b*) A coil of insulated wire of 500 turns and resistance of 4 Ω is closely wound on an iron ring. The ring has a mean diameter of 0.25 m and a uniform cross-sectional area of 700 mm^2. Calculate the total flux in the ring when a DC supply of 6V is applied to the ends of the winding. Assume relative permeability of iron is 500. (15)

(*c*) Determine the current I in the network shown in fig. by Thevenin's theorem. (10)

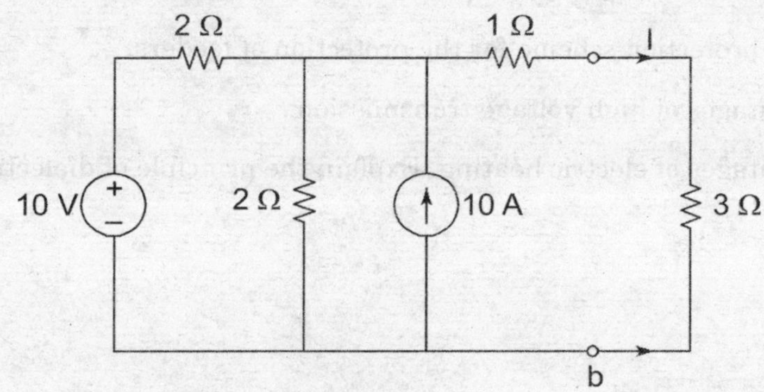

Fig.

2. (*a*) A coil of resistance 10 Ω and inductance 0.02 H is connected in series with another coil of resistance 6 Ω and inductance 15 mH across a 230 V, 50Hz supply. Calculate

(i) Impedance of circuit

(*ii*) Voltage drop across each coil

(*iii*) Total power consumed by the circuit (15)

(*b*) Describe with the aid of a carefully labelled diagram, the construction and working of electrodynamic type wattmeter. (10)

(*c*) Explain the working of single phase bridge rectifier. (5)

3. (*a*) Explain the tests to be performed on a transformer to determine the equivalent circuit parameters of transformer. (15)

(*b*) A 250 V DC shunt motor having an armature resistance of 0.25Ω carries an armature current of 50A and runs at 750 rpm. If the flux is reduced by 10%, find the speed. Assume that the load torque remains same. (15)

4. (*a*) A 3-phase star connected alternator is rated at 1600 KVA, 13500 V. The effective armature resistance and synchronous reactance are 1.5Ω and 30Ω respectively per phase. Calculate the percentage regulation for a load of 1280 kW at power factor of

(*i*) 0.8 leading

(*ii*) unity. (15)

(*b*) Describe with diagrams the working of the following induction motor starters: (15)

(*i*) Direct on-line starter

(*ii*) Autotransformer starter

(*iii*) Star-delta starter

5. (*a*) Define power factor and explain why in general, it should be kept as high as possible in power supply systems. Show with phasor diagram. How the power factor of load can be improved by connecting a capacitor in parallel with it. (15)

(*b*) With the help of labelled diagram explain the working of thermal power plant (15)

6. (*a*) Describe distance protection scheme for the protection of feeders. (10)

(*b*) Discuss the advantages of high voltage transmission. (10)

(*c*) Discuss the advantages of electric heating. Explain the principle of dielectric heating. (10)

EXPLANATIONS

1. (*a*) **Norton's theorem**

Nortons theorem states that " a linear two terminal circuit can be replaced by an equivalent current source in I_N parallel with a resistance R_N where R_N is the input or equivalent resistance at the terminals and I_N is the short circuit current through the terminals when all the independent sources are turned off.

Figure 1(a) circuit is a linear two terminal circuit, According to Norton's theorem we replace this circuit by a current source and a equivalent resistance that is figure (b).

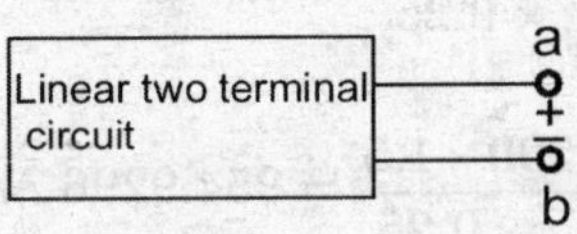

Figure 1(a)

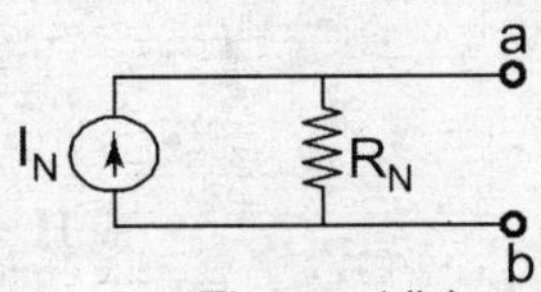

Figure 1(b)

From source transformation The Thevenin's and Norton's resistances are equal

$$R_N = R_{th}$$

As two terminal linear circuit is replaced to Norton's equivalent circuit so they are equal. To find Norton's current I_N from a to be terminal we have to short circuit and that is becomes figure below

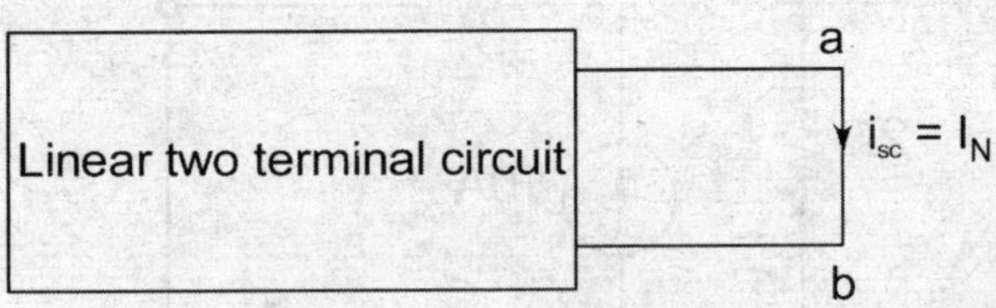

Norton's current I_N is equal to short circuit current, $I_N = i_{sc}$. Independent sources are turned off here as Thevenin's theorem. As we know $R_N = R_{th}$ and $I_N = V_{Th}/R_{Th}$

Norton theorem and Thevenin's theorem are related to source transformation. So source transformation often known as Thevenin-Norton transformation.

As we know $$V_{Th} = V_{oc}, I_N = i_{sc}$$

$$R_{Th} = V_{oc}/i_{sc} = R_N.$$

To find Thevenin's or Norton's equivalent short circuit and open circuit tests are sufficient if one side of the circuit contains at least one independent source.

(*b*) Number of turns = 500

Resistance of coil = 4Ω

Mean diameter of ring = 0.25m

Cross sectional area of ring

$$A = 700\text{mm}^2 = 700 \times 10^{-6}\ \text{m}^2$$

Supply voltage $V_{DC} = 6V$

Relative permeability of iron $\mu_r = 500$

$$\text{Current flowing in coil } I = \frac{V_{DC}}{R} = \frac{6}{4} = 1.5A$$

$$\text{Magnetic field strength } H = \frac{NI}{l} = \frac{500 \times 1.5}{l}$$

$$l = \text{mean circumference}$$

$$= \pi \times 0.25$$

$$H = \frac{500 \times 1.5}{\pi \times 0.25} = 954.9296 \text{ A/m}$$

$$\text{Flux density } B = \mu H = \mu_o \mu_r H = 4\pi \times 10^{-7} \times 500 \times 954.9296$$

$$= 0.6 \text{ wb/m}^2$$

$$\text{Total flux } \phi = B.A = 0.6 \times 700 \times 10^{-6} = 0.42 \text{ mwb}$$

(c)

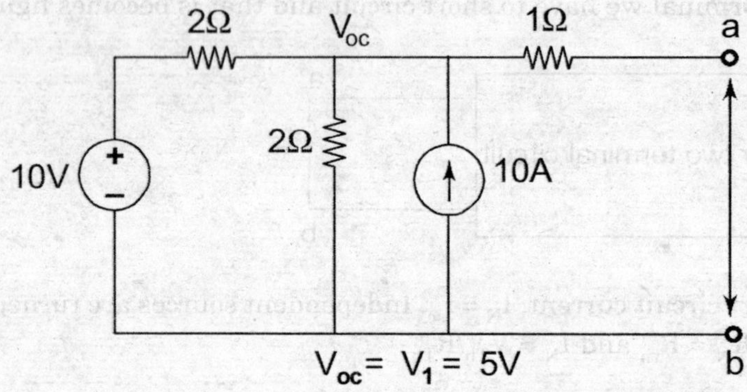

Step 1. Remove R_L 3Ω & find V_{oc}

At node 1,

$$\frac{v_1 - 10}{2} + \frac{v_1}{2} = 10$$

$$V_1 = 5V$$

$$V_{oc} = V_1 = 5V$$

Step 2. diactirate independent sources.

Voltage source – remove it by internal resistance current source – delete the source by open circuit & find internal resistance.

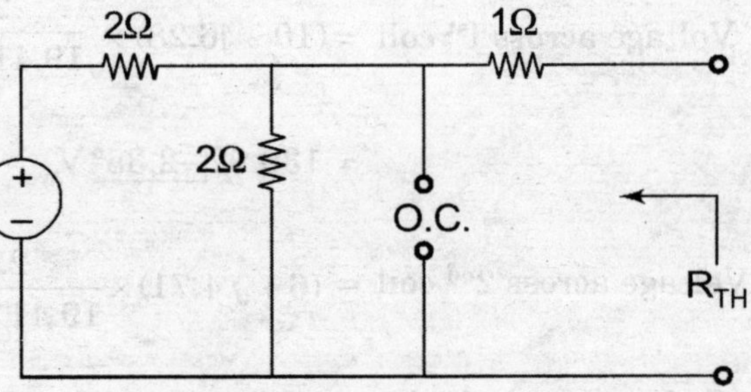

$$R_{Th} = (2 \parallel 2) + 1 = 2\Omega$$

Step 3. Obtain Thevenin's equivalent circuit.

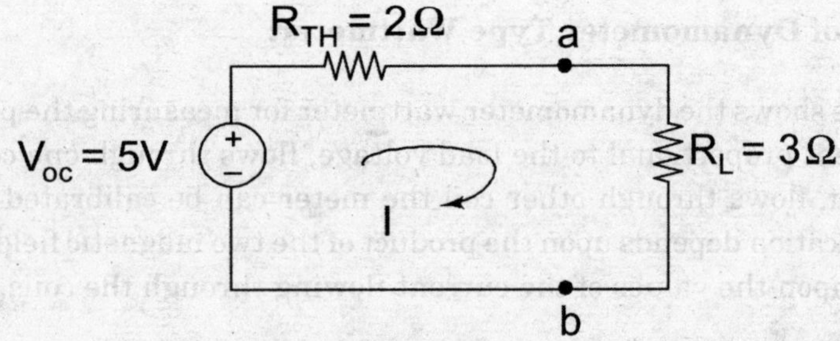

Step 4. Reconnect R_L

$$I = \frac{V_{oc}}{R_{Th} + R_L}$$

$$I = \frac{5}{2+3} = 1A$$

Hence current through 3Ω resistance is 1A.

2. (*a*) $R_1 = 10\Omega$ $L_1 = 0.02H$

$X_{L1} = W_{L1} = 2\pi \times 50 \times 0.02 = 6.283\Omega$

(i) Impedance $= 10 + j2\pi \times 50 \times 0.02 + 6 \times j2\pi \times 50 \times 0.015$

$= 10 + j6.28 + 6 + j4.71$

$R_2 = 6\Omega$

$L_2 = 15 \times 10^{-3}$

$X_{L2} = W_{L2}$

$= 4.71\Omega$

$= 16 + j10.99$

$= 19.41 \angle 34.48°\Omega$

(*ii*) Voltage across I[st] coil $= (10 + j6.28) \times \dfrac{230}{19.41\underline{|34.48^\circ}}$

$= 139.92\underline{|-2.35^\circ}\,V$

Voltage across 2nd coil $= (6 + j\,4.71) \times \dfrac{230}{19.41\underline{|34.48^\circ}}$

$= 90.38\underline{|3.65^\circ}V$

(iii) Total power $= \left[\dfrac{(230)}{(19.41)}\right]^2 \times 16 = 2246.6\ W$

(*b*) **Construction of Dynamometer Type Wattmeter:**

Following figure shows the dynamometer wattmeter for measuring the power. If two coils are connected such that, current proportional to the load voltage, flows through one coil and current proportional to the load current, flows through other coil the meter can be calibrated directly in watts. This is true because the indication depends upon the product of the two magnetic fields. The strength of the magnetic fields depends upon the values of the current flowing through the coils.

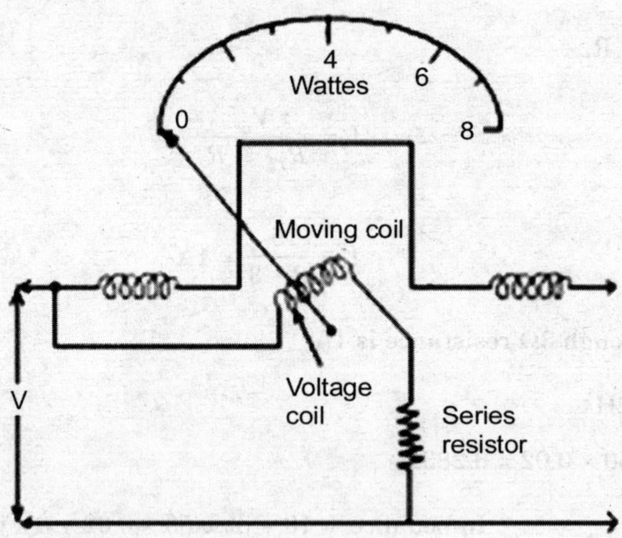

- v = supply voltage
- i = load current and
- R = resistance of the moving coil circuit
- Current through fixed coils, i(f) = I
- Current through the moving coil, i(m) = V/R

Deflecting torque,

$$T_d \ \alpha\ (i_f * i_m)\alpha \frac{iv}{R}$$

- For a DC circuit the deflecting torque is thus proportional to the power.
- For any circuit with fluctuating torque, the instantaneous torque is proportional to instantaneous power. In this case due to inertia of moving parts, the deflection will be proportional to the average power. For sinusoidal alternating quantities the average power is VI cos ϕ, where
- V = r.m.s. value of voltage,
- I = r.m.s. value of current, and
- ϕ = phase angle between V and I

Hence an electrodynamic instrument, when connected as shown in figure, indicates the power, irrespective of the fact it is connected in an AC or DC circuit.

Advantages :

1. In dynamometer type wattmeter, the scale of the instrument is uniform (because deflecting torque is proportional to the true power in both DC as well as AC and the instrument is spring controlled.)
2. High degree of accuracy can be obtained by careful design; hence these are used for calibration purposes.

Disadvantages :

1. The error due to the inductance of the pressure coil at low power factor is very serious
2. In dynamometer type wattmeter, stray field may affect the reading of the instrument. To reduce it, magnetic shielding is provided by enclosing the instrument in an iron case.

(*c*) Single-phase bridge rectifier

It is the most frequently-used circuit for electronic dc power supplies. It requires four diodes but the transformer used is not center-tapped and has a maximum voltage of v_{SM}. The full-wave bridge-rectifier is available in three distinct physics forms.

1. Four discrete diodes,
2. One device inside a four-terminal case,
3. As part of an array of diodes in an I_C

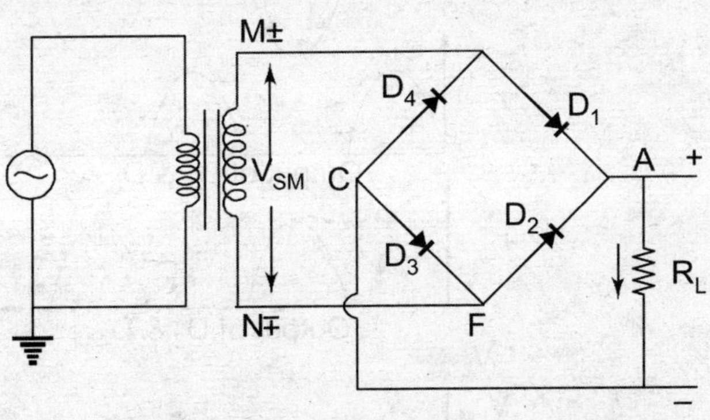

Figure: Single-Phase Bridge rectifier

Working of the circuit

During the positive input half-wave, terminal M of the secondary is positive and N is negetive as shown

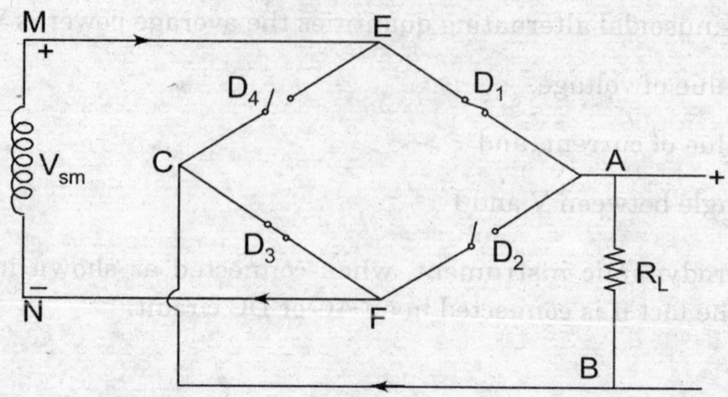

Diode D_1 and D_3 become forward-biased (ON) whereas D_2 and D_4 are reversed-biased (OFF). Hence, current flows along MEABCFN producing a drop across R_L.

During the negetive input half-cycle, secondary terminal N becomes positive and M negative. Now, D_2 and D_4 are forward-biased. Circuit current flows along NFABCEM as shown

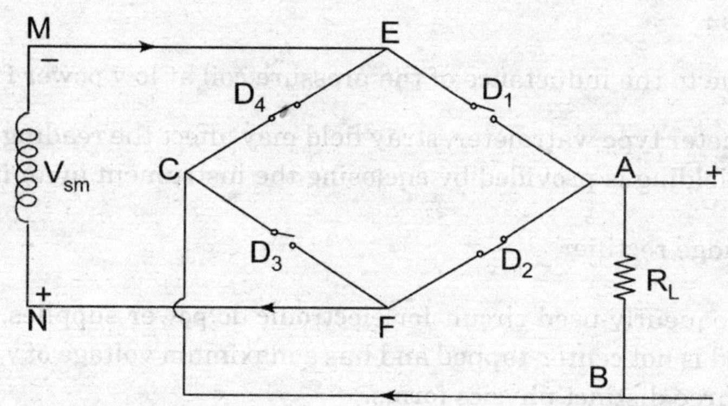

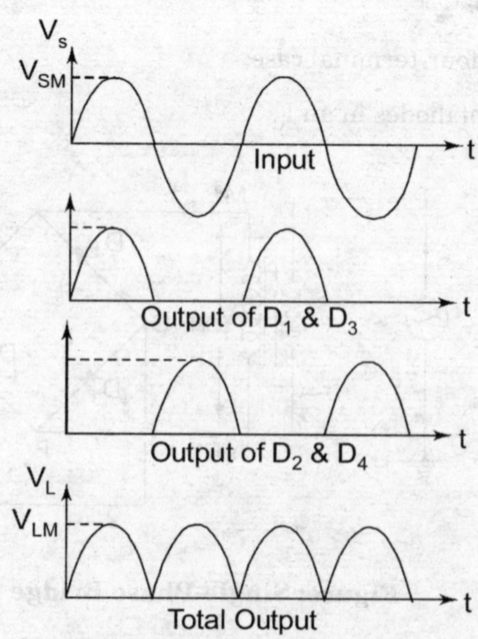

3. (*a*) **Open circuit and Short circuit Test on transformer**

These two transformer tests are performed to find the parameters of equivalent circuit of transformer and losses of the transformer. Open circuit test and short circuit test on transformer are very economical and convenient because they are performed without actually loading of the transformer.

Open circuit or No load test on Transformer

Open circuit test or no load test on a transformer is performed to determine 'no load loss (core loss)' and 'no load current I_0'. The circuit diagram for open circuit test is shown in the figure below.

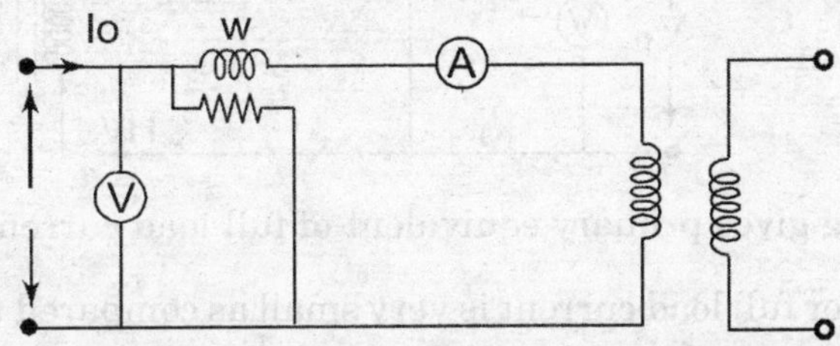

Usually high voltage (HV) winding is kept open and the low voltage (LV) winding is connected to its normal supply. A wattmeter (W), ammeter (A) and voltmeter (V) are connected to the LV winding as shown in the figure. Now, applied voltage is slowly increased from zero to normal rated value of the LV side with the help of a variac. When the applied voltage reaches to the rated value of the LV winding, readings from all the three instruments are taken.

The ammeter reading gives the no load current I_0. As I_0 itself is very small; the voltage drops due to this current can be neglected. .

The input power is indicated by the wattmeter (W). But, as the other side of transformer is open circuited, there is no output power. Hence, this input power only consists of core losses and copper losses. But as described above, short circuit current is so small that these copper losses can be neglected. Hence, now the input power is almost equal to the core losses. Thus, the wattmeter reading gives the core losses of the transformer.

Sometimes, a high resistance voltmeter is connected across the HV winding. Though, a voltmeter is connected, HV winding can be treated as open circuit as the current through the voltmeter is negligibly small. This helps is to find voltage transformation ration (K).

The two components of no load current can be given as,

$$I\mu = I_0 \sin\Phi_o \text{ and } I_w = I_0 \text{Cos}\Phi_0$$

$$\cos\Phi_0 \text{ (no laod power factor) } = W / (V_1 I_0). \qquad \text{... (W = wattmeter reading)}$$

From this, shunt parameters of equivalent circuit parameters of equivalent circuit of transformer (X_0 and R_0) can be calculated as

$$X_0 = V_1/I_\mu \text{ and } R_0 = V_1/I_w.$$

(These values are referring to LV side of the transformer.)

Hence, it is seen that open circuit test gives core losses of transformer and shunt parameters of the equivalent circuit.

Short circuit or Impedance test on Transformer

The connection diagram for short circuit test or impedance test on transformer is as shown in the figure below. The LV side of transformer is short circuited and wattmeter (W), voltmere (V) and ammeter (A) are connected on the HV side of the transformer. Voltage is applied to the HV side and increased from the zero until the ammeter reading equals the rated current. All the readings are taken at this rated current.

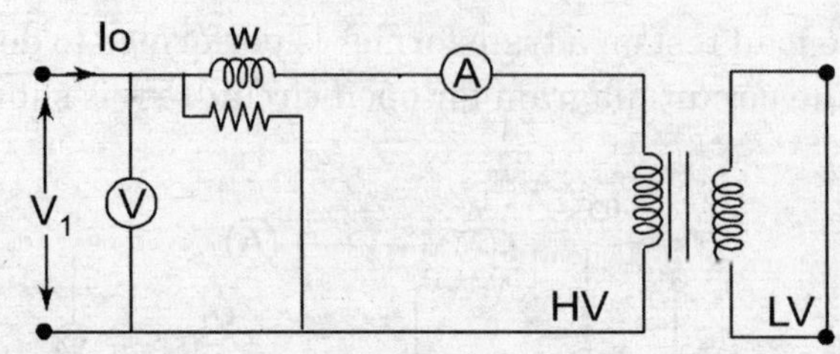

The ammeter reading gives primary equivalent of full load current (I_{sc}).

The voltage applied for full load current is very small as compared to rated voltage. Hence, core loss due to small applied voltage can be neglected. Thus, the wattmeter reading can be taken as copper loss in the transformer.

Therefore, $W = I_{sc}^2 R_{eq}$....... (where R_{eq} is the equivalent resistance of transformer)

$$Z_{eq} = V_{sc}/I_{SC}.$$

Therefore, equivalent reactance of transformer can be calculated from the formula $Z_{eq}^2 = R_{eq}^2 + X_{eq}^2$.

These, values are referred to the HV side of the transformer.

Hence, it is seen that the short circuit test gives copper losses of transformer and approximate equivalent resistance and reactance of the transformer.

(*b*)

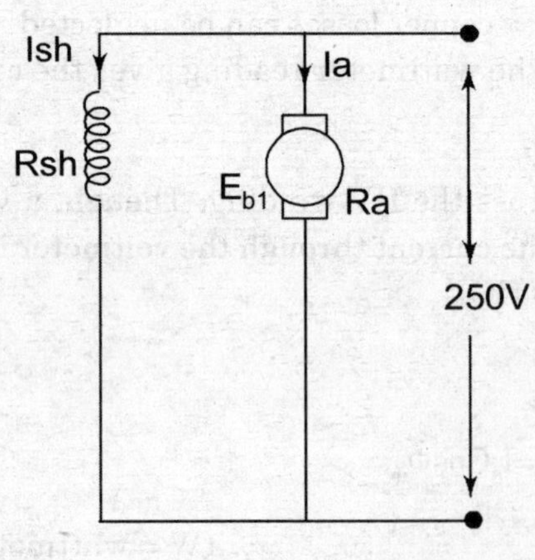

$$\text{Supply voltage} = 250\text{V}$$

$$R_a = 0.25\Omega$$

$$Ia_1 = 50\text{A}$$

$$N = 750 \text{ rpm}$$

$$E_b = V_s - IaRa$$

$$= 250 - 50 \times 0.25 = 237.5\text{V}$$

Now if flux. $\phi_2 = 0.9\phi_1$

and Torque = constant

$$T \propto \phi\, Ia$$

$$\phi_1\, Ia_1 = \phi_2 .\, Ia_2$$

$$Ia_2 = \left(\frac{\phi_1}{\phi_2}\right) Ia_1$$

$$= \frac{1}{0.9} \times 50 = 55.55\text{A}$$

$$E_{b_2} = 250 - 55.55 \times 0.25$$

$$= 236.11\text{V}$$

and $E_b \propto N.\phi$

$$\frac{E_{b_2}}{E_{b_1}} = \left(\frac{N_2}{N_1}\right) \times \left(\frac{\phi_1}{\phi_2}\right)$$

$$N_2 = N_1 \times \left(\frac{E_{b_2}}{E_{b_1}}\right) \times \left(\frac{\phi_1}{\phi_2}\right)$$

$$= 750 \times \frac{236.111}{237.5} \times \frac{1}{0.9}$$

$$= 828.46 \text{ rpm}$$

4. (*a*) $R_a = 1.5\ \Omega$ $X_S = 30\ \Omega$

Lower power = 1280 kw

Alternator KVA rating = 1600 KVA

supply volt line voltage = 13500V = 13.5 kV

(i) Power factor = 0.8 (leading)

$$\cos\phi = 0.8$$

$$P_{load} = \sqrt{3} V_L\, I_L \cos\phi$$

$$1280 \times 10^3 = \sqrt{3} \times 13.5 \times 10^3 \times I_L \times 0.8$$

$$\vec{I}_L \simeq 68.43 \angle 36.87^\circ$$

$$\vec{E}_f = \vec{V}_t + \vec{I}_L (R_a + jX_s)$$

$$= \left(\frac{13500}{\sqrt{3}}\right) + 68.43 \angle 36.87^\circ (1.5 + j30) \qquad \left[Vph = \frac{V_L}{\sqrt{3}}\right]$$

$$|E_f| = 6859.593 \text{ V}$$

$$\therefore \quad \text{voltage regulation} = \frac{|E_g| - |V_t|}{V} \times 100$$

$$= \frac{6859.593 - 7749.229}{7797.229} \times 100$$

(*ii*) Power factor

$$\Rightarrow \quad \cos\phi = 1$$

$$I_L = \frac{P_L}{\sqrt{3}V_L \cos\phi} = \frac{1200 \times 10^3}{\sqrt{3} \times 135 \times 10^3}$$

$$= 54.74 \text{ A}$$

$$\vec{E}_f = \vec{V}_t + \vec{I}_L \vec{Z}_S$$

$$= \left(\frac{13500}{\sqrt{3}}\right)\angle 0° + 54.74\angle 0°(1.5 + j30)$$

$$= 8045.715\angle 11.77°$$

$$|E_f| = 8045.715 \text{ V}$$

$$\therefore \quad \text{Voltage regulation} = \frac{|E_f| - |V|}{|V|} \times 100$$

$$= \frac{8045.715 - 7794.228}{7794.229} \times 100$$

$$= 3.226\%$$

(*b*) (*i*) **Direct on Line Starting Method**

This method is also known as the DOL method for starting the three phase squirrel cage induction motor. In this method we directly switch the stator of the three phase squirrel cage induction motor on to the supply mains. The motor at the time of starting'draws very high starting current (about 5 to 7 times the full load current) for the very short duration. The amount of current drawn by the motor depends upon its design and size. But such a high value of current does not harm the motor because of rugged construction of the squirrel cage induction motor. Such a high value of current causes sudden undesirable voltage drop in the supply voltage. A live example of this sudden drop of voltage is the dimming of the tube lights and bulbs in our homes at the instant of starting of refrigerator motor. Now let us derive the expression for starting torque in terms of full load torque for the direct online starter. We have various quantities that involved in the expression for the starting torque are written below: We define T_s as starting torque

T_f as full load torque

I_f as per phase rotor current at full load

I_s as per phase rotor current at the time of starting

S_f as full load slip

s_s as starting slip

R_2 as rotor resistance

W_s as synchronous speed of the motor

Now we can directly write the expression for torque of induction motor as $T = \frac{1}{W_s} I^2$ From the help of the above expression we write the ratio of starting torque to full load torque as $\frac{T_s}{T_f} = \left(\frac{I_s}{I_f}\right)^2 \times s_f$

Here we have assumed that the rotor resistance is constant and it does not vary with the frequency of the rotor current.

(*ii*) **Auto Transformer Starting Method**

As the name suggests in this method we connect auto transformer in between the three phase power supply and the induction motor as shown in the given diagram:

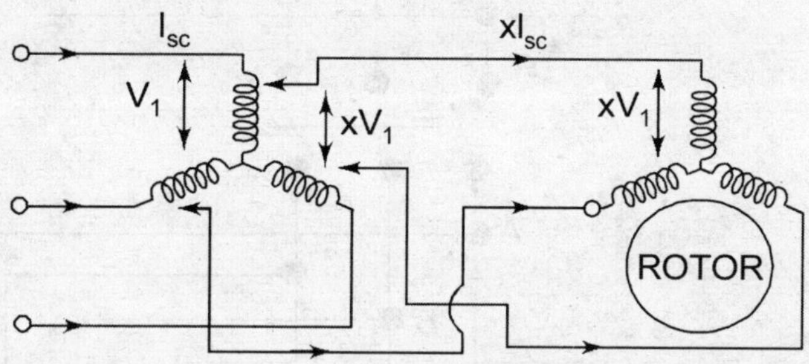

The auto transformer is a step down transformer hence it reduces the per phase supply voltage from V_1 to xV_1. The reduction in voltage reduces current from I_s to xI_s. After the motor reaches to its normal operating speed, the auto transformer is disconnected and then full line voltage is applied. Now let us derive the expression for starting torque in terms of full load torque for the auto transformer starting method. We have various quantities that involved in the expression for the starting torque are written below:

We define T_s as starting torque

T_f as full load torque

I_f as per phase rotor current at full load

I_s as per phase rotor current at the time of starting

s_f as full load slip

s_s as starting slip

R_2 as rotor resistance

W_s as synchronous speed of the motor

Now we can directly write the expression for torque of the induction motor as $T = \frac{1}{W_s} I^2$ From the help of the above expression we write the ratio of starting torque to full load torque as

$$\frac{T_s}{T_f} = \left(\frac{I_s}{I_f}\right)^2 \times s_f \qquad \text{...(i)}$$

Here we have assumed that the rotor resistance is constant and it does not vary with the frequency of the rotor current. From the above equation we can have the expression for the starting torque in terms of the full load torque. Now at the time of starting the per phase voltage is reduced to xV_1, the per phase starting current is also reduced to xI_s. On substituting the

$$\frac{T_s}{T_f} = \left(\frac{xI_s}{I_f}\right)^2 \times s_f$$

Value of I_s as xI_s in equation one. We have $\frac{T_s}{T_f} = \left(\frac{I_s}{I_f}\right)^2 \times s_f \times a^2$. This shows the variation of the starting torque with the value of x.

(*iii*) **Star Delta Starting Method**

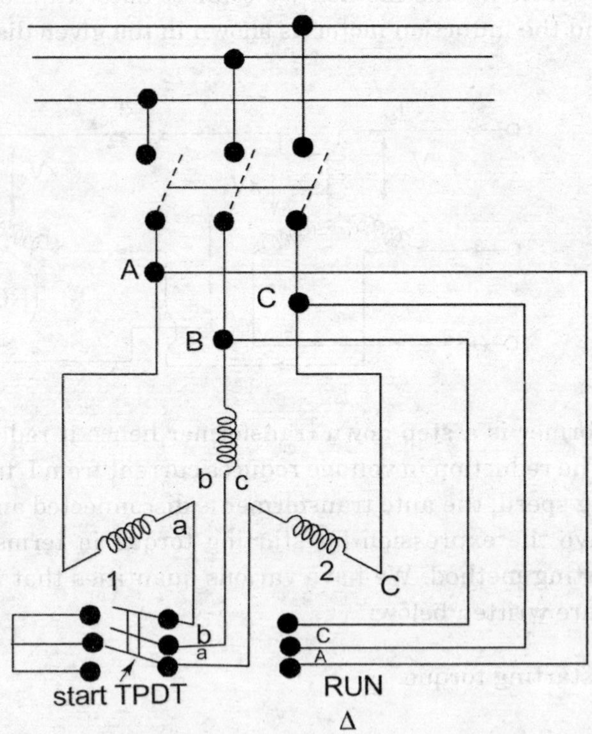

Connection diagram is shown below for star delta method,

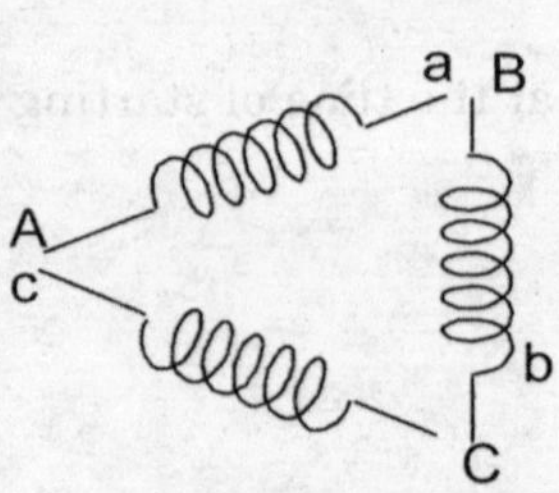

Star Delta

This method is used for the motors designed to operate in delta connected winding. The terminals are marked for the phases of the stator are shown above. Now let us see this method works. The stator phases are first connected to the star by the help of triple pole double throw switch (TPDT switch) in the diagram the position is marked as 1 then after this when the steady state speed is reached the switch is thrown to position 2 as shown in the above diagram.

Now let us analyze the working of the above circuit. In the first position the terminals of the motor are short circuited and in the second position from the diagram the terminal a, b and c are respectively connected to B, C and A. Now let us derive the expression for starting torque in terms of full load torque for the star delta starting method. We have various quantities that involved in the expression for the starting torque are written below

T_f as full load torque

T_s as starting torque

I_f as per phase rotor current at full load

1_s as per phase rotor current at the time of starting

S_f as full load slip

s_s as starting slip

R_2 as rotor resistance

W_s as synchronous speed of the motor

Now we can directly write the expression for Torque of induction motor as $T = \frac{1}{W_s} I^2$ From the help of the above expression we write the ratio of starting torque to full load torque as

$$\frac{T_s}{T_f} = \left(\frac{I_s}{I_f}\right)^2 \times s_f \qquad ...(ii)$$

Here we have assumed that the rotor resistance is constant and it does not vary with the frequency of the rotor current. Let us assume the line voltage to be V_1 then the per phase starting current when connected is star position is I_{ss} which is given by

$$I_{ss} = \frac{V_L}{\sqrt{3} \times Z}$$

When stator is in delta connected position we have starting current $I_{sd} = \frac{V_1}{Z}$ clearly. $I_{sd} = \sqrt{3} \times I_{ss}$ and $I_{fd} = I_{ss}$ From the above equation we have

$$\frac{T_s}{T_f} = \frac{1}{3}\left(\frac{I_{sd}}{I_{fd}}\right)^2 \times s_f \qquad ...(iii)$$

This shows that the reduced voltage method has an advantage of reducing the starting current but the disadvantage is that all these methods of reduced voltage causes the objectionable reduction in the starting torque.

5. (*a*) **Power Factor** is a measure of an electrical systems efficiency. The apparent or total electrical power (Kilo Volt Amperes or kVA) used in an electrical system by an industrial or commercial facility has two components:

- Productive Power (Kilowatts or kW) which produces work.
- Reactive Power (Kilo Volt Amperes Reactive or kVAR) which generates the magnetic fields required in inductive electrical equipment (AC motors, transformers, inductive furnaces, ovens, etc.)

Reactive Power (kVAR) produces no productive work. Because the inductive electrical equipment employing magnetic fields requires this Reactive Power, which produces no productive work, the Total Power (kVA) provided by the generating source (your utility) must always be greater than the Productive Power (kW).

The ratio of Productive Power (kW) to Total Power (kVA) is called the Power Factor (PF = kW / kVA). It is a measure of the systems electrical efficiency in an alternating current circuit and is represented as a % or a decimal.

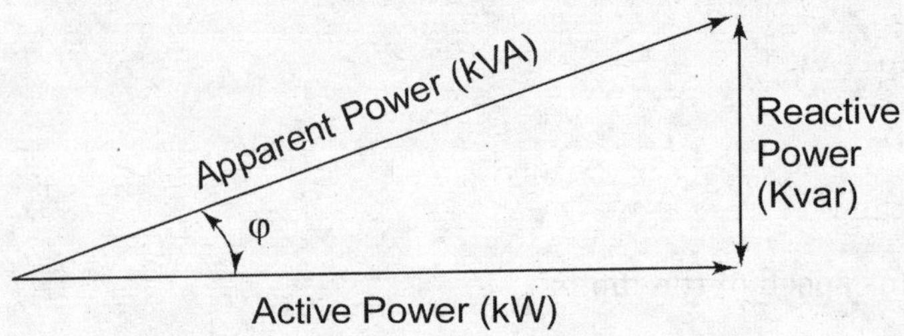

Power triangle

A power factor of less than unity (i.e. < 1) means that the voltage and current waveforms are not in phase reducing the instantaneous product of the two waveforms (v.i.).

In an electrical power system a load with low power factor draws more current than a load with a high power factor for the same amount a load with low power transferred.

The higher current increases the energy lost in the distribution systems and requires larger wires and other equipment. Because of the costs at utilities will reduce to keep high power factor in power supply systems.

$$S^* = P + jQ$$

$$S^* = \sqrt{P^2 + Q^2}$$

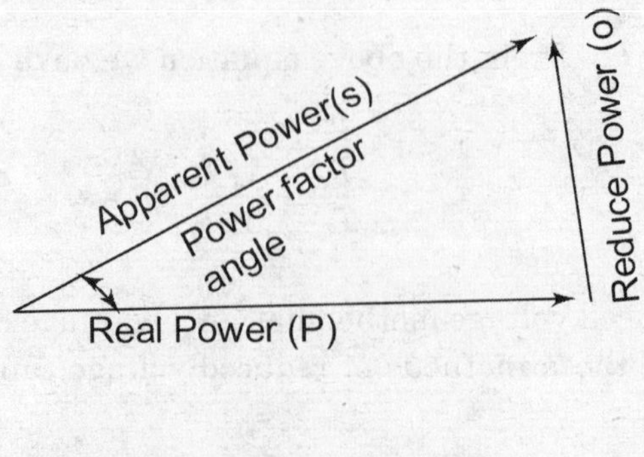

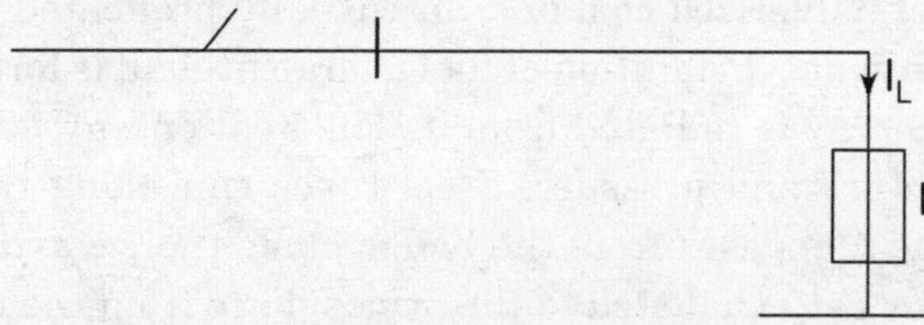

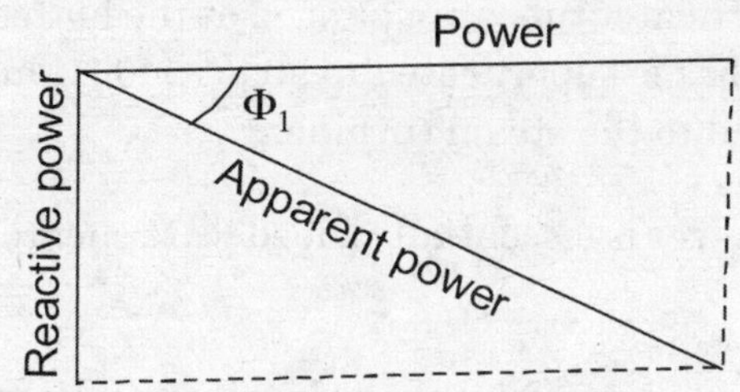

Take a lagging load supplied from a power system load power factor angle is Φ_1 as shown in above figure. Now to improve the power factor. Connecting a capacitor bank in parallel to load which drawn kVAR of approximately the same magnitude as the load kVAR but in phase opposition (leading). The resultant kVA is now smaller and the new power factor ($\cos\Phi_2$) is increased $\cos\Phi_2$ is controlled by the magntiude of the kVAR added. Thus any desired power factor can be obtained by varying the leading kVAR.

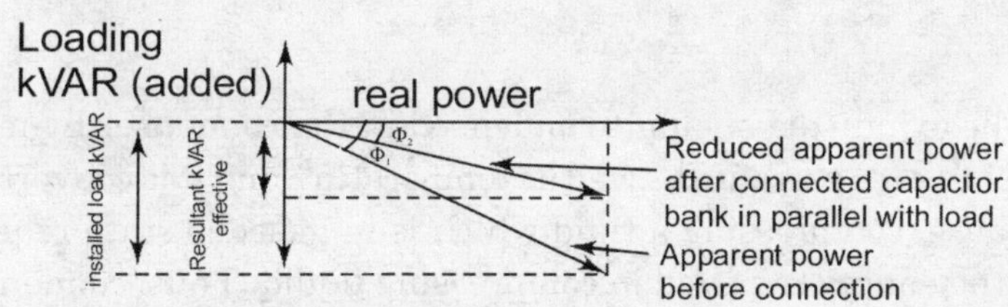

(*b*) Typical layout and working of a Thermal Power Plant

A simplified layout of a thermal power station is shown below.

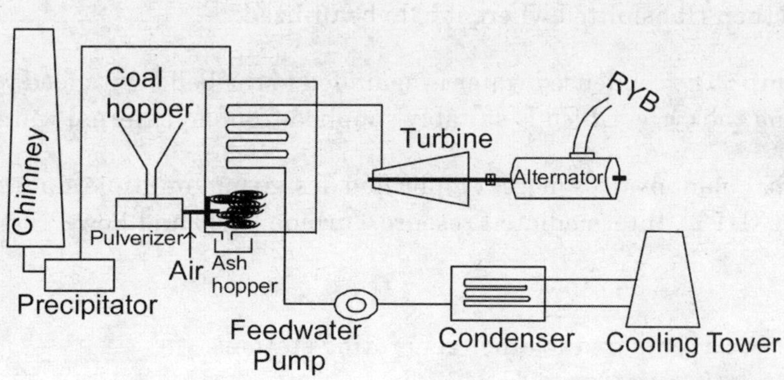

Coal : In a coal based thermal power plant, coal is transported from coal mines to the generating station. Generally, bituminous coal or brown coal is used as fuel. The coal is stored in either 'dead storage' or in 'live storage'. Dead storage is generally 40 days backup coal storage which is used when coal supply is unavailable. Live storage is a raw coal bunker in boiler house. The coal is cleaned in a magnetic cleaner to filter out if any iron particles are present which may cause wear and tear in the equipment. The coal from live storage is first crushed in small particles and then taken into pulverizer to make it in powdered form.

Boiler : The mixture of pulverized coal and air (usually preheated air) is taken into boiler and then burnt in the combustion zone. On ignition of fuel a large fireball is formed at the center of the boiler and large amount of heat energy is radiated from it. The heat energy is utilized to convert the water into steam at high temperature and pressure. Steel tubes run along the boiler walls in which water is converted in steam. The fuel gases from the boiler make their way through superheater, economizer, air preheater and finally get exhausted to the atmosphere from the chimney.

Superheater : The superheater tubes are hanged at the hottest part of the boiler. The saturated steam produced in the boiler tubes is superheated to about 540 °C in the superheater. The superheated high pressure steam is then fed to the steam turbine.

Economizer : An economizer is- essentially a feed water heater which heats the water before supplying to the boiler.

Air pre-heater : The primary air fan takes air from the atmosphere and it is then warmed in the air pre-heater. Pre-heated air is injected with coal in the boiler. The advantage of pre-heating the air is that it improves the coal combustion.

Steam turbine : High pressure super heated steam is fed to the steam turbine which causes turbine blades to rotate. Energy in the steam is converted into mechanical energy in the steam turbine which acts as the prime mover. The pressure and temperature of the steam falls to a lower value and it expands in volume as it passes through the turbine. The expanded low pressure steam is exhausted in the condenser.

Condenser : The exhausted steam is condensed in the condenser by means of cold water circulation. Here, the steam loses it's pressure as well as temperature and it is converted back into water. Condensing is essential because, compressing a fluid which is in gaseous state requires a huge amount of energy with respect to the energy required in compressing liquid. Thus, condensing increases efficiency of the cycle.

Alternator : The steam turbine is coupled to an alternator. When the turbine rotates the alternator, electrical energy is generated. This generated electrical voltage is then stepped up with the help of a transformer and then transmitted where it is to be utilized.

Feed water pump : The condensed water is again fed to the boiler by a feed water pump. Some water may be lost during the cycle, which is suitably supplied from an external water source.

A practical thermal plant possess more complicated design and multiple stages of turbine such as High Pressure Turbine (HPT), Intermediate Pressure Turbine (IPT) and Low Pressure Turbine (LPT).

Advantages:

- Less initial cost as compared to other generating stations.
- It requires less land as compared to hydro power plant.
- The fuel (i.e. coal) is cheaper.

Disadvantages:

- It pollutes the atmosphere due to the production of large amount of smoke. This is one of the causes of global warming.
- The overall efficiency of a thermal power station is low (less than 30%).

6. (*a*) **Distance protection scheme for protection of feeders:**

This scheme provides discrimination protection without making use of pilot wires. It is widely employed for protection without making use of pilot wires. It is widely employed for protection of high voltage ac transmission lines feeders.

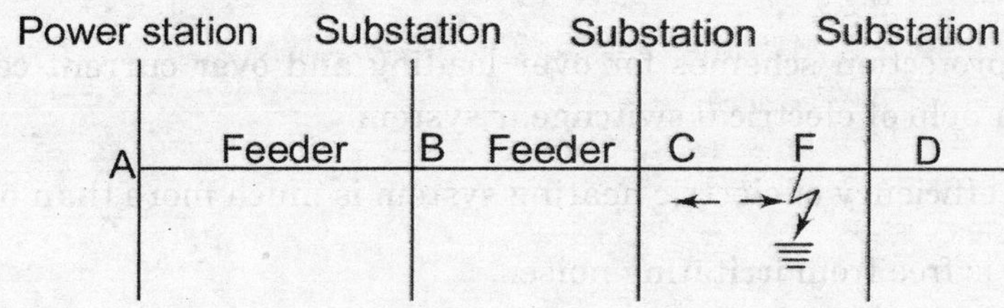

The relays at A, B, C and D are set to operate with impedance less than Z_A, Z_B, Z_C and Z_D respectively. For a short-circuit fault at point 'F' between substation Cand D, the fault loop impedances at power station *A* and substation B and *C* are $(Z_A + Z_B + Z)$, $(Z_g + Z)$ and Z respectively. It is obvious that only relay at substation C will operate. Similarly for short-circuit faults between substation B and Cand power station and substation B only relays at substation Band power station *A* respectively will operate.

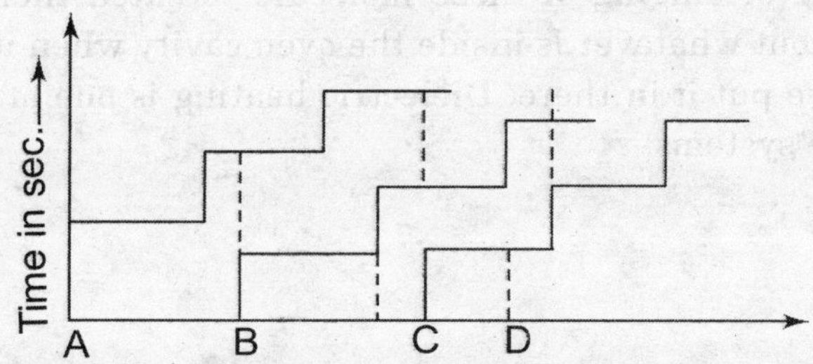

Modern practice is to employ definite distance method of protection applied in 3 zones. The zone-1 tripping which is instantaneous is normally set to 80% of the protected section. The zone-2 protection with a time delay sufficient for circuit breaker operating time and discriminating time margins covers the remain 20% portion of the protected section plus 25 to 50% of the next section.

Zone-2 also provide back up protection for the relay in the next section for fault case to the bus.

Zone-3 with still more time delay provides complete backup protection for all faults at all location.

(*b*) The choice of transmission systems and rated voltages for a transmission line is made from HV AC (220) EHV AC (400 – 750) UHVAC (above 760 AC) depending upon technical and economic consideration.

Advantages

- High power transferability of AC lines P α V^2.
- Line losses decrease with increase of transmission voltage and improvement of power factor for same power transfer.
- Bulk power transfer from large group of generating stations main transmission network.

(*c*) **Advantages of Electric Heating**

There are many process of producing heat energy but electric heating can be considered as superior of them because of many reasons.

1. This system is most clean system of heating. This is free from dirt.

2. This electric heating process does not produce any flue gas. So no additional arrangement is required to exhaust the flue gas.

3. This is much controlled method of heating. Temperature of the process can be accurately controlled as per requirement.

4. Initial and running costs of electric furnaces are much lower than other types of furnaces.

5. Automatic protection schemes for over loading and over current can easily be provided in this system with help of electrical switchgear system.

6. The overall efficiency of electric heating system is much more than other systems of heating.

7. The system is free from irritating noise.

8. There is no upper limit of producing temperature.

The dielectric heating as the generation of thermal energy or heat in a non-conducting material by the application of an electromagnetic force or field it. This is the way a microwave oven heats things placed in it.The microwaves electromagnetic energy cause water molecules, which are slightly polar, to flip back and forth in an attempt to align themselves with the magnetic field of the microwave energy. The flipping or ringing of these molecules created thermal energy in them, and this is transferred throughout whatever is inside the oven cavity when it's on. The result is that stuff gets hot, which is why we put it in there. Dielectric heating is one of the most common applications in domestic microwave systems.

Solved Paper 2008

Electrical Engineering

(Paper II)

1. (*a*) **Use Nodal analysis to find the currents in various resistors of the circuit shown in fig. 1.** (10)

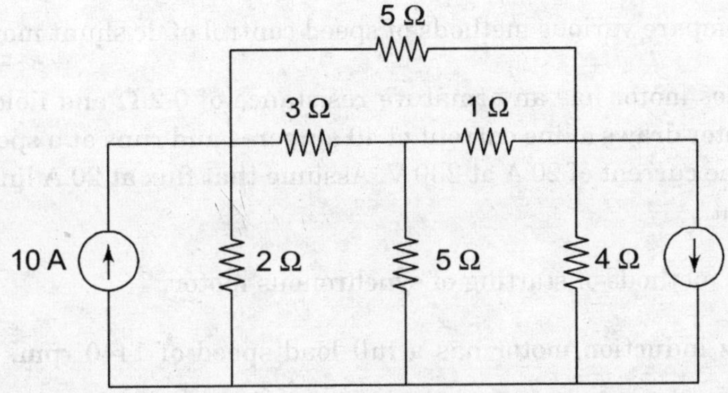

(*b*) **State and prove Maximum Power Transfer Theorem for dc circuits.** (10)

(*c*) **The self-inductance of a coil of 500 turns is 0.25 H. If 60% of the flux is linked with second coil of 10,000 turns then calculate**

(*i*) **the mutual inductance of the two coils.**

(*ii*) **the emf induced in the second coil when the current in the first coil changes at the rate of 100 A/s.** (10)

2. (*a*) **Calculate the rms and average values of current i represented by the waveform shown in figure 2.** (10)

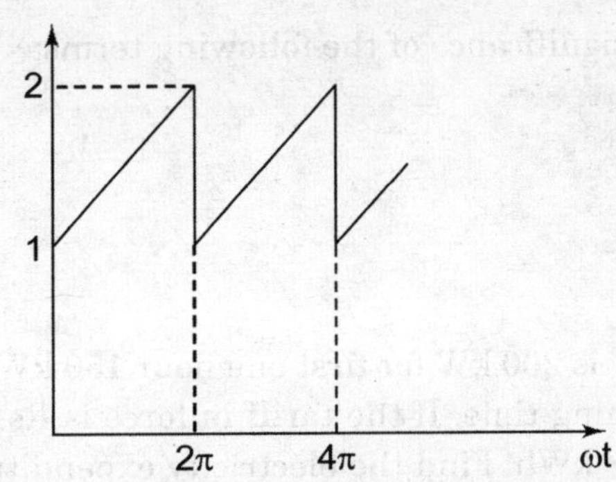

(*b*) **An iron choke coil takes 4A when connected to a 20V dc supply and takes 5A when connected to 65V, 50Hz ac supply. Determine.**

(*i*) **resistance and inductance of the coil**

(*ii*) **power drawn by the coil**

(*iii*) **the power factor** (10)

(c) With neat diagram explain the construction of moving coil instruments and derive the expression for deflecting torque of moving coil instrument. (10)

3. (a) Derive an expression for the emf induced in a transformer winding. Show that emf per turn in primary is equal to emf per turn in secondary. (10)

(b) Give the equivalent circuit of a transformer and define its various parameters. (10)

(c) Explain with neat diagram the differential protection scheme used to protect $\Delta - Y$ transformer. (10)

4. (a) Draw the external characteristics of various types of dc generators in one figure assuming the same no load terminal voltage. Compare these characteristics. (10)

(b) Describe and compare various methods of speed control of dc shunt motors. (10)

(c) A 230 V dc series motor has an armature resistance of 0.2 Ω and field resistance of 0.1 Ω at rated voltage. The motor draws a line current of 40 amperes and runs at a speed of 1000 rpm. Find speed of the motor for line current of 20 A at 230 V. Assume that flux at 20 A line current is 60% of the flux at 40 A line current. (10)

5. (a) Explain various methods of starting of synchronous motor. (10)

(b) A 3-phase 50Hz induction motor has a full load speed of 1440 rpm. For this motor calculate the following: (10)

(i) Number of poles

(ii) Full load slip

(iii) Rotor frequency

(iv) Speed of stator field w.r.t. rotor field

(v) Speed of stator field w.r.t. rotor structure

(c) Draw and explain the torque-slip characteristics of a 3-phase induction motor. Also explain the effect of rotor resistance on torque-slip characteristics. (10)

6. (a) Define and explain the significance of the following terms: (10)

(i) Load factor

(ii) Diversity factor

(iii) Demand factor

(b) Daily load of an industry is 200 kW for first one hour 150 kW for next 7 hours, 50 kW for next 8 hours and 1 kW for the remaining time. If the tariff in force is Rs. 1000/ per kW of maximum demand per annum plus Rs. 2.25 per kWh. Find the electricity expenditure for one year (365 days). (10)

(c) Explain different types of distribution systems with neat sketch. (10)

EXPLANATIONS

1. (*a*)

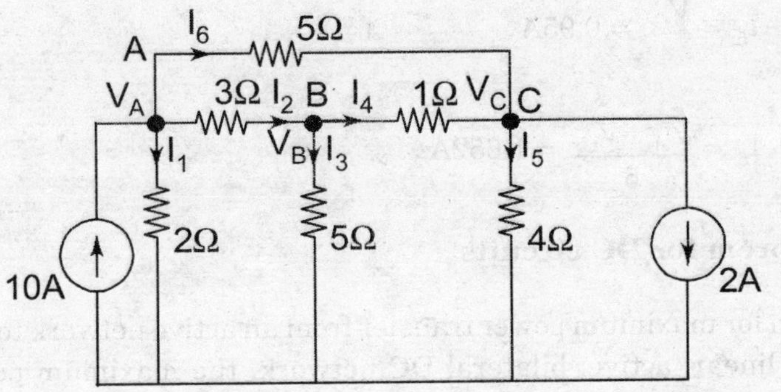

At node A,

$$\frac{V_A}{2}+\frac{V_A-V_B}{3}+\frac{V_A-V_C}{5}=10$$

$$31V_A-10V_B-6V_C=300 \qquad \text{...(A)}$$

At node B,

$$\frac{V_B-V_A}{3}+\frac{V_B}{5}+\frac{V_B-V_C}{1}=0$$

$$-5V_A+23V_B-15V_C=0 \qquad \text{...(B)}$$

At node C,

$$\frac{V_C-V_A}{5}+\frac{V_C-V_B}{1}+\frac{V_C}{4}+2=0$$

$$-4V_A-20V_B+29V_C=-40 \qquad \text{...(C)}$$

From (A), (B) and (C)

$$V_A=12\text{V}$$

$$V_B=5.1\text{V}$$

$$V_C=3.80\text{V}$$

$$I_1=\frac{V_A}{2}=6.03\text{A}$$

$$I_2=\frac{V_A-V_B}{3}=2.32\text{A}$$

$$I_3=\frac{V_B}{5}=1.02\text{A}$$

$$I_4 = \frac{V_B - V_C}{1} = 1.30\text{A}$$

$$I_5 = \frac{V_C}{4} = 0.95\text{A}$$

$$I_6 = \frac{V_A - V_C}{5} = 1.652\text{A}.$$

(*b*) **Maximum Power Transfer Theorem for DC circuits**

This theorem describes the condition for maximum power transfer from an active network to an external load resistance. It states that in a linear, active, bilateral DC network, the maximum power will be transferred form source to the load when the external load resistance equals to the internal resistance of the source. This theorem can be developed with reference to practical current or voltage source.

If the source is a practical or independent voltage source, its internal series resistance must match with load resistance to deliver maximum power. In case of practical or independent current source, parallel internal resistance should match with load resistance.

Explanation of Maximum Power Transfer Theorem

A variable resistance R_L is connected to a DC source network as shown in the circuit diagram in figure A below and the figure B represents the Thevenin's voltage V_{TH} and Thevenin's resistance R_{TH} of the source network. The aim of the Maximum Power Transfer theorem is to determine the value of load resistance R_L, such that it receives maximum power from the DC source.

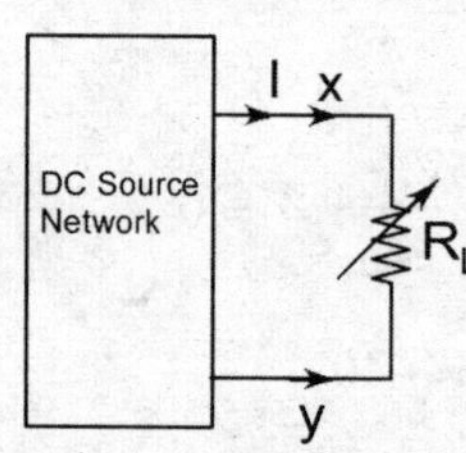

Figure A

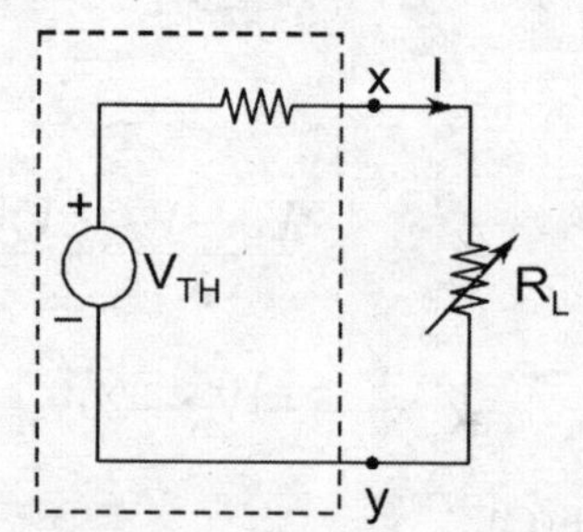

Figure B

Considering figure B the value of current will be calculated by the equation shown below

$$I = \frac{V_{TH}}{R_{TH} + R_L} \quad \text{...(1)}$$

While the power delivered to the resistive load is given by the equation

$$P_L = I^2 R_L \quad \text{...(2)}$$

Putting the value of I from the equation (1) in the equation (2) we will get

$$P_L = \left(\frac{V_{TH}}{R_{TH} + R_L}\right)^2 \times R_L$$

P_L can be maximized by varying R_L and hence, maximum power can be delivered when $(dP_L/dR_L) = 0$

However,

$$\frac{dP_L}{dR_L} = \frac{1}{[(R_{TH} + R_L)^2]^2}\left[(R_{TH} + R_L)^2 \frac{d}{dR_L}(V_{TH}^2 R_L) - V_{TH}^2 R_L \frac{d}{dR_L}(R_{TH} + R_L)^2\right]$$

$$\frac{dP_L}{dR_L} = \frac{1}{(R_{TH} + R_L)^4}\left[(R_{TH} + R_L)^2 V_{TH}^2 - V_{TH}^2 R_L \times 2(R_{TH} + R_L)\right]$$

$$\frac{dP_L}{dR_L} = \frac{V_{TH}^2 (R_{TH} + R_L - 2R_L)}{(R_{TH} + R_L)^3}$$

$$= \frac{V_{TH}^2 (R_{TH} - R_L)}{(R_{TH} + R_L)^2}$$

Therefore,

$$\frac{V_{TH}^2 (R_{TH} - R_L)}{(R_{TH} + R_L)^2} = 0$$

Which gives

$$(R_{TH} - R_L) = 0 \text{ or } R_{TH} = R_L$$

Hence, it is proved that power transfer from a DC source network to a resistive network is maximum when the internal resistance of the DC source network is equal to the load resistance.

Again with $R_{TH} = R_L$, the system being perfectly matched to the load and the source thus, the power transfer becomes maximum and this amount of power P_{max} can be obtained by the equation shown below

$$P_{max} = \frac{V_{TH}^2 R_{TH}}{(R_{TH} + R_{TH})^2} = \frac{V_{TH}^2}{4R_{TH}} \quad ...(3)$$

Equation (3) gives the power which is consumed by the load. The power transfer by the source will also be same as the power consumed by the load i.e., equation (3), as the load power and the power being the same.

Thus, the total power supplied is given by the equation

$$P = 2\frac{V_{TH}^2}{4R_{TH}} = \frac{V_{TH}^2}{2R_{TH}}$$

During Maximum Power Transfer the efficiency becomes

$$\eta = \left(\frac{P_{max}}{P}\right) \times 100 = 50\%$$

Steps for Solving Network Using Maximum Power Transfer Theorem

Following steps are used to solve the problem by Maximum Power Transfer theorem

Step 1 : Remove the load resistance of the circuit.

Step 2 : Find the Thevenin's resistance (R_{TH}) of the source network looking through the open circuited load terminals.

Step 3 : As per the maximum power transfer theorem this R_{TH} is the load resistance of the network i.e., $R_L = R_{TH}$ that allows maximum power transfer.

Step 4 : Maximum Power Transfer is calculated by the equation shown below.

$$P_{max} = \frac{V_{TH}^2}{4R_{TH}}$$

(*c*) Coil turns = 500 Self inductance = 0.25H

$$\text{Mutual inductance } M = \frac{N_2\phi_2}{I_1}$$

$$N_1 = 500\ L_1 = 0.25H\ \phi_2 = 0.6\phi_1\ N_2 = 10{,}000$$

$$L_1 = \frac{N_1\phi_1}{I_1};\ \frac{L_1}{N_1} = \frac{\phi_1}{I_1} = \frac{0.25}{500};\phi_2 = 0.6\phi$$

$$\frac{\phi_2}{\phi_1} = \frac{0.6\phi_1}{I_1} = \frac{0.6 \times 0.25}{500}$$

(*i*) $M = \frac{N_2\phi_2}{I_1} = 10{,}000 \times \frac{0.6 \times 0.25}{500} = 3H$

(*ii*) Emf induced

$$E_2 = -\frac{MdI_1}{dt} = -3 \times 100 \qquad \left(\frac{dI_1}{dt} = 100A/s\right)$$

$$= -300V$$

2. (*a*) Equation $i(\omega t) = \frac{1}{2\Omega}wt + 1$

This is a periodic waveform of period T = 2π

$$I_{avg.} = \frac{1}{T}\int_0^{2\pi} i(wt)\,d(wt)$$

$$= \frac{1}{2\pi}\int_0^{2\pi}\left(1 + \frac{wt}{2\pi}\right)d(wt)$$

$$= \frac{1}{2\pi}\left[wt + \frac{1}{2\pi}\frac{(wt)^2}{2}\right]^{2\pi}$$

$$= \frac{1}{2\pi}\left[(2\pi - 0) + \frac{1}{2\pi}\frac{(2\pi)^2}{2}\right]$$

$$I_{avg.} = \frac{1}{2\pi}(3\pi) = 1.5A$$

$$I_{rms} = \left[\frac{1}{T}\int_0^{2\pi} i^2(wt)\,d(wt)\right]^{1/2}$$

$$= \frac{1}{\sqrt{2\pi}}\left[\int_0^{2\pi}\left(\frac{1}{2}wt + 1\right)^2 d(wt)\right]^{1/2}$$

$$= \frac{1}{\sqrt{2\pi}}\left[\int_0^{2\pi}\left(\frac{(wt)^2}{4\pi^2} + 1 + \frac{2}{2\pi}wt\right) d(wt)\right]^{1/2}$$

$$= \frac{1}{\sqrt{2\pi}}\left[\frac{1}{4\pi^2}\frac{(2\pi)^3}{3} + 2\pi + \frac{1}{\pi}.\frac{(2\pi)^2}{2}\right]^{1/2}$$

$$= \frac{1}{\sqrt{2\pi}}\left[\frac{2\pi}{3} + 2\pi + 2\pi\right]^{1/2}$$

$$I_{rms} = \sqrt{\frac{7}{3}} = 1.527A$$

(*b*) (*i*)

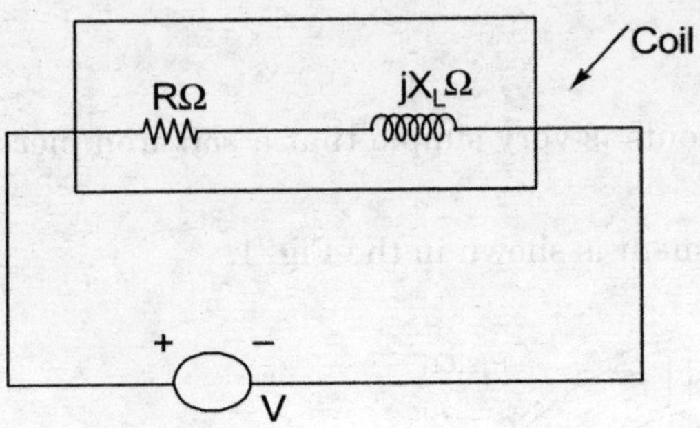

Case (i) When coil connected to 20V dc supply current I = 4A

For dc supply, f = oHz

$$I = \frac{V}{R}$$

$$\Rightarrow \quad R = \frac{V}{I} = 5\Omega$$

Case (ii) When coil is connected to 65V, 50Hz ac supply frequency f = 50Hz

$$I = 5A$$

$$Z = \frac{V}{I} = \frac{65}{5} = 13\Omega$$

$$X_L = \sqrt{Z^2 - R^2}$$

$$= \sqrt{(13)^2 - 5^2} = 12\Omega$$

$$2\pi fL = 12;$$

$$L = \frac{12}{2\pi \times 50} = 38.197 \text{ H}$$

(*ii*) Power factor

Case (i) For resistive circuit

$$\cos\phi = \frac{R}{Z} = \frac{R}{R} = 1$$

Case (ii)

$$Z = 13\Omega$$

$$\cos\phi = \frac{R}{Z} = \frac{5}{13} = 0.3846 \text{ (Lagging)}$$

(*c*) Moving Iron Instruments

The moving iron instruments are classified as:

(i) Moving iron attraction type instruments and

(ii) Moving iron repulsion type instruments

1. Moving iron attraction type instruments

The basic working principle of these instruments is very simple that a soft iron piece if brought near the magnet gets attracted by the magnet.

The construction of the attraction type instrument is shown in the Fig. 1.

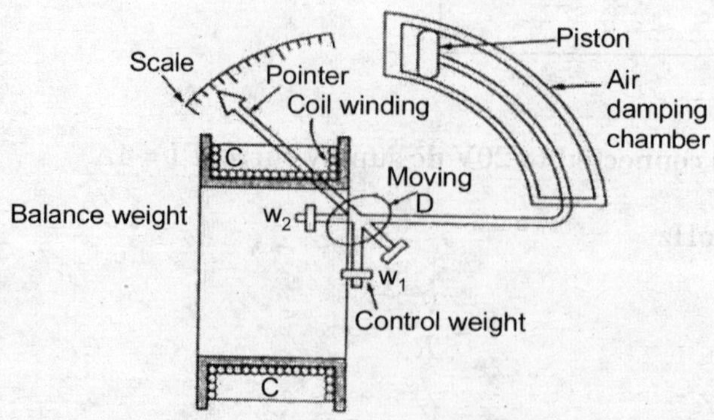

Fig. 1 Moving iron attraction type instruments

It consists of a fixed coil C and moving iron piece D. The coil is flat and has a narrow slot like opening. The moving iron is a flat disc which eccentrically mounted, on the spindle. The spindle is supported between the jewel bearings. The spindle caries a pointer which moves over a graduated scale. The number of turns of the fixed coil are dependent on the range of the instrument. For passing current through the coil only few turns are required.

The controlling torque is provided by the springs but gravity control may also be used for vertically mounted panel type instruments.

The damping torque is provided by the air friction. A light aluminium piston is attached to the moving system. It moves in a fixed chamber. The chamber is closed at one end. It can also provided with the help of van attached to the moving system.

The operating magnetic field in moving iron instruments is very weak. Hence eddy current damping is not used since it require a permanent magnet which would affect or distort the operating field.

2. Moving Iron Repulsion Type Instrument

These instruments have two vanes inside the coil, the one is fixed and other is movable. When the current flows in the coil, both the vanes are magnetized with like polarities induced on the same side. Hence due to repulsion of like polarities, there is a force of repulsion between the two vanes causing the movement of the moving van. The repulsion type instruments are the most commonly used instruments.

Torque Equation of moving iron instruments.

Consider a small increment in current supplied to the coil of the instrument, due to this current let dθ be the deflection under the deflecting torque T_d. Due to such deflection, some mechanical work will be done.

∴ Mechanical Work' $= T_d \, d\theta$

There will be a change in the energy stored i the magnetic field due to the change in inductance. This is ;cause the vane tries to occupy the position of minimum reluctance. The inductance is inversely proportional the reluctance of the magnetic circuit of coil.

Let I = initial current

L = instrument inductance

θ = deflection

dl = increase in current

dθ = change in deflection

dL = change in inductance

In order to effect and increment dL in the current, there must be an increase in the applied voltage given by,

$$e = \frac{d(LI)}{dt} = I\frac{dL}{dt} + L\frac{dI}{dt}$$

As both 1 and L are changing.

The electrical energy supplied is given by,

$$\text{eIdt} = \left(I\frac{dL}{dt} + L\frac{dI}{dt}\right)Idt$$

$$= I^2\,dL + IL\,dI$$

The second energy increase from

$$\frac{1}{2}LI^2 \text{ to } \frac{1}{2}(L+dL)(I+dI)^2$$

Hence the change in stored energy is given by,

$$= \frac{1}{2}(L+dL)(I+dI)^2 - \frac{1}{2}LI^2$$

Neglecting higher order terms, this becomes,

$$IL\,dI + \frac{1}{2}I^2\,dL$$

The energy supplied in nothing but increase in stored energy plus the energy required for mechanical work done.

$$\therefore \quad I^2dL + IL\,dI = IL\,dI + \frac{1}{2}I^2\,dL + T_d\,d\theta$$

$$\therefore \quad T_d \cdot d\theta = \frac{1}{2}I^2\,dL$$

$$\therefore \quad \boxed{T_d = \frac{1}{2}I^2\frac{dL}{d\theta}}$$

While the controlling torque is given by,

$$T_c = K\,\theta$$

where K = spring constant

$$\therefore \quad K\theta = \frac{1}{2}I^2\frac{dL}{d\theta} \quad \text{under equilibrium}$$

$$\therefore \quad \theta = \frac{1}{2}\frac{I^2}{K}\frac{dL}{d\theta}$$

Thus the deflection is proportional to the square of the currrent through the coil. And the instrument gives square law response.

3. (*a*) **EMF Equation of a Transformer**

When a sinusoidal voltage is applied to the primary winding of a transformer, alternating flux ϕ_m sets up in the iron core of the transformer. This sinusoidal flux links with both primary and secondary winding. The function of flux is a sine function. The rate of change of flux with respect to time is derived mathematically.

The derivation of EMF Equation of the transformer is shown below. Let

- ϕ_m be the maximum value of flux in Weber
- f be the supply frequency in Hz
- N_1 is the number of turns in the primary winding
- N_2 is the number of turns in the secondary winding

Φ is the flux per turn in Weber

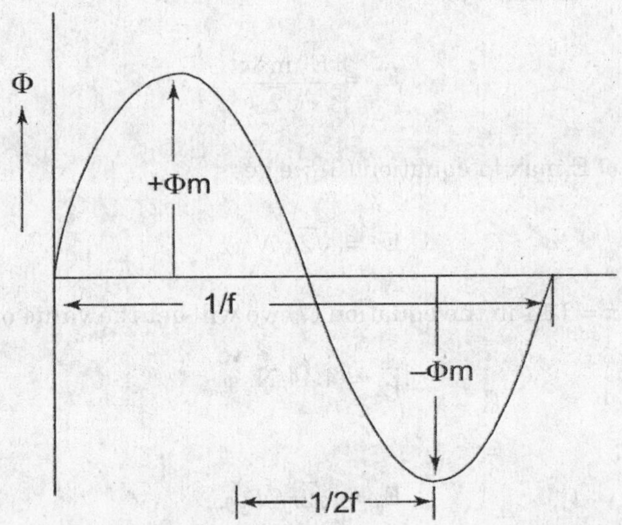

As shown in the above figure that the flux changes from + ϕ_m to – ϕ_m in half a cycle of 1/2f seconds.

By Faraday's Law

Let E_1 is the emf induced in the primary winding

$$E_1 = \frac{d\psi}{dt} \quad \text{...(1)}$$

where $\psi = N_1\phi$

Therefore $$E_1 = -N_1\frac{d\varphi}{dt} \quad \text{...(2)}$$

Since ϕ is due to AC supply $\phi = \phi_m$ Sinωt

$$E_1 = -N_1 \frac{d}{dt}(\varphi_m \text{ Sin}\omega t)$$

$$E_1 = -N_1 w\varphi_m \text{ Cos}\omega t$$

$$E_1 = N_1 w\varphi_m \text{ Sin}(\omega t - \pi/2) \quad ...(3)$$

So the induced emf lags flux by 90 degrees.

Maximum valve of emf

$$E_1\text{max} = N_1 w\varphi_m \quad ...(4)$$

But

$$w = 2pf$$

$$E_1\text{max} = 2pfN_1\varphi_m \quad ...(5)$$

Root mean square RMS value is

$$E_1 = \frac{E_1 \max}{\sqrt{2}} \quad ...(6)$$

Putting the value of E_1max in equation (6) we get

$$E_1 = \sqrt{2}\pi f N_1 \varphi_m \quad ...(7)$$

Putting the value $\pi = 3.14$ in the equation (7) we will get the value of E as

$$E_1 = 4.44fN_1 \varphi_m \quad ...(8)$$

Similarly

$$E_2 = \sqrt{2}\pi f N_2 \varphi_m$$

Or

$$E_2 = 4.44fN2\varphi_m \quad ...(9)$$

Now, equating the equation (8) and (9) we get

$$\frac{E_2}{E_1} = \frac{4.44fN_2\varphi_m}{4.44fN_1\varphi_m}$$

Or

$$\frac{E_2}{E_1} = \frac{N_2}{N_1} = K$$

The above equation is called the turn ratio where K is kown as transformation ratio.

The equation (8) and (9) can also be written as shown below using the relation

($\phi_m = B_m A_i$) where A_i is the iron area and B_m is the maximum value of flux density.

$$E_1 = 4.44N_1fB_mA_i \text{ Volts}$$

and $$E_2 = 4.44 N_2 f B_m A_i \text{ Volts}$$

For a sinusoidal wave

$$\frac{\text{R.M.S value}}{\text{Average value}} = \text{Form factor} = 1.11$$

(*c*) **Differential Protection Scheme in a Power Transformer**

Principle of Differential Protection

Principle of Differential Protection scheme is one simple conceptual technique. The differential relay actually compares between primary current and secondary current of power transformer, if any unbalance found in between primary and secondary currents the relay will actuate and inter trip both the primary and secondary circuit breaker of the transformer.

Suppose you have one transformer which has primary rated current Ip and secondary current Is. If you install CT of ratio Ip/lA at the primary side and similarly, CT of ratio *Is / 1A* at the secondary side of the transformer. The secondaries of these both CTs are connected together in such a manner that secondary currents of both CTs will oppose each other. In other words, the secondaries of both CTs should be connected to the same current coil of a differential relay in such an opposite manner that there will be no resultant current in that coil in a normal working condition of the transformer. But if any major fault occurs inside the transformer due to which the normal ratio of the transformer disturbed then the secondary current of both transformers will not remain the same and one resultant current will flow through the current coil of the differential relay, which will actuate the relay and inter trip both the primary and secondary circuit breakers. To correct phase shift of current because of star-delta connection of transformer winding in the case of three-phase transformer, the current transformer secondaries should be connected in delta and star as shown here.

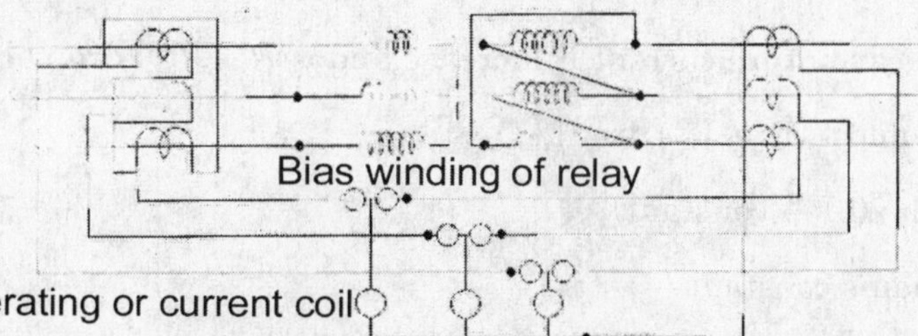

Schematic diagram of differential scheme

At maximum through fault current, the spill output produced by the small percentage unbalance may be substantial. Therefore, differential protection of transformer should be provided with a proportional bias of an amount which exceeds in effect the maximum ratio deviation.

4. (*a*)

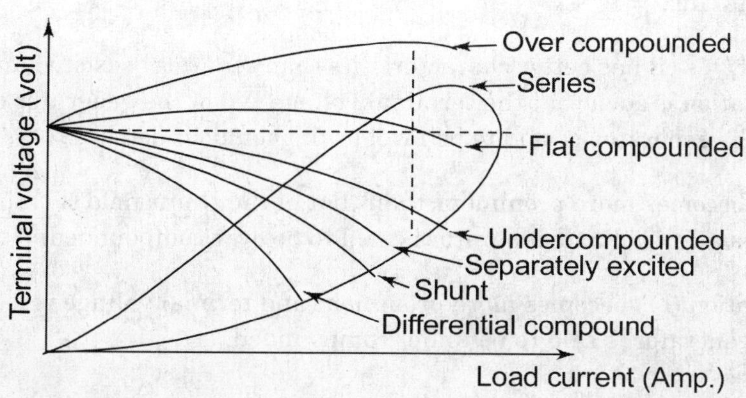

External characteristic is drawn between terminal voltage with load current for constant speed and field current (or excitation).

(*i*) **Separately excited dc Generator:** With the increase in load current, terminal voltage decrease slightly due to voltage drops cause by armature reaction and armature circuit resistance.

$$V_t = E_g - I_a R_a - \text{Armature reaction drop} - \text{Brush contact resistance drop}$$

(*ii*) **Shunt dc Generator:**

The drop in terminal voltage is due to

(*a*) Armature resistance drop $I_a R_a$

(*b*) Reduction in main field flux due to armature reaction

(*c*) Reduction in field current I_{sh}, since the terminal voltage has decreased because of the first two effects given in part (a) and (b).

A reduction in field current (I_f) cause the flux and therefore the generated emf to decrease. Thus the terminal voltage of the generator for a given load will be lower when shunt excited than when separately excited, provided no-load voltage is same in both the cases. If we further increase the load current, after breakdown point, the terminal voltages fall back rapidly.

(*iii*) **Series dc Generator:**

It has rising voltage characteristic in the operating region upto saturation. Series flux ϕ_{se} increase with load so terminal voltage V_t will increase as emf, E_g increase but $I_a(R_a + R_{se})$ drop will also increase. As increase armature current, armature reaction also increase i.e. $I_a \uparrow$, armature reaction$\uparrow$. Beyond saturation, it has shunt characteristics which is dropping in nature.

As load increase armature current I_a increase and $I_a(R_a + R_{se})$ drop also increase.

i.e.. Load$\uparrow$, and $I_a(R_g + R_{se})$ drop$\uparrow$

At saturation flux(ϕ) $\rightarrow$ constant

So, Emf E_g remains constant

$$\downarrow V_t = E_g - I_a (R_a + R_{se}) \uparrow$$

Terminal voltage V_t will decrease

(*iv*) **Cumulatively Compounded dc Generator:**

$$\text{Total flux} = \phi_{sh} + \phi_{se}$$

Since it has both flux f_{sh} and f_{se}, so it has better characteristics than separately excited and shunt dc generator if the series excitation is such that the terminal voltage (V_t) of the generator on full load is same as that of no-load the generator is said to be level or flat compounded.

If the series excitation (l_{se}) becomes more prominent than that of the shunt field (I_{sh}) the terminal voltage rises with the increase in load and generator is said to be over compounded.

When the shunt field excitation (I_{sh}) becomes more prominent and termial voltage is less than no-load terminal voltage, the generator is said to be under compounded.

(*v*) **Differential Compound dc Generator:**

In this case, with the increase in load, the series field flux oppose the shunt field flux and consequently the terminal voltage drop very rapidly.

(*b*) **Speed control methods of DC motor**

1. Flux control method

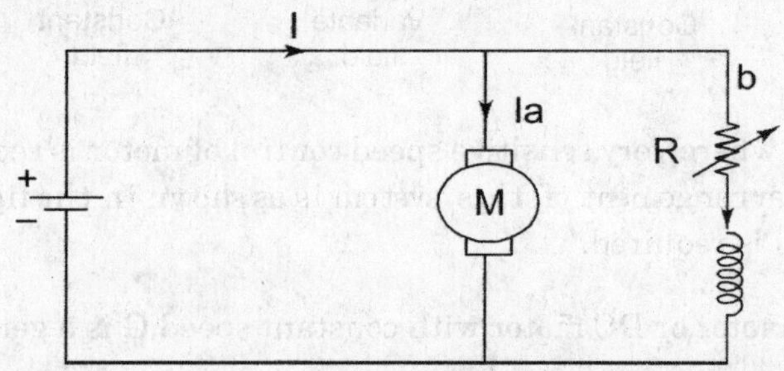

Speed of a dc motor is inversely proportional to the flux per pole. Thus by decreasing the flux, speed can be increased and vice versa. To control the flux, a rheostat is added in series with the field winding, as shown in the circuit diagram. Adding more resistance in series with the field winding will increase the speed as it decreases the flux. In shunt motors, as field current is relatively very small, $I_{sh}^2 R$ loss is small and, hence, this method is quite efficient. Though speed can be increased above the rated value by reducing flux with this method, it puts a limit to maximum speed as weakening of flux beyond the limit will adversely affect the commutation.

2. Armature control method

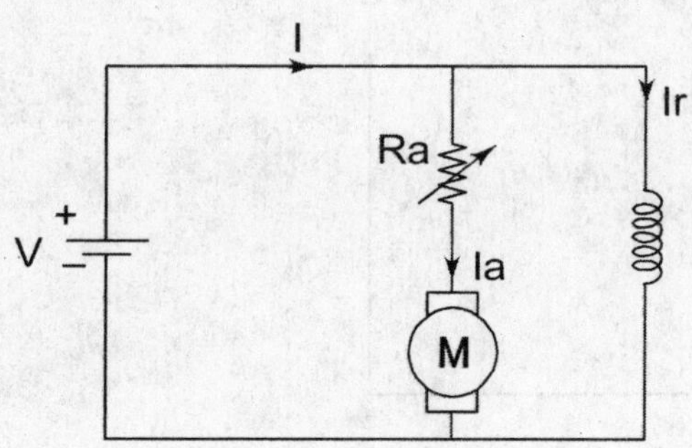

Speed of a dc motor is directly proportional to the back emf E_b and $E_b = V - I_a R_a$.

That means, when the supply voltage V and the armature resistance R_a are kept constant, speed is directly proportional to the armature current I_a. Thus, if we add a resistance in series with the armature, I_a decreases and, hence, the speed also decreases. Greater the resistance in series with the armature, greater the decrease in speed.

3. Voltage Control Method

(*a*) Multiple voltage control

In this method, the shunt field is connected to a fixed exciting voltage and armature is supplied with different voltages. Voltage across armature is changed with the help of a suitable switchgear. The speed is approximately proportional to the voltage across the armature.

(b) Ward-Leonard System:

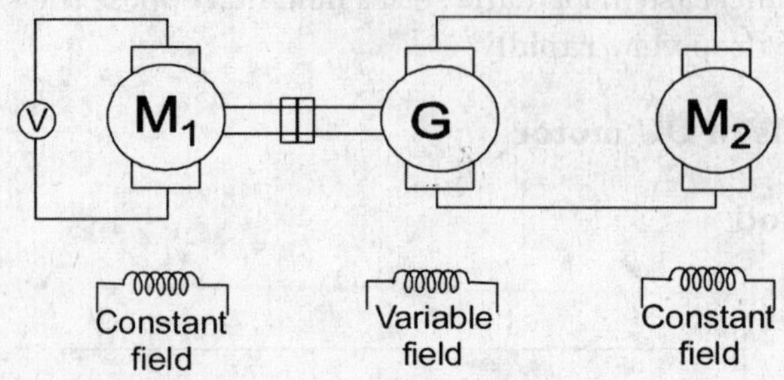

This system is used where very sensitive speed control of motor is required (e.g electric excavators, elevators etc.). The arrangement of this system is as shown in the figure at right. M_2 is the motor whose speed control is required.

M_1 may be any AC motor or DC motor with constant speed.G is a generator directly coupled to M_1.

In this method, the output from the generator G is fed to the armature of the motor M_2 whose speed is to be controlled. The output voltage of the generator G can be varied from zero to its maximum value by means of its field regulator and, hence, the armature voltage of the motor M_2 is varied very smoothly. Hence, very smooth speed control of the dc motor can be obtained by this method.

(c)

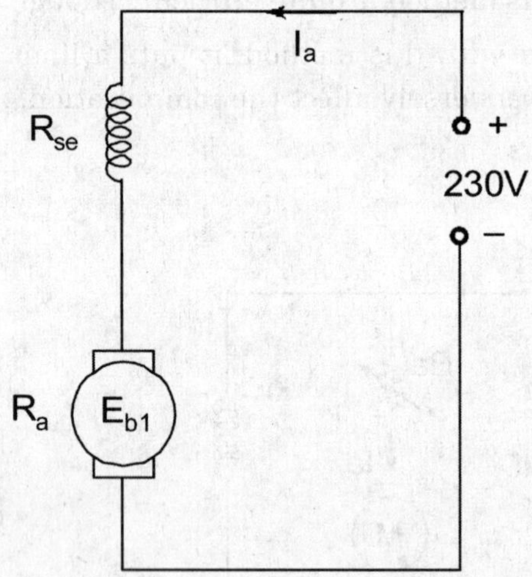

$$V_s = 230V$$

$$R_a = 0.2\Omega$$

$$R_{se} = 1\Omega$$

$$I_{a_1} = 40A$$

$$N_1 = 1000 \text{ rpm}$$

$$E_{b_1} = V_s - I_{a_1} \text{ (Rse + Ra)}$$

$$= 230 - 40\,(0.1 + 0.2)$$

$$= 218 \text{ V}$$

$$I_{a_2} = 20\text{ A}$$

$$\phi_2 = 0.6\phi$$

$$E_b \propto N\phi$$

$$\frac{E_{b2}}{E_{b1}} = \frac{N_2}{N_1} \times \frac{\phi_2}{\phi_1}$$

$$E_{b2} = V_s - I_{a2}(Rse + Ra)$$

$$E_{b2} = 230 - 20(0.1 + 0.2)$$

$$E_{b2} = 224V$$

$$N_2 = N_1 \times \left(\frac{E_{b2}}{E_{b1}}\right) \times \frac{\phi_1}{\phi_2}$$

$$= 1000 \times \frac{224}{218} \times \frac{1}{0.6}$$

$$= 1712.538 \text{ rpm}$$

Speed motor is 1712.538 rpm for line current of 2A at 230V

5. (*a*) **Methods of Starting Synchronous Motor**

As seen earlier, synchronous motor is not self starting. It is necessary to rotate the rotor at a speed very near to synchronous speed. This is possible by various method in practice. The various methods to start the synchronous motor are,

1. **Using pony motors:** In this method, the rotor is brought to the synchronous speed with the help of some external device like small induction motor. Such an external device is called 'pony motor'.

   Once the rotor attains the synchronous speed, the d.c. excitation to the rotor is switched on. Once the synchronism is established pony motor is decoupled. The motor then continues to rotate as synchronous motor.

2. **Using Damper Winding:** In a synchronous motor, in addition to the normal field winding, the additional winding consisting of copper bars placed in the slots in the pole faces. The bars are short circuited with the help of end rings. Such an additional winding on the rotor is called damper winding. This winding as short circuited, acts as a squirrel cage rotor winding of an induction motor. The schematic representation of such damper winding is shown below.

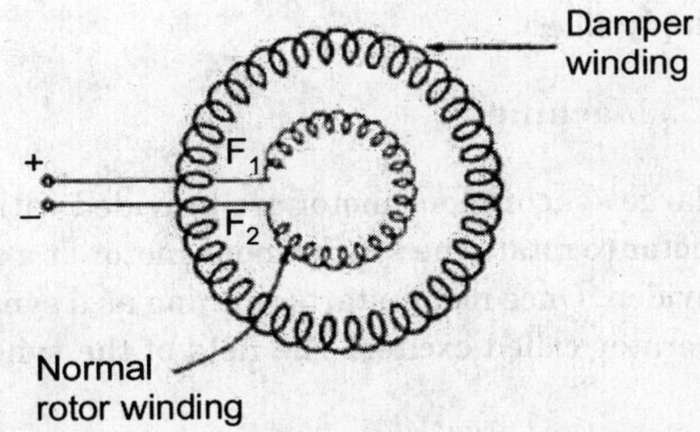

Fig. Starting as a squirrel cage I.M.

Once the rotor is excited by a three phase supply, the motors starts rotating as an induction motor at sub synchronous speed. Then d.c. supply is given to the field winding. At a particular instant motor gets pulled into synchronism and starts rotating at a synchronous speed. As rotor rotates at synchronous speed, the relative motion between damper winding and the rotating magnetic field is zero. Hence when motor is running as synchronous motor, there can not be any induced e.m.f. in the damper winding. So damper winding is active only at start, to run the motor as an induction motor at start. Afterwards it is out of the circuit. As damper winding is short circuited and motor gets started as induction motor, it draws high current at start so induction motor starters like star-delta, autotransformer etc. used to start the synchronous motor as an induction motor.

3. As a Slip Ring Induction Motor

The above method of starting synchronous motor as a squirrel cage induction motor does not provide high starting torque. So. to achieve this, instead of shorting the damper winding, it is designed to a form a three phase star or delta connected winding. The three ends of this winding are brought out through slip rings. An external rheostat then can be introduced in series with the rotor circuit. So when stator is excited, the motor starts as a slip ring induction motor and due to resistance added in the rotor provides high starting torque. The resistance is then gradually cut off, as motor gathers speed. When motor attains speed near synchronous, d.c. excitation is provided to the rotor, then motors gets pulled into synchronism ans starts rotating at synchronous speed. The damper winding is shorted by shorting the slip rings. The initial resistance added in the rotor not only provides high stalling torque but also limits high inrush of starting current. Hence it acts as a motor resistance starter. The synchronous motor started by this method is called a slip ring induction motor is shown in the Fig.l(b).

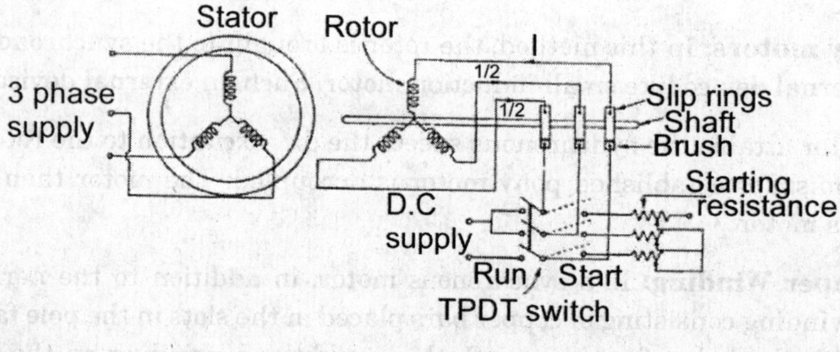

It can be observed from the above figure that the same three phase rotor winding acts as a normal rotor winding by shorting two of the phases. From the positive terminal, current T flows in one of the phases, which divides into two other phases at start point as 1/2 through each, when switch is thrown on d.c. supply side.

4. Using Small D.C.. Machine

Many a times, a large synchronous motor are provided with a coupled d.c. machine. This machine is used as a d.c. motor to rotate the synchronous motor at a synchronous speed. Then the excitation to the rotor is provided. Once motor starts running as a synchronous motor, the same d.c. machine acts as a d.c. generator called exciter. The field of the synchronous motor is then excited by this exciter itself.

(*b*) Full load speed of motor

$$N_r = 1440 \text{ rpm}$$

Synchronous speed of motor Ns

$$= \frac{120f}{P}$$

$$N_s > N_r$$

$$\text{Let } N_s = 1500 \text{ rpm}$$

(i) $1500 = \dfrac{120 \times 50}{P}$ so P = 4

(ii) Slip $s = \dfrac{N_s - N_r}{N_s} = \dfrac{1500 - 1440}{1500} = 0.04$

(iii) Rotor frequency

$$f' = sf = 0.04 \times 50 = 2\text{Hz}$$

(iv) Speed of stator field w.r.t. rotor field

$$= N_s - N_s = 0$$

(v) Speed of stator field w.r.t rotor structure

$$N_s - N_r = SN_s$$

$$= 1500 - 1440$$

$$= 60 \text{ rpm}$$

(*c*) **Torque Slip Characteristic of an Induction Motor**

The Torque Slip Characteristic is represented by a rectangular hyperbola. For the immediate value of the slip, the graph changes from one form to the other. Thus, it passes through the point of maximum torque when $R_2 = sX_{20}$. The maximum torque developed in an induction motor is called the Pull Out Torque or the Breakdown Torque. This torque is a measure of the short time overloading capability of the motor.

The torque slip characteristic curve is divided roughly into three regions. They are given below.

- **Low slip region**
- **Medium slip region**
- **High slip region**

The torque equation of the induction motor is g

$$\tau = \frac{k\ s}{R_2^2} \quad ...(1)$$

Low Slip Region

At the synchronous speed, s = 0, therefore, the torque is zero. When the speed i,s very near to synchronous speed. The slip is very low and $(sX_{20})^2$ is negligible in comparison with R_2. Therefore,

$$\tau = \frac{k_1 s}{R_2}$$

If R_2 is constant, the torque becomes

$$\tau = k_2 s \qquad ...(2)$$

When $k_2 = k_1/R_2$

From the equation (1) shown above, it is clear that the torque is proportional to slip. Hence, in the normal working region of the motor, the value of the slip is small. The torque slip curve is a straight line.

Medium Slip Region

As the slip increases, the speed of the motor decreases with the increase in load. The term $(sX_{20})^2$ becomes large. The term R^2_2 may be neglected in comparison with the term $(sX_{20})^2$ and the torque equation becomes as shown below.

$$\tau = \frac{k_3 R_2}{sX^2_{20}} \qquad ...(3)$$

At the standstill condition, the torque is inversely proportional to the slip.

High Slip Region

Beyond the maximum torque point, the value of torque starts decreasing. As a result, the motor slows down and stops. At this stage, the overload protection must immediately disconnect the motor from the supply to prevent damage due to overheating of the motor.

The motor operates for the values of the slip between S = 0 and S = S_M. Where, S_M is the value of the slip corresponding to the maximum torque. For a typical induction motor, the pull-out torque is 2 to 3 times the rated full load torque. The starting torque is about 1.5 times the rated full load torque.

The curve shown below shows the Torque Slip Characteristic of the Induction Motor.

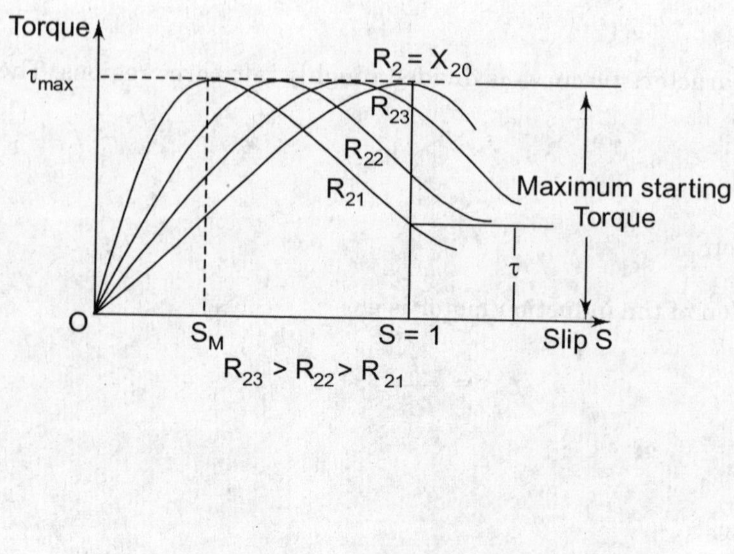

6. (*a*) It is ratio of average load to maximum demand during certain period of time (e.g. day/month/year) is called load factor. Following formula is used to calculate Load Factor.

Load factor

= Average Demand/Maximum Demand

Since average load is always less than maximum demand, hence load factor is always less than unity.

Demand Factor

The ratio of actual maximum demand on the system to the total ruled load connected with the system is called demand factor. It is always less than unity. Following formula is used to calculate demand factor.

Demand Factor

= Maximum Demand/Connected Load

Diversity Factor

The ratio of sum of individual maximum demand of all the consumers supplied by it to maximum demand of power station is called diversity factor. Following formula is used to calculate diversity factor.

Diversity Factor = (Sum of Individual Max. Demand)/(Max. Demand of Power Station)

(b) Load of an industry = 200kw for 1 hour

150 kw for 7 hour

50kw for 8 hour

1 kw for remaining time

Annual bill = b × maximum demand in kw + c × unit consumed in a year

$$\text{One day unit consumed} = 200 \times 1 + 150 \times 7 + 50 \times 8 + 1 \times 8$$

$$= 1658 \text{ kwh.}$$

For 365 days = 1658 × 365

$$= 605170 \text{ kwh}$$

Annual bill = 1000 × 200 + 2.25 × 605170

$$= \text{Rs } 1561632.5$$

(*c*) Distribution systems may be classified in various ways are followed:

1. According to current, the distribution systems are two types.

   (*a*) DC distribution system

   (*b*) AC distribution system.

(*a*) **DC distribution system:**

(i) 2-wire dc distribution system: This system of distribution consists of two wires, one is the positive and other Is the negative wire.

This system is never used tor transmission purpose due to low efficiency but may be employe for distribution of dc power.

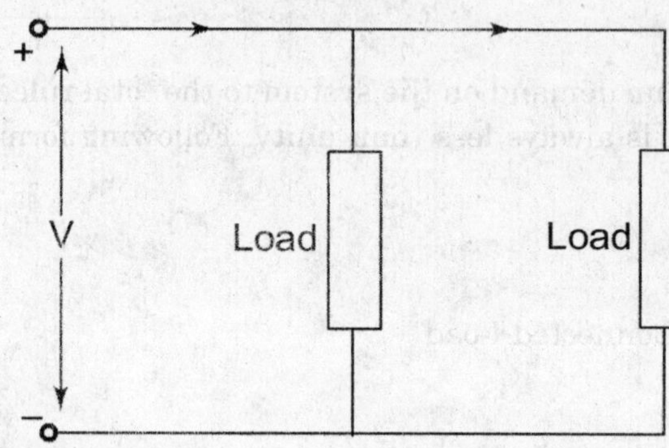

(ii) 3-wire dc distribution system: This system consists of two outers and a middle or neutral wire which is earthed at the substation. The voltage between the outer is twice the voltage between either outer and neutral wire.

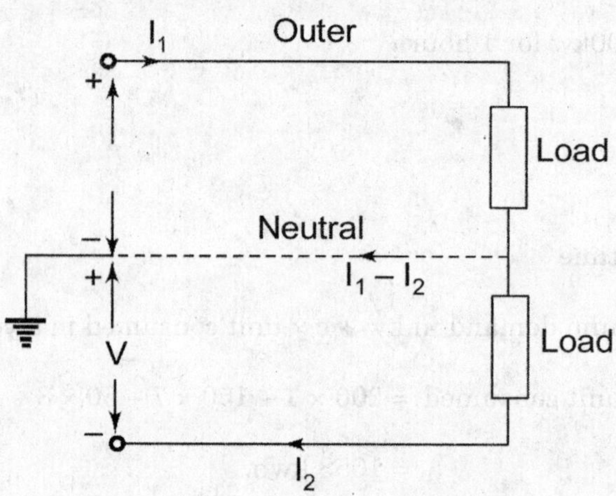

This system is used for transmission purpose.

2. According to types of construction of distribution systems:

(*a*) **Overhead**

(*b*) **Underground**

(*a*) The overhead system is generally employed for distribution as it is cheaper than underground system.

(*b*) The underground system is used at places where overhead construction is impracticable.

3. According to the scheme of connection of distribution system.

(*a*) **Radial system**

(*b*) **Parallel system**

(*c*) **Ring system**

(*d*) **Interconnected system**

(*a*) **Radial system :** In this system, separate feeder radiates from a substation and feed the distribution at one end only.

This system is simplest, most economical and most commonly used one.

(*b*) **Parallel system :** In this system, two radial feeders originated from the same or different substation are run in parallel. Each feeder, though cable of supplying the entire load, share the total equally in normal conditions.

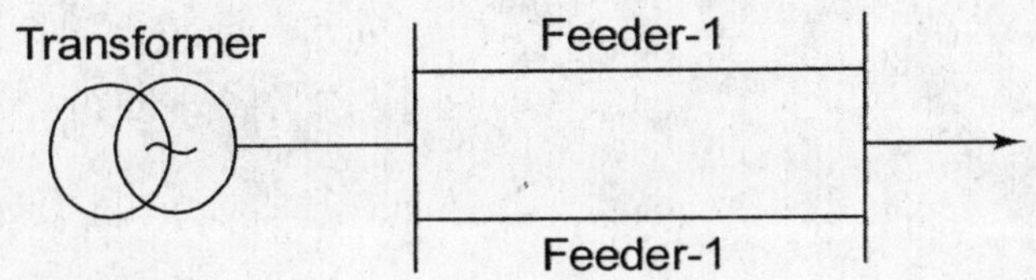

(*c*) **Ring system :** In this system, two or more radial feeders'originating from the same or different substations are laid on different routes of load areas.

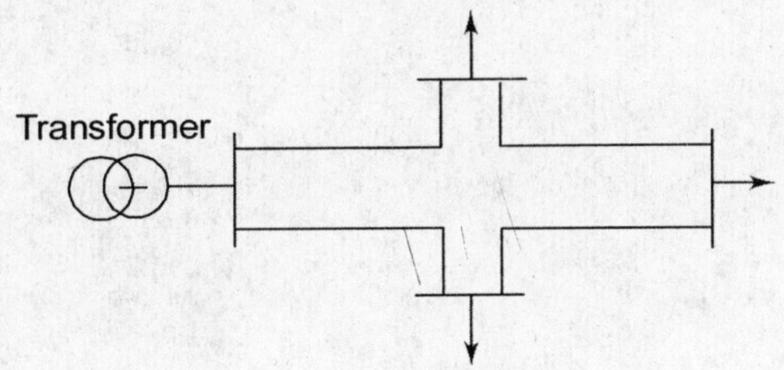

This system is most reliable for continuity of supply and gives better voltage regulation and power losses.

(*d*) Inter-connected system: When the feeder of ring main is energised from two or more than two generating stations or substations it is called the interconnected system.

This system provides better reliability and flexibility and is employed is large metropolitan cities where continuity of supply is the most important.

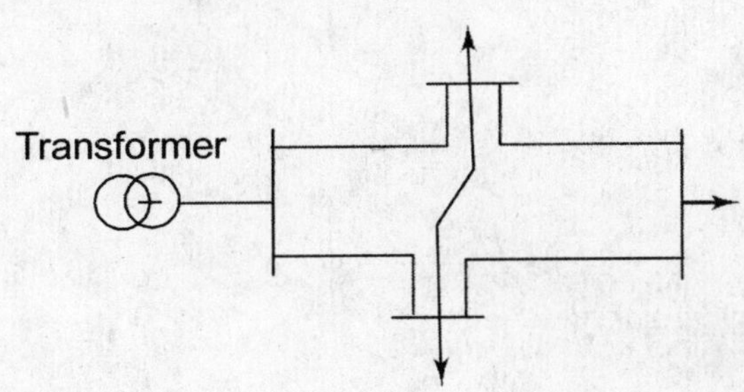

Solved Paper 2007

Electrical Engineering

(Paper II)

1. *(a)* **Draw-electrical analogue of the given magnetic circuit** **(15)**

(b) **In the magnetic circuit shown coil F_1 is supplying 4000 AT in the direction indicated. Find the AT of coil F_2 to produce air gap flux of 4 mWb from top to bottom and also current direction.** **(15)**

Core thickness = 8 cm

μ for Iron = 2500

$\mu_0 = 4\pi \times 10^{-7}$

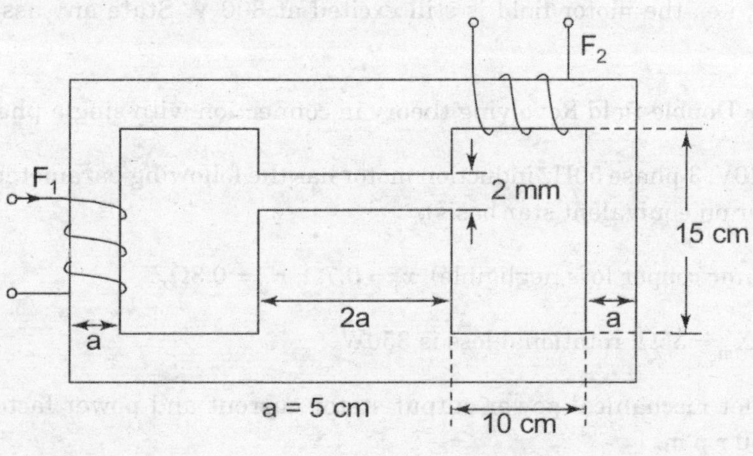

2. *(a)* **Explain the functioning of a permanent magnet type moving-coil instrument with suitable diagram**

(b) **A 25KVA, 230/115V, 50 Hz transformer has the following data:**

$r_1 = 0.12\ \Omega$, $r_2 = 0.04\ \Omega$

$X_1 = 0.2\ \Omega$, $X_2 = 0.05\ \Omega$

Find the transformer loading which will make the primary induced e.m.f. equal in magnitude to the primary terminal voltage when the carrying full load to the magnetising current. **(15)**

3. (*a*) State and explain Norton's theorem. (15)

(*b*) Use Thevenin's theorem to find the current through the switch S when it is closed. (15)

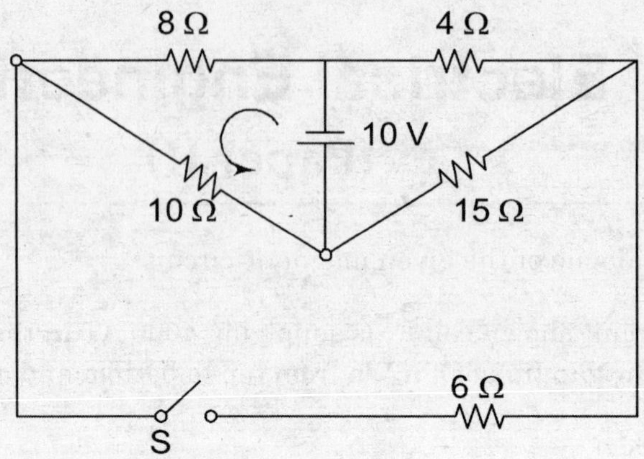

4. (*a*) Explain in detail about the Ward-Leonard system of speed control of DC motors. (15)

(*b*) A DC shunt motor is operated from 300 V mains. Its no-load speed is 1200 r.p.m. When fully loaded its speed drops to 1100 r.p.m., while it delivers a torque of 400 N.m. Find its speed and power when operated with an armature voltage of 600V, when delivering the same torque. Excitation is assumed unchanged, i.e., the motor field is still excited at 300 V, State any assumption you are required to make. (15)

5. (*a*) Explain the Double-field Revolving theory in connection with single-phase induction motor. (15)

(*b*) A 6-pole, 440V, 3-phase 50Hz induction motor has the following parameters of its circuit model (referred to the stator on equivalent star basis):

r_1 = 0.0 (stator copper loss negligible), $x_1 = 0.7\Omega$, $r'_2 = 0.3\Omega$,

$x'_2 = 0.7\Omega$, $X_m = 35\Omega$, rotational loss is 350W

Calculate net mechanical power output stator current and power factor when the motor runs at a speed of 950 r.p.m. (15)

6. (*a*) Explain in detail armature reaction is synchronous generators. (15)

(*b*) A 600V, 3-phase, 50Hz, star-connected synchronous motor has a resistance and synchronous reactance of 0.4Ω and 7Ω, respectively. It takes a current of 15 A at unity p.f. when operating with a certain field current. With the field current remaining constant, the load torque is increased until the motor draws a current of 50A. Find the torque (gross) developed and the new power factor. (15)

EXPLANATIONS

1. Given,

Core thickness = 8cm

μ_r for iron = 2500

$\mu_o = 4\pi \times 10^{-7}$

ϕ = 4mwb

F_1 = 4000 A.T

l_g = 2 mm (air gap length)

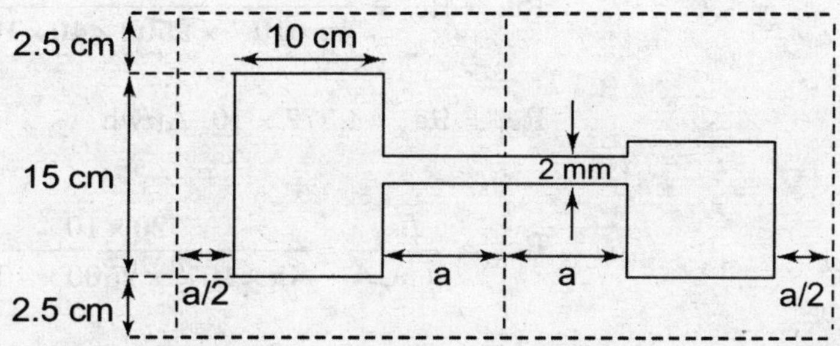

(*a*) Equivalent electrical analogue current

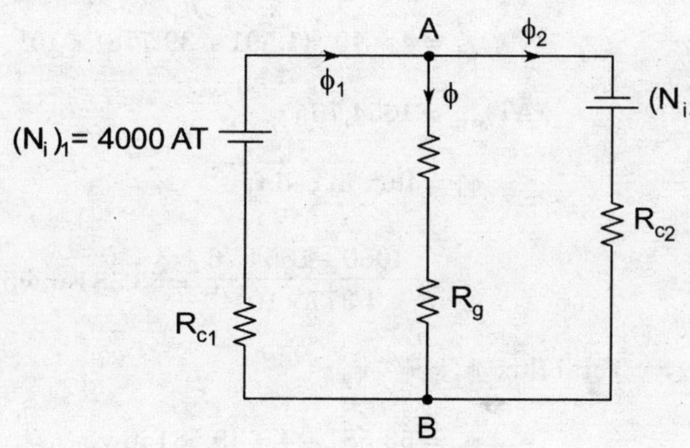

Rc_1, Rc_2, Rc_3 are core reluctance of the limbs.

(*b*) Mean length

$$Lc_1 = Lc_2$$

$$= (10 + 2.5) \times 2 + 2 \times 5 + 15 + 2.5 + 2.5$$

$$= 55 \text{ cm}$$

$$Rc_1 = Rc_2 = \frac{Lc_1}{\mu_0 \mu_r A}$$

A = core thickness × width through which flux is flowing

= 8 × a = 8 × 5 = 40 cm^2

$$R_g = \text{air gap reluctance} = \frac{l_g}{\mu_0 A}$$

$$= \frac{2 \times 10^{-3}}{4\pi \times 10^{-7} \times 40 \times 10^{-4}}$$

$$R_g = 39.788 \times 10^4 \text{ AT/wb}$$

$$Rc_1 = Rc_2 = \frac{55 \times 10^{-2}}{4\pi \times 10^{-7} \times 2500 \times 40 \times 10^{-4}}$$

$$Rc_1 = Rc_2 = 4.377 \times 10^4 \text{ At/wb}$$

$$Rc_3 = \frac{Lc_3}{\mu_0 \mu_r A} = \frac{20 \times 10^{-2}}{4\pi \times 10^{-7} \times 2500 \times 40 \times 10^{-4}}$$

$$Rc_3 = 1.591 \times 10^4 \text{ At/wb}$$

$$(AT)_{AB} = \phi\,(Rc_3 + R_g)$$

$$= 4 \times 10^{-3}(1.591 + 39.778) \times 10^4$$

$$(AT)_{AB} = 1654.76$$

$$\phi_1 = \text{flux in coil } f_1$$

$$= \frac{4000 - 1654.76}{4.377 \times 10^4} = 53.581 \text{ mwb}$$

$$\text{Total flux } \phi_1 = \phi - \phi_2$$

$$\phi_2 = 53.581 - 4 = 49.581 \text{ mwb}$$

and $$\frac{1654.76 + Ni_2}{4.377 \times 10^4} 4 = 49.581 \times 10^{-3}$$

$$\text{AT of coil } f_2 \; Ni_2 = 515.4 \text{ AT.}$$

2. (*a*) **Permanent magnet moving coil instruments (PMMC)**

The permanent magnet moving coil instruments are most accurate type for direct current measurements. The action of these instruments is based on the motoring principle. When a current carrying coil is placed in the magnetic field produced by permanent magnet, the coil experiences a force and moves. As the coil is moving and the magnet is permanent, the instrument is called permanent magnet moving coil instrument. This basic principle is called D'Arsonval principle. The amount of force experienced by the coil is proportional to the current passing through the coil.

The moving coil is either rectangular or circular in shape. It has number of turns of fine wire. The coil is suspended so that it is free to turn about its vertical axis. The coil is placed in uniform, horizontal and radial magnetic field of a permanent magnet in the shape of a horse-shoe. The iron core is spherical if coil is circular and is cylindrical if the coil is rectangular. Due to iron core, the deflecting torque increase, which increasing the sensitivity of the instrument.

The controlling torque is provided by two phosphor bronze hair springs.

The damping torque is provided by eddy current damping. It is obtained by movement of aluminum former, moving in the magnetic field of the permanent magnet.

The pointer is carried by the spindle and it moves over a graduated scale. The-pointer has light weight so that it deflects rapidly. The mirror is placed below the pointer to get the accurate reading by removing the parallax. The weight of the instrument is normally counter balanced by the weights situated diametrically opposite and rapidly connected to it. The scale markings of the basic d.c PMMC instruments are usually linearly spaced as the deflecting torque and hence the pointer deflections are directly proportional to the current passing through the coil.

The top view of PMMC instrument is shown in the below image.

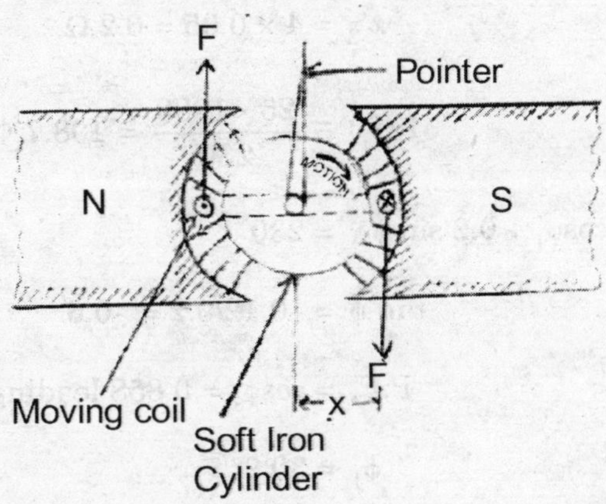

Advantages of PMMC

It has uniform scale.

With a powerful magnet, its torque to weight ratio is very high. So operating current of PMMC is small.

The sensitivity is high.

The eddy currents induced in the metallic former over which coil is wound, provide effective damping.

It consumes low power, of the order of 25 MW to 200 mW.

It has high accuracy.

Instrument is free from hysteresis error.

Extension of instrument range is possible.

Not affected by external magnetic fields called stray magnetic fields.

Disadvantages of PMMC

PMMC is Suitable for direct current measurement only. Ageing of permanent magnet and the control springs introduces the errors. The cost is high due to'delicate construction and accurate machining. The friction is due to jewel-pivot suspension.

(b)

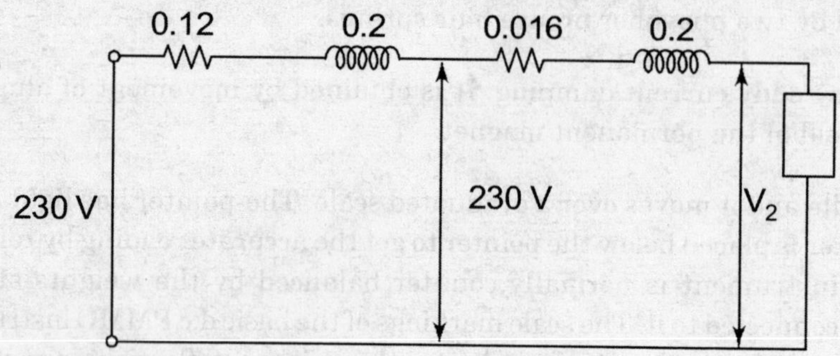

Referring to 230 V side

$$r'_2 = 4 \times 0.04 = 0.16\ \Omega$$

$$x'_2 = 4 \times 0.05 = 0.2\ \Omega$$

$$I_1(f_1) = \frac{25 \times 1000}{230} = 108.7\angle\phi\ \text{A}$$

$$230 - 108.7\,(0.12\cos\phi_1 + 0.2\sin\phi_1) = 230$$

$$\tan\phi = -0.12/0.2 = -0.6$$

$$\text{P.F.} = \cos\phi_1 = 0.858 \text{ leading}$$

$$\phi_1 = 30.9°$$

$$\bar{v}_2 = 230 - 108.7\angle 30.9° \times (0.66 + j0.2)$$

$$= 227.9\angle -6.9°$$

$$\phi_2 = 30.9° + 6.9° = 37.8°;$$

$$\cos\phi_2 = 0.79 \text{ leading}$$

$$\text{Load} = \frac{227.9 \times 108.7 \times 0.79}{1000} = 19.57 \text{ kw}$$

3. (*a*) Norton's Theorem

It states that a linear 2-terminal circuit can be replaced by on equivalent ckt consisting of current source I_N in parallel with R_N.

I_N =short circuit current through terminals

R_N =equivalent resistance at terminals when independent sources are turned off

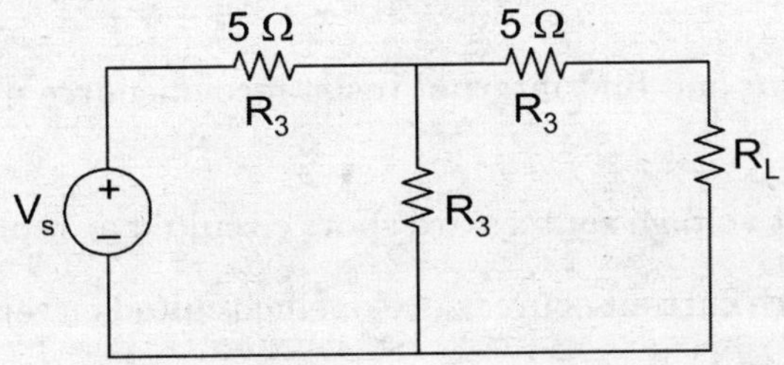

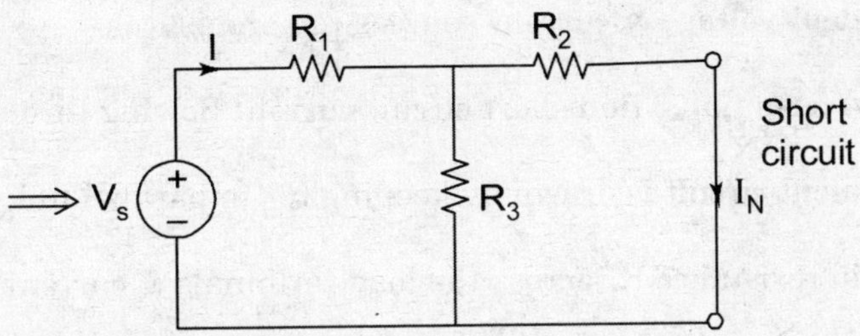

To find current through R_L, we short circuit it,

$$I = \frac{V_s}{R_1 + \left(\frac{R_2 - R_3}{R_2 + R_3}\right)} \;\&\; I_N = I\left(\frac{R_3}{R_2 + R_3}\right)$$

Then short circuit is removed & independent source is deactivated

$$R_{in} = R_2\left(\frac{R_1R_3}{R_1 + R_3}\right)$$

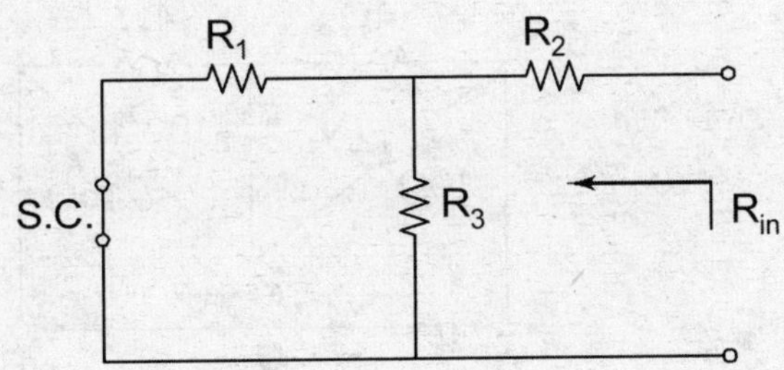

Norton's Equivalent circuit

$$I_L = I_N\left(\frac{R_{in}}{R_{in} + R_L}\right)$$

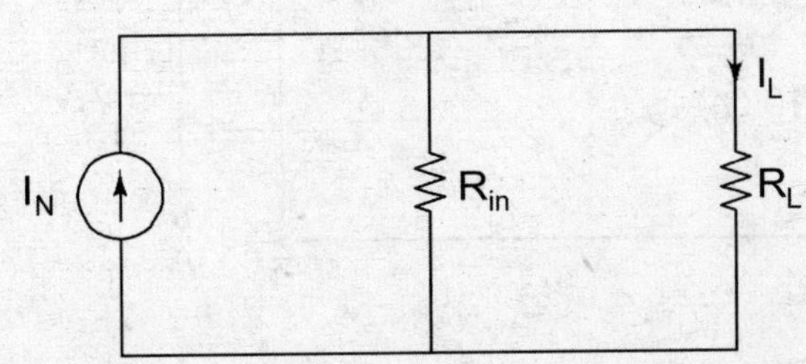

Steps :

1. Remove load resistor and find internal resistance of source network by deactivating independent sources.

   (a) all independent voltage sources are short circuited or replaced by their internal impedance.

   (b) all independence current sources are open circuited or replaced by their internal impedances

   (c) all dependent voltage & current sources remain as it is.

2. Short the load terminal & find short circuit current flowing through shorted loud terminals.

3. Norton equivalent circuit is drawn by keeping R_{in} in parallel to I_N.

4. Reconnect load resistance R_L across the load terminals & current through it is I_L.

$$I_L = I_N\left(\frac{R_{in}}{R_{in}+R_L}\right)$$

(*b*) **Step 1.** Remove 6Ω resistor and find V_{TH}.

$$V_1 = 10\times\left(\frac{8}{10+8}\right) = \frac{80}{18}V$$

$$V_2 = 10\times\left(\frac{4}{4+15}\right) = \frac{40}{19}V$$

$$V_{TH} = V_2 - V_1 = -2.339\text{ V}$$

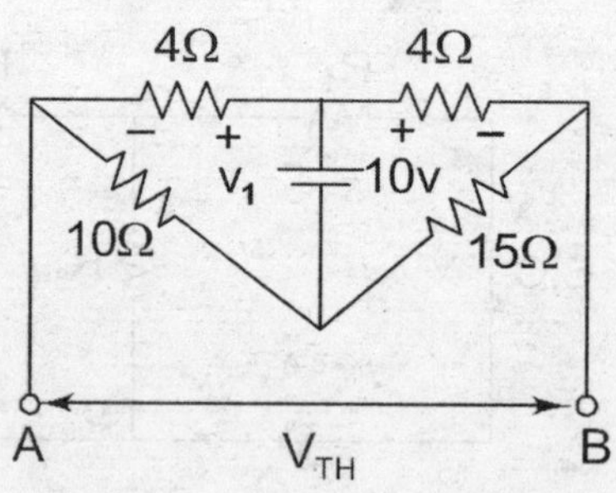

Step 2. Find Zeq after deactivating active sources.

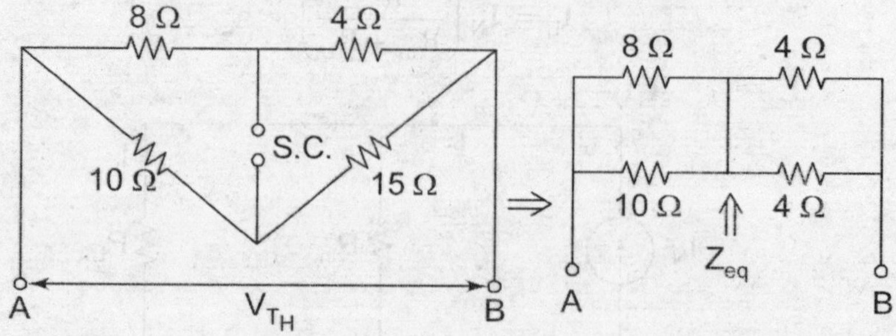

$$Zeq = (8 \parallel 10) + (4 \parallel 15) = 7.602\text{ W}$$

Step 3. Redraw Thevenin's equivalent circuit.

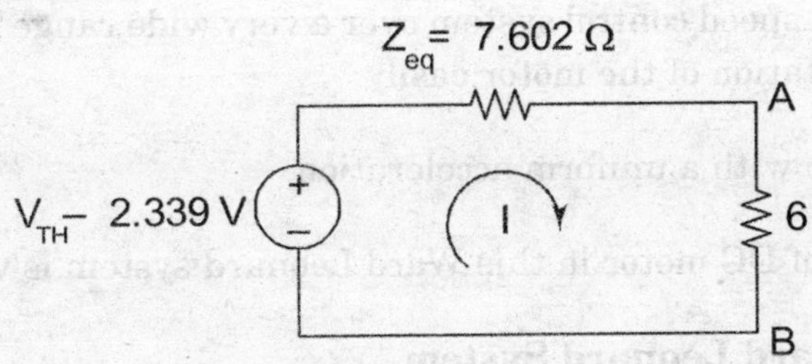

Step 4. Find I

$$I = \frac{V_{TH}}{Zeq + 6} = -0.17196 \text{ A}$$

–ve sign indicates current flowing from B to A

4. (*a*) **Ward Leonard control system**

Ward Leonard method of speed control is used for controlling the speed of a DC motor. It is a basic armature control method. This control system is consisting, of a DC motor M, and powered by a DC generator G. In this method the speed of the DC motor (M_1) is controlled by applying variable voltage across its armature. This variable voltage is obtained using a motor-generator set which consists of a motor M_2 (either AC or DC motor) directly coupled with the generator G. It is a very widely used method of speed control of DC motor.

Principle of Ward Leonard Method

The speed of motor M_1 is to be controlled which is powered by the generator G The shunt field of the motor M_1 is connected across the DC supply lines. Now, generator G is driven by the motor M_2. The speed of the motor M_2 is constant. When the output voltage of the generator is fed to the motor M_1 then the motor starts to rotate. When the output voltage of the generator varies then the speed of the motor also varies. Now controlling the output voltage of the generator the speed of motor can also be controlled. For this purpose of controlling the output voltage, a field regulator is connected across the generator with the dc supply lines to control the field excitation. The direction of rotation of the motor M_1 can be reversed by excitation current of the generator and it can be done with the help of the reversing switch R.S. But the motor-generator set must run in the same direction.

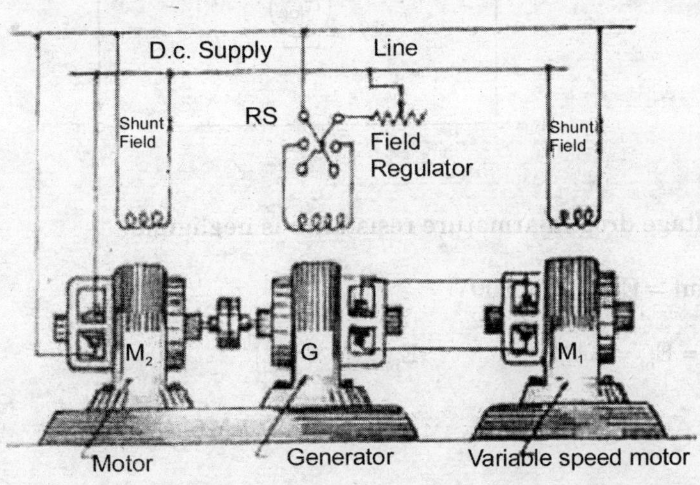

Advantages of Ward Leonard System

1. It is a very smooth speed control system over a very wide range The speed can be controlled in both the direction of rotation of the motor easily.
2. The motor can run with a uniform acceleration.
3. Speed regulation of DC motor in this Ward Leonard system is very good.

Disadvantages of Ward Leonard System

1. The system is very costly because two extra machines (motor-generator set) are required.
2. Overall efficiency of the system is not sufficient especially if it is lightly loaded.
3. Larger size and weight. Requires more floor area.

Application of Ward Leonard System

1. It is a very smooth speed control system over a very wide range (from zero to normal speed of the motor).
2. The speed can be controlled in both the direction of rotation of the motor easily.
3. The motor can run with a uniform acceleration.
4. Speed regulation of DC motor in this Ward Leonard system is very good.

(*b*) Supply voltage = 300 V

No load speed N_o = 1200 rpm

Full load speed N_{fL} = 1100 rpm

Full load torque T_{fL} = 400 Nm

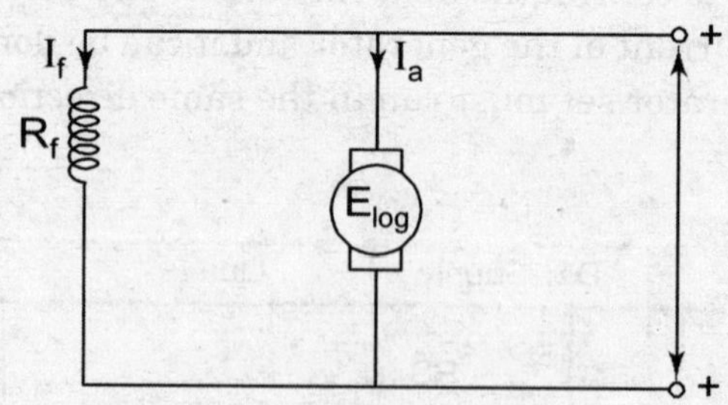

Assume no load voltage drop in armature resistance is negligible.

$\therefore$ No load back emf = $E_{bo} = V_t$ = 300V

Full load back emf = $E_{bf} = K\phi N$ $\{E_{bf} \times N \times w_m\}$

$$\frac{E_{bf}}{E_{bo}} = \frac{N_{fL}}{N_o} = \frac{w_{fL}}{w_o} \qquad \{\phi = \text{constant}\}$$

$$E_{bf} = E_{bo} \times \frac{N_{fl}}{N_o}$$

$$E_{b1} = E_{bf} = 300 \times \frac{1100}{1200} = 275 \text{ V}$$

Full load armature drop,

$$I_a . R_a = V_t - E_{bf}$$

$$= 300 - 275 = 25\text{V}$$

$$\text{Torque } T = K\,\phi\, I_a \text{ and } T = \frac{E_{b1} I_{a1}}{W_m}$$

$$I_{a1} = \frac{T.w_m}{E_{bf}} = \frac{400 \times 2\pi \times 1100}{275 \times 60}$$

$$I_{a1} = 167.5516 \text{ A}$$

Machine operated with V 600V & excitation is constant so flux ϕ is also constant.

Torque is same as before

$$\therefore \qquad I_a = I_{a1} = I_{a2} = 167.55 \text{ A}$$

$$V_{t2} = E_{b2} + I_{a2}\, Ra$$

$$E_{b2} = 600 - 25 = 575 \text{ V}$$

Speed,

$$N_2 = N_1 \times \frac{E_{b2}}{E_{b1}} = 1100 \times \frac{575}{525}$$

$$N_2 = 2300 \text{ rpm}$$

Power,

$$P_o = E_{b2}\, I_a, = 575 \times 167.5516 = 96.34217 \text{ kw}$$

5. (*a*) **Double Revolving Field Theroy**

According lo this theory, any alternating quantity can be resolved into two rotating components which rotate in opposite directions and each having magnitude as half of the maximum magnitude of the alternating quantity.

In case of single phase induction motors, the stator winding produces an alternating magnetic field having maximum magnitude of Φ_{lm}. According to double revolving field theory, consider the two components of the stator flux, each having magnitude half of maximum magnitude of stator flux i.e. ($\Phi_{lm}/2$). Both these components are rotating in opposite directions at the synchronous speed N_s which is dependent on frequency and stator poles.

Let Φ_f is forward component rotating in anticlockwise direction while Φ_b is the backward component rotating in clockwise direction. The resultant of these two components at any instant gives the instantaneous value of the stator flux at the instant. So resultant of these two is the original stator flux. The fig. 1 shows the stator flux and its two components Φ_f and Φ_b. At start both the components are shown opposite to each other in the Fig. (a).

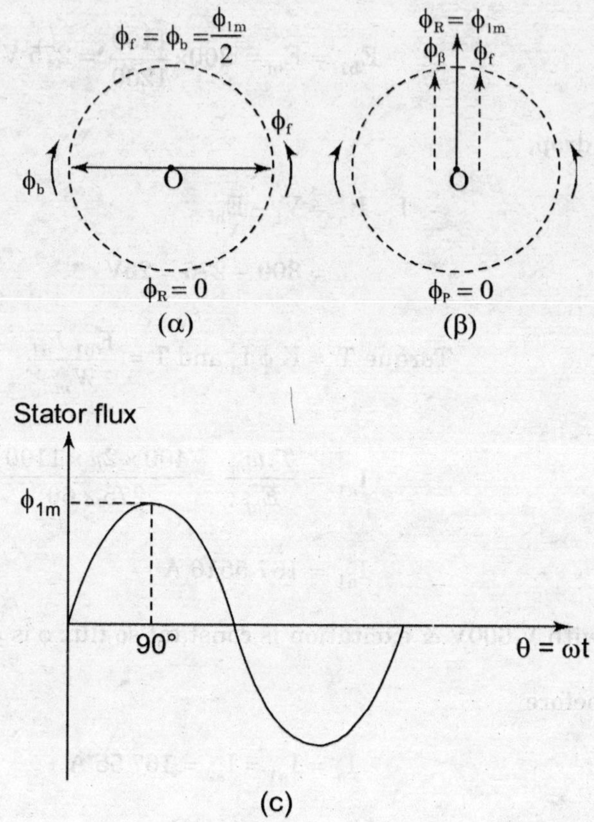

Figure 1

Thus the resultant $\Phi_R = 0$. This is nothing but the instantaneous value of the stator flux at start. After 90°, as shown in the Fig, the two components are rotated in such a way that both are pointing in the same direction. Hence the resultant Φ_R is the algebraic sum of the magnitudes of the two components. So $\Phi_R = (\Phi_{lm}/2) + (\Phi_{lm}/2) = \Phi_{lm}$. This is nothing but the instantaneous value of the stator flux at $\theta = 90°$ as shown in the Fig l(c). Thus continuous rotation of the two components gives the original alternating stator flux.

Both the components are rotating and hence get cut by the motor conductors. Due to cutting of flux, e.m.f. gels induced in rotor which circulate rotor current. The rotor current produces rotor flux. This flux interacts with forward component Φ_f to produce a torque in one particular direction say anticlockwise direction. While rotor flux interacts with backward component Φ_b to produce a torque in the clockwise direction. So if anticlockwise torque is positive then clockwise torque is negative.

At start these two torque are equal in magnitude but opposite in direction. Each torque tries to rotate the rotor in its own direction. Thus net torque experienced by the rotor is zero at start. And hence the single phase induction motors are not self starting.

Torque speed characteristics

The two oppositely directed torques and the resultant torque can be shown effectively with the help of torque-speed characteristics. It is shown in the Fig.2.

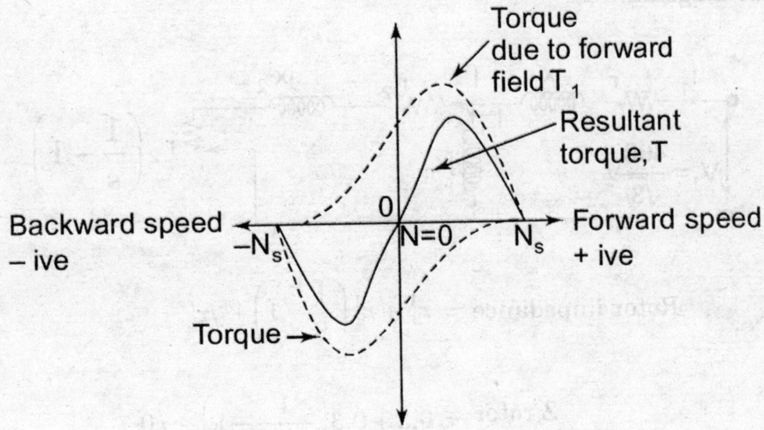

Fig. 2 Torque-speed characteristic

It can be seen that at start N = 0 and at that point resultant torque is zero. So single phase motors are not self starting.

However if the rotor is given an initial rotation in any direction, the resultant average torque increase in the direction in which rotor initially rotated. And motor starts rotating in that direction. But in practice it is not possible to give initial torque to rotor externally hence some modifications are done in the construction of single phase induction motors to make them self starting.

Another theory which can also be used to explain why single phase induction motors is not self starting is cross-field theory.

(*b*) Stator resistance = $r_1 = 0.05\ \Omega$ (Stator copper loss negligible)

Stator reactance = $x_1 = j0.7\Omega$

Rotor resistance referred to stator

$$r_2' = 0.3\Omega$$

Rotor reactance referred to stator

$$x_2' = j0.7\Omega$$

$$x_n = j3.5\ \Omega$$

Rotational loss = 350 w = 0.35 kw

Motor speed N = 950 rpm

Synchronous speed of motor,

$$N_s = \frac{120f}{P}$$

$$N_s = \frac{120 \times 50}{6} = 1000 \text{ rpm}$$

$$\text{Slip, s} = \frac{N_s - N}{N_s}$$

$$= \frac{1000 - 950}{1000} = 0.05$$

Equivalent circuit diagram

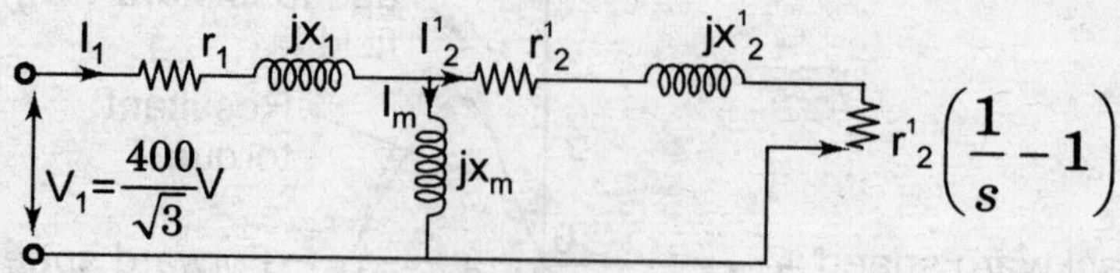

$$\text{Rotor impedance} = r_2^1 + r_2^1\left(\frac{1}{S} - 1\right) + jx_2'$$

$$\text{Z rotor} = 0.3 + 0.3\left(\frac{1}{0.05} - 1\right) + j\,0.7$$

$$= (6 + j0.7)\Omega$$

$$Z_{eq} = [(\text{Zrotor}) \parallel jXm\,] + (r_1 + jx_1)$$

(r_1 is neglected as given the stator copper losses are negligible)

$$= [(6 + j0.7) \parallel (j35) + (0 + j0.7)]$$

$$= 5.6086 + j2.3289$$

$$= 6.0729 \angle 22.55°\Omega$$

$$\text{Stator currents } I_1 = \frac{V}{Z_{eg}} = \frac{(4401\sqrt{3})\angle 0°}{6.0729\angle 22.55°}$$

$$= 41.8308\angle -22.55° \text{ A}$$

Using current division rule,

$$I_2' = I_1\left(\frac{jxm}{\text{Zrotor} + jxm}\right)$$

$$= 41.8308\angle -22.55° \times \frac{j\,35}{6 + j\,0.7 + j\,35}$$

$$= 40.44\angle -13.009°A$$

Mechanical power developed,

$$P_{mech} = 3(I_2')^2\, r_2\left(\frac{1}{S} - 1\right)$$

$$= 3 \times (40.44)^2 \times 0.3\left(\frac{1}{0.05} - 1\right)$$

$$= 27.9699 \text{ kw}$$

$$\text{Shaft power } P_{shaft} = P_{mech} - \text{Rotational loss}$$

$$= 27.9699 - 0.35 = 27.6199 \text{ kw}$$

$$\text{Power factor } \cos\phi = \cos(22.55°)$$

$$= 0.9235 \text{ (lagging)}$$

$$\text{Shaft Power, } P_o = 27.6199 \text{ kw}$$

$$\text{Stator current } I_1 = 41.80308 \text{ A}$$

$$\text{Power factor } \phi = 0.9235 \text{ lagging}$$

6. *(a)* **Armature Reaction in Synchronous Generator:**

The effect of armature (stator) flux on the flux produced by the rotor field poles is called armature reaction. When the current flows through the stator winding of an alternator, a flux isproduced by the resulting mmf. This armature flux reacts with the main pole flux, causing the resultant flux to become either less than, more than the original main field flux.

The armature reaction in synchronous generators are under following three conditions:

(i) unity power factor

(ii) zero power factor lagging

(iii) zero power factor leading

The power factor can be defined as the cosine of the angle between the armature phase current and the induced emf in the armature conductor in that phase.

(i) **Armature reaction at unity power factor:** Suppose that the alternator is supplying current at unity power factor. The phase current I_A, I_B and I_C will be in phase with their respective generated voltages i.e. E_A, E_B and E_C.

At ωt = 0, the instantaneous value of current and fluxes are

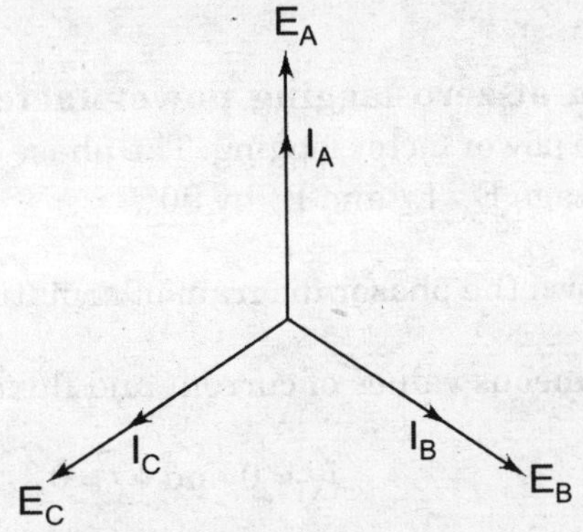

$$i_A = I_m \text{ and } \phi_A = \phi_m$$

$$i_B = -I_m \cos 60° = -0.5\, I_m \text{ and } \phi_B = -0.5\, \phi_m$$

$$i_C = -I_m \cos 60° = 0.5\ I_m \text{ and } \phi_C = 0.5\ \phi_m$$

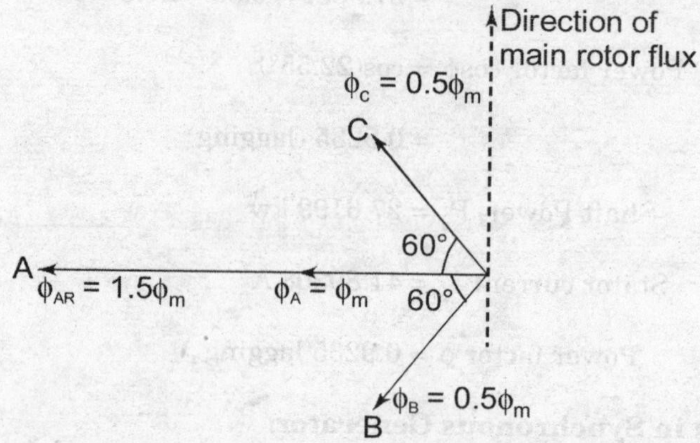

Resolving along horizontal direction, we get

$$\phi_H = -\phi_A - \phi_B \cos 60° - \phi \cos 60°$$

$$= -\phi_A - \left(\frac{1}{2}\phi_m\right)(0.5) - \left(\frac{1}{2}\phi_m\right)(0.5)$$

$$= -1.5\phi_m$$

Similarly, resolving along the vertical direction we get

$$\phi_V = -\phi_B \cos 30° + \phi_C \cos 30°$$

$$= 0.5\ \phi_m \cos 30° + 0.5\phi_m \cos 30° = 0$$

The resultant armature reaction flux is

$$\phi_{ar} = \sqrt{\phi_H^2 + \phi_V^2} = \sqrt{(1.5\phi_m)^2 + 0} = 1.5\ \phi_m$$

The armature reaction flux ϕ_{AR} lags behind the main field by 90°. This is called cross magnetizing flux.

(*ii*) **Armature reaction at zero lagging power factor:** If the alternator is loaded with an pure inductive load of zero power factor lagging. The phase current I_A, I_B and I_C will be lagging with their respective phase voltage E_A, E_B and E_C by 90°.

The figure below shows the phasor diagram of armature reaction as lagging load.

At t = 0, the instantaneous values of current and fluxes are given as

$$i_A = 0 \text{ and } \phi_A = 0,$$

$$i_B = I_m \sin(-120°) = -\frac{\sqrt{3}}{2} I_m$$

and $$\phi_B = -\frac{\sqrt{3}}{2}\phi_m$$

$$i_C = I_m \sin(-120°) = \frac{\sqrt{3}}{2} I_m$$

$$\phi_C = \frac{\sqrt{3}}{2}\phi_m$$

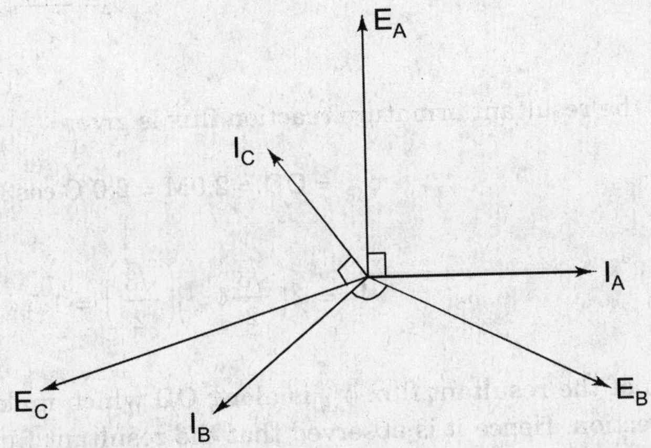

If the rotor is rotated at 30° in a clockwise direction, the corresponding phasor diagram is shown in below figure.

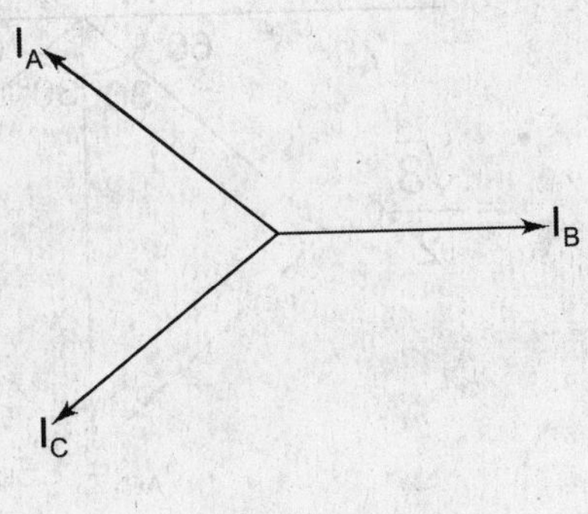

At $\omega t = 30°$; the instantaneous value of current and fluxes are

$$I_A = I_m \cos 30° = \frac{\sqrt{3}}{2} I_m \text{ and } \phi_A = \frac{\sqrt{3}}{2}\phi_m$$

$$I_B = 0 \text{ and } \phi_B = 0$$

$$I_C = -I_m \cos 30° = -\frac{\sqrt{3}}{2} I_m \text{ and } \phi_C = -\frac{\sqrt{3}}{2}\phi_m$$

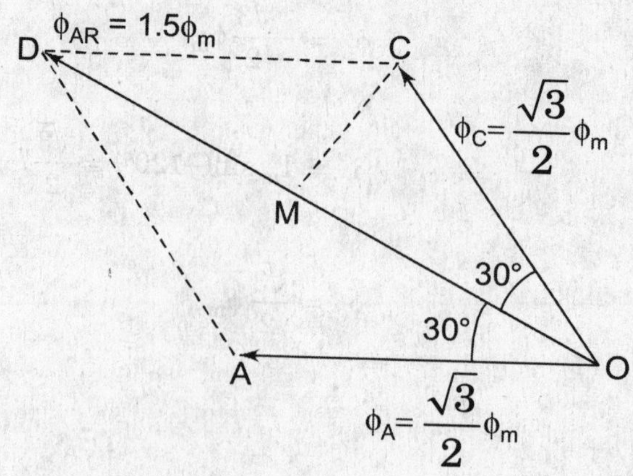

Here, $\phi_B = 0$, the resultant armature reaction flux is given

$$\phi_{AR} = OD = 2.0M = 2.0\ C\cos 30°$$

$$= 2\left(\frac{\sqrt{3}}{2}\phi_m\right)\left(\frac{\sqrt{3}}{2}\right) = 1.5\ \phi_m$$

The direction of the resultant flux ϕ_{AR} is along OD which makes an angle with horizontal in the clockwise direction. Hence it is observed that the resultant flux ϕ_{AR} sets up by the current in the armature remains constant in magnitude equal to $1.5\phi_m$ and it rotates at synchronous speed when the current is in phase with the induced voltage of the armature.

The space diagram of the magnitude fluxes is shown below:

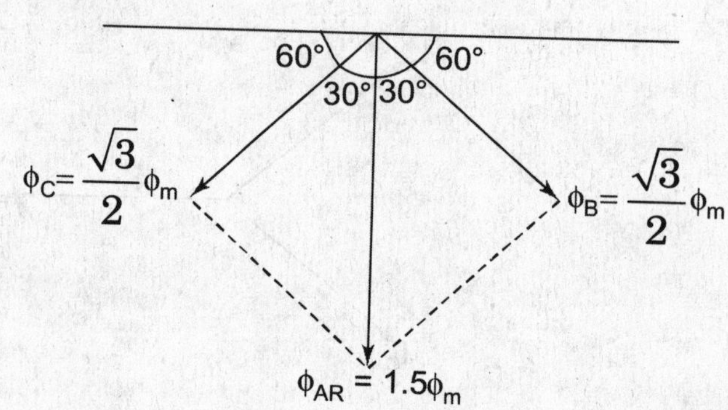

The resultant flux ϕ_{AR} is given by

$$\phi^2_{AR} = \phi^2_B + \phi^2_C + 2\phi_B\phi_C\cos 60°$$

$$\phi^2_{AR} = \left(\frac{\sqrt{3}}{2}\phi_m\right)^2 + \left(\frac{\sqrt{3}}{2}\phi_m\right)^2 + 2\left(\frac{\sqrt{3}}{2}\phi_m\right)\left(\frac{\sqrt{3}}{2}\phi_m\right)\times\frac{1}{2}$$

$$\phi_{AR} = 1.5\ \phi_m$$

The direction of armature flux is opposite to the main field flux. Therefore it will oppose and weaken the main field flux. it is said to be demagnetized.

(*iii*) **Armature reaction at zero leading power factor :** If the alternator is loaded with a load of zero power factor leading. The phase current I_A, I_B and I_C will be leading their respectiv phase voltages E_A, E_B, and E_C by 90°. The phase diagram is shown below.

At t = 0, the instantaneous values of currents and fluxes are given.

$$I_A = 0 \text{ and } \phi_A = 0$$

$$I_B = I_m \cos 30° = \frac{\sqrt{3}}{2} I_m \text{ and } \phi_B = \frac{\sqrt{3}}{2}\phi_m$$

$$I_C = I_m \cos 30° = -\frac{\sqrt{3}}{2} I_m \text{ and } \phi_C = \frac{\sqrt{3}}{2}\phi_m$$

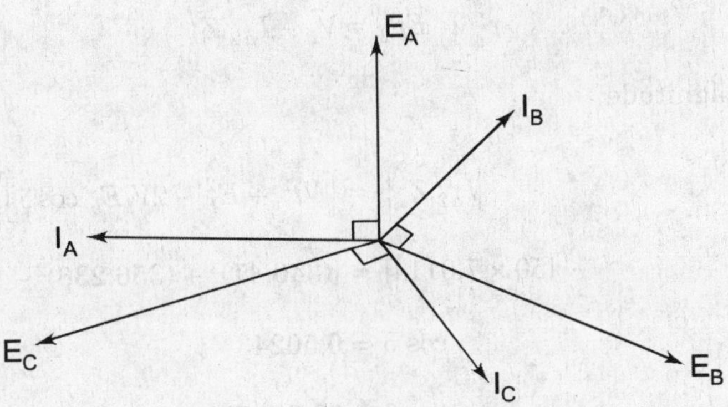

The direction of the flux is shown below in the phasor diagram.

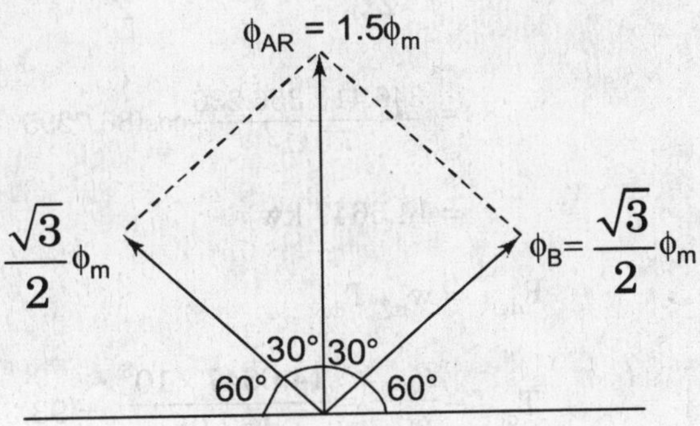

(*b*) Resistance of synchronous motor = 0.4W

Reactance of synchronous motor = 7W

Synchronous motor impedance,

$$Z_s = (0.4 + j7)\text{W}$$

$$\bar{Z}_s = 7.0119 \angle 86.729° \Omega$$

Current $\vec{I}_a = 15\angle 0°$

$$\vec{E}_f = \vec{V}_t - \vec{I}_a.\vec{Z}_s$$

$$= \frac{600}{\sqrt{3}}\angle 0° - (15\angle 0°)(7.0114\angle 86.7295°)$$

$$= 356.236\angle -17.142° V$$

Field current remaining constant so $|E_f|$ is constant

$$|E_{f1}| = |E_{f2}| = 356.236V$$

and
$$I_{a2} = 50A$$

$$\vec{E}f_2 = \vec{V}_t - I_{a2}.\vec{Z}_s$$

Taking only magnitude

$$\left|\vec{I}_{a2}.\vec{Z}_s\right| = \left[Vt^2 + E_f^2 - 2V_tE_b \cos\delta\right]^{1/2}$$

$$[50 \times 7.0114] = [(346.41)^2 + (356.236)^2 - 2 \times 346.41 \times 356.236 \times \cos\delta]V^2$$

$$\cos\delta = 0.50243$$

$$\delta = 59.8387°$$

Now developed power

$$P_{dev.} = \frac{V_tE_f}{Z_s}\cos(\theta_s - s) - \frac{E_{b2}}{Z_s}\cos\theta_s$$

$$= \frac{346.41 \times 356.236}{7.0114}\cos(86.7295° - 59.8397°) - \frac{(356.236)^2}{7.0114}\cos(86.7295°)$$

$$= 14.6647 \text{ kw}$$

$$P_{dev.} = w_m.\, T_{dev}$$

$$T_{dev} = \frac{P_{dev}}{w_m} = \frac{14.6647 \times 10^3}{157.08} = 93.355\ N_m$$

$$P_{dev.} = V_t\, I_a \cos\phi$$

$$14.6647 \times 103 = 346.41 \times 50 \times \cos\phi$$

Power factor $\cos\phi = 0.8466$ Lagging

$$\left\{\begin{aligned} \because w_m &= \frac{2\pi N_s}{60} = \frac{2\pi \times 120 \times f}{60 \times P} \\ &= \frac{2\pi \times 120 \times 50}{60 \times 4} = 50\pi = 157.08 \text{rad/sec} \end{aligned}\right\}$$

Practice Paper 1

1. (*a*) A copper wire has a resistance of 0.80 Ω at 20°C. What will be its resistance at 40°C? Temperature coefficient of resistance of copper at 0°C is 0.004°C. (10)

   (*b*) In the circuit shown in Figure, what is the value of V? (10)

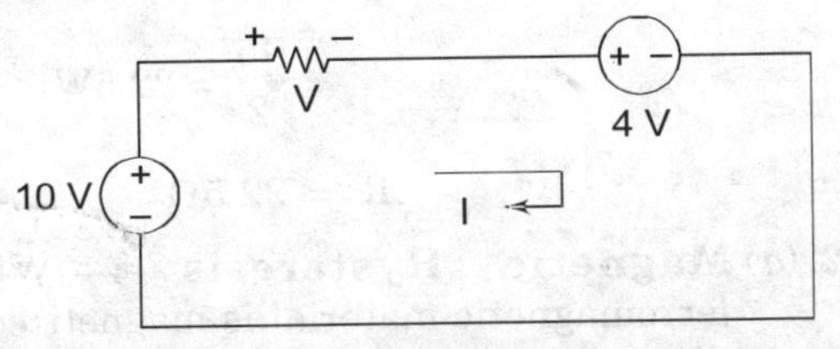

Figure 1

   (*c*) What is the value of Thevenin voltage V_{Th} in the given circuit of Figure? (10)

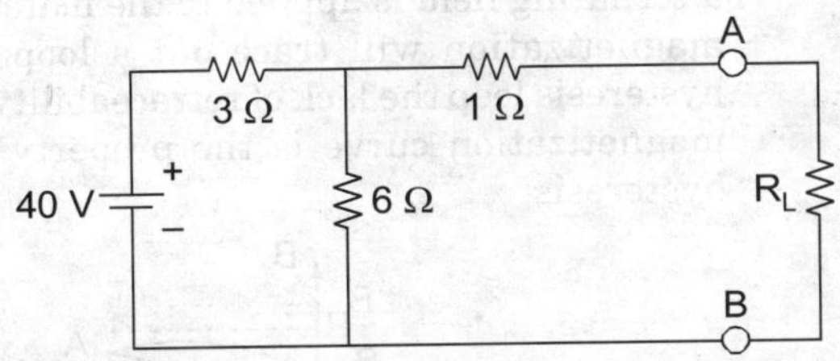

Figure 2

   (*d*) In Figure, find the value of resistance R. (30)

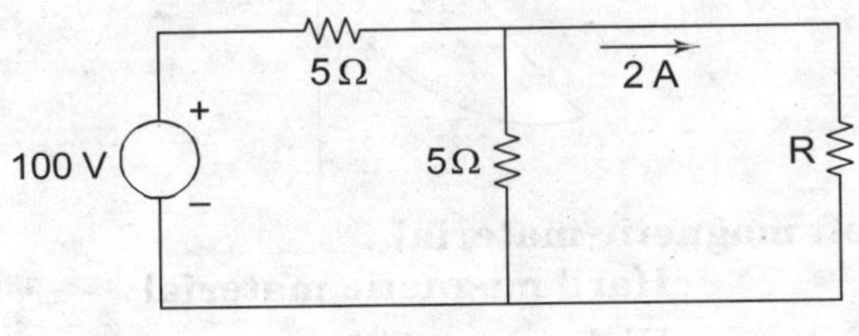

Figure 3

2. (*a*) What do you understand by magnetic hysteresis? Differentiate between hard and soft magnetic materials. (30)

   (*b*) Deduce an expression for the average power in a single phase RL circuit and hence explain the term power factor. (30)

3. (*a*) Describe the working principle and construction of an induction type wattmeter. What are the errors in induction type wattmeter, and how are they compensated? (30)

   (*b*) The four arms of a Maxwell A.C. bridge are as follows:

   AB and BC are non-inductive resistors of 100 Ω each, DA is a standard variable inductor L of resistance 38 Ω and CD comprises a standard variable resistor R in series with a coil of unknown impedance. Balance is obtained when L = 46 mH and R = 1.2 Ω. Find the resistance and inductance of the coil. (30)

4. (*a*) Explain the various losses in DC machines. (20)

   (*b*) A DC machine induces an EMF of 240 V at 1000 rpm. Find the developed torque for an armature current of 15 A. (10)

   (*c*) A 3300/300 V single phase transformer gives 0.5 A and 50 W as ammeter and wattmeter reading when supply is given to the low voltage winding and high voltage winding is kept open. What is the power factor of no load current? (15)

   (*d*) A 3 hp, 3-phase 4-pole, 400V 50Hz induction motor runs at 1220 rpm. What will be the frequency of the rotor-induced EMF? (15)

5. (*a*) What is loss load factor? Explain in detail how the loss load factor can be determined. (30)

   (*b*) Discuss various bus bar systems for distribution networks. (30)

6. (*a*) Discuss the laws of illumination and their limitations in actual practice. (30)

   (*b*) Draw the output characteristics of a common-emitter transistor. Show various regions of operation of the BJT on this characteristic. Describe the applications of operating the BJT into different regions. (30)

EXPLANATIONS

1. (*a*) Given:

at 20°C value of resistance is 0.80Ω

at 40°C change in temp Δt = 40–20 = 20°C

$$R_{40} = R_{20}(1 + \alpha\ \Delta t)$$

$$\therefore \quad \alpha = 0.004°C \text{ given}$$

$$R_{40} = 0.80(1 + 0.004 \times 20)$$

$$\boxed{R_{40} = 0.864\Omega}$$

(*b*)

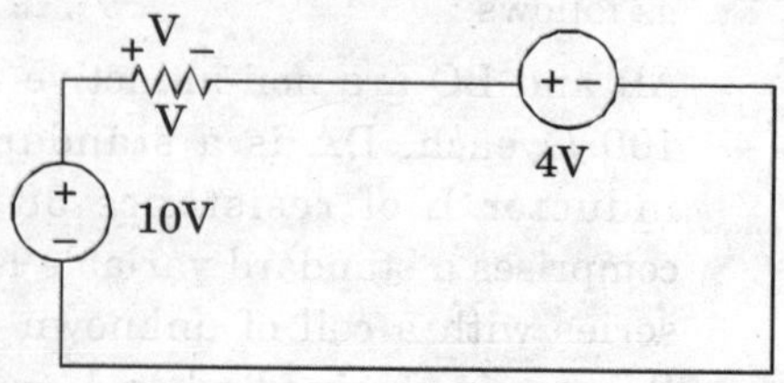

We have to find out the value of V in given circuit

On applying KVL

$$-10 + V + 4 = 0$$

$$\boxed{V = 6V}$$

(*c*) Find out the value of V_{TH} in given circuit

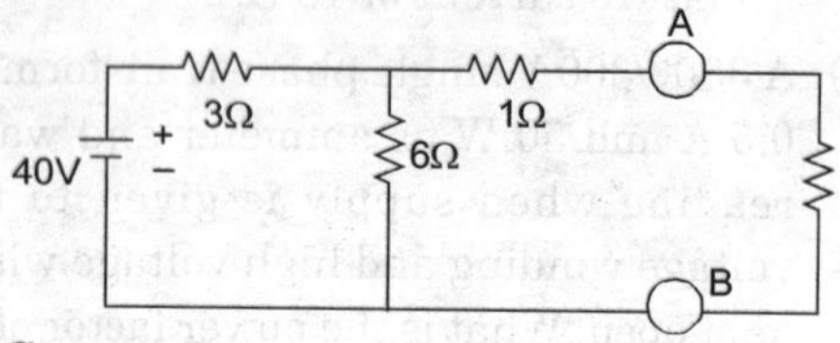

Step 1. Remove R_L

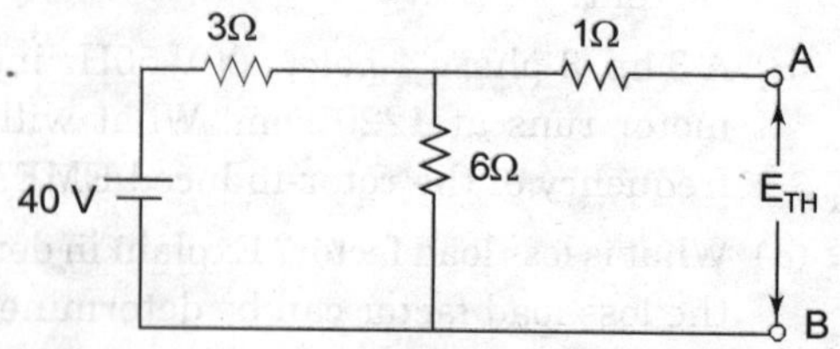

V_{TH} means voltage across 7W resistance

$$V_{TH} = \frac{6 \times 40}{6 + 3} = 26.66V$$

$$\boxed{E_{TH} = 27V}$$

(*d*) We have to find out the value of R in given circuit

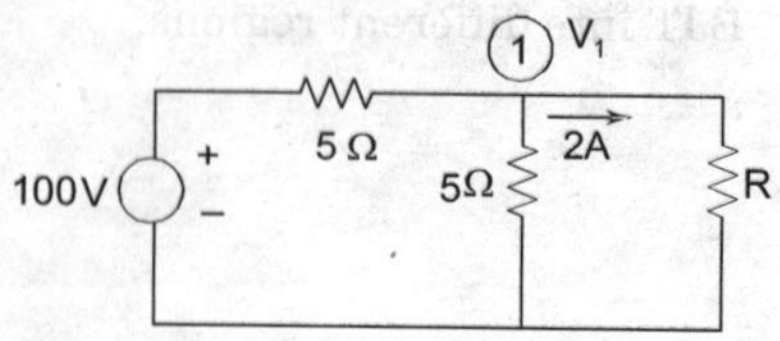

On applying KCL at node 1,

$$\frac{V_1 - 100}{5} + \frac{V_1 - 0}{5} + 2 = 0$$

$$\Rightarrow \quad 2V_1 - 100 + 10 = 0$$

$$\boxed{V_1 = 45}$$

$$\therefore \quad R = \frac{V_1}{2}$$

$$= \frac{45}{2} = 22.5W$$

$$R = 22.5\Omega$$

2. (*a*) **Magnetic Hysteresis :** When a ferromagnetic material is magnetized in one direction it will not relax back to zero magnetization when the imposed magnetizing field is removed. It must be driven back to zero by a field in the opposible direction. If an alternating field is applied to the materi-l its magnetization will trace out a loop called hysteresis loop the lack of retraceability of the magnetization curve is the property called hysteresis.

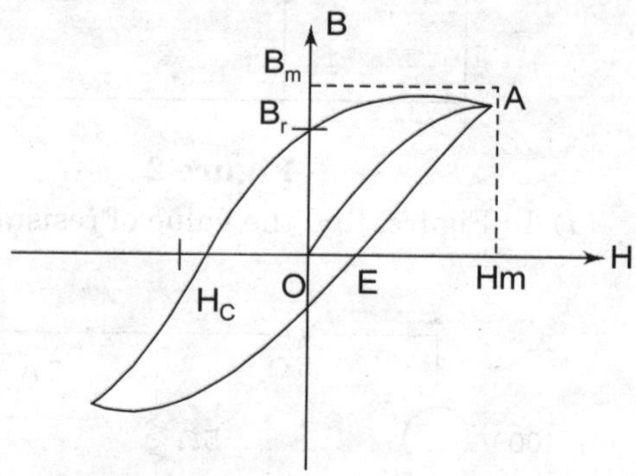

Soft magnetic material

Hard magnetic material

→ High permeability
→ High permeability
→ low retentivity
→ high retentivity
→ low coercivity
→ high coercivity
→ small hysteresis loop
→ large hystersis loop
→ suitable for making
→ high curve temp
→ transformer core, electromagnets
→ suitable for permanent magnet Ex: Alnico (used in magnetic shielding)

(*b*) Consider an R.L circuit shown below

V(t)= instantaneous supply voltage

V(t)= Vmsinωt

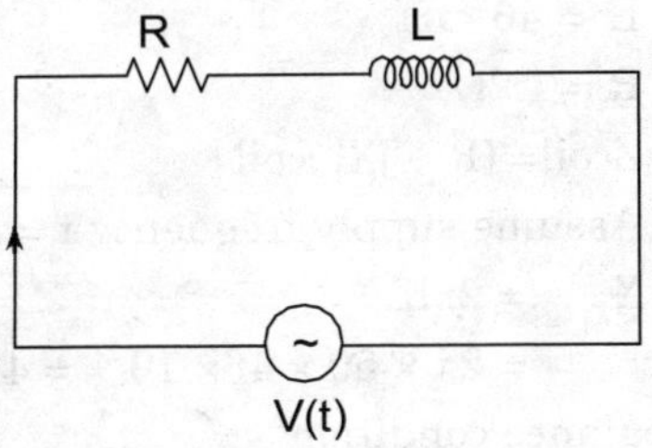

The angle between i and v which is in the Lagging nature is i.e. ϕ

$$\phi = \tan^{-1}\left(\frac{wL}{R}\right)$$

Instantaneous current i = Im sin (ωt – ϕ)

Instantaneous power p = v.i

$$= [V_m \sin \omega t]\ [I_m \sin (\omega t - \phi)]$$

$$= V_m\ I_m \sin \omega t \times \sin(\omega t - \phi)$$

$$= \frac{V_m I_m}{2}[\cos\phi - \cos(2\omega t - \phi)]$$

$$= V_{rms}\ I_{rms}\ [\cos\phi - \cos(2\omega t - \phi)]$$

Now average power P_{avg} =

$$\frac{1}{T}\int_0^T P.d(\omega t)$$

$$P_{avg} = \frac{1}{2\pi}\int_0^{2\pi} V_{rms}I_{rms}[\cos\phi - \cos(2\omega t - \phi)]d(\omega t)$$

$$P_{avg} = \frac{V_{rms}I_{rms}}{2\pi}\left[\cos\phi(\omega t) - \frac{\sin(2\omega t - \phi)}{2}\right]_0^{2\pi}$$

$$= \frac{V_{rms}I_{rms}}{2\pi}\ [\cos\phi(2\pi - 0) - 0]$$

$$= \frac{1}{2\pi}V_{rms}I_{rms}(2\pi\cos\phi)$$

$$\boxed{P = V_{rms}\ I_{rms}\cos\phi}$$

Power factor: The ratio of the actual electrical power dissipated by an AC circuit to the product of the r.m.s values of current and voltage. The difference between the two is caused by reactance in the circuit and represents power that does no useful work. It is denoted by cos ϕ

$$\cos\phi = \frac{P}{S}$$

$$S = \sqrt{P^2 + Q^2}$$

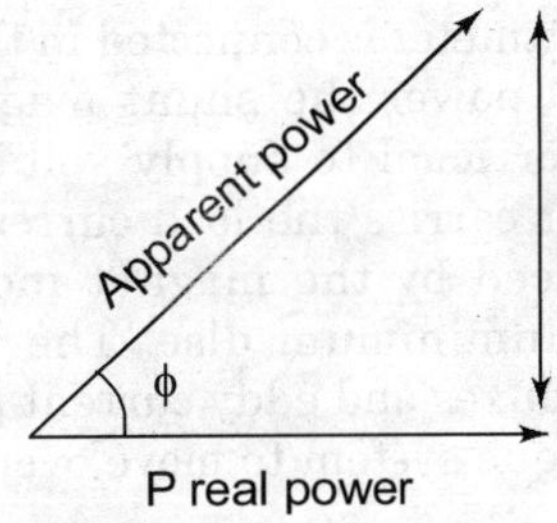

3. (*a*) **Induction type wattmeter:**

The induction type wattmeter is used to measure a.c power only

Principle of induction type wattmeters: The principle of operation of an induction type wattmeter is same as that of induction ameter and voltmeters i.e induction principle. However, it differs from induction ammeter or voltmeter in so far that separate two coils are used to produced the rotating flux in place of one coil with phase split arrangement

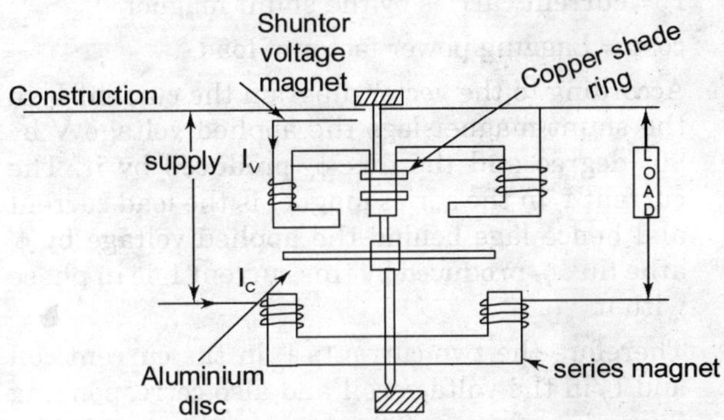

The principle parts of an induction wattmeter is shown above. It consist of two laminated electromagnets. One electromagnets called shunt magnet is connected across supply and carries current proportional to the applied voltage. The coil of this magnet is made highly inductive so that the current in it lags behind the supply and carries the load current. The coil of this magnet is made highly non inductive so that the angle of lag or lead is determined fully by load. A thin aluminium disc mounted on the spindle is placed between the twp magnets so that it cuts the fluxes of both the magnets. Thd controlling torque is provided by spirial springs. The damping is electromagnet and is usually provided by permanent magnet embracing the aluminimum disc. Two or more closed copper rings are provided on the central limb of shunt magnet. By adjunting the position of these rings, the shunt magnet flux can be made to lag behind supply voltage by 90 degree

Working of induction type wattmeter:

When the wattmeter is connected in the circuit to measure O.C power the shunt magnet carries current proportional to supply voltage and the series magnet carries the load current. The two fluxes produced by the magnet induced eddy current in aluminimum disc. The interaction between the fluxes and eddy current produce the deflecting torque system to move over the scale

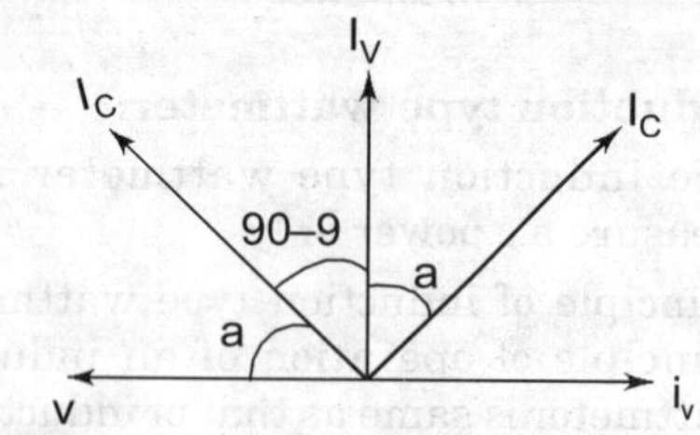

Deflecting torque of induction type wattmeter:

Let V = applied voltage

I_c = Load current carries by the series magnet

I_v = current carries by the shunt magnet

cosϕ = Lagging power factor of load.

According to the vector diagram the current I_v in the shunt magnet lags the applied voltage V by 90° degree and the flux ϕ_v produced by it. The current I_c in the series magnet is the load current and hence lags behind the applied voltage by ϕ' athe flux ϕ_c produced by this current I_c is in phase with it

Therefore the two currents I_c in the current coil and I_v in the voltage coil and also corresponding fluxes ϕ_v and ϕ_c are (90 – ϕ) apart.

The flux ϕ_c induced the eddy current iv in the aluminimum disc which lags behind the flux by 90°.

Similarly flux ϕ_c induce eddy current i_c which again lags behind the flux ϕ_c by 90 degrees

$$\boxed{T_d \alpha VI \cos\phi}$$

Errors in single phase energy meter. (Pg. 192-193 madeeary)

Last heading

Temp. Compensation:

(*b*)

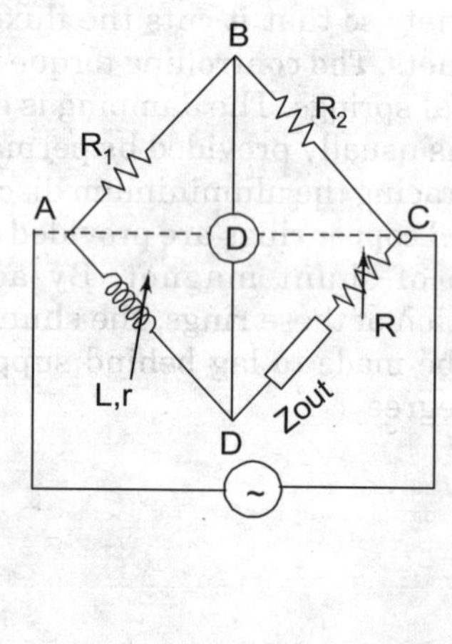

Given that

$R_{AB} = R_{BC} = 100\Omega$

r = 38 Ω

L = 46 mH

R = 1.2Ω

Zcoil= (R + jX_L)coil

Assume supply frequency f = 50Hz

X_L = 2πfL

= 2π × 50 × 46× 10^{-3} = 4.6 πΩ

In balance condition

R_1[Zcoil + R] = R_2[r + jX_L]

100[Zcoil + 1.2] = 100[38 + j4.6Ω]

Zcoil = 38 + j4.6π – 1.2

(R + jX_L) coil = 36.8 + j4.6

Resistance of coil = 36.8Ω

$$\text{Inductance of coil} = \frac{4.6}{2\pi f}$$

$$= \frac{4.6}{2\pi \times 50} = 14.6\text{mH}$$

4. (*a*) Losses in a rotating DC machine

(*i*) Copper loss

(*a*) Armature Cu loss

(*b*) Field Cu loss

(*c*) Loss due to brush contact resistance

(*ii*) Iron losses

(*a*) Hysteresis loss

(*b*) Eddy current loss

(*iii*) Mechanical loss

(*a*) Friction loss

(*b*) Windage loss

Copper losses: These losses occur in amature and field copper windings. Copper losses consist of armature copper loss field copper loss and due to brush contach resistance

Armature copper loss: $I_a{}^2R_a$

∴ I_a = armature current

R_a = armature resistance

This loss contributes about 30 to 40% of full load losses. The armature copper loss is variable and depends upon the amount of loading of the machine.

Field copper loss = $I_f{}^2R_f$

∴ I_f = field current

R_f = field resistance

In case of shunt wounded field, field copper loss is particularly constant. It contributes about 20 to 30% to full load losses.

- Brush contact resistance also contribution to copper loss generall his loss is included armature copper loss

Iron losses (Core losses) : As the armature core is made of iron and it rotates in a magnetic field, a small current gets induced in the core itself too. Due to this current eddy current loss and hysteresis loss occur in the armature iron core. Iron losses are also called as core losses or magnetic losses.

Hysteresis loss: Hysteresis loss in due to reversal of magnetization of the armature core. When the core passes under one pair of poles it undergoes one complete cycle of magnetic reversal. The frequency of magnetic reversal is f = P.N/120. P = no. of poles. N = speed in rpm

Hysteresis coss is given by steinmetz formula

$W_n = \eta B_{max}^{1.6} fv$ (watts)

where η = steinmetz hysteresis constt

V = volume of core.

Eddy current loss : When armature core rotates in magnetic field, an emf is also induced in the core. according to Faraday's law of electromagnetic induction. Though this emf is smalll it causes a large current to flow in the body due to low resistance of core. This current in known as eddy current. The power loss due to this current is known as eddy current loss

$Pe = Ke\, B^2max\, f^2t^2V$ watts

where ke = constt

Bmax = max flux density in wf/m²

f = frequency of magnetic reversal

t = thickness of lamination

v = volume of core

Mechanical loss: Mechanical loss consist of the losses due to friction in bearing and commutator and windie loss occurs due to air friction of rotating coil. This losses depends on the speed of machine.

(*b*) Given $E_b = 240V$

N = 1000 rpm

$I_a = 15$ amp

$$T = \frac{E_b I_a}{w} = \frac{E_b I_a}{2\pi N / 60} = \frac{240 \times 15}{2\pi\left(\frac{1000}{60}\right)}$$

$$\boxed{T = 34.394 \text{ N-m}}$$

(*c*) Given $I_o = 0.5$ amp

$P_{oc} = 50w$

$V_{oc} = 300V$

$P_{oc} = V_{oc} I_o \cos\phi_0$

$$\text{Cos } \phi_0 = \frac{P_{oc}}{V_{oc} I_o} = \frac{50}{300 \times 0.5}$$

No load power factor $\cos\phi_0 = 0.333$

(*d*) Given No. of poles p = 4

Supply frequency $f_s = 50Hz$

$$\text{Speed of induction motor} = \frac{120f}{P} = \frac{120 \times 50}{4}$$

$= 1500$ rpm

Slip = s

$$= \frac{Ns - Nr}{Ns}$$

$$= \frac{1500 - 1220}{1500} = 0.18$$

Frequency of rotor induced emf

$f_r = sf_s = 0.18 \times 50 = 9Hz$

5. (*a*) **Loss-load factor:** It is a factor which when multiplied by energy lost at time of peak and the no. of load periods will give overall average energy lost. It is calculated as the ratio of average load loss to the peak load loss.

or

It is defined as the ratio of actual loss during a period to the loss assuming maximum current to flow over the same period. It is denoted by G

Loss load factor

$$= \frac{\text{Actual loss(kwh) during a period}}{\text{loss (kwh) assuming maximum current to flow over the same period}}$$

If the load factor of the plant is 100% the copper loss will be at its full value throught the period approximately as the square of load.

The loss will occur with the same load factor it mean current flows continuosly except when a peak current I is reached movementairily and copper loss could be considered negligible under this condition

Loss α $I^2 F^2$= where F = Load factor

The greatest possible loss will occur it maximum current flow for fraction of the year and no current in the remaining part of year.

Under this condition Loss α I^2F

Now it is convieninent to neglect the effect of I^2 from both cases and express the losses as a fraction of those which would occur if the maximum current flows continuosly. This factor which is actually load factor of losses called load factor.

Loss factor formula

$$G = 0.5F+0.5F^2$$

The above formula gives a relativity of high value loss.

(*b*) **Bus bar:** Bus bars are the common electrical component that connects electrically number of lines which are operating at same voltage directly. Various bus bar distribution network are:

(*i*) single bus bar arrangement

(*ii*) single sub bar arrangement with bus sectionalized

(*iii*) Main and transfer bus arrangement

(*iv*) Double bus double breaer arrangement

(*v*) Ring main arrangement

(*vi*) Mesh arrangement

Single bus bar arrangement:

The arrangement of such type of system is very simple and easy. The system has only one bus bar along with the switch. All substation equipment like transformer, generator, the feeder is connected to this bus bar only. The advantages are

→ It has low initial cost

→ If requires less maintenance

→ It is simple in operation

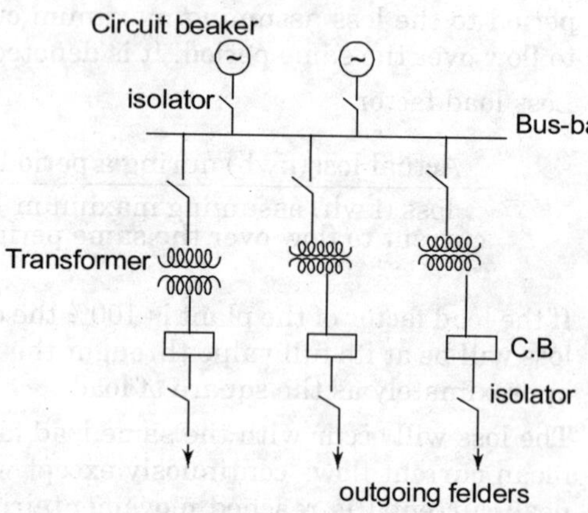

Single bus-bar arrangement with bus sectionalized:

In this type of arrangement, the C.B and isolating switches are used. The isolator disconnects the faulty section hence protect the system from complete shunt down. This type of arrangement uses one additional C.B which does not much increase the cost of system

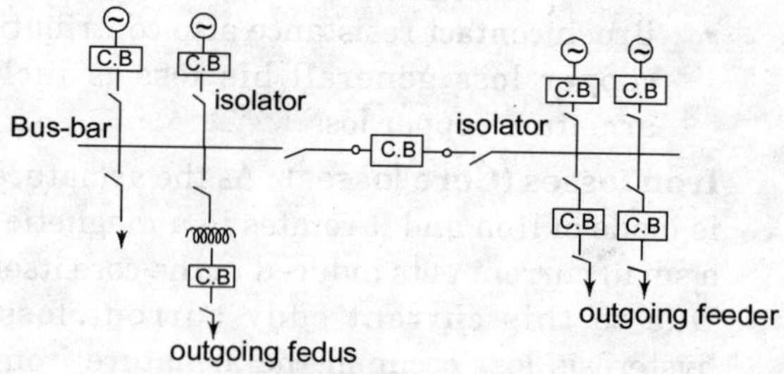

Main and transfer bus arrangement:

Such type of arrangement uses two types of bus bar mainly i.e. main bus bar and auxilary bus bar. The bus bar arrangement uses bus coupler which connects the isolating switches and circuit breaker to the bus bar. The bus coupler is also used for transfering the load from one bus to another in case of overloading. The following are the steps of transfering the load

→ The potential of both bus kept same

→ The bus bar on whcih the load is transfered kept close

→ open the main bus bar

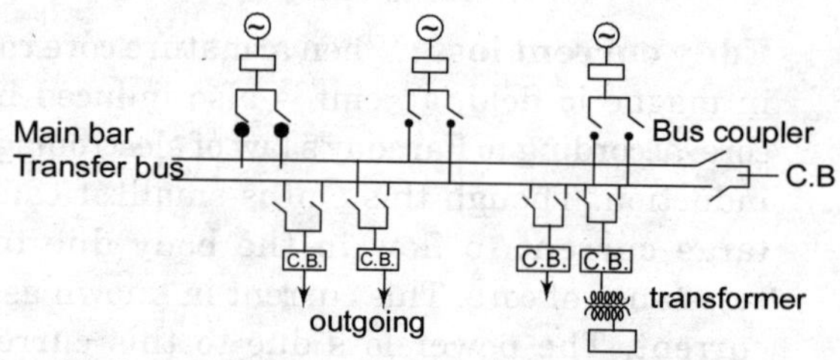

Double bus Double breaker arrangement

This type of arrangement requires two bus and two circuit breaker. It does not require any additional equiment like bus coupler and switch

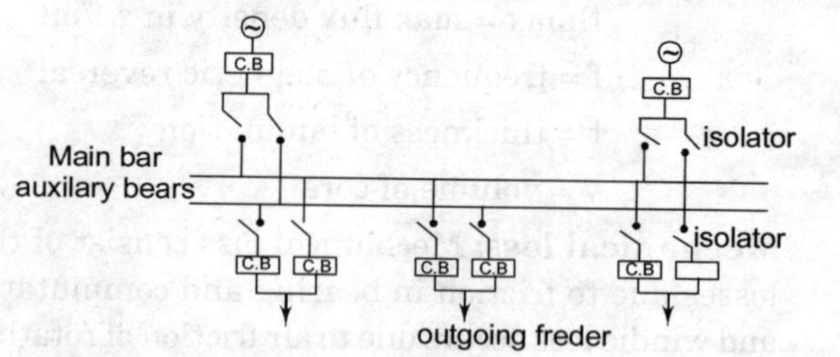

Ring main arrangement

In such type of arrangement the end of bus bar is connected back to the starting point of bus to form a ring

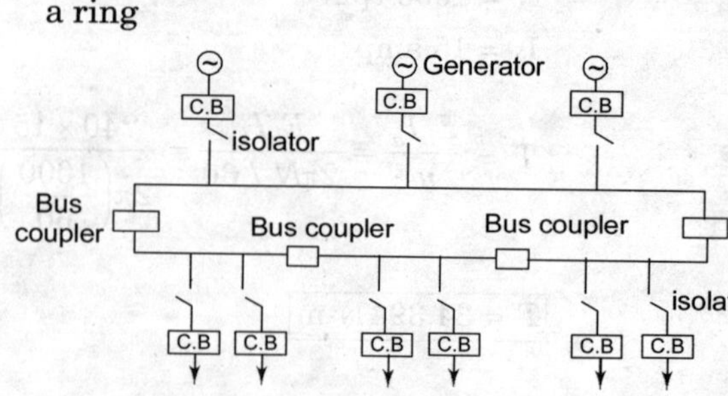

Mesh arrangement: In installed such type of arrangement the C.B are inslated in the mesh formed by the buses the circuit is tapped from the node point of mesh. such type of arrangement controlled by four C.B.

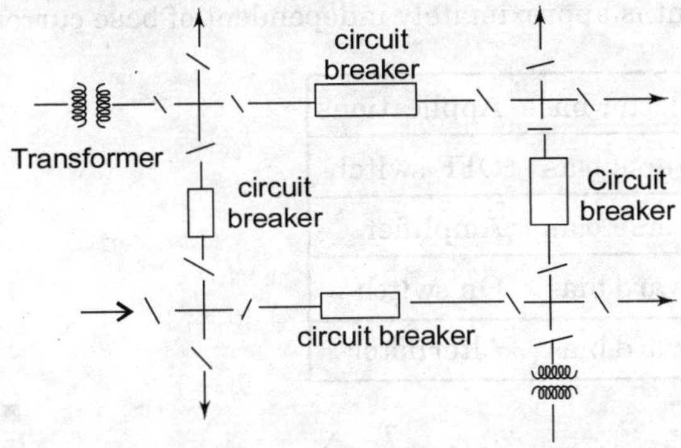

6. (*a*) Laws of illumination:

(*i*) Inverse law of square

(*ii*) Lambert's corine law

1. Law of inverse squares: The illumination of a surface is inversely proportional to the square of the distance between the surface and the light source provided that the distance between the surface and the source is sufficiently, large sot that the source can be regarded as point surface

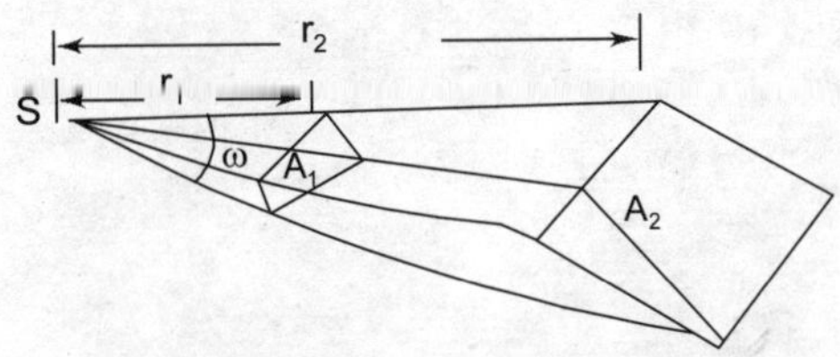

Consider surface area A_1 and the surface area A_2 at distance r_1 and r_2 respectively from the source point 's' of illumination intensity I and normal to the rays. The solid angle subtended be ω sterradian.

Iluminous on the surface area $A_1 = \frac{Iw}{A_1}$ Lumen/unit area

and $A_1 = \omega r_1^2$

$$E_1 = \frac{Iw}{A_1} = \frac{Iw}{wr_1^2} = \frac{I}{r_1^2} \text{ Lumens/unit area}$$

On area A_2 $E_2 = \frac{Iw}{A_2}$

$$= \frac{Iw}{wr_2^2} = \frac{I}{r_2^2} \text{ Lumen/unit area}$$

2. Lambert's cosine law:

According to this law the illumination at any point on a surface is proportional to the cosine angle of the angle between the normal at that point and direction of luminous flux

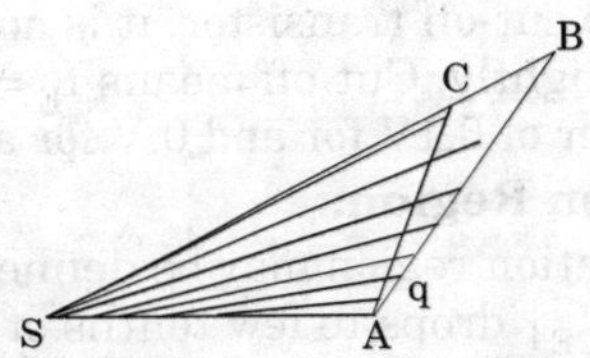

$$\frac{AB}{AC} = \frac{1}{\cos\theta} \text{ increase ratio}$$

and the illumination decreases in the ratio. Cosθ/p

$$\boxed{E = \frac{I\cos\theta}{r_2^2}}$$

(*b*) **Output characteristic of common emitter transistor**

The input is applied between base and emitter and output is taken between collector and emitter. Here emitter of the transistor is common to both input and output and hence the name common emitter contiguration.

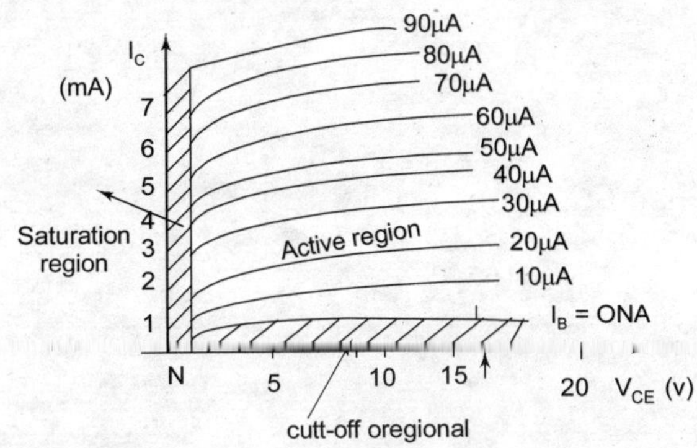

Active Region:

In this region the transistor output current respond most sensitively to an input signal. It must be operated to restric in this region if transistor is used to be an amplifying device.

According to figure, the active region is the area to the right of the ordinate V_{CE} = a few tenths of a volt and above $I_B = 0$

Cut-off region:

Cut-off region occurs at the interaction of load line with current $I_B = 0$ and hence we have to find out the collector current possible in this region

$$\boxed{I_c = -\alpha I_E + I_{co}}$$

From fig ∴ $I_B = 0$ that $I_E = -I_C$

Hence we have $I_C = -I_E$

$$= \frac{I_{co}}{1-\alpha} = I_{CEO}$$

The actual collector current with collector junction reverse biased and base open circuited is represented by symbol I_{CEO}

In order to cut-off transistor, it is not enough to reduce. I_B up to zero it is necessary to reverse bias the emitter junction slightly. Cut-off means $I_E = 0$, $I_C = I_{co}$, $I_B = -I_c = -I_{co}$ and V_{BE} is a reverse voltage whose magnitude is to the order of 0.1V for and 0 V for a silicon transistor

Saturation Region:

The saturation region may be defined as where collector junction an emitter junction is forward biased. In this region $|V_{CE}|$ drops to few tenths of a volt and collector current is approximately independent of base current

	Mode	Emitter bias	Collector base	Applications
(i)	cut-off	Reverse bias	Reverse bias	OFF switch
(ii)	Active	Forward bias	Reverse bias	Amplifier
(iii)	Saturation	Forward bias	forward bias	On switch
(iv)	Reverse active	Reverse bias	forward bias	Alternator

■■

Practice Paper 2

1. (*a*) Use Nodal analysis to find the currents in various resistors of the circuit shown in fig. 1. (10)

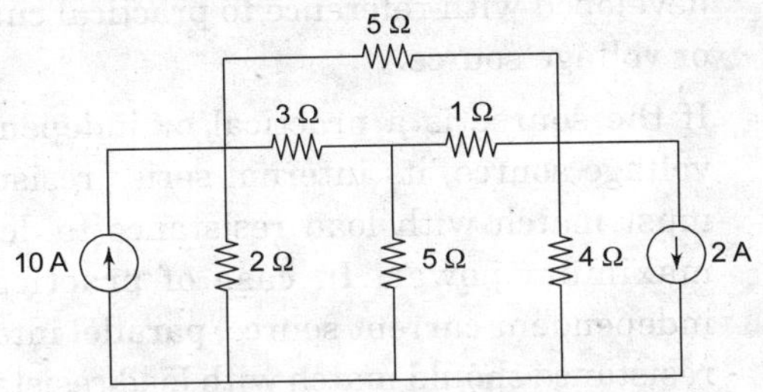

(*b*) State and prove Maximum Power Transfer Theorem for dc circuits. (10)

(*c*) The self-inductance of a coil of 500 turns is 0.25 H. If 60% of the flux is linked with second coil of 10,000 turns then calculate

(*i*) the mutual inductance of the two coils.

(*ii*) the emf induced in the second coil when the current in the first coil changes at the rate of 100 A/s. (10)

2. (*a*) Calculate the rms and average values of current i represented by the waveform shown in figure 2. (10)

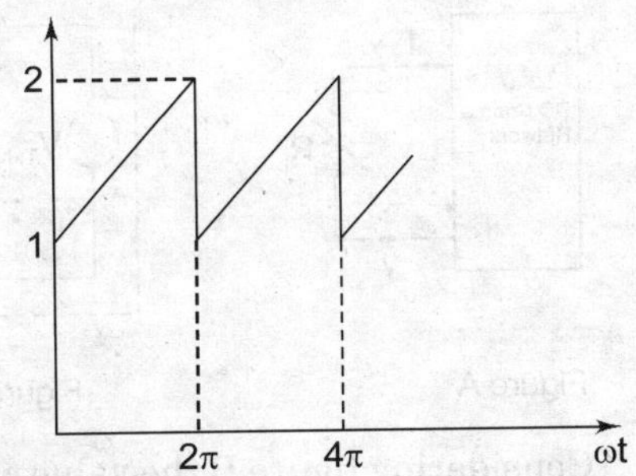

(*b*) An iron choke coil takes 4A when connected to a 20V dc supply and takes 5A when connected to 65V, 50Hz ac supply. Determine.

(*i*) resistance and inductance of the coil

(*ii*) power drawn by the coil

(*iii*) the power factor (10)

(*c*) With neat diagram explain the construction of moving coil instruments and derive the expression for deflecting torque of moving coil instrument. (10)

3. (*a*) Describe the construction and principle of working of a capacitor-start capacitor-run single-phase induction motor. (10)

(*b*) A 11000/400 V, distribution transformer takes a no load primary current of 1 A at a power factor of 0.24 lagging. Find (10)

(*i*) core loss current and magnetising current

(ii) core loss in the transformer.

(*c*) Explain different types of distribution systems with the help of neat sketches. (10)

4. (*a*) Describe the working of vacuum tube voltmeter VTVM. State the disadvantages of VTVM. (15)

(*b*) Describe the operation of PN junction diode under forward bias condition. (5)

(*c*) What is meant by doping in a semiconductor? How does the energy band structure of a semiconductor differ from that of a conductor and an insulator? (10)

5. (*a*) Explain the causes of low power factor in a power system. (10)

(*b*) Explain why a three-phase induction motor is self-starting and a single-phase induction motor is not. (15)

(*c*) Explain why a synchronous motor develops torque at synchronous speed, whereas an induction motor develops torque at all speeds except the synchronous speed. (15)

(*d*) Which fault in a power system is more severe as compared to other faults and why? (10)

(*e*) What are the necessary conditions to operate two alternators in parallel to supply a common load?(10)

6. (*a*) What are the advantages and disadvantages of BJT over JFET? (10)

(*b*) Explain clearly how a fuse rating is selected for the following: (20)

(*i*) Lighting circuit

(*ii*) Power circuit

(*c*) Name the different types of domestic wiring and compare their performance briefly. (15)

(*d*) What are the advantages and disadvantages of electric drives over conventional drives? (15)

EXPLANATIONS

1. (*a*)

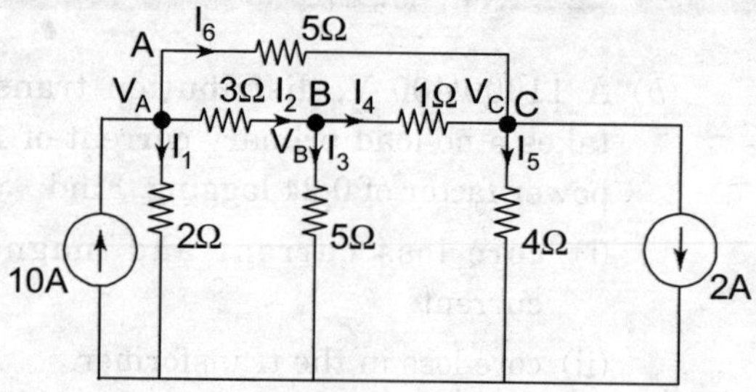

At node A,

$$\frac{V_A}{2}+\frac{V_A-V_B}{3}+\frac{V_A-V_C}{5}=10$$

$$31V_A - 10V_B - 6V_C = 300 \quad ...(A)$$

At node B,

$$\frac{V_B-V_A}{3}+\frac{V_B}{5}+\frac{V_B-V_C}{1}=0$$

$$-5V_A + 23V_B - 15V_C = 0 \quad ...(B)$$

At node C,

$$\frac{V_C-V_A}{5}+\frac{V_C-V_B}{1}+\frac{V_C}{4}+2=0$$

$$-4V_A - 20V_B + 29V_C = -40 \quad ...(C)$$

From (A), (B) and (C)

$$V_A = 12V$$

$$V_B = 5.1V$$

$$V_C = 3.80V$$

$$I_1 = \frac{V_A}{2} = 6.03A$$

$$I_2 = \frac{V_A-V_B}{3} = 2.32A$$

$$I_3 = \frac{V_B}{5} = 1.02A$$

$$I_4 = \frac{V_B-V_C}{1} = 1.30A$$

$$I_5 = \frac{V_C}{4} = 0.95A$$

$$I_6 = \frac{V_A-V_C}{5} = 1.652A.$$

(*b*) **Maximum Power Transfer Theorem for DC circuits**

This theorem describes the condition for maximum power transfer from an active network to an external load resistance. It states that in a linear, active, bilateral DC network, the maximum power will be transferred form source to the load when the external load resistance equals to the internal resistance of the source. This theorem can be developed with reference to practical current or voltage source.

If the source is a practical or independent voltage source, its internal series resistance must match with load resistance to deliver maximum power. In case of practical or independent current source, parallel internal resistance should match with load resistance.

Explanation of Maximum Power Transfer Theorem

A variable resistance R_L is connected to a DC source network as shown in the circuit diagram in figure A below and the figure B represents the Thevenin's voltage V_{TH} and Thevenin's resistance R_{TH} of the source network. The aim of the Maximum Power Transfer theorem is to determine the value of load resistance R_L, such that it receives maximum power from the DC source.

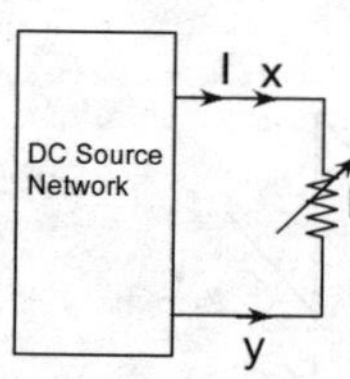

Figure A

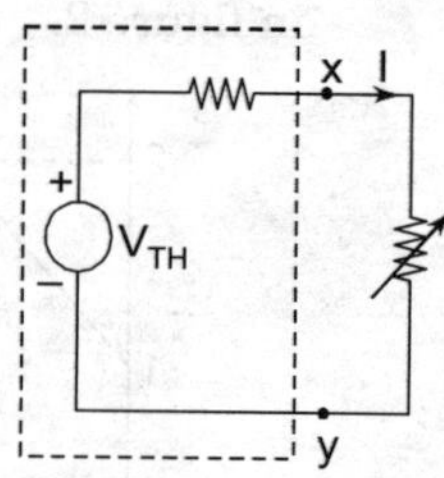

Figure B

Considering figure B the value of current will be calculated by the equation shown below

$$I = \frac{V_{TH}}{R_{TH}+R_L} \quad ...(1)$$

While the power delivered to the resistive load is given by the equation

$$P_L = I^2R_L \quad ...(2)$$

Putting the value of I from the equation (1) in the equation (2) we will get

$$P_L = \left(\frac{V_{TH}}{R_{TH}+R_L}\right)^2 \times R_L$$

P_L can be maximized by varying R_L and hence,

maximum power can be delivered when $(dP_L/dR_L) = 0$

However,

$$\frac{dP_L}{dR_L} = \frac{1}{[(R_{TH} + R_L)^2]^2}$$

$$\left[(R_{TH} + R_L)^2 \frac{d}{dR_L}(V_{TH}^2 R_L) - V_{TH}^2 R_L \frac{d}{dR_L}(R_{TH} + R_L)^2\right]$$

$$\frac{dP_L}{dR_L} = \frac{1}{(R_{TH} + R_L)^4}$$

$$\left[(R_{TH} + R_L)^2 V_{TH}^2 - V_{TH}^2 R_L \times 2(R_{TH} + R_L)\right]$$

$$\frac{dP_L}{dR_L} = \frac{V_{TH}^2 (R_{TH} + R_L - 2R_L)}{(R_{TH} + R_L)^3}$$

$$= \frac{V_{TH}^2 (R_{TH} - R_L)}{(R_{TH} + R_L)^2}$$

Therefore,

$$\frac{V_{TH}^2 (R_{TH} - R_L)}{(R_{TH} + R_L)^2} = 0$$

Which gives

$$(R_{TH} - R_L) = 0 \text{ or } R_{TH} = R_L$$

Hence, it is proved that power transfer from a DC source network to a resistive network is maximum when the internal resistance of the DC source network is equal to the load resistance.

Again with $R_{TH} = R_L$, the system being perfectly matched to the load and the source thus, the power transfer becomes maximum and this amount of power P_{max} can be obtained by the equation shown below

$$P_{max} = \frac{V_{TH}^2 R_{TH}}{(R_{TH} + R_{TH})^2} = \frac{V_{TH}^2}{4R_{TH}} \quad ...(3)$$

Equation (3) gives the power which is consumed by the load. The power transfer by the source will also be same as the power consumed by the load i.e., equation (3), as the load power and the power being the same.

Thus, the total power supplied is given by the equation

$$P = 2\frac{V_{TH}^2}{4R_{TH}} = \frac{V_{TH}^2}{2R_{TH}}$$

During Maximum Power Transfer the efficiency becomes

$$\eta = \left(\frac{P_{max}}{P}\right) \times 100 = 50\%$$

Steps for Solving Network Using Maximum Power Transfer Theorem

Following steps are used to solve the problem by Maximum Power Transfer theorem

Step 1 : Remove the load resistance of the circuit.

Step 2 : Find the Thevenin's resistance (R_{TH}) of the source network looking through the open circuited load terminals.

Step 3 : As per the maximum power transfer theorem this R_{TH} is the load resistance of the network i.e., $R_L = R_{TH}$ that allows maximum power transfer.

Step 4 : Maximum Power Transfer is calculated by the equation shown below.

$$P_{max} = \frac{V_{TH}^2}{4R_{TH}}$$

(*c*) Coil turns = 500 Self inductance = 0.25H

$$\text{Mutual inductance } M = \frac{N_2\phi_2}{I_1}$$

$N_1 = 500$ $L_1 = 0.25\text{H}$ $\phi_2 = 0.6\phi_1$ $N_2 = 10{,}000$

$$L_1 = \frac{N_1\phi_1}{I_1}; \ \frac{L_1}{N_1} = \frac{\phi_1}{I_1} = \frac{0.25}{500}; \phi_2 = 0.6\phi$$

$$\frac{\phi_2}{\phi_1} = \frac{0.6\phi_1}{I_1} = \frac{0.6 \times 0.25}{500}$$

(*i*) $M = \dfrac{N_2\phi_2}{I_1} = 10{,}000 \times \dfrac{0.6 \times 0.25}{500} = 3\text{H}$

(*ii*) Emf induced

$$E_2 = -\frac{MdI_1}{dt} = -3 \times 100 \left(\frac{dI_1}{dt} = 100A/s\right)$$

$$= -300\text{V}$$

2. (*a*) Equation $i(\omega t) = \dfrac{1}{2\Omega} wt + 1$

This is a periodic waveform of period $T = 2\pi$

$$I_{avg.} = \frac{1}{T}\int_0^{2\pi} i(wt)\, d(wt)$$

$$= \frac{1}{2\pi}\int_0^{2\pi}\left(1 + \frac{wt}{2\pi}\right) d(wt)$$

$$= \frac{1}{2\pi}\left[wt + \frac{1}{2\pi}\frac{(wt)^2}{2}\right]^{2\pi}$$

$$= \frac{1}{2\pi}\left[(2\pi - 0) + \frac{1}{2\pi}\frac{(2\pi)^2}{2}\right]$$

$$I_{avg.} = \frac{1}{2\pi}(3\pi) = 1.5A$$

$$I_{rms} = \left[\frac{1}{T}\int_0^{2\pi} i^2(wt)\, d(wt)\right]^{1/2}$$

$$= \frac{1}{\sqrt{2\pi}}\left[\int_0^{2\pi}\left(\frac{1}{2}wt + 1\right)^2 d(wt)\right]^{1/2}$$

$$= \frac{1}{\sqrt{2\pi}}\left[\int_0^{2\pi}\left(\frac{(wt)^2}{4\pi^2} + 1 + \frac{2}{2\pi}wt\right) d(wt)\right]^{1/2}$$

$$= \frac{1}{\sqrt{2\pi}}\left[\frac{1}{4\pi^2}\frac{(2\pi)^3}{3} + 2\pi + \frac{1}{\pi}.\frac{(2\pi)^2}{2}\right]^{1/2}$$

$$= \frac{1}{\sqrt{2\pi}}\left[\frac{2\pi}{3} + 2\pi + 2\pi\right]^{1/2}$$

$$I_{rms} = \sqrt{\frac{7}{3}} = 1.527A$$

(*b*) (*i*)

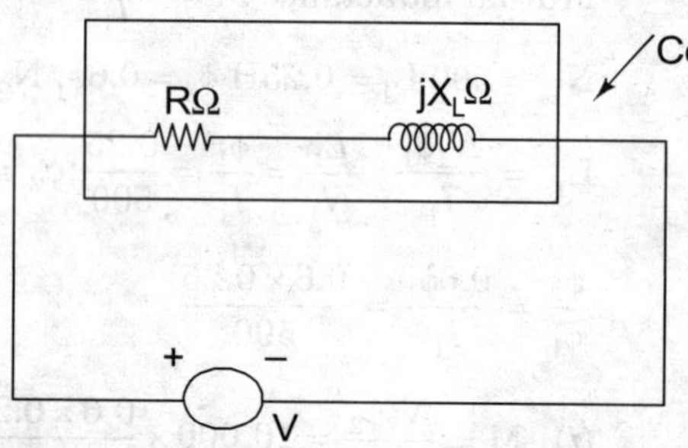

Case (i) When coil connected to 20V dc supply current I = 4A

For dc supply, f = oHz

$$I = \frac{V}{R}$$

$$\Rightarrow R = \frac{V}{I} = 5\Omega$$

Case (ii) When coil is connected to 65V, 50Hz ac supply frequency f = 50Hz

$$I = 5A$$

$$Z = \frac{V}{I} = \frac{65}{5} = 13\Omega$$

$$X_L = \sqrt{Z^2 - R^2}$$

$$= \sqrt{(13)^2 - 5^2} = 12\Omega$$

$$2\pi fL = 12;$$

$$L = \frac{12}{2\pi \times 50} = 38.197 \text{ H}$$

(*ii*) Power factor

Case (i) For resistive circuit

$$\cos\phi = \frac{R}{Z} = \frac{R}{R} = 1$$

Case (ii) Z = 13Ω

$$\cos\phi = \frac{R}{Z} = \frac{5}{13} = 0.3846 \text{ (Lagging)}$$

(*c*) Moving Iron Instruments

The moving iron instruments are classified as:

(i) Moving iron attraction type instruments and

(ii) Moving iron repulsion type instruments

1. Moving iron attraction type instruments

The basic working principle of these instruments is very simple that a soft iron piece if brought near the magnet gets attracted by the magnet.

The construction of the attraction type instrument is shown in the Fig. 1.

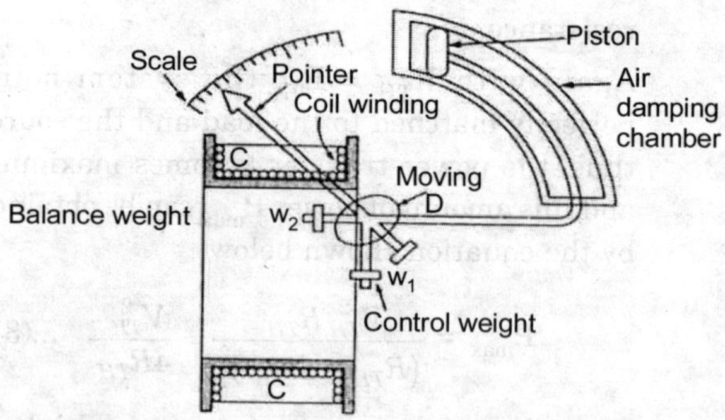

Fig. 1 Moving iron attraction type instruments

It consists of a fixed coil C and moving iron piece D. The coil is flat and has a narrow slot like opening. The moving iron is a flat disc which eccentrically mounted, on the spindle. The spindle is supported between the jewel bearings. The spindle caries a pointer which moves over a graduated scale. The number of turns of the fixed coil are dependent on the range of the instrument. For passing current through the coil only few turns are required.

The controlling torque is provided by the springs but gravity control may also be used for vertically mounted panel type instruments.

The damping torque is provided by the air friction. A light aluminium piston is attached to the moving system. It moves in a fixed chamber. The chamber is closed at one end. It can also provided with the help of van attached to the moving system.

The operating magnetic field in moving iron instruments is very weak. Hence eddy current damping is not used since it require a permanent magnet which would affect or distort the operating field.

2. Moving Iron Repulsion Type Instrument

These instruments have two vanes inside the coil, the one is fixed and other is movable. When the current flows in the coil, both the vanes are magnetized with like polarities induced on the same side. Hence due to repulsion of like polarities, there is a force of repulsion between the two vanes causing the movement of the moving van. The repulsion type instruments are the most commonly used instruments.

Torque Equation of moving iron instruments.

Consider a small increment in current supplied to the coil of the instrument, due to this current let $d\theta$ be the deflection under the deflecting torque T_d. Due to such deflection, some mechanical work will be done.

$\therefore$ Mechanical Work = $T_d\, d\theta$

There will be a change in the energy stored i the magnetic field due to the change in inductance. This is ;cause the vane tries to occupy the position of minimum reluctance. The inductance is inversely proportional the reluctance of the magnetic circuit of coil.

Let I = initial current

L = instrument inductance

θ = deflection

dl = increase in current

$d\theta$ = change in deflection

dL = change in inductance

In order to effect and increment dL in the current, there must be an increase in the applied voltage given by,

$$e = \frac{d(LI)}{dt} = I\frac{dL}{dt} + L\frac{dI}{dt}$$

As both 1 and L are changing.

The electrical energy supplied is given by,

$$eIdt = \left(I\frac{dL}{dt} + L\frac{dI}{dt}\right)Idt$$

$$= I^2\, dL + IL\, dI$$

The second energy increase from

$$\frac{1}{2}LI^2 \text{ to } \frac{1}{2}(L + dL)(I + dI)^2$$

Hence the change in stored energy is given by,

$$= \frac{1}{2}(L + dL)(I + dI)^2 - \frac{1}{2}LI^2$$

Neglecting higher order terms, this becomes,

$$IL\, dI + \frac{1}{2}I^2\, dL$$

The energy supplied in nothing but increase in stored energy plus the energy required for mechanical work done.

$$\therefore \quad I^2dL + IL\, dI = IL\, dI + \frac{1}{2}I^2\, dL + T_d\, d\theta$$

$$\therefore \quad T_d\, d\theta = \frac{1}{2}I^2\, dL$$

$$\therefore \quad \boxed{T_d = \frac{1}{2}I^2\frac{dL}{d\theta}}$$

While the controlling torque is given by,

$$T_c = K\,\theta$$

where K = spring constant

$$\therefore \quad K\theta = \frac{1}{2}I^2\frac{dL}{d\theta} \quad \text{under equilibrium}$$

$$\therefore \quad \theta = \frac{1}{2}\frac{I^2}{K}\frac{dL}{d\theta}$$

Thus the deflection is proportional to the square of the currrent through the coil. And the instrument gives square law response.

3. (a) **Capacitor Start Capacitor Run Motor**

The Capacitor Start Capacitor Run Motor has a cage rotor, and its stator has two windings known as Main and Auxiliary Windings. The two windings are displaced 90 degrees in space. There are two capacitors in this method one is used at the time of the starting and is known as starting capacitor. The other one is used for continuous running of the motor and is known as RUN capacitor.

So this motor is named as Capacitor Start Capacitor Run Motor. This motor is also known as Two Value Capacitor Motor. Connection diagram of the Two valve Capacitor Motor is shown below

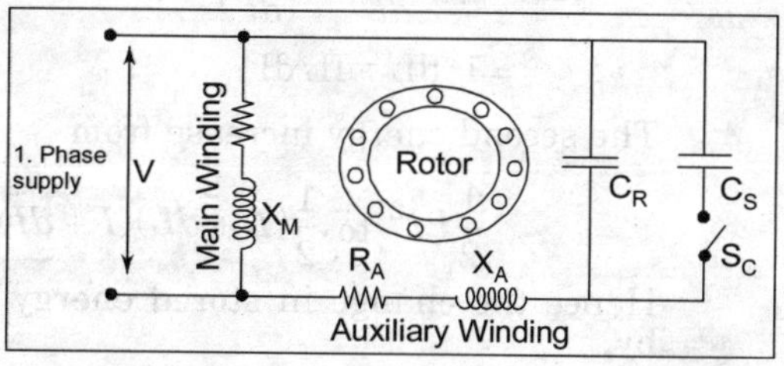

There are two capacitors in this motor represented by C_S and C_R. At the starting, the two capacitors are connected in parallel. The Capacitor Cs is the Starting capacitor is short time rated. It is almost electrolytic. A large amount of current id required to obtain the starting torque. Therefore, the value of the capacitive reactance X should be low in the starting winding. Since, $X_A = 1/2\pi fC_A$, the value of the starting capacitor should be large.

The rated line current is smaller than the starting current at the normal operating condition of the motor. Hence, the value of the capacitive reactance should be large. Since, $X_R = 1/2\pi fC_R$ the value of the run capacitor should be small.

As the motor reaches the synchronous speed, the starting capacitor Cs is disconnected from the circuit by a centrifugal switch Sc. The capacitor C_R is connected permanently in the circuit and thus it is known as RUN Capacitor. The run capacitor is long time rated and is made of oil filled paper.

The figure below shows the Phaser Diagram of the Capacitor Start Capacitor Run Motor.

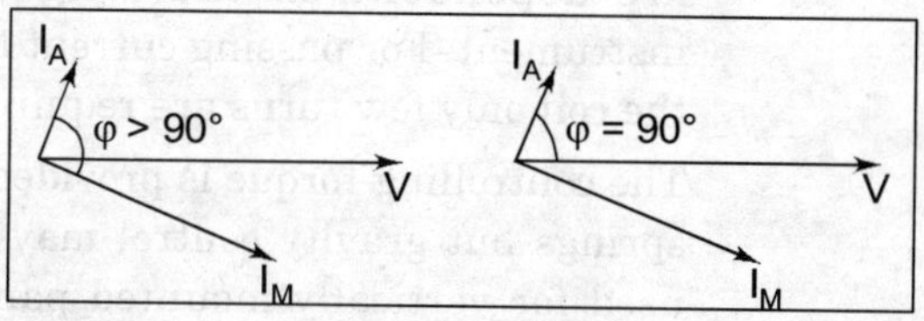

Fig. (a) shows the phasor diagram when at the starting both the capacitor are in the circuit and $\phi > 90°$. Fig

Fig. (b) shows the phasor when the starting capacitor is disconnected, and ϕ becomes equal to 90°.

The Torque Speed Characteristic of a Two Value Capacitor Motor is shown below.

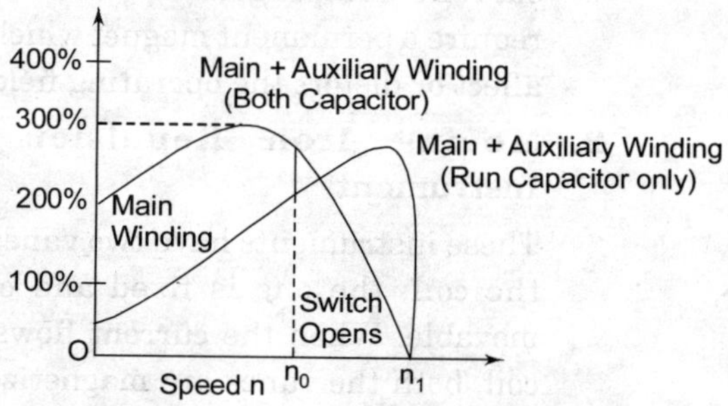

This type of motor is quiet and smooth running. They have higher efficiency than the motors that run on the main windings only. They are used for loads of higher inertia requiring frequent starts where the maximum pull-out torque and efficiency required are higher. The Two Value Capacitor Motors are used in pumping equipment, refrigeration, air compressors, etc.

(b) Given that :

No load curren,

$I_0 = 1$ A at power factor, $\cos\phi_0 = 0.24$ (lagging)

(i) Core loss current,

$$I_c = I_0 \cos\phi_0$$
$$= 1 \times 0.24 = 0.24\text{A}$$

Magnetising current,

$$I_\phi = I_0 \sin\phi_0$$
$$= 1 \times 0.97 = 0.97 \text{ A}$$
$$\therefore \quad \phi_0 = \cos^{-1}(0.24) = 76.113°$$
$$\sin\phi_0 = 0.97$$

(ii) Core loss in the transformer

Assume distribution transformer is 3-phase transformer,

$$P_0 = \sqrt{3}V_0 I_0 \cos\phi_0$$
$$= \sqrt{3} \times 11000 \times 1 \times 0.24$$
$$= 4572.614 = 4.5726 \text{ kW}$$

(*c*) Distribution systems may be classified in various ways as followed:

1. According to current, the distribution systems are two types:

   (a) **dc distribution system,**

   (b) **ac distribution system.**

   (*a*) **dc distribution system:**

   (*i*) 2-wire dc distribution system: This system of distribution consists of two wires, one is the positive and other is the negative wire.

   This system is never used for transmission purpose due to low efficiency but may be employed for distribution of dc power.

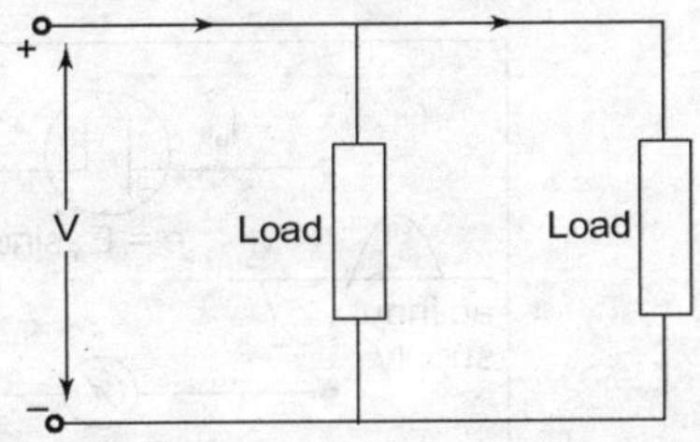

   (*ii*) 3-wire dc distribution system: This system consists of two outers and a middle or neutral wire which is earthed at the substation. The voltage between the outer is twice the voltage between either outer and neutral wire.

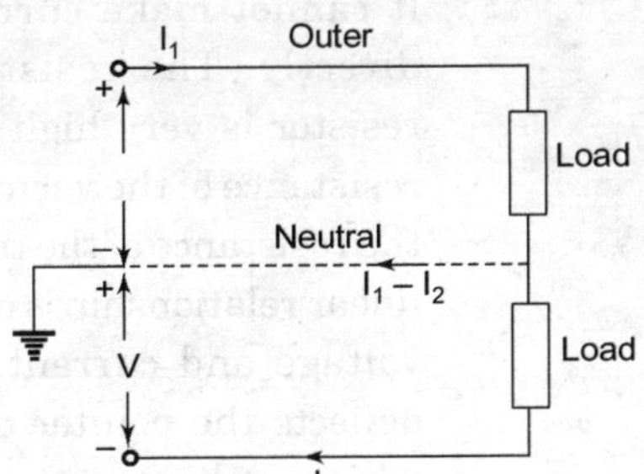

   This system is used for transmission purpose.

2. According to types of construction of distribution systems:

   (*a*) **Overhead**

   (*b*) **Underground**

   (*a*) The overhead system is generally employed for distribution as it is cheaper than underground system.

   (*b*) The underground system is used at places where overhead construction is impracticable.

3. According to the scheme of connection of distribution system.

   (*a*) **Radial system**

   (*b*) **Parallel system**

   (*c*) **Ring system**

   (*d*) **Interconnected system**

   (*a*) **Radial system:** In this system, separate feeder radiates from a substation and feed the distribution at one end only.

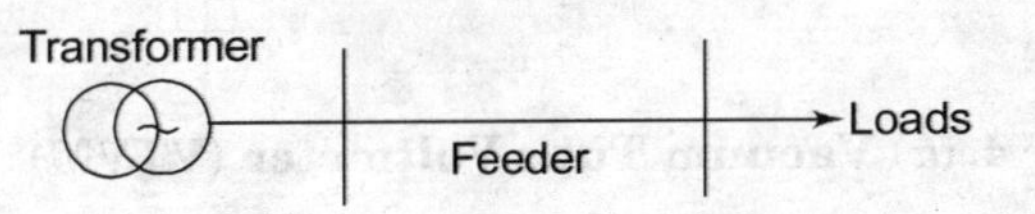

   This system is simplest, most economical and most commonly used one.

   (*b*) **Parallel system:** In this system, two radial feeders originated from the same or different substation are run in parallel. Each feeder, though cable of supplying the entire load, share the total and equally in normal conditions.

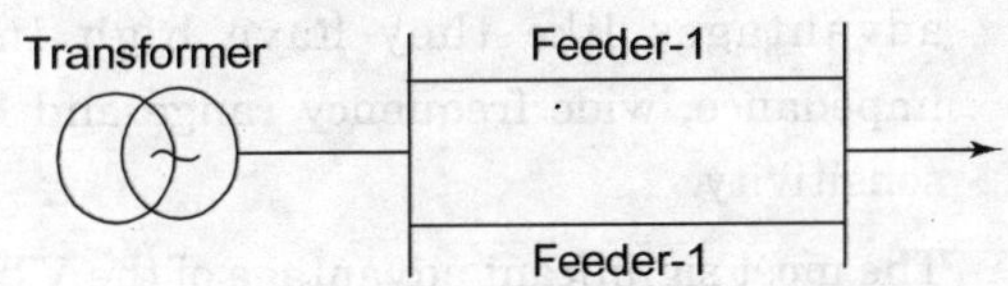

   (*c*) **Ring system:** In this system, two or more radial feeders originating from the same or different substations are laid on different routes of load areas.

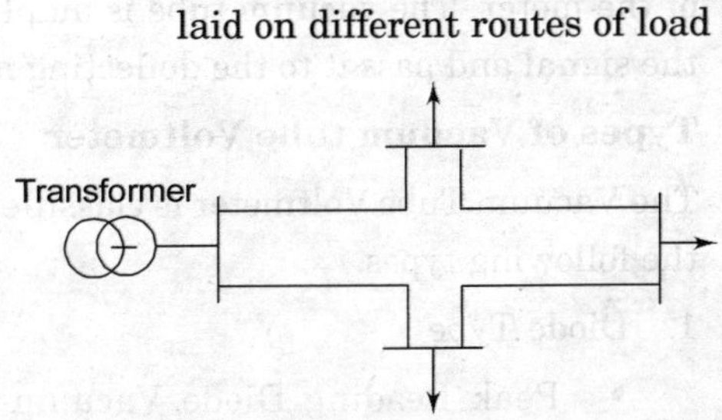

This system is most reliable for continuity of supply and gives better voltage regulation and less power losses.

(*d*) **Inter-connected system:** When the feeder of ring main is energised from two or more than two generating stations or substation it is called the interconnected system.

This system provides better reliability and flexibility and is employed is large metropolitan cities where continuity of supply is the most important.

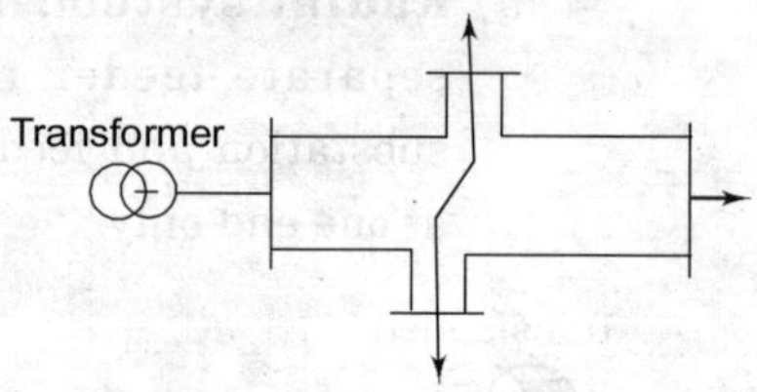

4. (*a*) **Vacuum Tube Voltmeter (VTVM)**

Definition : The voltmeter which uses the vacuum tube for amplifying the measurand AC and DC voltage is known as the vacuum tube voltmeter (VTM). The vacuum tube increases the sensitivity of the voltmeter because of which it can detect the signal of very weak strength.

The electronic voltmeter is used for measuring the voltage of direct, RMS and peak voltage of the system. The vacuum tube has many advantages like they have high input impedance, wide frequency range and high sensitivity.

The most significant advantage of the VTM is that it can draw very less current as compared to the other meter. In VTM, the measuring signal is directly supplied to the vacuum tube of the meter. The vacuum tube is amplifying the signal and pass it to the deflecting meter.

Types of Vacuum tube Voltmeter

The Vacuum Tube Voltmeter is classified into the following types.

1. Diode Type
   - Peak Reading Diode Vacuum Tube Voltmeter
2. Single Triode
3. Balanced Triode Type
4. Rectifiers Amplifier Type
5. Amplifier Rectifier Type

Simple Diode Type Voltmeter

The circuit of the diode voltmeter consists the PMMC meter, load resistor, vacuum tube diode. The vacuum tube diode connects in series with resistance raises the strength of the weak signal. Because of the vacuum tube, the system becomes more sensitive than the normal voltmeter.

For obtaining the accurate reading from the voltmeter, it is essential that their current and voltage are directly proportional to each other. This can be done by the help of the series resistor. The circuit diagram of the diode vacuum tube voltmeter is shown in the figure

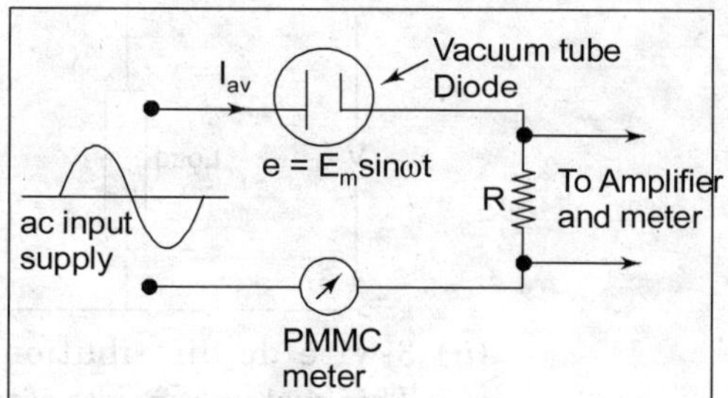

Vacuum Type Diode Voltmeter

Demerits:

* Accurate readings can be obtained only for sine waves.

* It cannot make current measurements directly. The resistance of the series resistor is very high as compared to the resistance of the vacuum tube diode. Thus the resistance of the tube is neglected. The linear relationship is obtained between the voltage and current. The input supply deflects the pointer of the PMMC meter which indicates the magnitude of the measured voltage.

In Diode vacuum voltmeter,

- The value of the input resistance of the voltmeter is equal to the series resistance because high voltage resistor decreases the sensitivity of the meter.

- The frequency range of the diode voltmeter depends on the value of the series resistance. The higher value of the series resistance decreases the frequency range of the meter.
- The vacuum tube voltmeter is used in limited applications because of the low input resistance and limited frequency range.

(*b*) **Forward Biased P-N Junction**

When we connect p-type region of a junction with the positive terminal of a voltage source and n-type region with the negative terminal of the voltage source, then the junction is said to be forward biased. At this condition, due to the attraction of positive terminal of source, electrons which participated in covalent bond creations in p-type material, will be attracted towards the terminal. As result numbers of covalent bonds are broken and, electrons are shifted towards the positive terminal. As a result, the concentration of electrons in the crystal nearer to the terminal increases and these electrons recombine with holes here. In this way, the number of holes increases in the portion of the p-type region away from the junction, and it is reduced in the portion of p-type region nearer to the terminal. As such holes are shifted from terminal to junction.

Due to the higher concentration of holes adjacent to negative impurity ions layer the electrons of negative ions come out and recombine with those holes and create new holes in the layer. Consequently, the width of this negative ions layer is reduced and finally this layer vanishes.

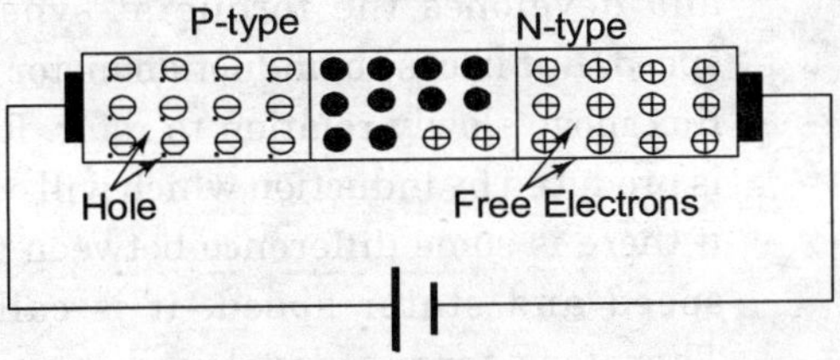

Similarly due to the negative terminal of source the free electrons in the n-type region will ripple towards junction where they will find the layer of positive impurity ions and start recombine with these ions and generate free electrons inside the layer. Consequently, the width of positive impurity ions is reduced, and finally, it vanishes.

In these ways, both layers of ions disappear, and there will be no more depletion layer. After the depletion layer disappeared, free electrons from the n-type region can easily drift to p-type region and holes from p-type region to n-type region in the crystal. Hence, ideally there will be no obstruction of flowing current and the pn junction behaves as the short circuit.

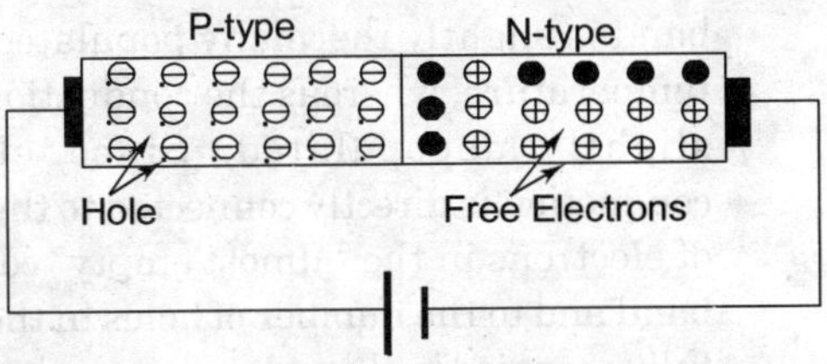

(*c*) **Doping**

In semiconductor production, doping is the intentional introduction of impurities into an intrinsic semiconductor for the purpose of modulating its electrical properties. The doped material is referred to as extrinsic semiconductors. A semiconductor doped to such high levels that it acts more like a conductor than a semiconductor is referred to as a degenerate semiconductor.

The electrical properties of a given material depend on the electronic populations of the different allowed bands. Electrical conduction is the result of electron motion within each band. When an electric field is applied to the material, electrons start to move in the direction opposed to the direction of the electric field. An empty energy band (in which there is no free electron) does not of course participate in the formation of an electric current. It is also the case for a fully occupied band. Indeed, an electron can move provided that, whenever it leaves its site, it can find some free space elsewhere (another available site within its energy band, called a "hole"), where it can go. A material with fully occupied or empty energy bands is then an insulator. This is the case when the gap energy exteeds ~9eV, because for such gaps, the thermal energy at 300K (~25 meV) is clearly insufficient to allow electrons from the valence band to be promoted to the conduction band. In this case the valence band (and all bands of lower energy) is fully occupied, and the conduction band is empty.

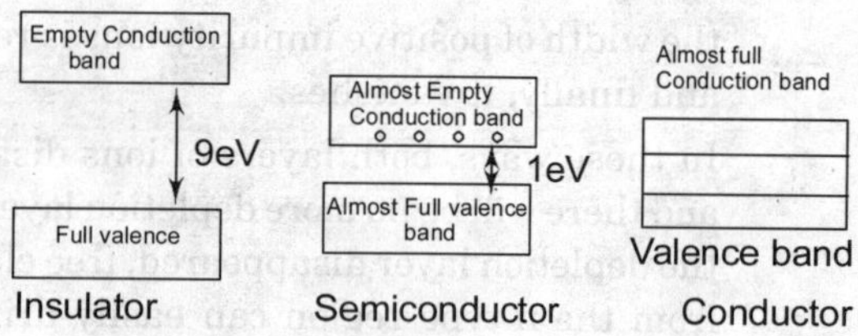

Representation of energy bands

A semiconductor is primarily an insulator at oK. However, since the energy gap is lower compared to insulators (~ leV), the valence band is slightly thermally populated at room temperature, whereas the conduction band is slightly depopulated. Since electrical conduction is directly connected to the number of electrons in the "almost empty" conduction band and to the number of holes in the "almost fully occupied" valence band, it can be expected that the electrical conductivity of such an intrinsic semiconducior will be very small.

For a conductor, conduction bands and valence bands are not separated and there is therefore no energy gap. The conduction band is then partially occupied (even at low temperatures), resulting in a "high"

5. (*a*) Cases of low power factor in a power system:

The main cause of low power factor is inductive load As in pure inductive circuit, current lags 90° from voltage, this large difference of phase angle between current and voltage causes zero power factor. Basically all those circuit having capacitance and inductance (except resonance circuit) where $X_L = X_C$, power factor would be exist over there becouse of capacitance and inductance causes difference of phase angle θ between current and voltage.

Main causes of low power factor:

1. Single phase and three phase induction motor usually induction motor works at low p.f. i.e. at full load p.f. = 0.8 – 0.9

   Small load p.f. = 0.2 – 0.3
2. Varying load in power system: During low load period, supply voltage in increased which increased the magnetizing current which cause the decresed power factor.
3. Industrial heating furnace
4. Transformers
5. Harmonic currents.
6. Electrical discharge lamp.

5. (*b*) Let us consider a 3-ϕ induction motor first and see how it rotates. A 3-ϕ supply is given to the armature of induction motor produces a rotating megnetic speed N_S = (120 f/P). This rotating magnetic field linked to the rotor coils and induces voltage which in turn produces current in the rotor. The current carrying rotor being placed in a magetic field experiences a torque being placed in a magnetic field experiences a torque and hence begins to rotate in the direction of rotating magnetic field. Thus we can say that 3-ϕ induction motor is self starting.

Single phase induction motor has distributed stator winding and a squirrel cage rotor, when fed from a flux which is only alternating i.e. are which alternate along one space axis only. It is not synchronously revolving flux as in case of a two or a three phase stator winding fed from a 2 of 3 phase supply. Now an alternating on pulsating flux acting on a squirrel cage rotor can not produce rotation. That is why single phase induction motor is not self starting.

5. (*c*) In an electric motor torque is developed by interaction of rotor flux and the stator flux. In order to develop a continuous torque the fluxes must be fixed value relative to one another as the motor rotates. It they are not fixed then the torque fluctuates both +ve and –ve and the net torque is zero, In case of synchronous motor the position of rotor flux is fixed relative to rotor Therefore rotor speed must be same as rotational speed of stator flux and in synchronous motor rotor is magnetically locked once approches the speed of stator flux and developes the torque at synchronous speed. But in case of induction motor the rotor flux move slowly relation to rotor. Rotor flux is produced by induction which will occur only if there is some difference between the rotor speed and stator speed. it is called slip. Therefore torque developed by induction motor is proportional to slip. At synchronous speed slip is zero and hence torque developed by the induction motor is zero.

5. (*d*) In case of power syntem single line to ground fault is most severe fault at the generator terminals than three phase fault become zero sequence impedance is less at the generator and fault current in case of line to ground fault is three times of +ve sequence current

$I_F (L - G) = 3I_{R1}$

I_{R1} = +ve sequence current

And if $Zn < \frac{1}{3}[Z_{G1} - Z\ G_0]$ the L–G fault is more severe where Z_{G1} is +ve sequence impedance of generator. Z_{G0} is zero sequence of generator Zn neutral grounding impedance

As the fault location moves away from generator, zero sequence impedance increases and 3–ϕ fault becomes more severe.

5. (*e*) The following conditions should be satisfied for parallel operation are as follows:

(i) The phase sequence of bus bar voltages and the incoming machine voltages must be some

(*ii*) The bus bar voltages and incoming machine terminal voltage must be in phase.

(iii) The terminal voltage of incoming machine and alternators which is to be connected in parallel or with the bus bar voltage should be equal.

(iv) The frequency of generated voltage of incoming machine and the frequency of voltage of bus bar should be equal.

6. (*a*) **Advantage of BJT over J.FET:**

(*i*) BJT having good voltage gain compared to J-FET

(*ii*) BJT having faster switching time compared to J.FET by preventing the device going into hard saturation.

(*iii*) BJT using amplifier circuit due to its high gain bandwidth product compared to J.FET

(*iv*) BJT shows good performance at high frequency compared to J.FET

Disadvantage of BJT over J-FET:

(*i*) BJT is less imune to radiation compared to J-FET

(*ii*) BJT is less stable than J-FET with respect to temperature variation

(*iii*) BJT occupies more space in integrated form compared to J-FET

(*iv*) BJT is more noisy compared to J-FET

(*v*) BJT has low input resistance compared to J-FET

6. (*b*) Fuses protect against overcurrent events by metting their elements and opening the circuit. Fuse must be applied at or below their specified voltage rating which differs between a.c and d.c currents.

Selection of fuse condition : In order to begin selecting the appropriate fuse, one needs to understand the nature of the circuit it power and protects. Basic operating factor such as maximum steady state voltage current value ambient temperature.

(*i*) **Voltage rating :** Fuses of lightning circuit are insensitive to voltage change within their ratings so selecting the proper voltage rating is necessary.

(*ii*) **Current rating :** The fuse element to be used in a fuse must be selected for a rated current large energy to ensure that the element will not fuse when the light circuit carrying its sustained maximum load current and when circuit is carrying a short time over load current

(*iii*) **Ambient temperature :** When a fuse is applied in an ambient temperature exceeding the standard 23°C. The fuse current rating should be durated

$$I_{rated} = \frac{\text{Input current (max)}}{K_{Temp}}$$

K_{Tempt} = Temperature derating factor

6. (*c*) **domestic wiring:**

1. **Lead and sheath wiring:** The wiring is similar to that of CTs but the conductors are individually insulated and converd with a common outer lead aluminium alloy sheath. The sheath protects the cable against dampness atmospheric extremities and mechanical damages. The sheath is earthed at every junction to provide a path to ground for leakage current. They are fixed by means of metal clips on wooden battens. The wiring system is very expensive It is suitable for low voltage installations.

2. **Casing and caping wiring :** As the name refered in this wiring. PVC insulated wires are placed in plastic

cashing and covered with cap. The casing is of rectangular cross-section. In this wiring no risk of electric shock due to covered wires and cables in casing and caping. The cables were carried through the wooden casing enclosers.

(3) Clear wiring : Cleat wiring temporary electrical wiring on building and construction sites is necessary to enable lightning and power to be provided for the various points on the site

Advantages:

(i) It is simple and cheap wiring system

(ii) Inspection is simple and easy

(iii) Cables and wires of cheat wiring system is in open air

(4) Conduit wiring : It conduits installed on root or wall. It is known as surface conduit wiring. In this wiring method they make holes on the surface or wall on equal distances and conduit is installed then with the help of rawal plugs.

Concealed conduit wiring : If the conduit is hidden inside the wall stock with the help of plastering it is called concealed conduit wiring. In other words, the electrical wiring system inside wall, roof or floor with the help of plastic or metallic piping is called concleared conduit wiring.

Advantage:

1. It is reliable and popular wiring system
2. It is very safe wiring system
3. No risk of electric shock
4. Sustainable and long-lossing wiring system
5. Battern wiring (CTs and TRs):

Single core or double core or three core TRs cables with a circular oval shape cables are used in this kind of wiring. Mostly single core cable are prefered

Advantages

(*i*) Strong and long lasting

(*ii*) Installation of wiring is simple

(*iii*) Less chance of leakage current in batten systems

(*iv*) Repairing is easy

6. (*d*) Advantages of Electric drive over conventional drive:

1. Electric drive is more reliable than conventional drives
2. It is smooth and easy control
3. Facility of remote control is avilable in electric drive.
4. Having long life than conventional drives
5. Electric drive has easy starting facilities.
6. It is more compact than conventional drives
7. Having low cost than conventional drives
8. More flexible than conventional drives

Disadvantage of Electric drives over conventional drives:

1. Having noise pollution.
2. It has poor dynamic response
3. To increase torque, a larger and havier motor must be used which is costly
4. It can not be employed at distant places
5. It's non availability on failure of supply